CW00558053

HEROES OF
POSTMAN'S
PARK

JOHN PRICE

HEROES OF POSTMAN'S PARK

HEROIC SELF-SACRIFICE IN VICTORIAN LONDON

Rear cover illustration: detail from 'Helping Hands',
a sculpture by Alec Peever, 2011.

First published 2015

The History Press
The Mill, Brimscombe Port
Stroud, Gloucestershire, GL5 2QG
www.thehistorypress.co.uk

© John Price, 2015

The right of John Price to be identified as the Author
of this work has been asserted in accordance with the
Copyright, Designs and Patents Act 1988.

All rights reserved. No part of this book may be reprinted
or reproduced or utilised in any form or by any electronic,
mechanical or other means, now known or hereafter invented,
including photocopying and recording, or in any information
storage or retrieval system, without the permission in writing
from the Publishers.

British Library Cataloguing in Publication Data.
A catalogue record for this book is available from the British Library.

ISBN 978 0 7509 5643 7

Typesetting and origination by The History Press
Printed in Great Britain

CONTENTS

Preface 7

Acknowledgements 11

Introduction: The Watts Memorial to Heroic Self-Sacrifice: Postman's Park, London . . . 13

CAUTION: MEN AT WORK

1. Made in London . . . . *(Griffin, Elliott, Nicholson, Underhill)* 17

2. 'Striving to save a comrade' . . . . *(Durrant, Mills, Jones, Rutter)* 28

3. Unsensational heroism . . . . *(Lucas, Rabbeth)* 39

RIVERS AND WATERWAYS

4. Lightermen and watermen . . . . *(Lowdell, Onslow)* 48

5. Messing about in boats . . . . *(Benning, Cazaly, Garnish)* 55

6. 'Dived in, but was drowned'. . . . . *(Blencowe, Donald, Emery, Farris)* 66

BOYS WILL BE BOYS

7. 'I saved him, but I could not save myself' *(Bristow, Fisher, Sisley, Gellman)* 80

8. His life for his friend . . . . *(Clinton, Morris, Selves, McConaghey)*. 92

A POLICEMAN'S LOT

9. 'On duty'. . . . . *(Funnell, Smith, Wright)* 104

10. Three in a row. . . . . *(Cook, Greenoff, Ricketts)* 118

NOBLE WOMEN

11. The stewardess of the *Stella*. . . . . *(Rogers)*. 133

12. 'Our Alice'. *(Ayres)* 143

TRAINS AND RAILWAYS

13. 'Heroism on the engine' . . . . *(Dean, Peart)* 154

14. Platelayers and flagmen . . . . *(Goodrum, Pemberton)* 172

15. One under . . . . *(Craft, Hewins)*. 179

LONDON'S BURNING

16. Firemen of the brigade. . . . . *(Ford, Lee)* 188

17. Friends and neighbours . . . . *(Bannister, Simons, Slade)* 202

18. The 'cult of domesticity'. . . . . *(Coghlam, Kennedy, Smith)* 215

19. Her life for her children . . . . *(Denman, Donovan, Jarman, Regelous)* 229

DEATH BY MISADVENTURE

20. 'Kicked by a horse' . . . . *(Boxall, Drake)* 246

21. Skating on thin ice. . . . . *(Clack, Simpson)* 253

BEYOND THE STREETS OF LONDON

22. 'A desperate venture'. . . . . *(Strange, Tomlinson)* 262

23. 'A stranger and a foreigner' . . . . *(Brown, Cambridge)* 268

    Afterword 275

    List of tablets and inscriptions 279

    Notes 285

    Bibliography 308

    Index 317

PREFACE

It must be nearly twenty years since I first visited Postman's Park and, like many other people, I was looking for a quiet spot to eat my lunch. It is difficult to sum up and convey first impressions of the Watts Memorial, certainly amazement, admiration, captivation and melancholy, but also intrigue, speculation, confusion and questions; lots and lots of questions. At the time, the only study of the memorial was a small self-published booklet by Harry Dagnall which, although admirable, was little more than a reproduction of an earlier 1930s publication and gave very little information about the memorial itself or details of the people commemorated. At that time, I was in no position to seek answers to my questions, but over the years, life moved on and new horizons appeared.

Since that first visit I have had the enormous privilege of being able to dedicate time and resources to researching and studying the memorial and the people who feature upon it in great detail. As a mature student studying history, it became the subject of my undergraduate dissertation, which grew into an article for an academic journal, then into a short book for the Watts Gallery. The monument inspired me to investigate the concept of 'everyday' heroism, which led to a Ph.D. in modern history, through which I gained the abilities and the time to explore the subject in depth and to write this book. This is the first study of all sixty-two people who feature on the memorial and it has become clear to me, while researching and writing it, why nobody had attempted it before.

The memorial tablets present single snapshot moments in the lives of otherwise unremarkable people who, predominantly, lived more than a hundred years ago and tended not to feature heavily in the records of the time; aside from the occasional census and the registers of births, marriages and deaths. As such, there is always going to be a limit to how much can be learned about their lives and their deaths. These problems were, however, further compounded by lax and inaccurate newspaper reporting, mistakes made by G.F. Watts when transcribing information, and the loss of records, particularly coroner's inquests. A few of the people proved relatively straight-forward to identify and locate, but the majority have required lengthy and protracted investigations. Even then, it has occasionally come down to educated supposition and settling for the 'most probable' candidate as conclusive proof has remained elusive.

My intentions throughout the book have been threefold: to provide a concise family history for each person, to detail fully the circumstances in which they lost their life and to provide some historical context to their life and death. I think it is important to know who each individual was and their background, so that each can be understood as a person, with a family and friends, rather than just a name on a memorial. To that end I have endeavoured to identify the parents and siblings of eve-ryone commemorated; for those who married, I have identified their spouse, and for those with families of their own, their children. I have also, where possible, tracked the lives of family members following the death of the hero; for unmarried heroes I have followed their parents and siblings but, for married individuals, I have focused on their spouse, their children and, in some instances, their grandchildren. Given the scope of this book, I have had to be selective and there have been some families where sheer numbers or commonality of surname has made it unfeasible for me to trace multiple siblings. I have, though, tried to provide sufficient information to allow others the pleasure and satisfaction of continuing that genealogical research.

When writing the stories of the incidents, I have aimed to balance the factual history with the drama of the situation and to construct narratives which are as accu-rate and detailed as possible, but still entertaining and engaging to read. Drama and spectacle were often central components to the 'heroism' of the events and this is something I have tried to reflect. The narratives have been constructed primarily from newspaper reports, and to make them straightforward to follow I have often compiled multiple accounts into a single story. In some instances, different reports provided slightly different accounts, and on those occasions, I have based my narrative upon the most frequently cited details or those which are most plausible in the light of other information. In the interests of readability, I have kept references to a mini-mum but those interested in sources will find everything meticulously documented in the endnotes.

This book could easily have been a straightforward directory or reference guide to the memorial, simply providing information about each individual and listing them alphabetically or in tablet order. However, as a historian, I have always been inter-ested in the memorial as a historical source and as a portal into the past, which is partly why I decided to approach things differently. Adopting a thematic approach and placing each individual within a historical context allows us to explore Victorian and Edwardian London and gain a better understanding of the city in which they lived. Again, as with documenting the family history of the individual, this histori-cal context helps to reveal the life and experiences of the individual, rather than just focusing on the circumstances of their death. This book is by no means intended to be a detailed history of London in the nineteenth and early twentieth centuries, but I do hope that readers discover interesting things about the city and the times while also learning about those commemorated on the monument.

During my research, I have really got to know each of the people commemorated on the memorial and I hope that readers will also come to know them through this book. Throughout the process, I have been struck time and time again by the fact that they were actual people, who lived real lives, and who, whatever the circumstances, experienced a sudden and untimely death that took them from their loved ones. As such, I have taken great care to treat them with the respect that they deserve, not because they were 'everyday heroes' but because they were genuine people. Where possible I have visited the graves of those commemorated and those have been inexplicably moving experiences which brought home the reality and gravity of otherwise distant events. The memorial is not a place for mourning, but it is a place for contemplation and remembrance; something which I hope visitors, perhaps inspired by this book, will bear in mind.

It has been at least ten years in the making, but this book is, essentially, the one I envisaged writing, and implausibly declared I would one day write, long before I really had the necessary skills or opportunities to do so. It is also very much the book I wanted to read all those years ago when I first came across the memorial, but which nobody at that time had written. It has been an enormous pleasure to write and I hope people will derive similar pleasure from reading it.

Acknowledgements

One does not research and write a book of this nature without accruing many debts, and I am immensely grateful for all the assistance and support I have received along the way. I would like to acknowledge the support of the Arts and Humanities Research Council, which sponsored my Ph.D. and laid the foundations for everything that has followed. I would like to thank the staff and students at Goldsmiths: University of London, King's College London, and the University of Roehampton who, over the years, have all provided an intellectually stimulating and supportive environment which has allowed me to pursue my research and writing. The Watts Gallery has always been, and continues to be, highly supportive and it is always a pleasure to work with everyone there. In the past, I relied heavily upon the staff at the British Library Newspaper Archive in Colindale and the Manuscripts Department at the Guildhall Library in the City of London, and I thank them for their patience and diligence. Numerous people have provided me with information about people on the memorial and I am particularly indebted to Rob Jeffries, Elizabeth Peacey and Helen Simpson for advice and copies of documents and images.

Finally, sincere and heartfelt thanks to friends and family who, over the years, have all spent many hours with me in the park, which is always chilly whatever the season, and have encouraged and supported me to pursue my research and writing; in particular, my partner, Tina, and my mother, Carol, without whom I could not have written this book.

INTRODUCTION

THE WATTS MEMORIAL TO HEROIC SELF-SACRIFICE: POSTMAN'S PARK, LONDON

In the shadow of the Museum of London and a short distance from St Paul's Cathedral there is a small public garden, adjacent to the church of St Botolph's Aldersgate, intriguingly named Postman's Park. The large building to the southern end of the garden was once the home of the General Post Office and the park became a regular spot for postmen to take their breaks, hence its unusual name. As with many green spaces in central London, the park was a by-product of the Metropolitan Burial Act of 1852, which led to the closure of burial grounds and graveyards, many of which were converted into gardens. Officially opened by the Lord Mayor of London on 30 July 1900, Postman's Park continues, to this day, to offer a beautiful oasis of tranquillity in the heart of the bustling city. It is, though, particularly well known for another reason, as the home of one of the most remarkable and enchanting monuments in London.[1]

The Watts Memorial to Heroic Self-Sacrifice in Postman's Park contains fifty-four ceramic tablets, each of which tells an evocative story about a person, or people, who lost their own life while attempting to save the life of another.[2] The tablets are fixed to a wall, approximately 50ft long, and protected from the weather by a wooden structure that stands about 9ft high and contains bench seating to encourage people to linger (see plate 1). The fifty-four memorial tablets are spread across two long rows of twenty-four, which span the length of the cloister wall, and a smaller row of six, starting from the left-hand side (see plate 2). Each tablet, manufactured using small glazed tiles, records the name of the individual and the date and details of the incident in which they perished (see plate 3). Illustrated tiles on either side act as a border and separate one tablet from another.

Every tablet has a unique story to tell and they are all fascinating in their own way. Some are truly heart-rending, such as in the case of Alice Denman who died, along with four of her children, all under 10, in a house fire in Hackney in 1902. Some are rather grizzly, like the deaths of Frederick Craft and James Hewins, both run over by trains while trying to pull people off the tracks. Others, though, are almost a comedy of errors, particularly in the case of some of the boating accidents where, in hindsight, easily avoidable and foolhardy mishaps end in dreadful and tragic catastrophes. Many of the stories illustrate the precarious nature of Victorian working-class life, with dangerous workplaces being the settings for many incidents, but also house fires started by oil lamps and young children being left to their own devices.

Sixty-two people are commemorated on the memorial: eight children, nine women and forty-five men. The ages range from 8-year-old Henry Bristow to Daniel Pemberton, who was 61 when he died. The earliest recorded incident is that of Sarah Smith, a pantomime artist who perished in 1863, and all but one of the people who feature died between 1863 and 1927. Six Metropolitan Police officers and two members of the Fire Brigade are commemorated, but essentially the memorial is dedicated to 'everyday' heroism; acts of life-risking bravery, undertaken by otherwise ordinary people, largely in the course of their everyday life, and usually within commonplace surroundings. Victorian heroes tend to be regarded as synonymous with military or imperial 'great men of history', but everyday heroism was also an important and prominent idea at the time, championed by some high-profile and influential figures, one of whom conceived and built the Watts Memorial in Postman's Park.[3]

The memorial takes its name from its creator, the Victorian artist George Frederic Watts. Considered by many to have been the greatest painter of the Victorian age, Watts enjoyed an unparalleled reputation as a portraitist, a sculptor, a landscape painter and a symbolist; talents and skills which earned him the title 'England's Michelangelo'.[4] In the 1860s, as incidents of everyday heroism became more widely reported, Watts became fascinated with the subject and began to formulate plans for a public sculpture or memorial to commemorate it. These initial plans did not come to fruition, but the artist's passion and commitment were undaunted and he kept the idea in mind for the next twenty years.

Watts' first tangible public suggestion for a monument to everyday heroism appeared in a letter to *The Times*, published on 5 September 1887 under the headline of 'Another Jubilee Suggestion'.[5] In this letter, Watts put forward his plans for a scheme to commemorate Queen Victoria's Golden Jubilee by declaring that 'The character of a nation as a people of great deeds is one, it appears to me, that should not be lost sight of. It must surely be a matter of regret when names worthy to be remembered and stories stimulating and instructive are allowed to be forgotten.' In order to prevent this, Watts suggested that details of cases of everyday heroism during Victoria's reign should be collected and compiled. These could then form the basis for monuments to commemorate those 'likely to be forgotten heroes' whose sacrifices were ephemerally reported in the newspapers. Regrettably, those planning the jubilee celebrations did not share Watts' vision and his plans for a national monument failed to get off the ground.

However, in 1898 Henry Gamble, the vicar of St Botolph's church, invited Watts to utilise a proposed extension to Postman's Park as the site for his monument and the artist gratefully accepted. Work began in 1899 and the wooden 'cloister' structure, constructed by J. Simpson and Son, was completed in time for the official opening of the park on 30 July 1900. At that time, there were only four tablets on the memorial and those had been manufactured by the noted ceramicist William De Morgan, who was a personal acquaintance of Watts'. These four tablets were followed in 1902 by a further nine, all of which were selected by Watts and manufactured by De Morgan. Watts had, for some years, been compiling long handwritten lists and transcriptions of acts of heroism from information collected for him from newspaper reports, so he had more than sufficient cases to fill his monument. It seemed he was perfectly poised to complete the project that had meant so much to him, but sadly it was something he would not live to accomplish. On 1 July 1904, George Frederic Watts died aged 87 at his London home, New Little Holland House, with his wife Mary by his side.

The Watts Memorial then developed in stages over the following thirty years.[6] In 1905, an additional eleven tablets, made by De Morgan, were erected which completed the first row of twenty-four. In 1908, a second complete row of twenty-four tablets, manufactured by Doulton of Lambeth, was fixed to the memorial wall, bringing the total number to forty-eight. In 1919, a single tablet, dedicated to a constable killed during an air raid, was installed, but after the First World War, interest in the memorial waned. In 1929, following some press attention on the lack of new commemorations, the committee made a public appeal for funds and raised £250 to recommence the erecting of tablets. The Metropolitan Police submitted three names and the tablets were erected and unveiled in a ceremony presided over by the Bishop of London on 15 October 1930. At the same time, a single tablet was installed on the same row to replace one that had been removed from the De Morgan row (see chapters 2 and 10). This more or less marked the end of developments with the memorial until 2009, when a single modern-day tablet was installed. This prompted speculation that further modern cases might be commemorated, but decisions were subsequently reached which now make that extremely unlikely (see the Afterword).

The Watts Memorial is a wonderfully 'historic' monument, suffused with Victorian language and redolent with the morals, values and beliefs of that society; it is something of a curiosity from a bygone era locked in the context of its time, and that is what makes it particularly interesting and valuable today. For while the heroic actions of those commemorated are still familiar enough to evoke emotions such as sadness, empathy and admiration, the tablets also generate another reaction: curiosity. Each short narrative provides just enough information to fascinate, but insufficient to elucidate, and, as with many historic monuments, the Watts Memorial frequently gives rise to more questions than answers. Many of these are curiosities about the people commemorated: who were they, where did they come from, who were their friends and family, what sort of life did they lead and, ultimately, what exactly happened in the incident which cost them their life? In this respect, the memorial continues to fulfil one of Watts's original objectives, in that it encourages the viewer to seek the person behind the act and to wonder what type of person would undertake it.

In the chapters that follow, many of those questions will be answered and, for the first time, the lives and deaths of all sixty-two people commemorated will be revealed. Each tablet focuses on the death of an individual, but behind each death there was a life and because it was a life lived in a different time to our own there is much we can learn from exploring it. What is more, the lives that feature on the Watts Memorial were the relatively unremarkable lives of otherwise ordinary working-class people; the kinds of people who would have remained 'hidden from history' were it not for the newsworthy circumstances of their death. They are the kinds of people who, historically, are notoriously difficult to locate because they tend not to feature in many records. Moreover, when they do feature, it is often in negative contexts: when they break the law, when they enter an institution like a workhouse or an asylum, or in surveys of their poverty and deprivation. The circumstances recorded on the memorial may not have been exactly 'positive', but the monument does arguably provide a more neutral or objective perspective from which to gain insights into everyday life in Victorian and Edwardian England.

This is one of the wonderful but often overlooked qualities of the memorial: its value as a historical source and its ability to forge links between the present and the past as well as between imagination and reality. It is fascinating, when reading each narrative, to speculate about the life of the individual, but even more satisfying to really know about them and who they were. The memorial commemorates (and to some degree celebrates) 'everyday heroes', people who gave their own life while trying to save others, and that is what ultimately draws people in. But behind each hero there was also an everyday life and, by and large, they were people who got up and got on with it, who did their jobs, earned their wages, raised their families, cared for their loved ones, perhaps went to the pub, or went to the seaside, or out on a boat trip or skating in the winter; they might be people who did well, people who got by, or people who had next to nothing. They were, essentially, 'people like us' and this is why, although they themselves are long since gone, their stories can continue to inform and educate, as well as to captivate and enthral. What follows, then, are their stories; the stories of the otherwise ordinary people who have come to be known as the Everyday Heroes of Postman's Park.

CAUTION: MEN AT WORK

1

MADE IN LONDON

There are two somewhat enduring myths about London and industrialisation: one is that London was more or less bypassed by the Industrial Revolution, with very little manufacturing taking place, and the other is that the limited manufacturing that did occur took place in tiny workshops or people's homes rather than in large factories. Both of these myths are exactly that, myths, and Jerry White, in his book *London in the Nineteenth Century*, offers excellent evidence to counter them.[7] White suggests that 630,000 Londoners – that is, one in three workers living in the county of London – made things in factories, in workshops or at home. He also estimates that 560,000 of those people worked in factories and workshops, and that a third of those, nearly 175,000 people, worked in factories employing more than 100 people. White argues that large factories were a central feature of London's working life, but the city was so vast that it 'swamped them and rendered them barely visible in the big picture'.

Almost anything might be 'made in London', but the capital was an especially ideal location for large-scale production of 'luxury' food and drink because there was a ready and prosperous consumer market right on the doorstep.[8] In terms of food, examples include Crosse and Blackwell pickling in Charing Cross, Bassetts making sweets in Wood Green, Keillers boiling jam in West Ham and Peak Frean baking biscuits in Bermondsey. To wash those down, there were numerous maltsters, distillers and mineral water manufacturers along the south bank of the Thames, and major brewers including Courage, Fuller's, Truman's, Watney's and Young's all established

their businesses in the capital. These large manufactories required considerable man-
power and they offered a range of employment opportunities to willing Londoners;
from white-collar jobs in the offices, down to labourers in the yards, plenty of people
clocked in at factories in London, but sometimes they did not clock out again.

In 1882, the pioneering sugar refiner William Garton moved his premises from
Canute Road in Southampton, where he had been based since 1847, to a new refinery at Southampton Wharf in Battersea.[9] Originally a brewer, Garton had developed
a type of invert-sugar, which he called saccharum, that was ideally suited for the
brewing industry, so he moved into producing that rather than the beer and he made
a fortune. The site at Battersea was known as the Garton, Hill and Company sugar
refinery and it was a large employer in the area.

One of its employees was **Thomas Griffin**, who, in 1899, had been working at
the refinery for around two years, having moved to London from Northamptonshire
(see plate 4). Thomas was born in the village of Sibbertoft near Market Harborough
in 1877. His parents were William Irson Griffin, a labourer, and Hannah Wilson,
the daughter of an agricultural labourer, who married in 1868. Their first child was a
daughter, Mary Jane, born in 1869, followed by another daughter, Hannah Elizabeth,
in 1873 and then Thomas in 1877. In 1881, Hannah and Thomas were living with
their parents in a house on Welford High Street but, presumably due to a lack of space,
Mary Jane was living nearby with her paternal grandparents, Isaac and Mary Griffin,
at their home on Front Street in Sibbertoft. By 1891, however, the family's living
arrangements had become even more complicated.

Between 1887 and 1891 William and Hannah had three more children: a set of
twins, Walter and Sarah Jane, in 1887 and then, in 1888, Margaret Ellen. William and
Hannah's home in Well Lane, Welford was simply not large enough to accommodate the sudden family increase and so a 'needs must' shuffling of family members
was undertaken. William and Hannah's son, Walter, lived with them and shared a
room with his 7-year-old cousin, Fred. Meanwhile, their eldest son, Thomas, went
to live with his maternal grandparents, John and Hannah Wilson, in their house on
Back Street in Welford.

This just left the couple's three youngest daughters, Hannah, Sarah Jane and
Margaret Ellen, who moved in with their paternal grandparents in Sibbertoft, Mary
Jane having already moved out and sought work in London by that time. It would
seem that the living arrangements were very much driven by practicalities, but the
relatively close proximity of the grandparents assisted greatly. Furthermore, by that
time William and Hannah's two eldest children were both working, Hannah as a
corset maker and Thomas as an agricultural labourer, so they were also able to help
financially support the two households in which they were living.

When Thomas and Hannah's eldest daughter, Mary Jane, left the home of her paternal grandparents, she headed for London and by 1891 she was working as a domestic servant for John and Ellen Dunn at 26 Santos Road in Wandsworth. Late in 1891, Mary married Edward Cronin in Wandsworth and the couple settled in the area, which is what then brought her brother, Thomas Griffin, to the south-western part of London. In around 1897, he secured work as a fitter's labourer at Garton's sugar refinery in Battersea, and by April 1899 he was living nearby at 75 Usk Road in Clapham Junction. It was an exciting time for Thomas, who was engaged to be married on 16 April, and on 11 April he travelled to Northamptonshire to discuss arrangements with his family and then back home to Battersea for work the next day. Griffin expected that by the end of the week he would be married; but that was not to be, and by the end of the following day, he was dead.

At Battersea Coroner's Court on 17 April 1899, Walter Schroeder, the deputy coroner for London, Middlesex and Surrey, opened the inquest into the death of Thomas Griffin.[10] Frederick Biggs, a friend and co-worker of Griffin's, told the court that at around 6 a.m. on 12 April he and several other men, including Thomas, were in the hydraulic room of the factory, changing into their work clothes. Biggs relayed how he then went into the adjoining boiler room to drain some water from a steam pipe, leaving the other men in the hydraulic room. His memory of the events that followed was hazy, but he recalled the pipe shaking slightly, then a loud noise, a sudden cloud of steam, and a blow to the chest which had knocked him off his feet and sent him tumbling into the corner of the room. Realising the room was quickly filling with steam, he had staggered to the nearest door, which led him out into a yard, and then he had gone in search of the main valve to turn the steam off.

Next up to give evidence was William Woodman, a steam-engine driver who had worked for Garton's for over thirty years. On the morning of the incident he had been getting changed with the other men when they suddenly heard a loud explosion, followed by a rush of steam from the boiler room. Woodman ran forward and pulled the door shut, telling the men that under no circumstances were they to go into the boiler room, and he then climbed out of a window and went to turn off the steam. When he returned a few minutes later, the hydraulic room was empty and, going to investigate, he found several of his workmates in an office tending to Griffin, who appeared to be badly scalded on his face and hands. Keen to establish what had happened, Woodman spoke to Samuel Tippler, who had been with Griffin at the time of the incident.

Addressing the coroner and the jury, Samuel Tippler explained how, shortly after Woodman had left the hydraulic room, Griffin, who was very agitated, suddenly cried out, 'My mate! My mate!' and before anyone could stop him, the young man disappeared into the boiler room. While waiting anxiously for Griffin to return, someone looking out through the window spotted a figure staggering around the yard and so Tippler and several other men climbed out and went to help. The figure was Thomas

Griffin, his hands so badly scalded that the skin was hanging from them, and the blistering on his face had closed up his eyes. Tippler and the other men carried Griffin to the office, where they applied wet cloths to his burns and made arrangements to have him conveyed to the local infirmary.

When Griffin arrived at the nearby Bolingbroke Hospital beside Wandsworth Common, he was examined by Dr Cecil Lister, one of the house surgeons, who told the inquest that he was impressed by the 'excellent first aid' that the victim had received at the refinery. Nonetheless, Griffin was 'severely scalded over the whole of his body', and although he was admitted and treated, he died later that day, the cause of death being 'shock and exhaustion'. As news filtered back to the refinery, there was dismay and sadness among the workers as they came to terms with what had happened; the only slight consolation was that Griffin had behaved so honourably. In Tippler's opinion, 'had he [Griffin] remained where he was before he entered the room he would have been perfectly safe', and Biggs testified that 'since the accident he had come to the conclusion that Griffin had run into the room to rescue him when he [Griffin] was scalded'.[11]

Because it was an industrial accident, the inquest was attended by Mr Arbuckle, a factory inspector from the Home Office, and Mr Harper, a legal representative acting in the interests of Garton, Hill and Company. Harper was quick to point out that it was the first incident of that nature which had ever occurred at the works, that the steam pipe had been fully pressurised for three days prior to the incident and that the pressure was relatively low at the time the pipe fractured. It was believed that a small crack in the pipe had allowed cold water to mix with the steam, which had then caused the catastrophic failure. Harper also expressed the company's sympathy with Griffin's relatives and declared that they 'fully realised the splendid conduct and high motive that prompted the deceased to act as he did'. With all the evidence heard, the jury delivered its verdict, 'that the deceased was killed through the bursting of a steam pipe and that he died at his post as a hero in trying to rescue his mate, the sad death being due to misadventure'.[12]

Schroeder formally released the body and announced that Griffin was to be buried near his family home in Welford, Northamptonshire. Following the death of their son, William and Hannah moved back to live in Welford High Street and continued to reside in the area until their deaths; Margaret in 1924 aged 76 and William in 1933 aged 85. All three of Thomas' sisters got married: Margaret Ellen wed William Rogers in 1911 and they had at least seven children, Sarah Jane married Charles Woolmer, a road labourer for the county council, in 1908 and they had at least two children, and Hannah married John Golby Meakins, an agricultural labourer, in 1904, after which the couple ran the Swan Inn in Welford.[13] Margaret died in 1969 aged 81, Sarah Jane died in 1962 aged 75 and Hannah died in 1956 aged 82. Thomas' brother, Walter Griffin, lived with his parents until at least 1901, and in 1911 he was working as a domestic horseman for the Stapleton-Bretherton family at Wheeler Lodge in Husbands Bosworth in Leicestershire. It is not entirely clear what happened to Walter after this.

When the coroner closed the inquest into Griffin's death, he lamented that 'the conduct of a man like him deserves to be recorded. No doubt there are heroes in everyday life, but they do not come to the front and so we do not hear of them.'[14] These could almost have been the words of G.F. Watts, who most certainly felt the same way, and just over a year after the incident at the sugar refinery, Thomas Griffin was among the first four people to be commemorated upon the newly opened memorial in Postman's Park. By the end of 1908, another forty-four tablets had been added, and among them was another to three men who died in an accident at a large industrial plant in London, manufacturing a product that had become synonymous with the capital: gin.

In the nineteenth century, the area commonly known as 'Three Mills' in Bromley-by-Bow, east London, derived its name, ostensibly, from the three mill buildings which had been erected there in living memory: the House Mill, built in 1776, the Clock Mill, built in 1817, and a windmill, which was replaced by a steam engine in the mid-nineteenth century.[15] However, the name 'Three Mills' had earlier origins, perhaps as far back as the fourteenth century, and the site, bordered by the River Lea to the west and the Channelsea river to the south, had been a location for milling since at least the eleventh century. In the fifteenth and sixteenth centuries, the mills were known for supplying flour to the bakers of Stratford-at-Bow, but in the 1730s they began milling for another purpose that would entirely alter the area.

In 1727, a consortium led by Peter Lefevre, the son of a Huguenot refugee, acquired the site for the purpose of building a distillery. It was the height of the so-called 'gin craze' in Georgian London and it was estimated that around 10 million gallons of the spirit were being distilled in the capital every year.[16] The mills ground the grain which formed the meal, and this was then brewed and distilled into base spirit, so it made sound business sense to build distilleries close to mills. Lefevre went on to set up another distillery nearby and the area became synonymous with producing alcohol for the gin trade. Daniel Bisson, Lefevre's former apprentice, took over the management of Three Mills and it was Bisson who built the House Mill in 1776. After a downturn in their fortunes, the consortium sold Three Mills and in 1872 the site was acquired by one of London's largest and best known distillers of gin: J. & W. Nicholson & Co. Ltd.[17]

Brothers John and William Nicholson began distilling gin in Clerkenwell in around 1802 through a partnership with their cousin, John Bowman, who had established himself as a distiller and brandy merchant some years earlier. They soon branched out on their own and built their own distillery, in Woodbridge Street, Clerkenwell, where they rectified, or re-distilled, base alcohol and added flavourings, predominantly juniper, to make gin. It is likely that the Nicholsons were already purchasing their base spirit from the Three Mills distillery, and acquiring the site in 1872 was a logical step to integrating the two stages in the process. Production of their trademark 'Lamplighter' gin was moved to Three Mills and for the next sixty years the Nicholsons continued to distil spirits on the site.[18]

J. & W. Nicholson & Co. was very much a family business, established by two brothers and then inherited by generations of their sons. John Nicholson (1778–1846) passed his share of the management of the business down to his son, William, who was born in 1824. William enjoyed a successful career as a first-class cricketer with the Marylebone Cricket Club (MCC) and the Middlesex County Cricket Club; he was said to be a free-scoring batsman and a competent wicket keeper.[19] Upon retirement from the sport he took over the management of the distillery but kept close links with his former club, donating large sums of money to the MCC to purchase the freehold of Lord's cricket ground and build the Lord's pavilion. It also seems likely that the famous 'egg and bacon' red and gold colour scheme of the MCC was adopted in honour of Nicholson's generosity, red and yellow being the brand colours of Nicholson's gin.

In August 1858, William Nicholson married Isabella Sarah Meek, whose family were business partners with the Nicholsons, and sometime before 1861 the couple moved into 25 Westbourne Terrace in Kensington. Over the next fifteen years, William and Isabella had fourteen children, the twelfth of which was **Godfrey Maule Nicholson**, born on 31 March 1872.[20] To accommodate their ever-expanding family, William and Isabella moved to 4 Sussex Square in Kensington, where Godfrey lived until at least 1881. By 1891, he had become a resident at the Grange in Hartley Witney near Farnborough in Hampshire, at what appears to have been a school or training establishment connected with the Militia. The Militia was a part-time voluntary defence force which had been created in 1757 and was organised on a county-by-county basis.

The school had three tutors: Samuel Kirchoffer, army school tutor, Frederick Brewer, mathematics tutor, and Gustavas Oierke, modern languages, and five young men between the ages of 11 and 20 were living there. Two of the men were described as 'students' and the other three, including Godfrey, were listed as 'militia officers'. Militia regiments, after 1881, were attached to units in the regular army, so it is possible that Godfrey may, at that time, have been considering a career as a military officer rather than following his father into the distilling trade.

Despite his spell in the Militia, Godfrey did, after all, follow his father into the family business and by the mid-1890s he was the managing director of the Nicholson gin distillery at Three Mills in Stratford. Godfrey was still in his mid-twenties and in many ways his lifestyle reflected his status as a young, wealthy metropolitan bachelor. In 1901, just three months before he died, he was living at 2 South Audley Street in fashionable Mayfair with a full household staff: a housekeeper, a kitchen maid, two housemaids and a manservant. However, it would appear that, in the day-to-day running of the distillery, Godfrey remained very much a 'hands on' manager and he was not averse to supervising his men personally, even in the most mundane and laborious of tasks.

It was 12 July 1901 and a group of men, supervised by Nicholson, had made their way to the north-west corner of the Three Mills site where there was an old well which had been dug about ten years earlier to collect ground water.[21] This waste water had been used in the distillery for cooling and condensing, but the well had been dry for about two years following the construction of a London County Council (LCC) sewer nearby. Nicholson had recently been informed that the LCC had suspended use of the sewer and so he wanted to check if sufficient water had accumulated in the well to make pumping it worthwhile. The work party consisted of Nicholson and three other men: Albert Dawkins, the yard foreman, and Thomas Pickett and Joseph Barber, both labourers. Dawkins had brought a ladder and an 11ft measuring pole, which would be dipped into the well to ascertain the depth of water.

The well was opened, the ladder was lowered in and Pickett descended with the pole to measure the depth. Having done so, he handed the pole to Dawkins who was in the process of checking the water mark when he saw Pickett fall limply backwards from the ladder and down into the well. Nicholson exclaimed, 'Good heavens' and, rushing to the ladder, he hurried to the bottom where he found Pickett unconscious in the water. Nicholson managed to get hold of him and was moving towards the ladder when he too suddenly lost consciousness and slid back down into the darkness. Dawkins too was about to climb into the well when Barber said he thought Pickett and Nicholson might have been overcome by gas and he should not go down without a rope, so he could be pulled up if he passed out. Looking around for ropes, Dawkins spotted another worker nearby and called to him for help. The man who responded and ran over was George Frederick Elliott, who worked as a tunman at the distillery.

George Frederick Elliott lived in Bow but he was not originally from the area. He had been born in the Huntingdonshire village of Swineshead, where he was christened on 13 May 1866. He was the eldest child of George Frederick Elliott senior, an agricultural labourer, and Hannah Bass, a lace maker, who had married in Risely in Bedfordshire on 24 July 1865. George junior had five siblings, Walter (b. 1870), James Alfred (b. 1873), Esther Emma (b. 1875), Rachel Mary (b. 1877) and Ellen Elizabeth (b. 1880), and sometime around 1877 the family moved from Swineshead to Raunds near Thrapston in Northamptonshire. Like his father, George worked for a short time as an agricultural labourer before moving to London, where he found work as a porter and settled in Camden Town. On 9 November 1890, George Elliott married Emma Neale, the daughter of a labourer, at the parish church of St Leonard and St Mary in Bromley, and shortly after the couple moved into 16 Goldington Street in St Pancras, where their first child, Dorothy, was born in 1891. The couple then had two more children, Frederick George, born on 9 August 1892, and Flora Ida Emma, born on 28 September 1894. To accommodate their growing family, George and Emma moved to 24 Imperial Street in Bromley and that was how George came to be working at the distillery, which was just around the corner from the house.

Hearing the cries for help, George ran over to the well, and realising what had happened, he said he would go down and help the men. Barber implored Elliott to wait until Dawkins returned with the ropes, but Elliott dismissed the risks by saying, 'I'll go down, I am used to a little gas.' Barber warned him not to descend too far until he had the measure of the situation, but Elliott went down to the bottom and Barber saw him pass out and disappear into the water below. Barber began shouting loudly for help and this roused the attentions of other men around the distillery grounds. Two men working in some nearby workshops heard the alarm and, wondering what the commotion was, they ran over to where a small crowd was gathering around the well. One of the men, a labourer named Smale, placed his head over the entrance of the well and, turning to his co-worker, cautioned, 'Good god, mate, it is full now,' referring to the level of gas. This did not, however, deter the other man – a labourer named Robert Underhill.

Evidence suggests that this labourer was **Robert Arthur Underhill**, who had been born in North Aylesford near Strood in Kent in 1877. His father, Robert senior, was a blacksmith who, on 29 December 1873, had married Eliza Mary Merritt in Rochester in Kent. The couple's first child, Richard William, was born the following year, then Robert Arthur in 1877 and Alice Maud in 1880. In 1881 the family was living at 2 Garden Row off Dunnings Lane in Rochester, but by 1891 they had moved to 18 Franklin Street in Bromley-by-Bow, a few streets away from the distillery, and a fourth child, May (b. 1892), had arrived. The family were still in the area ten years later, living at 38 Egleton Street, and Robert junior was working as a labourer at the Three Mills distillery. He was entered on the census by his middle name of Arthur, rather than Robert, and his age was incorrectly recorded as 19 when he was actually about to turn 24. He was also about to become a married man, with a wedding booked for 5 August, the bank holiday Monday. It was, however, a date he was sadly not going to keep.

The crowd watched on as Robert Underhill grasped the rails of the ladder and, drawing in a huge breath, descended down into the well. Within minutes, a splash was heard and then nothing; Robert too had been overcome by the gas and passed out in the water. Dawkins arrived with ropes and Job Vanning, a joiner at the distillery, was lowered down into the well under instructions to hitch the rope around whichever body he could find and then the two of them would be pulled back up again. He reported that he felt fine as he was being lowered into the well; he did not taste or smell any gas and he was not in any pain. He managed to locate one of the bodies but as he was trying to tie the rope he suddenly 'felt as though he was going to sleep' and, afterwards, did not remember being pulled unconscious from the well.

In the end, it was the fire brigade that recovered the four bodies, with firemen using smoke hoods, which trapped fresh air under them, as improvised breathing apparatus. A doctor, George Hilliard, had been called to the distillery at about 1 p.m., but as the bodies were recovered it was clear there was nothing he could do. He declared each man dead at the scene and, at the coroner's inquest held at Stratford Town Hall on 13 July, he gave the cause of death as asphyxiation caused by carbonic acid gas (carbon dioxide).[22] Evidence presented at the inquest suggested that in the time that the sewer had been sealed, rotting weeds had given off the gas, which had been exacerbated by recent hot weather, and it had accumulated under the water. As Pickett broke the surface with the measuring stick, some of the gas escaped, which suffocated him, and as he fell into the water he released more of the gas, which subsequently suffocated Nicholson, Elliott and Underhill.

The coroner, Walter Attwater, questioned Charles Drake, one of the senior distillers, about why the air had not been tested using a lit candle, as was common practice, before any of the men ventured in. Drake replied that there was no reason to suspect an accumulation of gas and nothing to indicate that gas was present when the well was opened. He agreed with the coroner that it would, in hindsight, have been better to have tested the air before anyone went down. However, given the way in which the gas had been trapped and then released, it was likely that the air would have initially appeared clean and the disaster would have unfolded in the same fashion. Verdicts of 'accidental death' were recorded for each of the men and the coroner 'warmly commended the courage of the men who successively went down the well to rescue the others' and said that 'much credit was due to Banning'. A Mr Soames, representing the distillery owners, expressed the Nicholson family's 'sympathy with the relatives of the three men, two of whom had made such gallant attempts to save the life of Mr Godfrey Nicholson, who too had done his duty as a man and a citizen'.

Godfrey Nicholson's family were very well connected in official positions and offices. His father, William, had been elected Liberal MP for Petersfield in Hampshire on two occasions: first in an 1866 by-election, after which he held the seat until 1874, and then in the 1880 general election, serving until 1885 when the seat was disenfranchised. He then stood as a Conservative Party candidate but was defeated in both the 1885 and 1886 general elections.[23] Godfrey's brother, William Graham, had also been elected as MP for Petersfield in 1897 and Godfrey's brother-in-law was Sir Edward Bradford, the Commissioner of the Metropolitan Police.[24] Consequently, Godfrey's funeral was quite a grand affair but also a relatively private one and not overly reported upon. He was laid to rest in the churchyard of Holy Trinity church in Privett near Alton in Hampshire, his father having been a major benefactor to the church. The other three men were all buried in Woodgrange Park Cemetery on Romford Road in East Ham.

Following her husband's death, Ellen Elliott continued to live at 24 Imperial Street with their two daughters and her sister until at least 1911, when Dorothy and Flora were both working as cardboard box makers. Dorothy Elliott, Frederick's daughter, married John W. Hawkes in Rochford in Essex in 1915 and the couple had at least three children: John W. junior (b. 1916), Norman (b. 1919) and Derek (b. 1925). Frederick's son, Frederick George Elliott, remained in London and in 1915 was working as a cinema attendant when he married Dorothy Maud Collier, the daughter of a clock maker, at Christ Church in Haringey on 16 August. At the time, the couple's address was given as 83 Avondale Road. Frederick appears to have died, aged 77, in Hitchin in Hertfordshire in 1970.

Robert Underhill's father, Robert senior, died aged 63 in Poplar in 1906 and by 1911 his wife Eliza was living at 24 Franklin Street with her two daughters Alice and May. Alice had married a lighterman, Richard Bailey, in 1898 and the couple had two boys, Arthur and Albert, as well as having had a daughter, Alice junior, who died in infancy. Eliza and May were both working as matchbox makers, which was generally quite exploitative and poorly paid piece-work which would probably have been undertaken at home rather than in a factory. Eliza Underhill, Robert's mother, died in 1928. May, Robert's youngest sister, married Joseph Stapleton in 1920. The couple do not appear to have had any children and May died, aged 43, in 1935.

Godfrey's father, William Nicholson, died in 1909 and his mother, Isabella, in 1934. Most notable among his sisters was Edith Mary, who married Sir Edward Bradford, the Chief Commissioner of the Metropolitan Police, 1890–1903. Most notable among his brothers, other than William Graham, was John, who became a brigadier-general in the British army, serving in India, and then a commandant-general of the British South Africa Police, succeeding Robert Baden-Powell as inspector-general in 1903. In 1921, he was elected as the MP for the constituency of Westminster Abbey and he was re-elected in the following two general elections. He did not marry and died aged 60, on 21 February 1924. Most of Godfrey's other brothers served in the military and five of his six sisters married.

As he does not feature on the Watts Memorial, Thomas Pickett tends to get overlooked in accounts of the Three Mills incident, and it is true to say that his actions were not necessarily heroic in comparison to those of his co-workers. He did, nevertheless, lose his life in the incident and, as such, he should also be remembered. Thomas was born in 1875 to John Pickett, a bricklayer, and Eliza Kidd. In 1898 Thomas married Eliza Knappett, and in 1901, just before the incident, the couple were living with Eliza's family at 20 Marcus Street in West Ham. They did not have any children.

In 2001, to commemorate the centenary of the Three Mills incident, a new memorial was erected on the site of the well, which was, by then, Three Mills Green. The memorial features a contemporary sculpture, *Helping Hands*, by the artist Alec Peever, which depicts two clasped hands, one lifting the other, alongside pieces of inscription from an older monument which had consisted of a stone cross (see plate 6). One of the panels reads:

Of your charity pray for the souls of Thomas Pickett, Godfrey Maule Nicholson, Frederick Elliott and Robert Underhill who lost their lives in a well beneath this spot on 12 July 1901. The first named while in the execution of his duty was overcome by foul air. The three latter, successively descending in heroic efforts to save their comrades, shared the same death. Godfrey Maule Nicholson rests in Privett churchyard Hants and the other three were laid in Wood Grange Park Cemetery.[25]

In 2011, this memorial was moved about 50m to the west of its original position and the exact site of the well is now marked with a small stone disc carrying the words 'in memoriam' and the initials of the four men who died. It is hugely evocative to stand at that spot and know of the drama and tragedy that unfolded there over 100 years ago, and to remember the four men who perished in such dreadful circumstances.

2

'STRIVING TO SAVE A COMRADE'

Disposing of sewage has always been something of an issue for London and certainly a pressing concern since the medieval period, as rapid and continued population growth has kept the city among the most densely populated in Europe.[26] Up until around the 1840s, waste was generally collected in cesspools, which were then emptied by 'nightsoil' men who sold the contents to farmers for use as manure. The rudimentary system of sewers that had developed in the capital in the early modern period largely consisted of various tributaries which flowed into the Thames, and it was only ever intended for surface water; in fact, up until 1815 it was illegal to discharge effluent from buildings into the sewers.

However, in the mid-nineteenth century, two factors combined which led to enormous problems with London's waste disposal system. Firstly, imports of guano from South America undermined the market for human waste, and as nightsoil men increased their removal fees to compensate for their losses, fewer people had their cesspools emptied regularly. Coupled with this was increased use of water closets, which 'flushed' the waste using water and thus caused cesspools to fill and overflow far quicker. In an attempt to relieve the pressure on the system, the prohibition on discharging waste into the sewers was lifted and the River Thames became the new destination for the bulk of London's sewage.

Over the next decade or so, the condition of the river worsened as increasing levels of waste drained into it. The smell and the appearance were highly unpleasant, but as the river was also the main source of water for most Londoners there were serious public health implications as well. In 1858, a particularly hot, dry summer led to the so-called 'great stink'; an almost unbearable stench that emanated from the festering waters of the Thames. Overlooking the river, MPs in the new Palace of Westminster were so appalled by the situation that, having spent years discussing options and aborting plans, they finally settled on a solution. The chief engineer for the Metropolitan Board of Works, Joseph William Bazalgette, was charged with the task of revolutionising London's sewage system, and it was a challenge he rose to with enormous success.

Bazalgette's scheme was described as 'the most extensive and wonderful work of modern times', and much of the system he designed and built still underpins waste disposal in twenty-first-century London.[27] For south London, a 12-mile network of tunnels running from Clapham, Putney and Bermondsey deposited the sewage at Deptford, where a pumping station with four huge beam engines lifted the waste into the southern outfall sewer for the 7-mile journey to Crossness. Upon arrival at Crossness, the sewage was either released directly into the Thames at high tide or pumped into a reservoir to await the next high water.

On the northern side of the Thames, 9 miles of tunnels carried waste from the Hampstead area out to Old Ford on the River Lea, and another 12 miles of tunnels delivered sewage from Kensal Green and Piccadilly to the same destination. Running parallel with the Thames, a low-level sewer between Vauxhall and Blackfriars was incorporated into the ambitious Victoria Embankment development and beyond there it continued eastwards to Stratford in east London. There, at Abbey Mills, a grand and ornate pumping station was built and eight large beam engines lifted the waste into the northern outflow sewer for its 5-mile journey to the East Ham Sewage Works, where it was held in reservoirs until hide tide and then released into the Thames at Beckton along with the sewage from the southern outfall. The idea was that the tide would then carry the sewage out to sea and away from the population of London.

The system was not without its teething troubles but, overall, it was a huge success and the Prince of Wales opened Crossness Pumping Station in April 1865. The northern system became operational in 1868 with the opening of the Abbey Mills Pumping Station, and thousands of gallons of sewage began arriving at the Beckton Sewage Works. By 1895, the practice of discharging raw sewage directly into the river had ceased and the waste was being treated and then taken out to sea. Nevertheless, Bazalgette's system was adaptable to this and the East Ham Sewage Works became a site for treating waste rather than expelling it. A large workforce was employed at the works, covering a wide range of different occupations from managers and engineers down to engine-drivers, stokers and labourers. For most of the workers, it was not a pleasant or particularly well-paid job, but it offered stable and regular employment with the local council and, as such, opportunities were much sought after. In August 1895, ninety men applied for a single vacancy, which might not necessarily sound that remarkable, until the circumstances behind the vacancy are revealed.

It was around 7 a.m. on Monday, 1 July 1895 and a labourer at the East Ham Sewage Works, Walter Digby, was given a particularly unpleasant job to do.[28] An engineer had identified a problem with the pressure in one of the pumping systems and the most likely cause was that the filter screen had become blocked. The screen needed to be manually cleaned and access was via an inspection chamber which was reached by descending into a brick shaft, similar to a well. Digby needed assistance to get into the shaft, so he enlisted the help of another labourer, Charles King, who helped him to remove the heavy manhole covers. Peering into the darkness, Digby grumbled as he realised that sewage had backed up into the chamber, which would make his job all the more disagreeable. Transit down the shaft was via a metal ladder fixed to the inside wall and King watched as Digby lowered himself down onto the first rung of the ladder and slowly descended, step by step into the gloom.

Digby had got about halfway down the ladder when King heard him shout, 'I feel faint; I'll come back up again,' but as Walter got within a few rungs of the top, he suddenly appeared to lose his balance and his grip and he fell backwards from the ladder and disappeared into the blackness of the shaft. Assuming he had slipped, King called down several times to see if Digby was all right, but receiving no reply he began shouting for help. A number of men were working nearby and several ran over to find out what was going on. When King explained to them that Digby had slipped and fallen, the most senior of the men, a chief engineer, took charge of the situation. He sent a labourer to fetch some ropes and said that, in the meantime, he would go down to the bottom of the shaft and tend to Digby so that when the ropes arrived they could both be pulled up.

That chief engineer was **Frederick Mills**, the son of Charles Henry Mills, a ship's mate, and Mary Ann Barnes who married in Barking in 1857. The couple moved to the Limehouse area of east London, close to the docks where Charles worked, and children duly arrived: Charles Henry, born in 1858, and Mary E., born in 1860. Frederick was their third child, born in 1868, and by 1871 the family were living at 21 Cotton Street, again very close to the docks where Charles was, by that time, working as a stevedore, unloading goods from cargo ships. Two schoolmasters, William Carver and Harry Sheppard, were also lodging with the family and it is likely they were employed at the Poplar and Blackwall Free School in nearby Woolmore Street.

Charles and Mary Ann clearly felt comfortable sharing their home with school-master lodgers, as they continued to rent rooms to men of that profession when they moved to 21 Locksley Street. In 1881, the couple and their two youngest children, Mary and Frederick, were living at that address with Charles's niece, Betsy, and three schoolmasters, James Simmonds, John Dowling and Jonathan Winkworth. By 1891, the reduced family, by then comprised of just Charles, Mary and Frederick, had moved a few doors along Locksley Street to number 41. The 60-year-old Charles was still working as a stevedore and Frederick was also contributing to the household income through his employment as an engine fitter, which was a fairly skilled job assembling and repairing parts of industrial steam engines. It was this trade that eventually secured Frederick his position as chief engineer at the sewage works; quite an achievement for a 27-year-old.

King and the other workmen looked on as Mills lowered himself into the opening of the shaft, but after just a couple of steps he too slipped from the ladder and fell. Again, it possibly did not occur to the workmen that anything other than a slippery ladder was to blame but, in actual fact, the men entering the shaft were all being overcome by sewer gas which had built up in the shaft. Modern technology means that workers today are equipped with monitors that signal to them if gas appears, but in 1895 men just took their chances and the first they tended to know of it was a feeling of light-headedness or nausea before they quickly passed out. At the sewage works that day, the men around the manhole did not realise that sewer gas had suffocated their two workmates, and this is why three more of them, one after the other, attempted to get down to the inspection chamber at the bottom of the shaft.

The first of these three victims was **Arthur Rutter** and, as with much of the capital's labour force, he was not a born-and-bred Londoner but had moved to the city from Ipswich in Suffolk to find work in the manpower-hungry metropolis. Arthur's father, George Rutter, was a butcher in Ipswich as had been his father before him. In 1868, George married Ellen Whiterod from Denston in Suffolk, but the couple must have been based in London at the time because their marriage took place in Southwark and their first child, George William, was born in Bermondsey in 1868. The couple were, however, back in Suffolk by 1870; the birth of their second child, Mary Amy, was registered that year in Ipswich and by 1871 they were living at 2 Victoria Street.

Arthur was the last of the couple's three children, born in Ipswich in 1872, and by 1881 the family were living at 3 Rope Walk in Ipswich. At some point before 1891, Arthur moved to West Ham in Essex and found work as a general labourer. He lodged for a while with the Vine family at 18 Grace Road and sometime around 1892 he managed to secure regular employment as a labourer working for the council at the sewage works. It was here that he met Walter Digby, who told him that there were good lodgings along the road from him in Wakefield Street. Rutter moved in shortly after and, on the morning of 1 July 1895, it is easy to picture the two men walking to work together; Walter, a married man, listening patiently but sagely as Arthur keenly outlined to him the plans and arrangements for his wedding later that month. Given that the two men were friends and neighbours, it is easy to see why Rutter was the second man who went down the well to try and rescue Digby.

The third person to try was known to everyone as **Robert Durrant** but, legally, his name was Robert George Mothersole, who had been born in Bury St Edmunds in Suffolk in 1869. His father was Robert George Durrant (b. 9 December 1830), the son of Augustin Durrant, a Suffolk brick maker. In 1853 Robert Durrant married Deborah Cross in Bury St Edmunds, but she appears to have died just two years later in 1855. Robert then moved to London, and in 1861 he was living at Sion College and employed as a railway inspector when, on 4 April, he married Jane Kerrison, the daughter of William Kerrison, a Suffolk farmer, at St Alphage church in Southwark. It is not entirely clear if Robert and Jane had any children or exactly what happened in their marriage, but by 1871 Robert had inherited his father's brickworks and was living, without Jane, back in Norfolk at 12 Nowton Road in Bury St Edmunds.

Living with him was Ellen Mothersole, who was recorded as Robert's domestic servant, and her two children, Robert George (b. 1869) and Ellen Elizabeth (b. 1871). It is not clear if Robert Durrant was the father of the two children; the couple were certainly not married and the births of both Robert George and Ellen Elizabeth were registered with the surname Mothersole. It seems likely, though, that he may have been because Robert senior and Ellen went on to have at least four more children together, Laura Maria (b. 1872), Maude Miriam (b. 1876), Flora (b. 1881) and Harry (b. 1883), but all of them were registered under the surname Mothersole, suggesting that Robert was still married to Jane.

By the time of the 1881 census, the family was still living at 12 Nowton Road, but with Ellen listed as Robert's wife and all the children with the surname Durrant, despite the fact that the couple had not married. This fact was reinforced when Robert senior died on 19 April 1885 and his estate of £1,461 passed to his brother Thomas rather than his 'wife' Ellen. The matter was confirmed once and for all when, in 1889, Ellen 'Mothersole', not Durrant, married Frederick Wheeler, an army pensioner, confirming that she and Robert had not been married and that, although the children continued to go by the name Durrant, they were technically Mothersoles. Ellen Wheeler, Robert's mother, continued to live in Suffolk until her death aged 59 in Bury St Edmunds in 1905.[29] Her husband, Frederick, entered the Royal Hospital for Army Pensioners in Chelsea and died there in 1911.

Robert George 'Durrant' left the family home and moved to London where, in 1891, he was lodging in the home of a widow, Eliza Rothery, and her family at 9 White Hart Lane in Tottenham and working as a railway porter. In 1893, Robert married Mary Ellen Garrard, the daughter of a shoemaker, in Braintree in Essex and the couple had their first and only child, Robert George Edward Durrant, later that year. By 1895, the family had moved to 2 Napier Road off the Barking Road in Essex, just a short distance from the sewage works where Robert was, by then, employed as a steam-engine stoker. He had been working in the engine shed when he heard the shouts for help, and upon being told that three men had fallen down the shaft, he too went down but was overcome by the gas.

The final man to share that fate was **Frederick David Jones** who, although his family were very much Londoners, was born in Doncaster in Yorkshire in 1866. His father, George Frederick Jones, was born in Southwark and worked as a house painter's assistant before becoming a material cutter for a clothing manufacturer. In 1864 George married Emma Clayden Corby, the daughter of a Southwark labourer, and they had their first child, Alfred William, in November that year. At the time, the couple were living in Gravel Lane in Southwark, but they must, for some reason, have been visiting Yorkshire in 1866 as Frederick, their second child, was born in Doncaster in the autumn of that year.[30] It must have been a relatively short visit as the couple's following two children, Ernest (b. 1868) and Emma Maria (b. 1871), were both born back in Southwark and by 1871 the family were living at 114 Rolls Street in Bermondsey. By 1881, they had moved again, to 3 Deverell Street in Southwark, following the birth of a fifth child, George William, in 1873.

Frederick Jones trained as an engine fitter, which was a relatively skilled trade and would have involved assembling, and possibly making, parts for industrial steam engines. In 1889, Frederick married Catherine Hayward Crutcher, the daughter of an engine driver, in Poplar, east London and by April 1891 the couple were living at 33 Uamvar Street in Poplar with their first child, Winifred Margaret, born earlier that year. It would appear that another child, Winifred Elsie, was born in the spring of 1873, but died almost straight away. This was followed, a month or so later, by the death of the couple's first child, Winifred Margaret, aged just 2; a double tragedy for the couple, but more heartache was sadly to follow. As with Frederick Mills, Jones' engine-fitting skills secured him a good job with the council and, by 1895, he was an assistant engineer at the sewage works, probably working under Frederick Mills, which might help to explain why he insisted on going down the shaft when four other men had already done so and not returned.

Not long after Jones had descended, a labourer named Robert Wheal returned with some lengths of rope and began preparing to go down. At that point another man, Herbert Worman, who was unknown to the sewage workers, stepped forward and explained that he worked for Mr Hollington at a neighbouring farm but had heard the commotion and come to see if he could help. In light of what had already happened, several people were trying to dissuade Wheal from entering the shaft, but Worman agreed that he could hear at least one of the men breathing and volunteered to help Wheal by taking it in turns to go down. Worman was first, and after a couple of failed attempts he managed to get a rope around Frederick Jones and the two men were hauled to the surface. Jones was unconscious but breathing, so he was taken straight to the nearby West Ham Hospital for treatment. There were also concerns for Worman, who was seen 'reeling like a drunken man', but after a few minutes he seemed to recover and then continued to help Wheal bring up the other men.

One by one, the four men were recovered from the well but, unlike with Jones, there were no signs of breathing and none of them responded to artificial respiration. There was much speculation among the bystanders as to the cause of the accident and Wheal told them he did not think it could be gas as he had not smelt anything or felt any symptoms. He also explained that 'he had crawled through sewage in some of the roughest sewers in London' but had never known gas to accumulate in a sewer or shaft like this one. Wheal was puzzled, though, because Worman's behaviour seemed to suggest gas and the men who went into the shaft certainly appeared to have been overcome by something, so he had to concede it was the most likely conclusion. In due course, a doctor arrived and after examining the four men he declared them dead at the scene. As each body was wrapped in a blanket to await transfer to the mortuary, thoughts turned to Jones in the hospital and hopes that he might prove to be at least one survivor of the terrible tragedy. Unfortunately, this was not the case and Frederick died in the West Ham Hospital the following morning.

Amidst much interest, the inquest into the deaths of Digby, Durrant, Mills and Rutter was opened by the Essex coroner, Charles Lewis, at a crowded room in the offices of East Ham Urban District Council on Tuesday, 2 July 1895.[31] News of Jones' death arrived while the court was sitting and the coroner announced that a separate inquest would be held for that particular case. Charles King then presented his account of the incident and told the jury that he 'had worked at the sewage works for three years and never seen anyone become insensible there before'. Under questioning, King explained that the manhole cover had been removed for about fifteen minutes before Digby went down, but also that there was an air vent in the cover which could not be shut and was designed to ventilate the shaft. Having heard King's evidence, the coroner announced that the inquest would be adjourned to allow the jury to visit the site of the incident and also for a post-mortem to be carried out on the body of Robert Durrant.

The inquest resumed on 11 July, but only briefly as Dr Smith, who had carried out the post-mortem, was not available to give evidence; he had been working in London covering for a colleague but had subsequently returned to Birmingham. The coroner, rather angrily, told the court that the inquest would have to be adjourned again because of Smith's absence: 'I have never heard such a thing before in all my experience, it is imperative that he should be here; he made the post-mortem and should not have undertaken it if he knew he could not be here.' The jurors did, however, hear evidence from Mr Savage, the council surveyor, who told them that there were no protective measures to prevent men falling into the shaft because none was ever considered necessary; there had never been the slightest mishap in the past and none of the men had ever complained about working in it. When questioned as to whether the council would now make safety provisions, Savage explained that a leather cradle for lowering the men into the shaft had already been purchased and there were plans to provide a respirator. At that point, the coroner adjourned the inquest to the following week.

The final session of the inquest into the deaths of Digby, Durrant, Mills and Rutter took place on 18 July when the previously absent and very contrite Dr Smith was present to give evidence.[32] During the post-mortem, Smith found Durrant's lungs full of water and sewage matter, leading him to conclude that the actual cause of death had been asphyxia from drowning, but that 'the deceased had probably been first overcome by sewer gas'. External examinations of the other men suggested a similar cause of death in each case. The council surveyor was recalled and questioned about the possible presence of gas, but he reiterated that there was more than adequate ventilation for the space and, in fact, far more than was usually the case for sewers of that size. If the men had been overcome by gas, he could not be sure how it had accumulated, but it might have been the effects of recent warm weather on sewage at the bottom of the shaft. The jurors then retired for over an hour and when they returned they delivered verdicts of 'accidental death' for each of the four men, adding 'a recommendation to the council to post up at the man-hole printed regulations to workmen, which should be rigidly enforced, and in dry weather to frequently flush the sewers with clean water'. The coroner thanked the jurors and closed the inquest.

It was 7 August before the inquest into the death of Frederick Jones was concluded and, as with the other proceedings, there had been several adjournments for evidence to be collected and presented.[33] Dr Stewart Blake, a house surgeon at the West Ham Hospital, told the court that Jones had been unconscious when admitted and that 'every remedy was applied, but with no success'. He had then undertaken a post-mortem, which was relatively inconclusive and only showed congestion of the brain and softening of the spinal cord. Despite the lack of evidence, Blake 'had not the slightest doubt that death was due to poisoning by sulphureted hydrogen gas', which was commonly found in the sewers. The jurors examining the case of Jones were far more scathing than their counterparts and found that 'the deceased died from inhaling noxious gas and expressed an opinion that the East Ham Council had shown neglect in not taking the necessary precautions to prevent such an occurrence'. No action, however, appears to have resulted from this declaration, although much controversy continued to stalk the council in the months following the incident.

At a meeting of the East Ham Urban District Council on 2 July, a series of resolutions were proposed and passed; letters of condolence were to be sent to the widows and relatives of the five victims, enquiries were to be made as to whether anything could be done to assist the families, and the funeral costs for each man should be paid.[34] Councillor Long declared that he had not known of anything in all his public life which had sent such a thrill of horror through the district and that the council should do everything it could to express its thanks to the men who had lost their lives in the well. In reply to this, Councillor Keys contended that 'thanks are very poor payment; I think the time must come when their services must be recognised in some other way'. A suggestion was made that a subscription fund could be started and this was wholeheartedly approved, with a total of £60 being subscribed by council members on the night.

Two days later, on 4 July, a letter appeared in the local press written by John Brooks, the vice-chairman of the council, in which he appealed for donations to the fund 'on behalf of the widows and orphans of the men who lost their life'. However, the letter contained an interesting statement which read, 'As the East Ham Urban District Council has no means of officially compensating the widows and orphans for the irreparable loss they have so suddenly sustained, a subscription has been opened.'[35] This comment implied that the council was not intending to pay compensation to the families, despite the fact that the men were its employees. In the weeks following the initial council meeting, further letters and comments in the press revealed that several of the families had been in touch with solicitors about issues including compensation for the widows and provision for other dependants such as Rutter's invalid mother. When it eventually closed, the fund had raised nearly £1,000 and the council began using it to pay 15s per week to each widow and 2s 6d for each child; however, the controversy over the money rumbled on.

Representatives from the East Ham District Ratepayers' Association accused the council of mismanaging the fund and using the money to avoid its own responsibilities. As one member wrote, 'I sincerely trust that the progressive Council of East Ham will not be mean enough to shelter itself behind this fund and escape paying due compensation.'[36] The Ratepayers' Association also alleged that when making payments from the fund 'members of the committee had entered the house of the widow and orphan with the weekly dole in one hand and a document in the other, coercing these poor people into saying they would not take legal action' against the council and then getting them to sign the document as proof.[37] In reply to the first of these charges, the council declared that it actually had no legal responsibility to compensate the families but that the matter would be revisited when the fund had been expended at its current rates. In answer to the second, the council maintained that the form being signed was simply a receipt; an acknowledgement from both parties that the money had been paid and received.

However, when a copy of the form emerged, it turned out to be far more than just a receipt, the full text reading 'in consideration of being allowed to share in the Relief Fund, raised by the members and officers of the East Ham Urban District Council for the widows and children of the men who lost their lives by the accident at the East Ham Sewage Works on July 1st, we withdraw all claim to compensation against the authorities and acknowledge the receipt of the following sums'.[38] This was quite damning evidence and it was clear that the council had, indeed, tried to induce people to sign away any legal claim against it when accepting payments from the relief fund. Furthermore, if the council was, as it had previously stated, so confident that it was not legally responsible for compensation, why was it so keen to secure waivers? In response to accusations of coercion, the council said it was simply trying to prevent the relief fund from being used by relatives to fund legal cases against the council, which was not why subscribers had made donations. However, many subscribers declared that, while they would prefer not to see their money handed over to lawyers, neither did they intend it to relieve the council from payment due as compensation.

It would appear that, ultimately, all of the dependants of the five men received some payment from the fund, certainly in the first year after the incident, and there do not appear to have been any legal challenges made against the council. Within two years of the incident, the Workmen's Compensation Act had been introduced, which certainly helped to clarify the legal position for employees. It was, though, initially restricted to those working in factories or in the railway, mining, quarrying and laundry industries, so it is debatable that the men at East Ham would have been eligible even if the legislation had been in place. Furthermore, even after the introduction of workmen's compensation, local communities continued to raise large public subscriptions for widows and dependants if there was an element of heroism to the incident in which the breadwinner died. Sometimes the proceeds of these subscriptions were paid out in large, one-off lump sums, but more often the middle-class custodians of the money would administrate it through a weekly pension to ensure it was not squandered. Also, payments usually stopped if and when the widow remarried and when the children entered full-time employment; at that point, the hero's dependants were considered to have become someone else's responsibility.

Following Robert's death, Mary Ellen Durrant married Frederick Thomas Garrett, a railway guard, in Braintree in Essex in 1899, and by 1901 she and Robert George junior were living with Frederick at 32 Beaconsfield Road in Leyton, Essex. They were still there in 1911 when 15-year-old Robert was attending school and in 1916 when he joined the 14th Reserve Battalion of the Rifle Brigade. Robert junior undertook active service in France, for which he received the British War and Victory Medals, before being medically discharged from the army in October 1919 with a hernia and receiving a one-off payment of £38 in compensation.[39] Robert married Ruth E. Paterson in December 1925 and the couple had one child, Joan, born in 1926. Ruth Durrant died, aged 80, in Brentwood in Essex in 1964 and Robert in Essex in 1979.

Robert George Durrant was not the only child of Robert and Ellen's to die an untimely death at a young age; their eldest daughter, Ellen Elizabeth, died in Bury St Edmunds in 1888, aged just 17. Of Robert's younger sisters, Laura Durrant worked as a domestic servant for the Cartwright family in Mileham in Norfolk and her younger sister, Maud, worked as a kitchen maid for the Turner family in Barrow in Suffolk. In 1898, the sisters had a joint wedding in Bury St Edmunds, with Laura marrying Arthur Leggett, a general farm labourer, and Maud marrying William Lee Paul, a furniture polisher. Laura and Arthur initially continued to live in Suffolk where they had their first child, but in 1903 they emigrated to Alberta in Canada where they had at least three further children.[40] Maud and William Paul moved to 203 Kilburn Road in Willesden and had four children in quick succession before William died aged 32 in 1906.[41] Miriam remarried to John William Bailey, a railway employee, on 27 January 1907 and the couple had at least six children.[42]

At the time of his death, Frederick Jones was living with his wife Catherine in Bendish Road in East Ham, but after his death Catherine moved in with her old neighbours, William and Mary Pearcy, at 31 Uamvar Street. Catherine Jones is not an uncommon name and without any further context such as spouse or children it is very difficult to say, with any degree of certainty, what happened to her after this. Fredrick's father, George, died aged 51 around the same time as his son, but Frederick's mother, Emma, lived to the age of 77 and died in 1920. Frederick's sister, Emma, married William James Adams, a railway clerk, in 1895 and the couple had two children, one of whom died in infancy.[43]

When he died, Arthur Rutter was engaged to be married, but no details of his fiancée were published so who his intended was remains unknown. Arthur's parents, George and Ellen, continued to live in Ipswich; at 72 St Helen's Street in 1891 and 5 Champion Cottages on Foxhall Road in 1901. George died in 1901 aged 55 and Ellen followed three years later. Their eldest son, George William, appears to have died in childhood and it is not entirely clear what happened to Arthur's sister, Mary.

Following the incident, the press reported that Frederick Mills was married but no details of his wife were published. The coroner's inquest revealed that Frederick's body had been formally identified by his elder brother, Charles, and the name of Frederick's widow was not mentioned in accounts of the funeral. Frederick Mills is not an uncommon name and with little additional information to work with it is very difficult to identify his wife or to say exactly when he married. Frederick's parents, Charles and Mary Ann Mills, continued to live in the East Ham area until 1907 when Mary Ann died. Charles moved in with his niece Betsy, who was living in Barnoldby le Beck in Grimsby, and he died aged 82 in 1913.

The incident at the East Ham Sewage Works attracted a lot of press coverage and several commemorations were undertaken in recognition of the men who died and the men who tried to recuse them. Robert Wheal and Herbert Worman both received the high accolade of a silver medal from the Royal Humane Society and the organisation awarded 'in memoriam' testimonials to the families of Durrant, Mills, Jones and Rutter.[44] The four men were also honoured on a striking brass memorial plaque, erected in Newham Town Hall, which carried the inscription: 'This tablet is placed here to commemorate an act of heroism by four brave men, Frederick Mills (supt.), Robert G. Durrant, Frederick D. Jones and Arthur C. Rutter of East Ham who sacrificed their lives, 1st July 1895, in the attempt to save the life of a fellow workman, Walter Dibgy, in the council's employ. "He that loseth his life shall find it"' (see plate 7).

The Postman's Park memorial tablet commemorating the four men was installed in 1902, but it had to be removed several years later when it was realised that the details it provided were wrong.[45] When compiling his volume of heroic incidents, Watts had mistakenly transcribed the newspaper cutting from which he was working and the narrative he composed for the tablet stated that it occurred at West Ham in 1885, when it had actually been at East Ham in 1895. These mistakes were corrected on a new tablet that was manufactured in 1930 and erected on the top row of the second bay alongside the three tablets dedicated to Metropolitan Police officers (see Chapter 10). It had taken thirty-five years, but finally Robert Durrant, Frederick Jones, Frederick Mills and Arthur Rutter were correctly and publicly recognised for their brave attempt to rescue a co-worker who had been overcome by sewer gas.

3

UNSENSATIONAL HEROISM

The term 'heroism' is perhaps most often associated with dramatic acts of life-risking bravery undertaken by people in sudden, unexpected and trying circumstances, where the object is to save the life of someone in perilous danger. The Watts Memorial has no shortage of such acts, with people running into burning buildings or jumping onto railway tracks to try and rescue unfortunate victims. Most of those who feature on the memorial had no official duty or responsibility to try and save life, and it was often a matter of reacting to a situation in which they suddenly found themselves. Their actions were determined and driven by the urgency and jeopardy of the situation and characterised, to some extent, by the drama and spectacle that underpinned it.

The monument does, however, commemorate some individuals who more clearly died in the line of professional duty and, in addition to firemen and policemen, this includes doctors. What is especially interesting about these medical cases is the nature of the heroism involved. It is the heroism of careful and dedicated devotion, of professional commitment and responsibility, and of quiet, measured actions; not necessarily attributes that are readily thought of as 'heroic'. Nevertheless, these medical men lost their own life while trying to save the life of another and, as such, they appealed to Watts as suitable candidates for inclusion on his memorial.

It can be argued that the middle of the nineteenth century saw the emergence of a distinct medical 'profession' as opposed to the unregulated system which had previously existed. There was, undoubtedly, still something of a divide between the metropolitan, semi-aristocratic membership of organisations like the Royal College of Physicians and Surgeons and the everyday practitioners working in the provinces.[46] This distinction was not helped by the broad range of dubious and sometimes poisonous patent medicines that were energetically marketed and sold by people claiming to be 'doctors'.

However, the formation of the British Medical Association in 1856 and the creation of the General Medical Council, leading to statutory registration of medical practitioners, in 1858 really helped to secure the professional status of medicine and elevated doctors in terms of social status and respectability. It was a profession that required a high level of education and, as such, it was largely populated by the sons of reasonably affluent middle-class families, such as the two young men commemorated on the Watts Memorial.

William Freer Lucas was born on 24 August 1870 and was the eldest son of William and Miriam Lucas. William senior was the son of another William Lucas and the family had been gentleman farmers in the Funtington area of West Sussex for many years. William senior married Miriam Cartwright, the daughter of Richard Cartwright, a 'gentleman', on 13 May 1868 at St James' church in Toxteth, Liverpool, where Miriam was living at the time. Once married, the couple took over the management of Rooks Hill Farm in Alfold, Surrey, comprised of 500 acres of land and employing eleven men and eight boys. They also started a family; Catherine Mary arrived in 1869 and then William Freer in 1870.

William Freer became part of a large family as his parents went on to have a further eleven children; James Hubert (b. 1872), Richard Clement (b. 1873), Frances Miriam (b. 1874, d. 1879), Charlotte Elizabeth (b. 1876), Charles Frederick (b. 1878), Walter Sheward (b. 1880), Alice Gertrude (b. 1881), Thomas Riley (b. 1883), Dorothy Joan (b. 1887), Ella Cartwright (b. 1888) and then another William Lucas, born in 1899, six years after the death of his elder namesake. The farming business kept the family on the move; in 1881 they were living on the 420-acre Moor Farm in Petworth, Surrey, and by 1891 they were resident in the manor house in the village of Treyford in Surrey.

During this time, William junior was acquiring the education that would gain him entry to the medical profession. His early schooling was at the Churcher's College in Petersfield, founded in 1722 from the will of Richard Churcher. The college was originally established as a non-denominational foundation to educate children for maritime apprenticeships and William would probably have entered around the age of 9 years. Following his time at Churcher's, William moved to the Royal Medical Benevolent College at Epsom, which had originally been established in 1855 to educate the sons of retired practitioners but by 1864 had expanded beyond that remit. William excelled at Epsom, winning the Senior School Scholarship Prize in 1886 and the Anne Hood Exhibition Prize in 1887, and he was the highest placed pupil from Epsom College in the University of London's matriculation examinations.

In 1888 William passed his preliminary scientific examinations and became a medical student at the Middlesex Hospital in Fitzrovia where he continued to shine. He was awarded the institution's highest undergraduate award, the Broderip Scholarship, and also the Lyell Medal for Surgery and Surgical Anatomy. After a short spell as house physician, William was appointed to the position of casualty medical officer in July 1893. He was then awarded his initial medical qualifications, Membership of the Royal College of Surgeons (MRCS) and the diploma of Licentiate of the Royal College of Physicians (LRCP), and was due to gain his final degree in medicine (MB) later in 1893 but tragic circumstances intervened.

Samuel Rabbeth, in contrast to Lucas, was born in the St Pancras area of London in 1858 and was the only child of John Edward and Hannah Rabbeth (see plate 5). John Rabbeth was a clerk for the prestigious Coutts Bank and in 1857 he married Hannah Court, but she died either giving birth to Samuel or very shortly afterwards. In 1861, when Samuel was 2, he was living with his father, his aunt Annie and Mary Shaw, a house servant, at 15 John Street in Westminster. In 1869, aged 12, Samuel entered King's College School, where he studied until 1876. During this period of study, the family moved from Westminster to 14 Spencer Road in Putney; Annie moved with them and a new house servant, Caroline Sharpe, was employed.

Samuel joined the medical department at King's College London in 1877, where he passed his preliminary examinations and, in 1880, was awarded a prize in clinical surgery. Around 1881, Samuel undertook a medical diploma and, at that time, was lodging at 15 Featherstone Buildings in Holborn with another medical student and several other young professionals. After completing his diploma, Samuel was appointed assistant house physician at King's College Hospital and, after a short spell, he was promoted to house physician. King's College Hospital had been established in 1840 on the site of a former workhouse on Portugal Street, close to Lincoln's Inn Fields, and was used as a training hospital for King's College medical students as well as developing into a major infirmary for the surrounding area. Samuel gained his Membership of the Royal College of Surgeons (MRCS) while working at King's, and in 1883 he obtained a gold medal in midwifery and passed his final MB examinations. He was then elected an Associate of King's College London and in April 1884 appointed senior resident officer at the Royal Free Hospital. It was in that post at the hospital that he undertook the treatment which would cost him his life.

Both of the medical cases commemorated on the Watts Memorial relate to the treatment of diphtheria, which is a contagious bacterial disease of the upper respiratory tract, usually contracted through direct physical contact with the infection or through breathing in infected particles. Symptoms include a sore throat, fever and difficulty in swallowing, but in severe cases the lymph nodes in the upper part of the throat swell, which then obstructs breathing. In these cases, it is necessary to perform a tracheotomy operation, whereby a breathing tube is inserted directly into the windpipe below the obstruction, allowing the patient to continue breathing through the tube until the nodes contract again. Due to the contagious nature of the disease, doctors and nurses were at risk of infection during the operation itself but also after the operation, as mucus and other fluids often had to be cleared from the breathing tube to prevent suffocation.

For William Lucas, it was during the operation itself that he contracted the disease. A child being treated for diphtheria at the Middlesex Hospital in September 1893 had started to suffer severe breathing problems and the decision was taken to perform an emergency tracheotomy.[47] The resident medical officer, Dr Edward Fardon, was absent at the time and so Lucas took responsibility for the procedure. He was in the process of administering chloroform as an anaesthetic when the child coughed or sneezed and his face was peppered with infected mucus. Well aware of the dangers of infection in this manner, Lucas insisted on continuing with the operation rather than stopping to clean himself and the surgery was able to go ahead as planned. A few days later it became clear that Lucas had contracted the disease and he was admitted to the hospital and treated for it. Within days, however, it had spread to his lungs and he died on 9 October 1893. It is not known if the child survived but the operation offered the best chance and William Lucas would have known this when he chose to put the success of the procedure before his own safety and well-being.

The circumstances of Samuel Rabbeth's death were slightly different and it was while treating a patient *after* a tracheotomy operation that he was fatally infected.[48] The patient was 4-year-old Leon Rex Jennings, the son of Walter and Elizabeth Jennings who lived at Crescent Place, just off the Euston Road. Walter was a gas fitter and the couple had four other children: Fredericka (b. 1868), Jessie (b. 1870), Henry (b. 1879) and Elizabeth (b. 1883). Leon had been admitted to the Royal Free Hospital in October 1884 suffering from diphtheria and had successfully undergone a tracheotomy operation after developing breathing problems. However, following the operation some infected mucus blocked the breathing tube and, to prevent Leon from suffocating, Rabbeth had used his mouth to apply suction and clear the blockage. This was not an unusual procedure, but it did carry high risks of infection which were well known to medical staff at the time. As a result of his actions, Rabbeth contracted the disease and, although intensively treated at the Royal Free, he died on 20 October 1884. Despite the tracheotomy and Rabbeth's selfless actions, Leon Jennings also died a few days later.

On 12 October 1893, a funeral service for William Lucas, led by the Rev. W. G. Deighton at the Middlesex Hospital, was attended by numerous members of the medical and nursing staff including Mr Clare Melhado, the secretary superintendent, and Miss Thorold, the lady superintendent. The following day, 13 October 1893, the body of William Freer Lucas was transported to Shamley Green near Guildford in Surrey, where he was buried in the churchyard of Christ Church. The *British Medical Journal (BMJ)*, recounting the funeral, reported that 'the handsome and numerous floral tokens from members of the medical and nursing staffs, the resident officers and the students of the hospital, speak with greater eloquence than words of the high esteem in which he was held by all'.[49] The *BMJ* also published a five-verse poem composed, entirely in Latin, by 'one who was well acquainted with Mr Lucas', signed simply 'N. M. M. P.'. The final verse of the poem translates roughly as:

He led a fruitful life,
full of faith,
and fell asleep,
but he has not died.
His ship has a safe haven,
in the garden of heaven.[50]

Some months after the funeral, a handsome monument was erected over Lucas' grave, consisting of a cross, embellished with a Christogram and mounted upon a three-stepped plinth with the inscription: 'William Freer Lucas, M. R. C. S., L. R. C. P. Passed away at the Middlesex Hospital in the path of duty. Oct 9th 1893 aged 23 years' (see plate 8).

Samuel Rabbeth was similarly mourned by his family and friends and he was buried in Barnes Cemetery near to the family home in Putney (see plate 5). A large and imposing headstone was placed at the grave which, in addition to a quote from Matthew 25:37–40, carried a full and detailed account of Samuel's life and death, including the lines:

His bright and cheerful disposition, his earnest and sincere character endeared him to numerous friends by whom his memory will be cherished with lasting affection. A little child suffering from diphtheria was brought to the hospital whom he endeavoured to save by an act of heroism that cost him his life but which has forever linked his name with the names of the brave and good of all time who have proved by their bright example how the grace of Christ-like self-sacrifice can ennoble humanity.

As with Lucas, poems were composed in memory of Samuel Rabbeth and one, signed C. C. L., published in *The Spectator* included a verse which captures the quiet and measured nature of medical heroism:

No cry of battles rousing thy young blood,
urged thee to valorous deeds and hopes of fame.
Lowly to objectness thy loving task,
humble thy path, unknown 'til now thy name'.[51]

Following his son's death, John Rabbeth continued living with his sister Annie, and sometime between 1871 and 1881 they moved a short distance from Spencer Road to Middleton Lodge on the Upper Richmond Road near Barnes. They lived there together, with a cook and a domestic servant, until 16 August 1900 when John died, aged 77. He was buried with his son Samuel in Barnes Cemetery and a bevelled tombstone was added to the grave with the inscription 'In loving memory of John Edward Rabbeth born Jan 10th 1823, died Aug 16th 1900. "He giveth his beloved sleep".' John left an estate valued at £10,975 to his sister Annie but also to George Michael Rabbeth and Charles Frederick Dafforne, both described as gentlemen. Annie continued to live at the lodge with servants until Christmas Day 1916, when she passed away at the age of 80. She joined her brother and nephew in the family burial plot and the tombstone was appended with 'In loving memory of Annie Rabbeth, born May 12th 1826, died Dec 25th 1916.' Her estate, valued at £6,222, passed as before to George Rabbeth and Charles Dafforne.

Both William Lucas and Samuel Rabbeth were highly praised and much lamented for their actions. Referring to Lucas, *The Illustrated Police News* concluded that the sad circumstances of the case reflected the highest honour upon the doctor, while his obituary in the *BMJ* highlighted his athleticism as well as his 'gentlemanly bearing, uprightness and candour', which had gained him many friends.[52] Rabbeth was similarly lauded and a particularly melodramatic editorial in the *BMJ* declared:

> Mr Rabbeth did manfully what he felt was his duty … he did not flinch from the sacrifice which professional responsibility impelled him to undertake. A good and true and earnest man has fallen, close up the ranks! There will not be wanting men to obey the call or impulse of duty as promptly and unselfishly as the dear brother whom we mourn.[53]

In both cases, it was felt that the specific sacrifice made by the individual was indicative of the wider bravery and heroism in the medical profession which often went unnoticed. The *Hampshire Advertiser* summarised it thus:

> All honour to our hospitals that they are full of men ready to run such risks for the saving of life and the relief of pain. Their heroism is seldom recognised. Modest as they are brave, these men are heroes without knowing it, but when such a record as this does reach us we pay eager tribute to its nobility.[54]

'Eager tribute' was most certainly paid to Rabbeth in particular, and on 6 November 1884 a committee was formed 'to consider the best means of commemorating his name and sacrifice'.[55] The committee was formed of senior medical luminaries including the epidemiologist Sir William Jenner, best known for his work on typhus and typhoid; the ophthalmologist Sir William Bowman; the surgeon Sir Joseph Lister, who, appropriately, was a pioneer of antiseptic and antibacterial practices; and Sir William Gull, who furthered knowledge on a range of diseases, including anorexia nervosa, but who is now perhaps more infamously known for his links to the Whitechapel murders in 1888.[56] The committee established a subscription fund which over the next few months raised in excess of £850, roughly equivalent to £40,000 in modern terms, including a donation of £100 from John Rabbeth, Samuel's father.

The committee was keen to ensure that this benevolence was expended purposefully as well as commemoratively and so a range of initiatives were undertaken. Funds were allocated to purchasing and staffing a cot or child's bed at both the Royal Free and King's College hospitals and medical scholarships were established at King's College London and the University of London.[57] Two commemorative tablets were also installed, one in the chapel at King's College London, which is still in place, and another in the inquest room of the Gray's Inn Road site of the Royal Free Hospital, which is now the Eastman Dental Hospital. A notable recipient of the Rabbeth Scholarship was Peter Hansell, who in 1945 established the first department of medical photography and illustration in the UK at Westminster Hospital Medical School.

While there was most certainly no shortage of tributes to Lucas and Rabbeth, the adulation was not universal and alongside the praise there was also harsh criticism, and to some degree disdain, for the way in which the two men had behaved. With regard to Lucas, there was some disbelief that he had not taken even the most rudimentary precautions during the operation. Dr Horace Dobell, writing in *The Times*, remarked that deaths such as Lucas' were quite unnecessary and easily preventable:

> during my professional career I was often called upon to examine infectious throat affections and ... I always adopted a simple expedient of tying my pocket handkerchief across my nose and mouth before looking into a suspicious throat. In this way, without in the least bit inconveniencing the patient or myself, I entirely escaped infection from diphtheria.[58]

Another correspondent offered a similar solution, 'a light band of carbolized [soaked in carbolic acid], or even ordinary, cotton wool over the mouth and nose of the operator would have saved a valuable life by arresting the poisonous germs and so preventing their inhalation'.[59] Similar safeguards are second nature in medical practice today and it would seem as though they could have saved Lucas' life on that occasion, had he applied them.

It was, though, Rabbeth's actions which attracted the most critical commentary and, in particular, prompted a flurry of heated correspondence in *The Times*. This began with a letter published on 27 October 1884 and signed 'E.W.F', which questioned why Rabbeth had used his mouth to clear the blockage.[60] The letter explained that hospitals were equipped with various devices, ranging from simple pipettes and syringes through to more complex pumps and suction devices, that were routinely used for removing or taking samples of poisonous tissue without risk to the physician. It seemed implausible, the letter suggested, that the Royal Free did not have any such equipment, and therefore why had it not been used? Two days later, Frederick Gant, a senior surgeon at the Royal Free, responded to the letter by stating that the hospital was 'fully equipped with the appliances requisite for all surgical operations and emergencies', but that pipettes and syringes were often unsuitable in diphtheria cases because of the thickness and toughness of the poisonous membrane.[61] In these instances, the only option open to the doctor was to apply suction with the mouth, hence Rabbeth's behaviour.

However, Gant's defence was quickly disputed by William Stone, a fellow of the Royal College of Physicians, who, in a letter published the following day, wrote: 'there can be no hesitation in stating that, for infectious cases, an inanimate air pump should be used instead of that with which nature has endowed us'.[62] Stone did agree that pipettes and syringes were often unsuitable, but claimed that an ordinary stomach pump or an aspirator could easily be adapted to suit the conditions and clear the airway. Stone also highlighted that, although much was being done to prevent infections in patients, there needed to be more precautions in place for medical staff. He cited his own practice at St Thomas's Hospital as an example, where diphtheria patients were housed within a small tent of carbolised gauze to prevent the dispersal of poisonous matter.

The opinion that Rabbeth acted rashly and unnecessarily was reinforced by another letter from Dr Scott-Battams, the resident medical officer at the East London Hospital for Children in Shadwell.[63] While accepting that every case was individual, Battams reported that syringes, pipettes and air pumps were frequently used to remove matter from the air tube following a tracheotomy. Furthermore, he stated that:

> speaking from my own experience, which has been a fairly large one, I should say that those cases are extremely rare in which it would be necessary to apply the mouth for suction purposes and, speaking for myself with a full knowledge of the difficulties and dangers of tracheotomy in diphtheria, I must say that I would not, in 'cold blood', do what Dr Rabbeth did.

Despite the criticisms levelled at both men for their professional misjudgements, it must be noted that every censure was laced with praise for the motivation and courage that underpinned their actions; commentators may not have agreed with what the men did, but they were deeply reverential of their sacrifice. Referring to Rabbeth, William Stone began his letter 'with all respect for the memory of a good man who has died at the post of duty' and Gant referred to 'the deep regret felt … at the unfortunate result of Dr Rabbeth's self-sacrificing devotion to duty'.[64] Lucas was equally praised for his intentions, if not his actions, with the treasurer of the Royal Medical Benevolent College at Epsom writing: 'he left a most excellent record for ability and industry and had won the warm regard and esteem of the staff and his fellow students; his future was most promising and was eagerly looked forward to by all who knew him'.[65] It was, however, Dr Scott-Battams from the East London Hospital who best summed up the heroic impulse that motivated Rabbeth, Lucas and other doctors to risk their own lives when caring for others:

there are moments when the devotion and enthusiasm of the surgeon domi-
nate all selfish considerations: in such moments, men like Dr Rabbeth, seeing
life and death struggling for mastery, act quickly and without stopping to count
the cost. We are proud of such men and, while there are such, medicine will
always have its ever growing roll of heroes and martyrs.[66]

RIVERS AND WATERWAYS

4

LIGHTERMEN AND WATERMEN

The River Thames runs for 215 miles, from its source in Gloucestershire to its North Sea estuary, winding its way through nine English counties on its journey. However, as the historian Peter Ackroyd has observed, 'the closer the Thames advances towards London, the more historical it becomes … the Thames has been a highway, a frontier and an attack route; it has been a playground and a sewer, a source of water and a source of power';'No one' he concludes, 'would deny the central importance of the Thames to London.'[67]

The Thames also played an important role in the history of the Watts Memorial or, more specifically, in the lives and deaths of the people commemorated upon it. Seven of the individuals died in the Thames: two children who were swimming in it, two men who were pleasure-boating on it, a man who was travelling via it, and the two men who feature in this chapter, both of whom were working on it. The Thames undoubtedly brought wealth, prosperity, trade and opportunity to the people of London, but for many it also harboured risk, danger and ultimately tragedy.

Both of the men discussed in this chapter worked on the Thames and both could be broadly categorised as bargemen or lightermen, occupations which took their name from particular vessels. The flat-bottomed sailing barge, known commonly as the 'western barge', would have been the most familiar craft on the river and they were very much the work-horses, carrying every conceivable cargo in quantities ranging from 60 to 200 tons.[68] The sail gave them a good range and their exceptionally low draught meant they could operate in shallow water, making them ideal for reaching the upper stretches of the navigable river. Lighters were generally smaller craft, still flat-bottomed but known as 'dumb' barges because they did not have sails. Instead, lighters were propelled and steered using long oars called 'sweeps', but the real skill of the lightermen who piloted these vessels was being able to use the tides and currents of the river itself to provide motive power.[69]

Before the advent of the enclosed dock system on and around the Isle of Dogs in the early nineteenth century, cargo ships entering the 'pool of London' between Bermondsey and Tower Bridge would moor in mid-river and wait to be unloaded. If the goods were destined for the local wharfs and warehouses that lined the riverside, a lighter would be employed to shuttle small loads back and forth. If a longer journey upriver was required or the cargo was beyond the capacity of a lighter, a barge was employed. It is important to note the distinction between lightermen, who transported goods, and watermen, who carried and ferried passengers. As bridges were increasingly built across the river, the waterman's business declined, but the booming commercial economy bringing thousands of ships into the capital meant that lightermen and bargemen were in high demand and it could provide a good living to those willing to undergo the training.

In order to work on the river, a person had to be licensed by the Company of Watermen and Lightermen, which had been formed in 1700 when the Woodmongers Company, which regulated lightermen, amalgamated with the Company of Watermen.[70] Obtaining a licence involved a seven-year apprenticeship during which time the apprentice was bound to a master who was responsible for teaching him the skills of the trade as well as providing board and lodging. Apprentices were not officially permitted to marry, although many did, and once the seven years were completed, the apprentice would undergo an examination at the Watermen's Hall in St Mary-at-Hill when, upon passing, they would gain the Freedom of the Company. It was common for men to be apprenticed to their fathers and therefore, as with many long-standing trades or professions, lightering was something that tended to run in the family. This was not, though, the case with **Joseph William Onslow**, the lighterman commemorated on the Watts Memorial, and his family business was something very different.

Joseph's father, John Goodacre Onslow, was a hairdresser, as had been his father before him. John Onslow married Sarah Brown, the daughter of a baker, at the parish church of St John in Wapping on 11 August 1851, at which time John was living with his widowed mother at 25 Red Lion Street, also in Wapping. John and Sarah's family began with twins, Sarah Ann and Jane Louisa, who arrived in 1853, followed by John Bowen in 1856 and then Elizabeth Ann in 1858. According to the census, in 1861 the family were living at 3 Green Bank, a small alley off Tooley Street and close to the River Thames near London Bridge. Joseph William Onslow was born on 7 June 1862 and when he was baptised at St John's church in Wapping on 6 July that year, the address recorded in the parish register was 16 Red Lion Street, so the family appear to have moved back to nearby John's original address.

The Onslow family were still living at 16 Red Lion Street in 1871 and six years later, on 13 November 1877, the 15-year-old Joseph was bound to Calvin Lawrence Hedges to begin his seven-year apprenticeship to become a licensed lighterman. Unusually, rather than living with his master, Joseph continued to reside with his parents who, in 1881, were still living in Red Lion Street with two lodgers, Walter Myers, a lighterman, and John Cronin, a wharf labourer. Joseph also broke with convention by marrying while still apprenticed and, on 3 June 1883, he tied the knot with Mary Ann Plant, the daughter of a builder, at St Thomas's church in Stepney. At the time of his wedding, Joseph was living at 27 York Place, just a couple of streets north of Red Lion Street, but it is not clear if this was with his master or as a lodger.

Within a year, on 8 April 1884, Joseph completed his apprenticeship and a week later, on 13 April, he and Mary had their first (and only) child, Beatrice Louisa. Beatrice was baptised at St John's church in Wapping on 7 December 1884, at which time the couple were living at 10 Calvert Street, which ran parallel to York Place. A regularly employed lighterman could earn between 25s and 30s a week, with night work attracting a bonus of 2s or 2s 6d for each shift. For a 'jobbing' lighterman, work could be irregular, thus reducing his income, but if a man could get a small amount of capital behind him, he could buy his own lighter and become a master. It must, therefore, have been quite a prosperous and satisfying time for Joseph with a new family and the promise of a reasonable livelihood working on the river, but it all ended tragically in May the following year.

It was 5 May 1885 and Onslow was working on a barge with another lighterman, William Dare, the two men busily going about their usual duties.[71] Dare lived at 7 Broad Street off Old Gravel Lane and was a neighbour and friend of Onslow's as well as a co-worker. Giving evidence at the coroner's inquest, held at the Gunn Hotel in Wapping on 8 May, Dare described how, alerted by screaming, he and Onslow became aware of a boy who had fallen from Wapping dock stairs and was struggling to stay afloat in the water.[72] Apparently without hesitation, Joseph Onslow dived from the barge and began swimming to the lad, who was about 60yds from the vessel. He was within about 3yds of the boy when Onslow appeared to suffer from cramp and, to the horror of the crowd who had gathered on the bank, he sank beneath the surface before anyone could reach him.

A worker on another barge managed to save the boy by scooping him out of the water with a boat-hook, while other barges joined the search for the stricken lighterman, but it was to no avail; Joseph Onslow, aged just 22, had drowned. The inquest jury recorded a verdict of 'accidental death' and it was revealed that Onslow 'had previously jumped into the river in the same daring manner and saved no less than three lives' – something which they all greatly commended. Perhaps it even provided some comfort to his grieving widow to know not only that her husband had died trying to save another, but that more people had previously been saved by his bravery.

Following Joseph's death, Mary Ann was left alone with a 1-year-old daughter to support and on 28 February 1887 she married Montague Byatt Peaper, a lighterman, at the parish church of St James the Great in Bethnal Green. Montague and Mary Ann's first child, John William, was born on 1 October 1886 and baptised at the parish church of St Dunstan and All Saints in September 1888, at which time the family was living at 57 Knott Street in Stepney. By 1891, Montague, Mary Ann, Beatrice (Joseph's daughter) and John had moved in with Montague's mother at 13 and 15 New Gravel Lane in Shadwell, and Beatrice was recorded on the census with the surname Peaper rather than Onslow, suggesting that Montague had informally adopted her as his own. He and Mary Ann went on to have at least five more children: Henry Charles Frederick (b. 1891), Agnes Lucy (b. 1895), John Montague (b. 1896), Frederick George (b. 1897) and Ernest Nelson (b. 1903). Mary Ann, Joseph's wife, died in 1932, aged 69, and Montague Peaper died in 1940, aged 72.

Beatrice, Joseph Onslow's daughter, lived with her mother and step family, and in 1901 they were resident at 10 Herbert Road in Edmonton. Despite having lived the majority of her life as one of the Peaper family, Beatrice married under her birth name of Onslow and on Christmas Day 1904 at the parish church of St George in the East she tied the knot with George Land, a carman, living in Red Lion Street. The couple went on to have at least nine children and in 1911 the family were living at 40 Bloomfield Road in Mile End.[73] Beatrice died aged 89, in Southend-on-Sea in Essex, in 1973.

Less than two years after Joseph's death in 1885, another young woman, also with a recently born daughter, would be placed in more or less exactly the same situation as Mary Ann Onslow and the similarities between those two incidents on the Watts Memorial are remarkable. That woman was Ellen Lowdell, the wife of **Samuel Champion Lowdell**, a Thames bargeman who died on 25 February 1887.

Samuel Lowdell was born on 7 February 1864, the third son of John Champion Lowdell, a ship's caulker, and Emma Wood, the daughter of a painter, who married at St Thomas' church in Stepney on 6 November 1856. They had their first child, John William, in 1858 and then a second, Joseph Thomas in 1861. The census for 1861 shows the Lowdell family somewhat dispersed. John senior's job, which was essentially maintaining and repairing watertight seals on ships, had taken him overseas and he was living and working on HMS *St Jean d'Acre*, a battleship which had served in the Crimean War and was at that time stationed in the Bay of Cádiz on the southwest coast of Spain.

His wife, Emma Lowdell, was living with their newborn son, Joseph, at her parents' house, 3 James Street in Poplar, while the couple's eldest child, John, was living a few streets away, at 35 Manor Street, with his paternal grandparents, John and Mary Ann Lowdell. By 1871, the family were reunited and, after living in Walker Street for a while, they moved to 85 Augusta Street in Poplar with their three additional children, Samuel Champion (b. 1864), Charles Clemens (b. 1866) and George (b. 1869) as well as John senior's mother, Mary Ann.

On 16 March 1885, Samuel Lowdell married Ellen Moore, the daughter of a labourer, at the parish church of St James the Great in Bethnal Green. This date suggests that Samuel was bound to a master at the age of 14 and that, having completed his seven-year apprenticeship, he had gained his Freedom of the Company in 1885, which then left him free to marry. The occupation listed on Samuel's wedding banns was 'riveter', so it would appear that he did not immediately find work as a bargeman or that the work was irregular. An interesting insight into the life of a river worker can be gained from the Victorian journalist and social investigator Henry Mayhew who, in the 1850s, interviewed a range of London workers for his study *London Labour and the London Poor*.

Mayhew spoke to one lighterman who told him, 'I should be right well off if that [work] lasted all the year through, but it don't … that's the mischief of our trade.'[74] The worker concluded, nevertheless, that he was 'not badly off' and Mayhew tended to agree that lightermen and bargemen were fairly well paid. Assessing their character, Mayhew concluded that they differed little from watermen, they were a 'sober class of men, both the working masters and the men they employ', and with very few exceptions they could all read and write. He did, though, feel that lightermen and bargemen lived more comfortably than watermen, most of them residing near to the docks on the Middlesex side of the river. Mayhew also noted the increasing level of risk in the job; economics and competition often led men to take vessels out in unsuitable weather and rough waters, while the introduction of steamboats was causing swells and wakes which unsettled the flat-bottomed craft. The river was a dangerous place, as the families of the men who worked it knew only too well.

It was around 6.30 p.m. on the evening of Friday, 25 February 1885, and the 34-ton spritsail barge, *William and Mary*, was moored at Bankside near Falcon Dock. The crew were in the cabin 'having their grub' when a shout of 'man overboard' was heard.[75] A boy named Buck, probably an apprentice, had fallen into the water and, having rushed up onto the deck and seen that the lad was in trouble, Lowdell jumped in from the bow of the barge with the intention of helping him. The bargeman, however, quickly got into difficulties and became trapped underneath a lighter that was moored alongside the barge. While his crewmates and others tried desperately to free him, another boat nearby was able to reach the boy and pull him from the water. Lowdell, though, had now disappeared completely and after extensive searching it was concluded that he must have drowned.

It was over a month later when a lighterman, James Law of Bull Court, Tooley Street, recovered Lowdell's body. Giving evidence at the coroner's inquest, held on 26 March at the Old King's Head pub, Law reported finding the body floating in the river and towing it to the shore, where the police then conveyed it to the local dead-house.[76] Lowdell's trousers were apparently around his knees, suggesting that he had been trying to get out of his clothing when he drowned. The body was examined by a Dr Fitzrayne, who noted that Lowdell was 'tattooed about the arms' and that, although the corpse's nose was broken, this had happened post-mortem; Fitzrayne recorded the cause of death as drowning. Other evidence presented at the inquest revealed that Lowdell was considered to be a good swimmer and, as with Joseph Onslow, he had previously saved several people from drowning in the river. Samuel Lowdell's funeral was held on 3 April 1887 and he was buried in a common grave at Manor Park Cemetery in Forest Gate. Shortly after this, the Royal Humane Society awarded a testimonial on parchment and a sum of money to Lowdell's widow, Ellen, in honour of her husband's attempt to save life.[77]

The testimonial may have been some consolation for Ellen Lowdell, but the money would certainly have been most needed. On 23 February 1887, just two days before Samuel's death, the couple had baptised their first child, Emma Jane, who had been born two weeks earlier. As with Mary Ann Onslow, Ellen Lowdell suddenly found herself widowed, with a young child to support, and she followed the same course as Mary Ann. On 3 June 1888, Ellen married Joseph Sharp, a carman, at the parish church of St James the Great and the couple went on to have at least three children of their own: Elizabeth (b. 1890), Richard Joseph (b. 1892) and Doris Catherine (b. 1901).

It is not entirely clear what happened to Samuel and Ellen's daughter, Emma Jane, in the immediate years after her father's death. She does not appear to have lived with her mother, and when she attended Alton Street School in Tower Hamlets in 1892 her father was listed as John, which could mean she was informally adopted by her grandfather. It cannot have been Samuel's elder brother John, as he had died in 1873. Emma Jane reappeared in the records in 1905 when she married William Oliver, a crane driver, and they had several children: William (b. 1907), Ellen (b. 1908), Rose (b. 1915), Jane (b. 1916) and Arthur (b. 1918). Emma Oliver died, aged 66, on 18 October 1953 at 69 Friendly Street in Deptford.

Samuel's mother, Emma Lowdell, died in 1888 and his father John died in 1912 after spending some time in the Poplar workhouse. Samuel's elder brother Joseph married Sarah Ann Curtis at St Paul's church in Bow on 14 November 1880 and the couple initially settled in the Poplar area, where they had two children, Annie (b. 1881) and Sarah (b. 1883), before moving to Pembrokeshire, where they had a third daughter, Alice Matilda, in 1885. The family then moved again, this time to South Shields, where they had two more children, Ethel Maud in 1890 and Mary Jane in 1895. Joseph died, aged 45, in South Shields in 1905. Mary Jane, the youngest of Samuel's siblings, married Arthur John Smith, a farmer, at St Saviour's church in Poplar on 3 July 1894 and the couple appear to have had at least seven children.[78]

In 1861 Henry Mayhew estimated that the total number of bargemen, lighter-men and watermen working on the River Thames was around 3,157.[79] This marked a significant decline from the seventeenth and eighteenth centuries, but the river was still, nonetheless, a prominent place of work for a great many people. Steam power had also transformed the river into a viable highway for the modern city and regular 'commuter' services were conveying thousands of people up and downriver every day. Life on the Thames was not, however, 'all work and no play' and in the latter half of the nineteenth century the river became as much a place for recreation as it did for work and transport – an aspect explored in the next chapter.

5

MESSING ABOUT IN BOATS

The Victorian River Thames was undoubtedly a place of trade, commerce, employment and transport, but it was also a place of recreation and pleasure. As Peter Ackroyd has noted, 'The rising population of London throughout the nineteenth century helped to turn the Thames into a river of pastime and exercise. It seemed that everyone wanted to be on the river, an atavistic movement that has had no parallel.'[80] The Pool of London and the central stretches of the Thames were noisy, bustling places where steamboats, barges and lighters crisscrossed the waterway and vied for every inch of open water; they were certainly not places for plucky amateur boatmen. For pleasure-boaters, the 'pleasure' was to be had upstream, where wharfs and warehouses gave way to tree-lined tow-paths, and pleasant afternoons could be spent 'messing about in boats' and enjoying the hospitality of village pubs dotted along the riverbank.

By the 1880s, the phrase 'going up the river' became part of the popular repertoire in music-hall songs and sketches, and in 1889 Jerome K. Jerome famously portrayed the joys and entertainments of boating on the upper Thames in his comic novel, *Three Men in a Boat*, which had started life as a serious travel guide.[81] Destinations much beyond Kingston-upon-Thames or Hampton Court were out of reach to all but the most hardy of day-tripping leisure rowers, but suburban hamlets such as Putney, Mortlake, Richmond and Kew were within easier reach of the boat-hire companies at Waterloo and Westminster. One such company was Searle's which, as early as 1844, was being heartily endorsed in guides to London:

> For the convenience of all who would enjoy the splendid scenery of Richmond, and the river Thames, it is deemed proper to State that pleasure-boats, for large or small parties, may be obtained of Mr. Searle, at his justly celebrated and well-known establishment, about a minute's walk from the Surrey side of Westminster Bridge. Here may be had beautiful boats, at the following very reasonable rates; a four-oared boat, 1s. 6d. for the first hour, and 1s. for every hour after.[82]

Hiring a boat was not cheap but, with the cost split between two or four people, it was an affordable treat for many working-class Londoners, particularly those who were regularly employed in skilled or semi-skilled occupations. Rowing the boat themselves, rather than employing a boatman, also reduced costs and had the added advantage, for single men, of providing an opportunity to impress young ladies with demonstrations of skill and strength. Boats trips were, in fact, ideal opportunities for Victorian courting; the venue was respectably public but still relatively intimate and private, it was a constructive activity rather than simply 'loafing', the trip could include the added incentive of lunch or tea, and there was plenty of stimulus and opportunity for conversation with a 'captive' audience. However, masculine bravado and a desire to impress, coupled with the technicalities of rowing a small, unsteady boat on a busy tidal river, was a potent combination and it was not uncommon for pleasurable jaunts upriver to end in tragedy.

It was around 4 p.m. on a sunny late-summer Saturday afternoon, 25 August 1883, when four young friends decided to hire a boat from Audsley's boathouse at Waterloo Bridge.[83] They rowed upstream to Kew, where they stopped to have afternoon tea and the time soon ran away with them. Suddenly realising it was gone 7 p.m., they all clambered back into the boat and began the return journey, mindful that it would soon be dusk and the boat was unlit. To speed their passage, two of the men, Herbert Brooks and Francis Palmer, took an oar each and they made good progress downriver, reaching Pimlico by about 9 p.m. In the bow of the boat was a young woman, Jeanette Simmonds, and she was deep in conversation with the fourth occupant, a 21-year-old colleague of Palmer's who worked with him at the printing firm Spottiswoode & Co. in Fleet Street. **Ernest Bradley Benning** had been posted in the bow as a 'lookout', but the eligible young bachelor's attentions were far more focused on Simmonds than on the river up ahead.

Benning had been working at Spottiswoode's for several years, having started as an apprentice and then qualified as a compositor. Ernest was following in the footsteps of his father, Charles Benning, who worked as a printer and a printer's reader. On Christmas Day 1852, Charles had married Harriett Abbott, the daughter of a Norfolk gentleman, in St Pancras parish chapel and the couple settled in Clarence Road in Kentish Town, where they started a family. First born, in October 1853, was Edith Frances Jane, soon followed in 1855 by Charles Barlas and then in 1858 by Frederick William. The family was living on Albert Road in Islington in 1862 when Ernest Bradley was born, and he was baptised at St John Islington on 16 February that year. Charles and Harriett had another daughter, Margaret Ethel, in 1864, by which time the family had moved to 7 Wolsey Road in Stoke Newington.

The couple's last child, Albert Edward, was born in 1867 and his birth was registered in Sunderland, Durham, although it is not clear why the family was living there at the time. By 1881, they were all back in London and living at 14 Blurton Road in Clapton. Ernest's elder brother, Charles, was working as a shipping clerk, and in 1875 he had married Alice Freegard in Hackney and the couple were living at number 14 with their three children, Alice (aged 5), Charles (aged 4) and Albert (aged 1). Frederick, Ernest and Margaret were all working in the printing business; Frederick and Margaret as binders and Ernest as a compositor.

Ernest's occupation tells us a lot about him because, as Jerry White has pointed out, 'the intelligence and high degree of literacy of compositors put them in the vanguard of the London working class; at the very top of the aristocracy of labour in the nineteenth century'.[84] In 1810, a compositor on night work was guaranteed a wage of 48s per week, a huge sum for a manual worker, and the job remained among the highest-paid artisan occupations. Spottiswoode's was also a prestigious company to work for; known as the 'Printers to the Queen', it undertook the production and printing of vast quantities of parliamentary paperwork from Acts and bills to bluebooks and advice literature. Ernest was at the top of his trade, working for one of the leading firms, and he was an intelligent, well-paid, smartly dressed and erudite young man.

As the conversation flowed between Simmonds and Benning, Brooks and Palmer continued to dig in with their oars and push the boat onwards to its destination. Night had fallen and, with darkness all around, the small unlit rowboat was all but invisible to other larger vessels, including the paddle steamer *Wedding Ring* which was heading upstream to its overnight moorings. It was probably the noise and wash of the paddles that first attracted Ernest's attention and, peering into the dim light, he suddenly saw the steamer looming out of the darkness and bearing down on the boat. There was little time for them to take evasive action and so the occupants of the rowboat stood up and began waving frantically to attract the attention of the steamboat crew, hoping that they would be able to swerve around them. However, the sudden movement and elevated centre of gravity unbalanced the rowboat, which lurched violently from side to side before tipping over, throwing all four passengers into the water and into the path of the steamer. The rowboat was torn apart as the steamboat's heavy paddles churned up the thick, muddy water and then silence fell as the *Wedding Ring* ploughed on into the night, leaving a trail of wreckage floating upon the inky black waters of the river.

A short distance away, William Large, an engineer who worked at Muggeridge's steam mills a bit further downstream, was in a boat with his wife, one of his children and another young man named John Corking. Large saw the collision and hastily rowed to the spot to see if any of the people in the rowboat had survived. He soon spotted a couple in the water; Ernest Benning was holding on to a floating oar with one arm while helping to support Jeanette Simmonds with the other. Both were struggling to stay afloat and so, as Large drew alongside, he shouted at them to get hold of the side of his boat. As Simmonds reached up and grabbed on, Benning somehow lost his grip on the oar and before anyone could reach him he drifted away from the boat and disappeared under the water.

Large then heard a shout of 'Make haste! Make haste!' from another part of the river and, rowing towards the sound, he located an exhausted Henry Brooks and instructed him to hold on to the boat next to Simmonds. Other vessels in the area also came to assist with the rescue and Large heard that the crew of a fishing boat had pulled Francis Palmer out of the water. Nobody, though, had seen Benning since he let go of the oar and, after spending some time searching, Large concluded that the young compositor must have drowned. Simmonds, Brooks and Palmer were all conveyed to the shore while a Thames division police cutter set about the grim task of continuing to search the water for Benning's body. It was not, though, until thirteen days later that it resurfaced and was recovered from underneath Waterloo Pier.

The inquest into Ernest's death was convened by Samuel Langham at the Vestry Hall of St Martin-in-the-Fields church on 11 September 1883.[85] Alfred Pendrill, captain of the *Wedding Ring*, and his first mate, William French, both gave evidence in the presence of a solicitor representing their employer, the London Steamboat Company. William Large also testified and, in the opinion of all three witnesses, the incident had arisen 'due to the occupants of the small boat losing their presence of mind on seeing the steamer approach' and the boat capsized because they had stood up and unbalanced it. It was concluded that the collision was unavoidable on the part of the steamboat crew and the jury returned a verdict of 'accidental death', with a rider stating, 'we desire to express our admiration for the coolness and bravery shown by the witness [William] Large and John Corking in saving the lives of two of the occupants of the boat'. There was no mention, at the inquest, of the sighting of Benning supporting Simmonds which had been reported in *The Times* on 8 September and from which Watts obtained his understanding of the incident.

Ernest's father, Charles Benning, had died aged 54 in the spring of 1883, just a few months before his son, and Harriett Benning, Ernest's mother, died four years later in 1887 at the age of 56. Just three years after that, in 1890, their eldest son, Charles Barlas Benning, died at the age of 34, leaving his wife, Alice, and at least three children.

Of Ernest's other brothers, Frederick Benning followed his father into the book trade and became a bookbinder, initially living with his parents but later moving to Hackney where, in 1891, he was boarding with Stephen Peale, also a bookbinder, and Stephen's family at 99 Overbury Street. Frederick did not marry and died in Islington in 1894. Albert Benning, like his sister Margaret, moved south of the river and became a groom and cab driver in and around the Kew area. On 9 March 1891, he married a local girl, Ada Neal, the daughter of a gardener and, initially, the couple moved in with Ada's parents, Frederick and Charlotte, at 29 St John's Place on the Kew Road. Shortly after this, they started a family and went on to have at least four children, Frederick (b.1892), Emily (b.1895), John (b.1899) and Charlie (b.1910). Albert died in Ealing in 1949, a year after his wife Ada.

Both of Ernest's sisters married and had families. Edith Benning married her cousin, Granger William Benning, in West Ham in 1878. The couple went on to have five children and lived in the West Ham area until at least 1901. Sometime after that, they moved to Hampshire, perhaps to live with one of their children, and Edith died in South Stoneham, near Eastleigh, in 1901. Margaret Benning worked briefly as a bookbinder before marrying Walter Badkin in Westminster in 1888. By 1891 the couple had a 5-year-old son, Alleyne Shafto, and were living in Twickenham, Middlesex. The couple do not appear to have had any further children and Margaret died in Brentford in 1898, aged just 34.

Kew in Surrey was a popular destination for pleasure-boaters who, like Ernest Benning, hired a boat and rowed there from somewhere downstream. The area was, and still is, famed for its botanical gardens, but there were also tea rooms, pubs and cafés to attract and cater for weary day-trippers in need of refreshment before the return leg of their journey. The river at Kew, though, was also a popular spot for local boating, and numerous watermen would hire out boats by the hour to those who just wanted to enjoy a brief spell on the water. Many of these boats would have been small gigs or skiffs which would have been straightforward for watermen to use but were not the most stable vessels for people with little or no experience. Nevertheless, at peak times, such as Saturday afternoons, Sundays and especially bank holidays, whatever was available would be hired out to satisfy and capitalise upon the high demand. Overcrowded waters, inexperienced rowers, unstable boats and local hostelries serving alcohol; what could possibly go wrong?

The deposit of 5s 6d for the hire boat seemed rather high for the size and quality of the vessel, but Francis Moore and his friend Joseph Gerety very much wanted to spend an hour or so on the river and the 1s for the actual hire itself represented good value, especially split between the two of them.[86] Moore and Gerety were both single men, and well-paid printers who lived and worked in and around the Westminster area of central London, so the expense was not really an issue for them. It was Easter Monday, 22 April 1889, and the two pals were making the most of their bank holiday with an excursion to Kew, where a jaunt in a boat seemed a pleasurable way to end the day. It was about 6.45 p.m. in the evening when they hired the boat from a waterman named Pierce, based at Tyrell Dock, and it did not appear to matter to him that neither man had any real experience on the water. Moore and Gerety had each had about three half-pints of beer during the day, but both men felt perfectly sober as they climbed into the boat and Pierce pushed them out from the pier into the river.

Around two hours earlier and about 5 miles downstream from Kew at Putney, another group of friends were also hiring a boat for an early evening trip upriver. Among them were Henry Jeffries, a fine art dealer, and his friend **Herbert Peter**

Cazaly, who worked as a clerk for a firm of stationers in Hatton Garden. The two men knew each other because they were neighbours; Jeffries lived in Tudor Street in Whitefriars and Cazaly lived around the corner at 39 Hutton Street.

Herbert Cazaly had been born on 13 January 1859 and baptised at St Leonard's church, Shoreditch, on 17 July that year. His father, Peter, was a debt collector and in 1856 he married Charlotte Whaley at St Martin-in-the-Fields. Their first child, James Adolphus, was born in 1857, followed by Herbert Peter in 1859, Henrietta Charlotte Elizabeth in 1861 and Marianne Jane in 1864. In 1859 the family were living at 23 Stangate Street in Lambeth, but by 1864 they had moved to 6 Charles Street off Southgate Street in Shoreditch. Peter had moved from collecting debts to working as a linen draper, and with a reasonable income and a young, fast-growing family, he and Charlotte would probably have been fairly positive about their future prospects.

The Cazaly family did not, however, live happily ever after and Charlotte Cazaly bore the brunt of the tragedies that befell it. Her husband, Peter, died in 1864 and the family moved to 4 Bonverie Street off Fleet Street. Four years later, in 1868, Charlotte's daughter, Henrietta, died at the age of just 7. By 1871, the remaining family members were still living at Bonverie Street, with a housemaid, Elizabeth Moore, and a lodger, William Cooper; Charlotte was working as a housekeeper to support the family while the three children were listed as scholars. By 1881, the two boys were both working for a newsagents, James as a packer and Herbert as a clerk, while Charlotte was earning her living as a dressmaker.

Tragedy, though, continued to beset the family and, in 1882, Marianne Cazaly, Charlotte's youngest daughter, died at the age of 18. At that point, the family moved again, but only a couple of streets away to 39 Hutton Street, and Charlotte's 10-year-old niece, Kathleen, came to live with them. It was around that time that Herbert became acquainted with Henry Jeffries and by 1889 Cazaly had left the newsagents and was working at the stationers in Hatton Garden. Charlotte Cazaly must have hoped that the family had, by then, seen the last of its ill fortune but, unfortunately, further heartbreak was on the horizon.

Unlike Moore and Gerety, Jeffries and Cazaly were both confident and experienced in boats, so they were able to ensure that the craft they hired was large enough and suitable for their party. They set off from Putney at around 4.45 p.m. and were nearing Kew at around 6.45 p.m., just as Moore and Gerety were rowing out into the busy throng of pleasure boats. Patrolling nearby in a Thames division cutter was Police Constable Minnett and at about 6.50 p.m. he noticed Moore and Gerety's boat cutting across stream, apparently slightly out of control, so he shouted to them to take more care and keep to their proper course. This seemed to do the trick and the two men rowed steadily away, but after about 200yds they found themselves passing close by another boat and Gerety, who was rowing, had to lift his oars suddenly out of the water to avoid a collision. This was all it took to unbalance the small boat and, as Moore leant forward to help Gerety control the oars, the whole craft tipped up and deposited the two men into the water. Moore could swim a little and managed to get back to the boat where he clung on to the upturned hull, but Gerety could not swim at all and began shouting for help and waving frantically as he struggled to stay afloat.

Jeffries and Cazaly had watched in slight amusement as the two men were tipped into the water but, suddenly realising that neither of them could swim, Herbert threw off his coat and his waistcoat and dived into the river. Jeffries rowed after him, with the intention of retrieving everyone into his boat, but the river was so crowded with vessels that he could not get close to anybody, at which point, he also stripped off his jacket and waistcoat and plunged into the river. Cazaly was able to get hold of Gerety and, meanwhile, Jeffries, while swimming towards Moore, found an oar floating in the water which he tried to shove in Cazaly's direction to help him and Gerety stay afloat. However, as he was trying to get hold of the oar, Jeffries got tangled in a coat which was in the water and while he was trying to free himself from that, he was struck on the head and knocked unconscious by a passing boat that was trying to assist him. While Jeffries floated limply in the water, Moore clung on to his upturned boat and Cazaly struggled to keep himself and Gerety alive.

On the Brentford side of the river was the Bunch of Grapes pub, and the landlord, Sydney Bridgeman, also operated the ferry which transported people across the water to the Surrey bank where there was, among other things, a riverside gate into Kew Gardens. Around 7 p.m., Bridgeman was just setting off with some passengers when he noticed some commotion and saw an upturned boat in the middle of the river. He could see one man clinging to it and, suddenly realising that there were three other men in the water, he steered his boat across towards them, but struggled to get through because of all the holidaymakers boating in the area. Eventually he managed to reach both Jeffries and Moore, whom he hauled into his boat, but he could not get to Gerety and Cazaly, who were still clinging to one another but starting to sink. Bridgeman shouted and gestured to PC Minnett, who had turned around the cutter and was trying to help, but the constable was also unable to reach the two men and before any more could be done, they both sank.

More officers from the Brentford station of Thames division were drafted in to help with the search but, at around 8 p.m., the body of Gerety was found about 100yds downstream of the ferry crossing. The search for Cazaly continued but was called off for the night when it became too dark to work safely. It was not until 5.45 a.m. the following morning that PC William Warman spotted Herbert's body in about 10ft of water by the Surrey bank opposite the Grapes pub; Cazaly was fully clothed apart from his coat, hat and waistcoat. Both bodies were taken to Kew mortuary and examined by Dr Gardner, the police surgeon, who concluded that all marks and abrasions were post-mortem and that the cause of death was suffocation by drowning.

The inquest into both deaths took place at the Kings Arms pub in Kew on 25 April 1889 and was presided over by Athelstan Braxton-Hicks, the son of John Braxton-Hicks, the physician who gave his name to the phenomenon of phantom pregnancy.[87] Moore, Jeffries, Bridgeman and Minnett all gave evidence and recounted their memories of the incident, which more or less corroborated each other. Evidence was then received from a witness, Charles Spittles, described as 'an evangelist', who was leaving Kew Gardens at the time of the incident and watched from the bank as events unfolded. Spittles told the jury that:

> he saw two men in one of the small boats which was swaying, either from difficulty in rowing or the restlessness of the men. The boat suddenly turned upside down. No other boat was in collision with it at the time and he did not notice any of the oars of any boat go up into the air.

When questioned directly by the jury on the subject of drink, Charles Spittles said he 'did not form an opinion that any of the men were intoxicated'. Having heard all the evidence, the jury returned verdicts of 'accidental death' in both cases and 'commended the gallant action of the ferryman Bridgeman and of [Henry] Jeffries'. They also 'endorsed the opinion of the coroner with regard to the carelessness of watermen in the letting out of boats, particularly at holiday times' and Inspector Rowley of Thames division said 'he would communicate the suggestion to the proper quarter'.

Herbert Cazaly was buried in Abney Park Cemetery on 29 April 1889, in a family plot which already contained his sister Marianne, who had died in 1882. The grave was marked with a large headstone but the cemetery has since become very overgrown and access to the site is difficult. In another plot at the cemetery, Peter Cazaly, who died in 1864, was buried with his 7-year-old daughter, Henrietta, who had died in 1868. James Cazaly, Herbert's older brother, became an actor or performer and was working at the Empire Theatre in 1889 when Herbert died. On 14 December 1890 at St Peter's church, Regent Square, James married Rosalie Louisa Henrietta Archdeacon, the daughter of Montague Aloysius Archdeacon, a painter. The couple had at least three children, Herbert Peter Adolphus (b. 1892), Edward John (b. 1894) and Bessie Marian (b. 1897). Once again, though, the Cazaly family had happiness snatched from them when, in 1904 at the age of 47, James died. Charlotte Cazaly, Herbert's mother, ultimately suffered the agony of burying every member of her immediate family and one can only imagine the sadness that must have haunted her as one by one her loved ones were taken; she then died aged 61 in 1909. Initially buried in Tottenham and Wood Green Cemetery, Charlotte was later disinterred and finally laid to rest in the plot at Abney Park with her daughter Marianne and her two sons, James and Herbert.

There is a third incident recorded on the Watts Memorial relating to an individual who reportedly lost their life in a boating accident on the River Thames, and it could be said to be the most remarkable case on the wall. The tablet commemorates 'G. Garnish, a young Clergyman, who lost his life in endeavouring to rescue a stranger from drowning at Putney, January 7 1885' and in many ways the event appears to share much in common with the other two incidents described in this chapter. On 7 January 1885, a man named Mr Mackenzie, who was reported to reside in 'the Laburnums' in Twickenham, was in a boat on the Thames at Putney with four other passengers when, suddenly, it overturned, spilling all the occupants into the river. In another boat nearby, the press reports continued, was the **Rev. G. Garnish**, a recently ordained curate, who 'sprang overboard to his assistance', but Mackenzie gripped Garnish so tightly around the neck that both men sank and drowned.[88]

The details of the story were picked up and reprinted in numerous newspapers including the local *Putney and Wandsworth Borough News* and the London-based *Reynolds's News*, but also as far afield as the *Leeds Mercury* and even the *Aberdeen Weekly Journal*.[89] The press cutting that Watts acquired was taken from the *Lloyd's Weekly* newspaper published on 11 January 1885 and, as he did with many other cases, Watts recorded and transcribed the information in his volume of heroic incidents. It was not, though, until 1902 that the case was selected for inclusion on the memorial, at which time Watts simply chose it from his list of cases. He then sent the wording to William De Morgan who, in turn, made the ceramic tablet which was installed on the memorial by 4 May 1902. The tablet has, of course, remained there ever since, but what is truly remarkable about the case is that the incident did not actually happen and the Rev. G. Garnish does not appear to have been a real person.

The reporting of the incident itself does initially appear unusual because the information provided is so sparse and lacking in detail; no forenames are given and the only two people named, out of seven who were apparently involved, are Garnish and Mackenzie. Dramatic and heroic incidents of that nature usually attracted plenty of press coverage and, even if details did not emerge from the event itself, the witness statements and accounts provided at the coroner's inquest filled in the gaps. But in this case, there was no coroner's inquest, which immediately raises suspicions. With an incident of that kind resulting in two sudden, unnatural and unexplained deaths of people who were not visited by a doctor before they died or within fourteen days prior to their death, there would undoubtedly have needed to be an inquest and yet there are no records of one ever taking place. There were also no deaths registered in 1884 or 1885 for either a Garnish or a Mackenize anywhere in Surrey or Middlesex remotely connected to the Putney area.

The fact that the incident did not occur is confirmed by a statement that appeared in the *Mid-Surrey Gazette* on 10 January 1885; a statement that G.F. Watts clearly did not see, as he only collected the initial cutting about the incident itself.[90] The statement was headlined 'Bogus Boat Accident' and continued:

A sensational and circumstantial account has appeared in several of our contemporaries of a collision between two boats, on Wednesday, at Putney, one of
which was capsized, five persons thrown into the river and two drowned. Our
contemporaries have been the victims of a hoax and no such incident occurred
anywhere near Putney.

On its own this might not appear entirely convincing, but when coupled with the
absence of a coroner's inquest and the lack of any death registrations it begins to look
far more likely that the incident was, indeed, some sort of deception. There were also
no reports around the same time of similar incidents elsewhere in London.

Trying to prove that someone did not exist is, in many ways, far harder than prov-
ing that they did, and their absence from historical records is not necessarily cast-iron
proof that they were entirely fictional. That said, there is no record of an ordination
of anyone called Garnish into the Anglican Church, so if he was a real person, he was
not a recently ordained clergyman, although this does not discount the unlikely possibility that he could have been a Catholic priest.[91] That is, of course, if he even
existed. In terms of registered births for people with the surname Garnish, the initial
'G' can only have stood for George or Golding and there were only six births registered between 1837 and 1865, all of which can be traced through the census and none
of which concur with the facts of the incident. The only G. Garnish in the Putney
area around the same time was a Golding Albert Garnish who lived at Battersea, but
he was a coal porter and died in 1892.

All of the evidence suggests that the boating incident at Putney on 7 January 1885 did
not occur and no incident of a similar nature was reported to have happened elsewhere.
There was an admission that the reporting of the incident had resulted from a hoax
and this explains why there was no coroner's inquest and no registration of relevant
deaths in or around the area at the time. The G. Garnish who was referred to in the
press reports, and whose name was recorded on the Watts Memorial, does not appear
to have been a real person and, if he was, he was certainly not an ordained member
of the Church of England. This is not to say, for definite, that there was not a genuine
G. Garnish somewhere in the country who was the subject of the hoax, but there
appears to have been only a handful of possible candidates, none of which was entirely
plausible and, certainly, none of them died in a boating accident at Putney in 1885.

Why someone would concoct such a hoax and why they created that particular
story remains a mystery, but they could never have known that their prank would
continue to deceive people over a hundred years later. It is, perhaps, surprising that
the error went unnoticed and that the facts of the case were not double-checked
before the tablet was installed in 1902. However, as discussed in other chapters, Watts
was not particularly fastidious about details and, more crucially, the report had been
published in the press seventeen years earlier, so the details would have been long
forgotten by the time the tablet appeared on the memorial. In many ways, apart from

it being in the depths of winter, the incident was plausible and similar to numerous other cases, so it must have aroused little suspicion and simply slipped through with the eight other tablets made in 1902. Thus, the 'Rev. G. Garnish' took his place alongside the other everyday heroes of Postman's Park, despite the fact that he was almost certainly the fictional creation of a mischievous Victorian prankster.

The Thames 'boating craze' of the late nineteenth century gradually subsided as other year-round attractions gained prominence, but pleasure boats can still be hired at places including Richmond, Teddington and Hampton. On sunny bank holidays, stretches of the suburban-London river are still to be found crowded with couples and families 'messing about on the river', although life jackets now help to ensure that pleasure boating is a largely safe and pleasurable pastime. This was not, though, always the case, and as the incidents in this chapter demonstrate, even relatively minor mishaps could quickly escalate into serious and tragic episodes which cost people their lives. Part of the reason for this was simply that many people could not swim and so, if they did find themselves unexpectedly out of their depth in water, they were reliant upon someone else to help them. What is more, it was not always falling from boats that led to those situations, as the next chapter illustrates.

6

'DIVED IN, BUT WAS DROWNED'

Writing in 1858, the journalist James Ewing Ritchie claimed that 169 people died every day in London; a figure of around 61,685 deaths every year.[92] Of those deaths, around 500 were people who drowned in the Thames, but the total figure for drowning must have been far higher, given the amount of open water in London. The Royal Humane Society (RHS) was formed in 1776 for the purposes of 'affording immediate relief to persons apparently dead from drowning' and by the middle of the nineteenth century it was the largest organisation bestowing awards on people who had acted to save life from drowning and asphyxiation.[93] Working from their annual reports, it is possible to get a very broad impression of how common incidents of drowning were in the mid to late Victorian period.

Between 1840 and 1850, the RHS made an average of 100 awards each month, rising to 112 in the 1850s and 166 in the 1860s. Between 1870 and 1880 the average number of awards each month climbed to 202, rising sharply to 334 in the 1880s.[94] By the end of the century the RHS was making, on average, 536 awards every month, predominantly to people involved in incidents of drowning. Some of the increase over the sixty years was undoubtedly due to the growth of the organisation itself, but the figures still provide an interesting benchmark for how prolific drowning was at the time, especially considering that the RHS only recognised noteworthy incidents which were brought to its attention, rather than every incident which occurred. Given the figures, it is likely that hundreds, if not thousands, of people every month were involved in some sort of potential drowning situation.

There were many reasons why drowning in London was so prolific and certainly far more common than today. There was a lot more open water, such as canals, reservoirs, lakes, ponds and rivers which have since dried up or been covered over; so there was much more available water to fall into. Also, Victorian clothing and footwear was much heavier and made of material that easily became saturated with water. Women, in particular, wore many layers of clothing and garments which were much more difficult to get out of in a hurry. Men too would often wear a vest, a shirt, a waistcoat, a jacket and a top-coat, whereas today two or possibly three layers are much more common. Swimming was not readily taught and comparatively few people could swim more than a few yards, if they could swim at all, and that would be without the encumbrance of clothes.

There was a lot less safety advice and awareness of the dangers of open water than there is today and, although the RHS did its bit, there was a lot less rescue equipment available to assist those who got into problems. Many Londoners, especially the poorer inhabitants, also had a much closer relationship with open water, particularly rivers like the Thames in which they might wash, bathe, swim and clean clothing, but also scavenge along the shoreline or mudlark at low tide. Rivers like the Thames and the Lea were also very much working rivers and part of the capital's transport network, so a great many people worked and travelled on the water, even if they had no other direct contact with it. It is not altogether surprising, then, to discover a high incidence of people getting into difficulty in water, and where there were people in difficulty in the water, there would invariably be other people going in to try and help them.

For centuries, watermen had been conveying Londoners up, down and across the River Thames, surviving and adapting as each new bridge nibbled away at their monopoly; the advent of steam-powered riverboats, however, took huge chunks out of the business. London's first steamboat 'packet' line running a regular passenger service undertook its maiden voyage on 23 January 1815 when the *Margery* left London Bridge at 10 a.m. bound for Gravesend. By 1830 there were fifty-seven steam packets plying their trade on the Thames and by the 1840s steamboats were carrying several million passengers every year.[95] The fare to Gravesend was around 1s, tickets to Greenwich could be purchased for 5d, the short hop from London Bridge to Westminster cost just 1d and, in 1846, a 'halfpenny' steamer started chugging between Hungerford Pier and the City.[96]

Writing in 1861, the journalist Henry Mayhew described the business in some detail.[97] Each vessel had a captain, who earned around 35s per week, an engineer and Stoker both earning around 30s, a first-mate and three crewmen on 25s, and a call-boy who took home about 7s. The steamers operated between Easter and 1 October, or a little later if the weather remained fine, and as most of the crew were also watermen they tended to run a small skiff or wherry themselves during the winter months. Mayhew was informed that the men who worked the steamers were all of good character and the men themselves told him that, as a body, they felt fairly treated and were never dismissed without reason and due inquiry.

Of the passengers who used the vessels, Mayhew had this to say:

The class of persons travelling by these steamboats is mixed. The wealthier not unfrequently use them for their excursions up or down the river; but the great support of these boats is the middle and working classes, more especially such of the working classes (including the artisans) as reside in the suburbs and proceed by this means of conveyance to their accustomed places of business.

It was, then, upper-working-class and middle-class 'commuters', who lived in the quieter suburbs of west London and travelled in and out of central London for work, who most frequently used the steamers which operated upstream of London Bridge; people, in fact, just like Charles Emery.

Charles Edward Emery was commemorated on the Watts Memorial as Edmund Emery, but this was an error, derived from an inaccurate newspaper report. Charles Emery was the son of Edward Emery, from Northamptonshire, and Jane Elizabeth Badger, from Lambeth, who married in Marylebone on Christmas Eve, 24 December 1842. By 1851, Edward was employed as a schoolmaster and the couple were living in Stow-on-the-Wold in Gloucestershire with their three children, Jane Elizabeth (b. 1844), Joseph Rudolph (b. 1848) and Charles Edward (b. 1850), as well as a lodger and a domestic servant. Another son, Frank Frewin, was born in 1852, followed quickly by Octavius William (b. 1853) and then Lionel Frederick (b. 1856). The following year, however, would deliver a sequence of dreadful events for Edward and his family.

At the beginning of 1857, Octavius passed away at the age of 4, followed shortly afterwards by Edward's wife, Jane, who possibly died as a result of complications during childbirth. A few weeks later, Edward's daughter, Jane, who was living in Marylebone, died and towards the end of the year his youngest son, Lionel, also passed away in infancy. Within the space of twelve months, Edward went from being a married man to being a widower with three young children to raise, and so, in 1858, he married Susannah Sellwood in Marylebone. By 1861, the family were living together at a boarding school in Stow-on-the-Wold, where Edward was the schoolmaster, with eight male pupils between the ages of 12 and 15 and two domestic servants. Tragedy, however, never seems to have been far away for Edward Emery, and his second wife, Susannah, died at the beginning of 1868.

At this point, Edward and his two youngest sons moved to Birmingham and took up residence at 26 St Marks Road West. Frank was working as a telegraph operator while Charles was employed as a lithographer, a skilled profession that, shortly after, secured him a job as an artist and illustrator with the *Illustrated London News* (*ILN*). Charles left his father and younger brother in Birmingham and sometime in late 1873 or early 1874 he moved to London where he rented accommodation at 272 King's Road in Chelsea. The offices of the *ILN* were on the Strand and after work Charles was in the habit of walking to London Bridge where he would board a Citizen steamboat with its distinctive black and red livery and City coat of arms on the paddle-boxes. The steamer would then convey him upriver to Cadogan Pier, where he would disembark and walk a short distance along Oakley Street to his lodgings. The boat journey took about an hour and it was an efficient and reasonably priced alternative to the omnibus as well as a pleasant and relaxing way to travel home from work.

It was a Friday afternoon, 31 July 1874, and Charles was aboard a Citizen steamboat on his usual journey home to Chelsea.[98] As the heavy iron paddle-steamer chugged past Pimlico Pier, Emery suddenly spotted a young boy fall into the river from the embankment. The tide was high and as the boy struggled in the water Emery surveyed the embankment for people who might be able to help. With nobody in sight, the young illustrator climbed up onto the bulwark and jumped into the water from the slow-moving vessel. Charles was, apparently, a strong swimmer and it was later reported that he probably would have been able to reach and rescue the boy had he not struck his head against something in the water as he jumped from the boat. Losing consciousness, Charles tried to swim against the tide and was seen to make two or three uncertain and faltering strokes before he was swept away downstream.

On the embankment, the boy's cries were heard by James Levett, who lived nearby at 2 Cheyne Walk, and he managed to lower himself down into the water where, holding on to some metal railings, he was able to pull the desperate lad from the river. It turned out that the boy's surname was Tomlinson and he lived with his parents a few streets away at the Royal Military Stores on Chichester Street. He seemed unscathed from his ordeal and a constable took him home. Attention then turned to finding Emery and Thames division police began dragging the river. At around 8 p.m. that evening, the dead body of Charles Emery was lifted from the water about 20yds downstream from where he was last seen struggling to stay afloat.

Three days later, in the boardroom of the St George's Hanover Square Workhouse in Mount Street, John St Clare Bedford presided over the inquest into Charles Emery's death.[99] Witnesses described how a 'tall gentlemanly young man' had jumped overboard, but the fast-running tide had 'turned him over and over, and after a few fruitless efforts by the young fellow, it carried him beneath the surface, to the horror of the spectators'. Levett gave evidence confirming that he was on the embankment when he heard Tomlinson shouting, which cleared up some confusion, generated by the press, that Levett was a crewmember of the steamer who had jumped in after Emery. The inquest also revealed that a constable on the embankment had witnessed the whole incident but did not report it to his superiors when he returned to the station. The jury listened attentively to all the evidence and then, after a short deliberation, returned a verdict that 'the deceased [Emery] was accidently drowned while attempting to save the life of a fellow creature' and they also expressed an opinion that the constable on duty should have communicated with the station inspector.

Charles Edward Emery was laid to rest on 5 August 1874 in a common grave in Brompton Cemetery on the Fulham Road. There is no evidence that a headstone was erected and the plot has subsequently become overgrown. The *Illustrated London News*, as might be expected, published several articles on Emery's death and in one it was stated that:

> he was unmarried, but supported an invalid father, and gave some aid to others of his family, by his earnings as an artist. It is proposed by several of his friends to raise a subscription for the benefit of those whom this good son so dutifully cared for and an account has been opened at the Union Bank, where payments may be made.[100]

It is not clear how much the subscription fund raised, as no further details were published. Edward Emery, Charles' father, continued to live in Birmingham where, in 1881, he was lodging with the Grimsley family at 31 Newhall Hill; he died three years later, in 1884, at the age of 74.

Frank Emery, Charles' younger brother, married Alice Mary Clements in Marylebone in 1880. Frank worked for a while as a salesman before becoming the landlord of the Town Hall Tavern on Kensington High Street where, in 1891, he was living with his wife and two children, Alice May (b. 1882) and Frank junior (b. 1883). By 1901, the family had moved to the Prince of Wales pub at 8 Church Street in Kensington and two further children had arrived, Edward and Charles. In 1911, Frank, Alice, Edward and Charles were living at 1 Bessborough Place in Pimlico, ironically just a short distance from where Charles Emery had drowned thirty-seven years earlier. Frank died in 1937 aged 85.

The Thames is, without doubt, the most significant of London's rivers but many tributaries run into it and each has contributed to the history of the metropolis. The fast-flowing Lodden and Wandle powered industry through networks of watermills, the Ravensbourne refreshed the rebellious followers of Wat Tyler, and the once mighty Fleet ignominiously decayed into one of the capital's most notorious and disease-ridden sewers.[101] To the east of the city, at Bow Creek, the River Lea merges seamlessly with the Thames, yet its 40-mile journey from Leagrave near Luton is anything but straightforward.

Below Hertford, large sections of the River Lea were canalised to form the Lee Navigation and then, as the river approaches London, it forks into numerous creeks and man-made channels known as the Bow Back Rivers, which include the Three Mills Back River, the Waterworks River, Abbey Creek, and Prescott Channel.[102] This network of waterways twisted and turned through a highly industrial landscape where the chemical works and factories of Stratford, Bow and Old Ford employed the rivers for water, transport and waste disposal. In one spot, it was said that 'a match factory on its banks lent the water a urinous taste and appearance, while the smell of the whole area became offensive'.[103] These were tremendously unhygienic places and yet local people, especially children, could often be found bathing and swimming in the Lea and its back rivers. Disease and infection must have been potent risks to health and well-being, but there was also the omnipresent threat that lurked around all open water in the capital: drowning.

It was 16 July 1876 and 18-year-old **William Percy Donald** had travelled from his west London home in Hammersmith to have Sunday lunch with his cousin, Thomas Percival Yull, a clerk for the Prudential Assurance Company, who lived at 10 Frederick Place on the Bow Road in east London.[104] William knew the area well as he had been born in Mile End Old Town near Stepney on 22 July 1857 and spent the first ten years of his life living in and around Bow. William's father was William Donald senior, a London jeweller, and his mother was Maria Marian Grimes. Before she married William Donald, Maria had previously been the wife of Aylmer Horatio Wabe, whom she married in 1847. Maria and Aylmer had three children, Aylmer junior (b. 1848), Aylmer Horatio junior (1849) and Alfred John (b. 1851), but by 1853, Maria's husband and all three children were dead; Alymer junior died in infancy and the other two boys and their father passed away in the spring of 1852.

Sometime between 1852 and 1856, Maria Wabe married William Donald and William Percy was their first born. Three more children followed, Marian junior (b. 1859), Amy (b. 1860) and John (b. 1863), and the family lived at 7 Mostyn Road in Bow. In 1864, Maria senior died, leaving William senior with four young children to raise. Consequently, on 25 April 1866 at St Stephen's church in Bow, William married Mary Clay, the daughter of a commercial clerk. Around 1866, the family moved from east London to west London, and by 1871 they were living in Melina Road in Hammersmith. William and Mary had their first child, Helen, in 1868 and the three youngest of William's other children were living with the couple.

William Percy was not, though, living with them and was, instead, resident at the Gloucester House Academy in Doddington in Kent with thirty-three other boys between the ages of 8 and 15. This education served him well and on 23 October 1872, aged 15, he began working for the London and North Western Railway Company (LNWR). William was employed as an apprentice clerk in the corresponding office at the commercial handling department, which was based in Broad Street Station, adjacent to Liverpool Street Station. His starting salary was £25 per annum, rising around £10 per annum for each year of satisfactory service, and by 1875 he was earning £50 per annum; a good income for a single man in his teens. In 1876 William was living at 1 Askew Crescent in Hammersmith and this is where he set off from on 16 July to visit his cousin.

After lunch, Thomas wanted to take his dog, a large retriever, for some exercise and William suggested they should walk up to Old Ford and see his uncle, Samuel Clay (the younger brother of Mary Clay, William's stepmother), who lived at Woodland

Cottage in Wick Lane. They arrived an hour or so later and, as the land behind the cottage was bordered by the River Lea, it was decided to take Yull's dog down to the water and give it a bath. However, it was a warm summer day and when they reached the river, near to Old Ford Lock and a paper-staining factory, Thomas and William decided that they would also go in for a swim. Samuel tried to dissuade them, saying that the weeds in that stretch of the Lea made bathing dangerous, but the two lads, assuring Clay that they were both excellent swimmers, stripped off and jumped in. While they were trying to swim, Yull's increasingly overexcited retriever became a nuisance and kept getting in the way, so William swam back to the shore, climbed up onto the bankside, and pulled the drenched dog out after him. He was just settling the animal and asking Clay to hold onto it, when he heard his cousin shouting for help; Thomas was in mid-stream but his legs had become entangled in weeds and the current was dragging him under.

William immediately jumped back into the water and was in the process of trying to free Yull when he too became tangled in the weeds and, unable to free themselves or each other, both young men started shouting for Clay to help them. In panic, Samuel Clay waded fully clothed into the river but, quickly realising that he was out of his depth and in danger of drowning, he struggled back to the shore to take his clothes off. Donald and Yull fought vigorously with the weeds but the flow of the river was relentless and as they became more and more exhausted they found it increasingly difficult to keep their heads above the water. Finally removing the last of his garments, Clay turned to make his way back into the river, but Donald and Yull were nowhere to be seen; although he swam out to where he had last seen them, Samuel could find no trace of the two young men and was eventually forced to abandon his search due to fatigue. Later that evening, further downstream, two bodies were found and identified as Thomas Yull and his cousin William Donald; both men had drowned.

The inquest into the two deaths was held at the White Horse pub in Bow Road on 18 July 1876 and Mr Donaldson, the deputy coroner for East Middlesex, heard evidence from Clay and relatives of the deceased.[105] Inquests were often held in pubs, particularly if they concerned working-class individuals, primarily because they offered large and accommodating indoor public spaces in the vicinity of the incident. They were also used, though, because working-class people were generally familiar with the pub and comfortable to give evidence there in a way they would not have been in the formal setting of a coroner's court.[106] For many, the term 'court' was loaded with all kinds of assumptions and fears about the police and the authorities that might prevent witnesses from coming forward to testify. Having heard all the evidence, the jury in the White Horse returned verdicts of 'accidental death' for both men, after which the coroner closed the case and formally released the bodies for burial.

William Donald's father and his stepmother, Mary, had at least eight children, who would have been his half-siblings, and then William Donald senior died in 1895 or 1896.[107] Mary continued to live in Hackney until around 1910 when she moved to Bognor Regis in West Sussex to live with her married daughter, Annie. William Donald's three full siblings, particularly his sisters, are problematic to trace, given the variable nature of the recording of the surname 'Donald' and the lack of context once they moved out of the family home. William's brother, John, joined the Royal Navy and undertook various duties including mess officer. In 1894 he married Ada Lily Eames, who was fourteen years his junior and appears to have been his cousin, which might explain why the couple decided not to have any children. William's sister, Marian, was living with her father and stepmother in 1881, but her movements after that are unclear, as are those of Amy Donald.

William Donald is not the only person who drowned in the River Lea to be commemorated on the Watts Memorial. Four years after William perished, another young man, just 16 years old, also died in similar circumstances. On the afternoon of Monday, 6 September 1880, two boys, who were friends and neighbours, were playing near the Lead Mill Stream or 'back river' close by to the old wooden bridge that crossed the River Lea by Temple Mills Lane and the White Hart Inn.[108] One of the boys was 12-year-old Walter Sale, the son of Thomas Sale, a greengrocer, who lived at 98 St Ann's Road in Mile End Old Town, and the other was Stephen Webb, also 12, the son of Richard Webb, a blacksmith, who lived at either 7 St Ann's Road or 5 Edinburgh Road, which was just around the corner.[109]

Walter suggested that they play in the river, but Stephen was unable to swim and so he offered to stay on the side and look after Walter's clothes while he went in. Sale duly stripped off and plunged into the water, where he swam to the opposite bank and then, turning around, waved to Webb before starting out on the return journey. About halfway back, Sale started to flag and as he struggled in the flow of the river he started shouting for help, but Stephen, unable to swim, was powerless to do anything but watch and cry out for assistance.

Passing by at the time was **George Blencowe**, who lived a mile or so east of Temple Mills in Stratford New Town at 3 Maryland Road. George's father, George senior, was born in Barnet and as a young man had served in the Metropolitan Police. On 28 July 1859 he married Elizabeth Alger, the daughter of a cabinet maker, at St Dunstan and All Saints church in Stepney, and by 1863 the couple had moved to 11 Bright Street in Poplar with their two children, Elizabeth Charlotte Ann (b. 1860) and Louisa Edith (b. 1862). Their first son, George Blencowe junior, was born in 1864 and then five more children followed over the next fourteen years.[110] In 1871, the family were living at 39 Glengall Road in Poplar, but by 1880 George senior had left the police so the family had to move to 3 Maryland Road and George found work as a greengrocer to support his ever-growing household.

George junior was walking near the River Lea when, alerted by shouting, he ran to the bankside and found Webb, highly distressed, screaming and pointing into the river where Sale was battling to stay afloat. Quickly slipping off his boots and his coat, George waded into the river and swam out to Sale who, in a state of sheer panic, grabbed on to Blencowe and wrapped himself around him, which prevented George from swimming. A brief struggle ensued but, with Sale hanging on for his life and Blencowe unable to loosen the boy's grip, the two of them sank beneath the surface and disappeared. Stephen Webb continued screaming in the hope that further help would arrive and, a few minutes later, it did. Working nearby was Stephen Jones, who like Blencowe lived in Stratford New Town, and hearing screams in the distance he went down to the bank of the Back River to see what the problem was. On the other side of the narrow stream and beyond some marshland, Jones could see a very agitated boy waving and crying for help. The shortest route to reach him was across the river, so Jones stripped off, swam across the stream, climbed out the other side and ran through the marshland to reach Webb, who explained to him that his friend and another man had sunk in the river.

Jones then swam out into the Lea and, diving under, was able to feel two bodies on the riverbed, one of which he was able to bring to the surface and drag back to the shore, where Webb identified it as his friend Walter Sale. By this time several other men had gathered on the bank and a couple of them were wading in the water, trying to help with the search. Jones also went back in and, diving down again, he spotted Blencowe's body but was unable to reach it because, inexplicably, one of the other men in the water was inadvertently standing on it. Coming to the surface, Jones remonstrated with the man, who at first ignored him but then tried to grab hold of him, and so Jones, exhausted and fearing he would be pushed into the water, was forced to back away and return to the shore. With the alarm raised it was not long before two constables arrived and the men were told to get out of the water, which was then dragged and Blencowe's body brought to the surface. A local physician, Dr Mallam of Hackney Wick, was summoned and attempted artificial resuscitation, but to no avail, and after a short time he reluctantly declared both Sale and Blencowe dead from drowning.

An expectant and interested crowd filled the King's Head Tavern in Hackney on 8 September for the inquest into the two deaths which was conducted by George Collier, the deputy coroner for east Middlesex.[111] Stephen Webb recounted how Sale had got into difficulty in the water and that Blencowe had gone in to help him, but that both had then sunk after a brief tussle. Jones' evidence caused quite a stir when he explained how he was unable to recover Blencowe's body due to the man standing on it. In answer to questions from the jury, it transpired that the man was intoxicated and did not appear to understand what he was doing. At the conclusion of the inquest, the jury returned a verdict of 'accidental death' in both cases and said they 'could not speak too highly of the courage of the poor youth Blencowe for his heroic, though unsuccessful, attempt to save the life of Sale at the risk of his own'.

The court then asked for Jones to be recalled and, addressing him, the jury said that they planned to open a subscription to reward him, but Jones replied that 'he considered it his duty to save a life if he could do so'. The coroner then announced 'that this was the third body Jones had either saved or attempted to save' and he would take steps to ensure that his heroic conduct was brought before the Royal Humane Society. This may well have resulted in a certificate or monetary award but Jones did not receive either the society's bronze or silver medal, which were its primary accolades for heroic lifesaving. With the inquest complete, the coroner released the bodies for burial and Walter Sale was buried in a common grave in Manor Park Cemetery in Forest Gate on 12 September 1880. George Blencowe was laid to rest the following day in a common grave in West Ham Cemetery in Newham. There is no evidence that a headstone was ever erected, but if one was, it has not survived to the present day.

George's parents both lived into their seventies and enjoyed a reasonable income from George senior's police pension; he died in 1911 at the age of 78 and his wife Elizabeth outlived him by three years, dying at the age of 80 in 1914. Of George's sisters, the eldest, Elizabeth, married Albert Ernest E. Watts in 1895; he was around twelve years younger than her. By 1901, the couple were living at 20 Haringey Grove in Hornsey with their son, Edward G. Watts, born in 1898. In 1903, George's sister Ellen moved in with Elizabeth and her family at 20 Haringey Grove, and on 26 December that year she married Charles Frank Moore, a shop assistant, at St James' church in Edmonton. Their first child, Vera Beatrice, was born in July 1906 while the couple were still living at 20 Haringey Grove. By 1911, the family had moved to 2 Linden Road in Tottenham. Elizabeth Watts died in Willesden in December 1952.

George's sister Louisa married Charles Henry Runnalls, a gas fitter, in 1889 and the couple moved to East Grinstead where they had their first child, also Charles Henry, in 1890. By 1901, the family had grown through the addition of three more children and had moved to 44 Beahill Road in Sutton, Surrey. Another child arrived in 1903 and by 1911 all five children were living with their parents at 6 St Margaret's Villas, St Barnabas Road, Sutton.[112] Louisa was still living in St Barnabas Road, number 11, on 22 December 1940 when she passed away. Her husband Charles died twenty-six years later in 1966. George's sister Alice became a milliner and on 19 September 1903 she married Clement Hugh Stone, a monumental mason and son of a gentleman, at St Peter's church in Hornsey; as with her sister Ellen, Alice was living at 20 Haringey Grove when she got married. Margaret Blencowe married Walter Cromwell Davies in 1903, but it is problematic to trace her any further than that.

George's only brother, Albert William Blencowe, found work as a stationer's assistant and on 17 August 1898 he married Bathsheba Mary Tollett in Islington; their first child, Ethel May, was born in 1899. In 1901, when their second child, George Henry Albert, was born, the family was living at 80 Packington Street in Islington and Albert had progressed to an estimating clerk at the stationers. By 1905, when their third child, Ivy Ada Bathsheba, was born, the family had moved out to Finsbury and was living at 40 Chatterton Road. This outward migration continued to Ilford, and in 1911 the family was living at 188 Hampton Road, with Albert working as a department manager. Albert died in Ilford in Essex on 15 April 1955, leaving £1,860 to an Albert William Blencowe, presumably his son. Albert's wife, Bathsheba, died in Rayleigh in Essex in July 1966.

Rivers were not, of course, the only bodies of water in London and by no means the only ones that posed a danger to residents. In the present day it is difficult to picture Peckham in south-east London as a 'waterside' community, but that was very much the case in the nineteenth century and the history of the area really illustrates the extent to which open water was so much more a part of everyday life in Victorian London than it is today. In 1801, plans were agreed to build a new waterway, the Grand Surrey Canal, to connect a new commercial dock at Rotherhithe with lucrative areas of south-east London and Surrey.[113] By 1826, the canal had carved its way through Deptford and Bermondsey to Camberwell where, at a junction near Glengall Road, a Peckham extension branched off and ran parallel to Hill Street before terminating at Peckham High Street. For over a hundred years the canal was part of people's lives, with houses and businesses built alongside it and bridges carrying people back and forth across it. It was a busy, bustling commercial waterway in the heart of a densely populated urban district; something which we seldom see in London today.

Around 1970, the canal was filled in, partly to eliminate the dangers of people drowning in it, and the area was redeveloped. The southern side of Burgess Park, along St George's Way, now stands on what would once have been the Grand Surrey Canal, and the Peckham branch has been transformed into the Surrey Canal Walk which connects the park with Peckham Square. The walk is now a 'greenway' footpath and cycle path, but it retains much of its canal infrastructure, including two ornately decorated bridges which would have once spanned the waterway. One of these is the Commercial Way Bridge and every day thousands of cyclists and pedestrians pass under it as they enjoy a traffic-free passage through Peckham. Few will know that the crossing was once known as Globe Bridge and even fewer will be aware that, in May 1878, it was the scene of a dreadful incident in which two people lost their lives; one while trying to save the other from drowning in the canal.

It was around 10 p.m. on Monday, 20 May 1878, and Thomas Hudson, a labourer, was making his way through Peckham to his home at 29 Stanton Street when he decided to stop in at the Surrey View Tavern for a drink.[114] The pub was adjacent to Globe Bridge, which crossed the canal, and as Hudson approached he noticed a young woman on the bridge 'who appeared in great distress of mind, with her elbows resting on the parapet and her face covered by her hands'. Hudson paused, considered the situation, and decided to ask the woman if she was all right, but as he turned to walk towards her his attention was attracted by someone calling to him from the other side of the road. Looking over, he spotted one of his neighbours who was also standing and intently watching the woman, so Hudson crossed the road to talk to him.

Hudson's neighbour was **Richard Farris**, a 44-year-old stonemason who lived at 43 Stanton Street. Richard was the son of Henry Farris, a labourer, and Lucy Catlin who had married in Bishopsgate on 8 November 1824. Their first child, James, was born in 1825, followed by Henry in 1827 and Eliza in 1830. Richard was born in 1833 and baptised in Hackney on 7 April that year. After that, two more daughters arrived, Sarah, born in 1837, and Charlotte, born in 1840. By 1841, the family was living at 23 Cock and Castle Lane in Stoke Newington, but in June that year Lucy died at the age of 41. With a small baby and two young children to raise, Henry married again in 1842 to Elizabeth Baker and the couple went on to have three children of their own, who would have been half-siblings to Richard.[115]

In 1851, Henry and Elizabeth's living arrangements were somewhat unconventional. Henry was living in Clapham with his four youngest children from his first marriage, while Elizabeth was working as a laundress and living with their three children at 9 Mellon Place, a couple of streets away from New Road, which would later become Stanton Street. By 1861, Henry and Elizabeth were reunited and were living at 26 Lyham Road in Brixton with their three children. It was, however, a short-lived reunion as Henry died in 1869.

Meanwhile, Richard Farris was working as a brickmaker and living with his elder brother, Henry (also a brickmaker), at Bloomfield Cottages in Chelsea. Henry had married Ann Thompson in 1857 and by 1861 when Richard was living with them the couple had three children, Henry junior (c.1857), Catherine (c.1858) and James (c.1860). Evidence suggests that sometime between 1868 and 1872, Henry Farris and his family travelled to Canada where their son, Walter, was born in 1872. It is highly plausible that Richard Farris travelled to Canada with his brother, as he does not appear to be recorded on the 1871 census. By 1878, however, Richard had returned to Britain and, on 20 May 1878, he found himself on a canal bridge in Peckham watching a young woman who, he suspected, was intending to try and commit suicide.

The distressed woman standing on Globe Bridge was 20-year-old Eliza Sarah Arlott, a laundress's assistant, who lived at 10 York Terrace in Basing Road, which was just a couple of streets from the canal. Her father, Thomas, was a bricklayer's labourer who had married Sarah Hume in 1848. Eliza had been born in 1857 in Clapham, where the family was living at the time, but by 1860 they had moved to York Terrace. It is interesting that both the Arlott and Farris families had been living in Clapham at around the same time, that they both had connections with Peckham at the same time, that men in both families were employed in brickmaking and bricklaying, and that Eliza was employed as a laundress's assistant while Elizabeth Farris worked as a laundress. There are no explicit or obvious associations between the families, but their movements and occupations do seem slightly too similar to be entirely coincidental.

Perhaps Richard Farris even knew Eliza Arlott and that is why, when he saw her on the bridge, he stopped and started to watch her, unsure exactly what he should do. While he was standing there, he spotted a neighbour of his, Thomas Hudson, who also seemed to be watching the girl, so Richard called to him and beckoned him over. 'I have been watching that woman,' Farris told Hudson, 'and believe she intends to throw herself into the canal. If she does, I will go in after her and save her.'[116] After a short discussion, Hudson left Farris on the bridge and proceeded to the Surrey View Tavern as planned, but he had barely ordered his drink when he heard urgent cries from outside that a man and woman were in the canal. Waterside taverns often acted as Royal Humane Society receiving houses for treating people who had been pulled from the water and, as such, they also tended to keep a set of 'drags' (ropes or chains with metal hooks at one end) for getting bodies out. Suspecting that the people in the water might be Farris and Arlott, Hudson grabbed the drags from the pub and ran out to the canal side.

Witnesses told Hudson that the woman had jumped from the bridge and, as promised, Farris had then jumped in after her. Both of them were now in the water and Arlott, who had her arms clamped around Farris' neck, was screaming, 'Save me! Save me!' as the two of them struggled in the water. People on the bank were calling out for help and Hudson was trying to figure out if he could do anything useful with the drags, but before he had a chance, the two victims disappeared under the water. On the bank, people waited anxiously for the couple to resurface, but after several minutes it was clear that all hope was lost. Several constables arrived and, using the drags from the pub, they began the all too common task of finding and recovering the bodies from the canal.

About twenty minutes later, Arlott was first to be lifted out and she was taken straight to the Surrey View Tavern where a local doctor, who attended at the receiving house, tried to resuscitate the young woman but was forced to conclude that she was dead. A short time later, the body of Richard Farris was pulled from the canal and, although he too was conveyed to the receiving house, it was clear to those who lined the towpath that he was very much dead, something quickly confirmed by the physician. Arlott's parents were sent for and later that night, as Hudson walked slowly home to Stanton Street, he could hear the gossip and rumours spreading about his friend and neighbour Richard Farris, who, it was said, had lost his life while trying to save a 'poor distracted girl'.

The Marlborough Arms Tavern on South Street in Camberwell was full to capacity on Friday, 24 May, to hear the coroner, William Carter, convene the inquest into the two deaths.[117] After Hudson had given his testimony about his conversation with Farris prior to the incident, Eliza Arlott's mother was called to give evidence as to her daughter's state of mind at the time. Sarah Arlott told the court that Eliza 'had been in very low spirits and greatly distressed about something her sweetheart had said to her'. After all the witnesses had been heard, the jury deliberated and reached a verdict that 'Farris lost his life accidentally while humanely trying to save the life of Eliza Sarah Arlott, who had committed suicide while in a state of unsound mind'.

Undoubtedly, Farris performed bravely and his actions ultimately cost him his life, but there are a few things about the event which leave room for some speculation. It seems odd that Farris stood back and watched Eliza until she jumped and then went in to try and save her, rather than trying to talk her round or actually trying to stop her from jumping. It must be remembered that suicide was illegal until 1961 and aiding and abetting someone to commit suicide remains a criminal offence, so why did Farris not try to prevent Arlott or, at the very least, try to find a constable? Thomas Hudson testified that he was about to speak to Eliza, so there were clearly no Victorian 'protocol' issues about approaching a distressed woman. Furthermore, when Hudson went to approach Arlott, Farris called him to one side and prevented him from doing so; why was Farris so keen to wait and see what Arlott did before trying to help her? There are also Arlott's actions to consider and, although she was clearly distressed when she jumped and may have instantly regretted it, screaming 'Save me! Save me!' at Farris hardly seems like the actions of someone intent on suicide.

Eliza Arlott was said to have 'quarrelled with her sweetheart', which is why she jumped, but what if her sweetheart was Richard Farris? It was around 10 p.m. when Hudson saw Eliza on the bridge and perhaps she and Farris had been together that evening and had an argument which caused her to storm off. Perhaps she was pregnant and he was unwilling to support her. After they argue, he follows her, they argue again and she says that she has had enough and is going to throw herself into the canal. Not knowing if she is serious, he keeps his distance and watches, but suddenly she does actually jump, so he goes in after her and she screams for him to save her. This scenario does not necessarily fit with what Farris told Hudson, but perhaps he did not want his neighbour to know that he was involved with Eliza; after all, she was nearly twenty-five years younger than him. Perhaps, however, there was no connection between them and the incident was exactly how it was reported; a kind and humane man trying to save the life of a distressed young girl who had broken up with her boyfriend and did not want to carry on living.

Ultimately, it will remain a mystery and the nagging questions will go unanswered because people like Eliza Arlott, Richard Farris and most of the others commemorated on the Watts Memorial lived their lives below the level at which history thought them fit to record. Apart from the decennial census, the registers of hatching, matching and dispatching, or criminal proceedings when folks strayed into trouble, everyday people living everyday lives tended to feature very lightly in the historical records. This is one of the reasons why the Watts Memorial is such an important and rewarding piece of historical evidence, because it briefly illuminates the lives of 'ordinary' people and, however briefly and tragically, brings them into focus, where we can finally get a better look at them. From the single 'snapshot' moment of their death, some sense of the life can be reconstructed – and not just the individual life but the lives around it, the communities in which that life was lived and the times that person experienced. When it comes to 'everyday' heroes, the *everyday* aspect is every bit as important and valuable as the heroic.

Boys Will
Be Boys

7

'I saved him, but I could
not save myself'

When Victorian social investigators, such as Henry Mayhew and Charles Booth, encountered working-class children, what appears to have struck them most was their lack of 'childlike' qualities. As the historian James Walvin has concluded of children in this period, 'they worked, they were worldly wise, often economically independent, sometimes sexually experienced – they even *looked* older than their years. Yet, they were, at the age of say eight or nine, children nonetheless.'[118] There is also, perhaps, a tendency to imagine and picture Victorian children, particularly boys, at the polar opposites of the social spectrum; from Tom Brown at one extreme to the Artful Dodger at the other.[119] In the popular imagination, Victorian boys are either knickerbocker-clad sons of empire or grubby semi-criminal street urchins. As with most things, though, the reality was far different and much more nuanced with most children falling somewhere in the middle ground.

There is also the thorny issue of exactly what constitutes a 'child' and modern western concepts are often quite different from attitudes and definitions in the past. Legal distinctions have altered immeasurably over the years, and social and cultural distinctions are equally problematic. Economic independence, often regarded today as a 'coming of age' marker, is less useful in the Victorian era as many children worked and earned. Physical maturity has also differed greatly over time, with indicators such as height and puberty ceasing to offer suitable points of comparison. Even something like education provides little guidance as experiences were highly variable, particularly across social classes. Taking issues such as these into account, an upper age limit of 14 would seem to be an appropriate point at which to define a Victorian 'child'. There are, of course, clear inadequacies and weaknesses of such an arbitrary line in the sand, and as Walvin has argued, 'by that age millions of Victorian children had long since lost any characteristics of childhood'.[120] Nevertheless, 14 appears to be a useful rule of thumb, as long as it is viewed as an indicator rather than a cut-off point.

Based on this definition, there are eight children commemorated on the Watts Memorial and they range in age from 8-year-old Henry Bristow to 13-year-old Herbert McConaghey. A further distinction can be made in that four of those commemorated, who feature in this chapter, died while trying to save a sibling, while the other four, documented in the following chapter, lost their life while trying to save a friend. The incidents featuring children are, perhaps, the most moving of those on the memorial, and the very fact that there is less to say about them is a stark reminder of the short lives they led. Most were too young to have official occupations and, of course, none of them married or had children, so there were no widows or direct descendants. There were, though, grieving parents and siblings who, despite the appalling high levels of child mortality, would have been deeply and profoundly affected by the loss.[121] It is tempting to imagine that day-to-day familiarity with death may have induced a sense of helpless resignation, but that did not mean that the death of a child was any less painful for the family.

There are several striking things that stand out about the incidents which feature in this chapter. One is the relative freedom that the children were given and the distances from home which they were permitted to travel. When discussing the children of London street-sellers and the propensity for them to be out on the streets on a daily basis, the journalist Henry Mayhew estimated the figure to be somewhere between 10,000 and 20,000.[122] This presents a picture of London's streets, especially in working-class areas, teeming with children, working, travelling or simply passing their time. In modern terms, these children seem to have had quite a high degree of autonomy. Another striking feature is the frequency with which children were given responsibility for looking after their younger siblings, either in the home or on the streets. For working-class families it was usually a financial necessity for both parents to work, and often to work long or irregular hours, so children were often required to assume the mantle of carer. No doubt this practice was commonplace and widespread, and, for the most part, it probably presented little in the way of drama beyond scuffed knees or broken ornaments. Sometimes, though, the consequences of leaving one child to care for another, no matter the shortness of time, were more serious and far more tragic.

Jessie Eliza Bristow lived with her husband and her four children at 7 Hawkesley Terrace in Walthamstow, east London. Her husband, Henry James Bristow, was a cabinet maker earning a reasonable income and the family lived in relative working-class comfort. Jessie had moved to London from Woodbridge in Suffolk in around 1855 when her parents, James and Emily Arnold, had relocated to Hoxton; James was a coach painter keen to capitalise on the growth of London transport. Jessie and Henry met and married in Shoreditch in 1879, after which they moved into rooms at 107 Haggerston Road in Hackney and started a family. Their first child, Emily Sophia Bristow, arrived early in 1880 and then they had a son, **Henry James Bristow**, in 1882. Two more daughters followed, Beatrice Maud in 1884 and Jessie Louisa in 1888, and then a second son, Sydney Albert, born in 1889. It was around this time that the family moved to Hawkesley Terrace and settled into everyday life.

It was around 5 p.m. on 30 December 1890 and Jessie had some errands to run. Her husband was at work but she intended to be back within the hour so she left the children alone in the house.[123] Eight-year-old Henry was in a room with his 2-year-old sister Jessie, who had reached an age where she was able to pull herself up on the furniture. A small paraffin lamp had been hung over the mantelpiece and as the flickering light danced across the ceiling of the room it caught the attention of the little girl. A nearby chair provided all the height she needed, but as she clambered up and reached out for the lamp, she upended it, tipping flaming paraffin over herself. Her clothing quickly caught fire and as she screamed Henry ran to her and tore off the burning garments, but in doing so he set fire to himself. He eventually managed to extinguish the fire, but not before he and his sister had both been badly burned.

His mother, returning from her errand and alarmed by the smoke, ran into the room to find the two children 'quite naked and very much burned', at which point she raised the alarm and a doctor was summoned. The doctor advised Jessie to get a cab and take the children to the nearest infirmary, which was the German Hospital in Ritson Road. This had originally been established in 1845 to offer, as the name suggests, free treatment to German-speaking immigrants, but by 1890 it was mostly treating the poor of the local area. Henry and his sister were both admitted and treated by Dr Lacher, the house surgeon. At the coroner's inquest into Henry's death, held at the German Hospital on 9 January 1891, Dr Lacher reported that Henry 'had severe burns over the arms, neck, chest, abdomen and legs … he never recovered from the shock and died last Monday (5 Jan. 1891) as a result of his injuries'.[124] The inquest jury returned a verdict of 'accidental death' and the coroner commented, 'it is a sad case, the little fellow was quite a hero', to which Henry's mother added, 'he did his best to save his sister'. He did indeed and she recovered from her injuries, going on to marry Thomas Sanders Rolls, a carman and son of a mechanic, at St Peter's church in Edmonton on 31 July 1910. The couple had at least four children, Beatrice (b. 1911), William (b. 1914), Jessie (b. 1921) and Henry (b. 1931), and Jessie Louisa died, aged 57, in 1945.

Following their son's death, Henry and Jessie had four more children: Edward James (b. 1892), Elizabeth Winifred (b. 1895), Elsie Florence (b. 1898) and Rose Olive (b. 1899), but loss and bereavement were never far from their door. Their son Sydney died aged 4 in 1893, whilst Jessie (Henry's mother) died, aged 46, in 1903. Their youngest daughter, Rose, died in 1904, aged 5, and then their eldest daughter, Emily, died in 1907, aged 27. Emily had previously been sent to live with her step-grandmother, Sophia, and her maternal great uncle, William, at 54 De Beauvoir Road in Hackney, where she worked for them as a domestic servant. Sophia was 60 and William 70, so it is easy to imagine that Emily would have been doing much of the manual labour required to run the household and this may have taken its toll on her, hence her relatively young death.

There were, though, some happier stories for the Bristow family. On 5 March 1911, Beatrice Bristow married Alfred Thomas Jiggins, a painter and son of a tram driver, at St Peter's church in Edmonton, and the couple moved into rooms at 49 Gordon Road in Lower Edmonton. A family followed, with Florence (b. 1912) and then Winifred (b. 1916). Elsie Bristow, Beatrice's younger sister, lodged with the couple for a while, during which time she came to know Alfred's brother, Walter John Jiggins, and the two were married in 1922. They had at least one child, Marie (b. 1926). Alfred saw action in the First World War and was discharged in 1918, following which he and Beatrice do not appear to have had any more children. Alfred Jiggins died in an ambulance on the way to St Leonard's Hospital in Shoreditch, on 16 April 1945, Beatrice Jiggins died in Edmonton nineteen years later, Walter Jiggins died on 7 April 1945 and Elsie died in Exeter in 1965.

Of the eight cases which featured children, Henry Bristow's was the only one that took place indoors. All of the others occurred on the streets and waterways of the capital, underlining the itinerant nature of everyday life for working-class children. Two of the incidents in particular are strikingly similar; in fact, almost exactly alike. Both feature a pair of brothers who were returning home from an excursion, and the journey required them to cross a busy road when misfortune struck. The coming of the railways in 1863 is, undoubtedly, a landmark in London transport history, but it tends to overshadow the pre-steam era where four legs were the norm. Furthermore, while not every thoroughfare resembled Ludgate Hill as depicted by the illustrator Gustave Doré in 1872, there is little doubt that London's roads were frantic and dangerous places.[125]

Horse-drawn vehicles of every size and shape literally 'jockeyed' for position on the cobbled streets. For passengers, there were fast and nimble two-wheeled hansom cabs pulled by a single steed, four-wheeled 'growlers' with a pair of horses, four-horse and even six-horse coaches crossing London on longer journeys and, from the 1830s, the London Omnibus. A wide variety of goods were also being carried in an array of vehicles, drays delivering beer, pantechnicon vans moving furniture, milk floats, trollies and wagons of varying descriptions, all thundering along with work to do and places to be. In 1861, Mayhew estimated that there were 3,000 omnibuses, 5,000 hackney cabs, and somewhere around 8,000 carriages, carts and wagons in London, all with at least one, and more often, two or four horses pulling each one.[126] Horse-drawn vehicles posed a range of hazards to pedestrians, not least the propensity for horses to bolt out of control, taking their carriage or wagon with them, and cases of this nature feature on the Watts Memorial.[127] Furthermore, pedestrians struck by the vehicles were doubly at risk; firstly, of being knocked down and trampled by the horse, and then of being run over by the heavy iron-rimmed wheels. It would appear, then, that crossing a busy London thoroughfare in the mid-Victorian period was fraught with potential disaster, and it could be argued that these were certainly not places for children to be negotiating alone.

The Rodney Road runs through Walworth in south-east London and the Victorian social investigator Charles Maurice Davies once described it as 'anything but a romantic thoroughfare, leading out of the New Kent Road, a little way from the Elephant and Castle'.[128] The Rodney Road is also near to Brandon Street, and in July 1886, number 35 Brandon Street was home to the Fisher family. William Joseph Fisher was a brass finisher, originally from Westminster, and in 1867 he had married Eliza Marian Ayres, the daughter of a waterman, in Lambeth. Initially, the couple moved into 4 Hughes Place in Newington, where they had their first child, Eliza Ann, born in 1867. A son, Henry George, arrived next in 1870 and at that point the couple moved to 35 Brandon Street in Newington to accommodate their expanding family. Another daughter, Annie Caroline, was born in 1873, then William in 1876, Jane Elizabeth in 1880, James Charles in 1884 and Florence Maud in 1887.

On 12 July 1886, the 9-year-old **William Fisher** was returning home to Brandon Street with his 2-year-old brother James.[129] It is not clear exactly where the two boys had been, but it was around 6 p.m. and the roads in the area were busy with traffic. As the two brothers were waiting for an opportunity to cross the Rodney Road, the younger boy ran out into the roadway just as a horse and delivery van was approaching. William was quick to see the danger and, rushing after James, he seized him by the shoulder to pull him back out of the way. The vehicle, though, was upon them and one of the shafts clipped James, spinning the two boys around, and they both fell under the van. As the vehicle rattled on, both the front and rear wheels passed over the boys, who then became tangled in the undercarriage of the vehicle. Realising what had happened, the van driver pulled up the horses and horri-fied onlookers ran to the back of the van and dragged the boys out.

James was the first to be extricated and he was carried to the pavement and laid on the ground. As William was pulled out, he spotted James lying on the street and tried to run to him, but he staggered, lost his balance and collapsed against some hoardings that lined the road. Both boys appeared badly injured and they were quickly conveyed to Guy's Hospital in Great Maze Pond, where James was admitted but William was pronounced dead on arrival. The boys' parents were contacted and they rushed to the hospital where they were given the mixed news; one son killed but the other one alive, although the prospects looked slim. James' injuries did indeed prove to be fatal and he died on 14 July, two days after his brother. The inquest into both deaths was held at Guy's Hospital on 16 July and, after evidence had been given by witnesses James Banham and a Mrs Howe, verdicts of accidental death were returned and the van driver exonerated from any blame.[130] Witnesses said there was nothing he could have done to avoid the boys. The two brothers had lived together, grown up together, played together and died together, so it was fitting that they were also buried together. The funeral took place on 20 July 1886 and the two boys were buried in a common grave in Manor Park Cemetery in Forest Gate.

To some extent, the elaborate and prolonged mourning customs of the earlier Victorian period were still practised by the middle classes and these would have prescribed a period of around six months of full mourning for William and James' siblings.[131] In reality, for working-class families, there was seldom the time or money for such rituals, but it is likely that they would have worn dark colours or sombre dress for a period of time as a mark of respect and so not to attract the scorn of their neighbours. Life, however, went on. William, Eliza and the remaining family moved to 1 Albion House on Amelia Road in Newington and, as the children grew up and moved out, the couple continued to downsize, moving to 22 Olney Street in Newington by 1900. Eliza Fisher, William and James' mother, died aged 58 in Southwark in 1904, and sometime after this, but before 1911, their father William entered the Christchurch Workhouse in Gray Street, Southwark. He appears to have died, aged 77, in Camberwell in 1922.

The couple's only surviving son, Henry George Fisher, followed his father's trade and became a tinplate worker. He married Annie Emma Walsh, the daughter of a cooper, at St John the Evangelist church in Walworth on 1 August 1897. In 1901, they were living at 73 Lion Street, just off the Old Kent Road, with their two children, Florence Alice (b. 1899) and Henry (b. 1900). Another child, Doris Beatrice, arrived in 1904 and by 1911 the family had moved to Tooting and were living at 14 Mellison Road. Annie died, aged 52, in Wandsworth in 1927 and Henry died, aged 66, in 1936.

William and James' sister, Eliza Ann Fisher, married George Jarlett, a tanner, on 3 June 1888 at All Saints church in Walworth. In 1891, they were living at 26 Fort Road in Bermondsey with their first child, Eliza Clara, born in 1889, and over the next eighteen years they had a further six children.[132] In 1901, the family was still living in Bermondsey, at 34 Larnaca Street, but by 1907 they had moved to 7 Matthews Place in Dover, Kent. Both George and Eliza Ann died in Exeter; George aged 82 in 1948 and Eliza aged 91 in the City Hospital in 1958. The boys' other sister, Annie Caroline Fisher, worked for some years as a book folder before marrying

Henry Reynolds, an engineer and son of a commercial traveller, at St Mary's parish church in Newington on 5 August 1900. Their first child, Florence Adelaide, was born in 1901 and at least three more followed: Henry William (b. 8 October 1902), Henry Frederick Fisher (b. 26 July 1904) and Doris Marian Annie (b. 1906).

Just over five years after William Fisher was killed trying to stop his brother James from being hit by a vehicle in the Rodney Road in Walworth, almost exactly the same thing happened to another pair of brothers. It was, though, on a different road and the boys involved appear to have come from quite a different background, although uncovering the full story is far from straightforward.

The tablet on the Watts Memorial states that **Solomon Galaman** was killed trying to save his brother from being run over in Commercial Street on 6 September 1901, and the report of the incident in the *East London Advertiser* the following week provided key details of the incident. Galaman was reportedly 11 years old and 'the son of a journeyman tailor residing at 73 Cable Street, St George's East'. His mother's name was Becky Galaman, whose evidence at the coroner's inquest had to be translated, and he had been to visit his grandmother when the accident occurred.[133] The 1901 census had been conducted just five months earlier and so it should provide an ideal source to corroborate the information given in the press and reveal more details about Solomon and his life.

There was, however, no Solomon Galaman recorded on the 1901 census (or for 1891) and 73 Cable Street was, in March 1901, occupied by Lazarus Breitman, a boot maker from Turkey, and his family. There was a Becky Galman living in Cable Street; she and her sister Sarah were boarding with the Rosenthal family at number 59, but she was recorded as being 20 years old and therefore too young to be Solomon's mother. As for his grandmother, there were no Galamans or Galmans of a suitable age in the area and no clues to a possible maternal surname.

Casting the net a little wider and allowing for phonetic spellings and not uncommon errors and mistakes in press reporting reveals an 11-year-old Solomon Gellman, the son of Nathan Gellman, a master tailor, and Elizabeth (Leah) Gellman living, in 1901, at 35 Red Lion Street behind Farringdon Street Station in Clerkenwell. Nathan and Leah were both Russian Jewish immigrants and four of their five children, including Solomon, were born in Russia. The youngest, Israel, was born in Bethnal Green in 1899, while the next eldest, Samuel, was born in Russia in around 1894. This provides a five-year window in which the Gellman family entered Britain and this was towards the tail end of a significant period of eastern European migration.

The Russian famine of 1869–70, conscription for the Russo-Turkish War of 1877–8 and the repression of Jews in Russia following the assassination of Tsar Alexander II in 1881, along with the economic pressures and disadvantages of an increasingly proletarian employment structure, led many Russians, Poles and Austrians, among others, to settle in Britain.[134] The 1881 census recorded 8,700 Russians and Poles living in London; by 1901 the figure was around 53,000.[135] Indicative of this, also living with Nathan and his family were his father David, his widowed sister Annie, his brother Benjamin, his brother's wife Sarah and their 3-year-old son Charles. All were born in Russia and all the adults were described as tailors. David Gellman was recorded as being married, rather than widowed, which suggests that there was a paternal grand-mother living somewhere else whom Solomon and his brother could have been visiting in the Commercial Street area on the day of the accident.

Evidence of family links to the Whitechapel area can also be drawn from the records of Solomon's school attendance. On 22 October 1900 he was admitted to the Roseberry Avenue School on Laystall Street, formerly the Laystall Street School built by the London School Board and opened in 1876. The Register of Admissions and Discharges for the school recorded his father as Nathan Gellman and his address as 35 Red Lion Street, which was just a short walk along the Clerkenwell Road, and it tallies with the 1901 census. However, the register also notes that Solomon had attended another school, Old Castle Street, for two years prior to entering Roseberry. Old Castle Street ran adjacent to Commercial Street, close to its junction with Whitechapel High Street, and the board school was an imposing building adjacent to the public baths. Henry Walker, in his *Sketches of Christian Work and Workers* (1896), described a Sunday morning visit to the area thus:

> The capacious new school-buildings of the London School Board have during the last few years been readily offered and eagerly accepted for the Sunday use of Jewish children. A visit from a stranger never fails to excite his astonishment at the number of children in attendance. At Whitechapel, the large Board schools in Settle Street, Old Castle Street, and Berner Street, Commercial Road, stand, perhaps, at the head of the list as regards children attending for instruction in the Scriptures and knowledge of Hebrew. At Old Castle Street School the number of Jewish children attending religious classes on the Sunday is often one thousand.[136]

It would appear that around the time of 1897–1900 Solomon had been attending Castle Street School in an official capacity as a school board pupil and this would place the family as living in the Whitechapel area at that time. By October 1900, something had caused a move to Clerkenwell, but the family clearly had roots in and around Commercial Street.

The report in the *East London Advertiser*, which documented the coroner's inquest held at the London Hospital on Saturday, 7 September, related that Solomon had left home on Tuesday, 3 September, not 6 September as recorded on the memorial tablet, with his 4-year-old brother to visit their grandmother.[137] Solomon had two younger brothers, Samuel, aged 7, and Israel, aged around 2, so neither fits exactly with the published story. Israel was born in Bethnal Green and his birth registered in 1899, so his age is verifiable. The journey on foot between Red Lion Street and Commercial Street was around a mile and a half, and it seems improbable, even in 1901, that an 11-year-old would have been tasked with taking a 2-year-old on such a trip. More likely it was Samuel who accompanied Solomon that day and he may well have been 4 years of age rather than 7, but this cannot be easily verified. It is therefore not unfeasible that the brothers could have covered the distance, although if they were heading for Cable Street it is unlikely their journey would have taken them via Commercial Street.

Nevertheless, this is where witnesses saw them sometime later and it would appear that, while trying to cross the road, the younger of the two brothers slipped and fell. The road had recently been watered and this had left the surface slippery. Seeing that his brother had fallen into the path of an approaching cart, Solomon rushed into the road and successfully pulled him out of the way. He was, though, unable to move quickly enough to avoid the vehicle himself, which knocked him down and dragged him beneath the wheels, where, according to the witnesses, he received 'terrible injuries', much the same as the Fisher brothers. Solomon was quickly conveyed to the nearby London Hospital on the Whitechapel Road and a police constable took Samuel home and informed his mother, Elizabeth, that the elder boy had been injured. By the time she reached the London Hospital it was clear that little could be done for Solomon. As his mother leant over him, he reportedly looked up and whispered, 'Mother, I am dying. Have they brought my little brother home? I saved him, but I could not save myself.' He kissed her, laid back in the bed and, a short time later, died.

Following Solomon's death, the hustle and bustle of everyday life continued for the Gellman family. Solomon's uncle Benjamin and Benjamin's wife Sarah had at least two more children, Israel (b. 1901) and Alexander (b. 1907). By 1911, they were living at 41 Walgrave House on the newly built Boundary Road estate in Bethnal Green. Nathan and Elizabeth had also moved there and were living at 6 Hurley House with their daughters Tilly, aged 26, and Annie, aged 9, and their sons Samuel, aged 17 and employed as a carpet maker, and Israel, aged 11, who was attending school. Nathan Gellman, Solomon's father, died in 1933, aged 71, and his mother, Elizabeth, died in 1936, aged 76.

Of the other Gellman siblings, Ethel, Solomon's elder sister, married Isaac Morgenstein, a clerk, in Whitechapel in 1910. In 1911, they were living at 129 Englefield Road off the Essex Road in Islington, and they had their first child, Hannah, in 1912. Tilly Gellman, Solomon's eldest sister, took up the family tailoring trade and lived with her parents until 1919 when she married Abraham Cohen in Bethnal Green. They had at least two children, Ruth (b. 1922) and Maurice (b. 1927). There is evidence to suggest that Samuel Gellman, Solomon's younger brother, may have emigrated to New York, and there is no evidence of him marrying or dying in Britain. Israel Gellman also travelled to New York in 1931 and there is evidence of him travelling to Argentina, although he died in Hendon, north London, in 1970.

The final incident in the quartet of sibling heroism recorded on the Watts Memorial was undertaken in slightly different circumstances from the other three and arose from what can best be described as youthful 'high jinks'. In St Mary's fields, close to Kilburn High Road, some building works had been taking place and, as a result, several large deep pits had been dug which had subsequently filled with water to a depth of around 8ft. There can be few things more enticing to young boys, particularly Victorian boys, than the prospect of an 'adventure', and several large ponds surrounded by offcuts of wood and other building materials added up to one pursuit: raft building. On the afternoon of 24 May 1878, four schoolboy friends decided upon this course of action and they set off for the makeshift ponds; the four were Frank Sisley, aged 12, his 10-year-old brother, **Harry Sisley**, and two other boys of around the same age, one with the surname Pye and another called Webb.[138]

The Sisley brothers, Frank and Harry, were respectively the fourth and fifth sons of George and Sophia Sisley. George was an east London cab driver who came from a line of transport proprietors; his father, William, had also been a coachman and a cab driver. Sophia Lewis, the boys' mother, was born in Deptford in Kent and was the daughter of George Lewis, an auctioneer, and his wife Matilda. On 7 March 1859, Sophia had married George Sisley at St Mary's church in Marylebone, and their first child, George William, arrived a little over nine months later on 20 December.

The family moved into rooms at 9 Clarendon Street in Somerstown behind Euston Station and more children followed: Edwin Charles (b. 1862), Arthur Sidney (b. 1864), Frank Herbert (b. 1866), Harry (b. 1868) and Maud Sophia (b. 13 February 1870). Sometime before the early 1870s, the family moved westwards to 9 Victoria Mews off Victoria Road on the border of Kilburn and Willesden. On 20 October 1872 another daughter, Alice Olivia, was born, followed by Matilda Amelia in 1876, and to accommodate the increase, the Sisley clan moved a short distance to 7 Linstead Street in Kilburn, a short distance from St Mary's fields, where, in May 1878, an enticing prospect for adventure had presented itself.

Arriving at the ponds, the boys constructed a crude raft and launched it upon the water. At first, they took turns one at a time, but as they became more confident Frank and Harry decided to attempt a dual voyage and, sliding their craft into the water, they clambered aboard and set out to paddle across. While they were paddling, Frank spotted something enticing in the water and, leaning down to grab it, he lost his balance and toppled in. The water was deep and, unable to swim, Frank called frantically for help. Harry quickly jumped into the water and grabbed on to his brother, but the two of them sank beneath the surface. On the bank, Pye and Webb watched the drama unfolding and, fearful that he would get into trouble, Webb ran off, but Pye waded into the water and swam out to where the Sisley brothers had sunk.

Pye managed to get hold of Harry and drag him to the shore before returning to the water in search of Frank. He got hold of Frank, but as he turned to swim back he realised that Harry was back in the water, crying 'Oh, Oh, Frank!' and splashing towards them. Whether Harry was trying to help or was in shock is not clear, but when he grabbed hold of his brother and 'cuddled to him', the two of them promptly sank. Pye was by now exhausted and thought it best to go for help rather than continue alone. He fetched a constable and another man, named Redwood, who, it was reported, 'after some difficulty' managed to recover Frank and Harry from the water. A local GP, Dr Hills of Abbey Road, had been called and he tried artificial respiration but 'all efforts to restore animation proved fruitless'; both the boys had drowned. An inquest into the deaths was held at the Duke of Hamilton Tavern in Hampstead on 28 May and the jury, returning a verdict of 'accidental death', expressed their 'admiration of the conduct of Pye' and praised Redwood and the constable for their actions.[139]

As with the Fisher brothers, Frank and Harry Sisley were laid to rest together in the same grave. On 29 May 1878, family and friends gathered at Hampstead Cemetery in Fortune Green Road to say goodbye as the two small coffins were lowered into the ground. Unlike in the case of the Fisher brothers, the Sisley family had been able to purchase the burial plot and also to erect a headstone, the inscription of which read 'in fond remembrance of Frank Sisley, aged 12 years and Harry Sisley, aged 10 years, died May 24 1878'. There was also a quote from Psalms 90:6, 'in the morning it flourisheth and groweth up, in the evening it is cut down and withereth'; a melancholy but fitting tribute to two brothers who died at such a young age in such unnecessary circumstances.

Following the sudden and untimely deaths of their two sons, George and Sophia Sisley had one more child, Thomas Henry, in 1878. The family continued to live at 7 Linstead Street and life carried on despite the tragedy they had experienced. Maud, Alice, Matilda and George all attended the Netherwood Street School, opened in 1881, which backed onto Linstead Street, so they did not have far to walk. George continued to work as a cab driver and the two elder boys still living at home were gainfully employed and supporting the household, Edwin working as an oilman and Arthur as a carpenter.

Heartbreak struck the family again in 1888, when Alice Olivia died at the age of just 16. She was buried in Hampstead Cemetery in the same plot as her brothers, Harry and Frank. The family also purchased the adjacent grave and this is where the boys' mother, Sophia, was buried on 5 November 1902 and then their father, George, on 17 July 1924; Sophia was 61 and George, 86. All three names were subsequently added to the headstone.

The other boys in the Sisley family all married and had families. Edwin Sisley married Charlotte May Ada Chandler at the Jesus Chapel in Enfield on 14 April 1884 and the couple had at least five children.[140] Edwin Charles died, aged 79, on 3 February 1942 at 58 Park Parade in Harlesden. His wife Charlotte had predeceased him in 1940, so his estate of £192 passed to his daughter, Elsie Ellen, who had married George Stansfield in 1922. Thomas Sisley developed a successful career, working in the accounts department of the local council, and in 1900 he married Elizabeth Coe in Hampstead. Their first child, Kathleen Irene, was born in 1901, followed by Marjorie Jessie in 1904 and Alice Mary in 1908. Arthur Sisley married Fanny Smith at Christ Church in Brondesbury on 4 August 1888 and evidence suggests that in 1891 they emigrated to the USA, where they had at least two children, George and Leslie. Fanny and the children were resident in Willesden in 1901, but there is no record of Arthur or Fanny dying in the UK, so it seems likely that they moved back to the USA after 1901.

Of the Sisley girls, Maud Sisley married William Frost in 1892 and the couple moved to Derbyshire where they had a daughter, Alice, and then back in Hampstead they had another daughter, Hilda. Matilda Sisley became a dressmaker and lived with her parents until at least 1901. In 1911 she was lodging with the Whitethorn family at 129 Kilburn High Road along with another dressmaker of the same age, Jessie Cook. Matilda did not marry or have children, but when she died, on 27 January 1957 at Flat B, Galsworthy Close in Cricklewood, her estate of £218 passed to Jessie Cook, who was also still a spinster. For the two women to be still so closely associated after over forty years certainly shows that they were very close friends, but also perhaps suggests that they may have been a couple.

By collecting together these four cases of young boys who died while trying to save their siblings, the wider family context comes into focus. The Watts Memorial commemorates the bravery of Henry Bristow, William Fisher, Solomon Gellman and Harry Sisley, but uncovering the full stories also reveals the loss of James Fisher and Frank Sisley – those families having to bury not just one, but two of their sons. On the other side of the coin were those who were saved and who went on to enjoy fruitful lives as a result of their brother's sacrifice: Jessie Bristow marrying and having four children and Samuel Gellman emigrating to the 'land of opportunity'.

8

HIS LIFE FOR
HIS FRIEND

The Watts Memorial is unique in many ways, but something particularly noteworthy is that it publicly commemorates acts of heroism undertaken by children and women. To modern readers, this may not seem particularly remarkable, but the Victorians had quite different and somewhat compartmentalised attitudes towards heroism. Broadly speaking, heroism was generally regarded to be the natural and innate domain of adult men, particularly in relation to life-risking acts of bravery. Much of this stemmed from the fact that the public understanding of heroism had traditionally been fostered in arenas dominated by adult men, such as the military, the police, the fire brigade and overseas service or exploration in the British Empire.

The introduction of decorations such as the Victoria Cross in 1856 and the Albert Medal in 1866 paved the way for a more democratic understanding of gallantry and heroism.[141] Later on, the increasingly publicised work of charitable organisations like the Royal Humane Society and the Society for the Protection of Life from Fire, coupled with the ideas of people like G.F. Watts and Andrew Carnegie, widened the understanding of how and where heroism could be performed.[142] This did a great deal to widen the spheres in which heroism was recognised, thus fostering the idea of 'everyday' heroism and opening the door for the recognition of heroic women and children alongside their male counterparts. This is not to say, though, that the ideas of everyday heroism were universally adopted, at least not to begin with and, in particular, not in relation to children. For example, prior to 1914, only one of the 238 Albert Medals awarded by the government for civilian gallantry went to a boy and that was not until 1911.[143]

There was one area, however, where the heroism of children was championed and celebrated and that was children's literature, especially prescriptive literature designed to instil character and sound morals. Books with titles including *Heroism of Boyhood*, *Fifty-Two Stories of Heroism in Life and Action for Boys*, and *Deeds of Daring: Stories of Heroism in Every Day Life* all contained dramatic tales of heroic boys.[144] Girls were also catered for in books such as *Heroines: True Tales of Brave Women – A Book for British Girls* and *A Book of Brave Girls at Home and Abroad: True Stories of Courage and Heroism*.[145] What is particularly interesting about the stories which feature in these publications is that they were almost always instances of children rescuing other children, and this seems to have been an acceptable construction of heroism for the Victorian palate. Men saving men was heroic, men saving women was heroic, women saving children was heroic, and children saving children was heroic; anything outside of these patterns presented a challenge to the status quo.

These attitudes are all clearly reflected in the cases on the Watts Memorial, so while it is nevertheless unusual to see women and children so publicly commemorated on a Victorian monument to heroism, all of the incidents did, essentially, conform to accepted models of behaviour at the time. All of the nine women commemorated died while trying to save either other women or children in their care, and, aside from this, women feature mainly as the objects of male heroism. Similarly with the eight children who feature on the monument, all of them perished while trying to save another child rather than an adult. In four cases, covered in the previous chapter, the other child was their sibling, but this was not always the case, and in four other cases, discussed in this chapter, it was a friend or playmate.

In the summer of 1894 there was some consternation among people in the riverside district of Southwark, on the southern side of the River Thames, regarding the behaviour of some children in the area. It was reported that most nights around fifty or sixty boys would go down onto the foreshore near to London Bridge at low tide and could be seen wading, swimming and playing in the water.[146] Local people were concerned that, as the tide turned and the strong currents drove the North Sea back upriver, there was a real danger that boys could be swept away and drowned. The local police had been informed and Inspector Pritchard of the Thames division had repeatedly sent constables to the area to warn off the children, but they persisted in returning. Local feeling was that it was only a matter of time before something dreadful happened, and on 16 July 1894, it did.

Two of the boys who had taken to playing on the foreshore were 8-year-old Campbell Mortimer and 10-year-old **John Clinton**. The boys were friends through living in the same building at 51 Brandon Street in Walworth, a short walk from the Thames at London Bridge. John Clinton had been born in Lambeth on 17 January 1884. His father, Thomas, born in Ireland in around 1853, was a carman who, in 1882, had married Harriett Fry, originally from Devon, who at that time was working as a domestic servant in the Kensington area.

John was the couple's first child and then five more followed: Thomas (b. 1 July 1885), Arthur (b. 1 September 1887), Theresa (b. 1889), Frederick Fry Joseph (b. 1893) and May Florence (b. 1896). The family initially lived at 66 Waldeck Buildings in Windmill Street, Lambeth, before moving to 48, and then 51, Brandon Street. Both John and his brothers Thomas and Arthur attended St John and All Saints School in Lambeth: John when he was 5, Thomas when he was 4, and Arthur was admitted when he was just 3. John's playmate, Campbell Mortimer junior, was the son of Campbell Mortimer, a butcher, and his wife Margaret, who also had three other children: Margaret junior, Willie and Daisy.

On the evening of 16 July 1894 the two friends were playing, along with many other children, on the beach at London Bridge.[147] Both had taken off their shoes and stockings and were wading through the water when suddenly Campbell lost his footing and, caught by a current, was carried out beyond his depth. Heeding his shouts for help, John swam out to him and with difficulty just managed to get Campbell back into shallow water and the youngster scrambled to the shore. However, as he turned to look for John, he saw that his rescuer had fallen back into the water and was, himself, being pulled out into the stronger currents. Exhausted from retrieving Campbell, John was unable to swim against the tide and the children on the shore watched helplessly as the lad was dragged beneath the surface.

A nearby lighterman, James Palmer, saw John in trouble and tried to steer his craft towards the boy, but the tide was also against him and he was unable to reach Clinton before the stricken youth was washed under the steamboat pier. About ten minutes later, in the backwash of an approaching steamer, Clinton's body emerged from beneath the pier and was washed up onto the shore. A Dr Pearce from nearby Guy's Hospital applied artificial respiration and 'tried every means in his power to restore animation', but nothing could be done; John Clinton had drowned.

On 23 July, the Southwark coroner, Samuel Frederick Langham, held an inquest at Guy's Hospital on the death of John Clinton.[148] Campbell Mortimer gave evidence, as did James Palmer, Dr Pearce and Inspector Pritchard. The foreman of the jury questioned Pritchard, asking him why the police did not prevent boys from entering the water, but the inspector replied that they could not be there all the time and they had frequently warned the boys about the dangers. The foreman suggested that a warning noticeboard might be erected at the site in the hope that 'a little trouble might save many a life'. The jury returned a verdict of accidental death, adding that 'no blame was attributable to anyone'.

The inquest also revealed that John Clinton had previously saved the life of his younger sister, Theresa, in circumstances reminiscent of those in which Henry Bristow died. The infant girl had been playing with some matches and had set fire to the curtains, which had then ignited her clothing. John had grabbed hold of his little sister and rolled her on the carpet to extinguish the flames before pulling down the curtains, thus preventing the fire from spreading. In doing so John had suffered severe burns to his hands and arms, but the incident clearly did not deter him from also trying to save his friend.

John was buried in Manor Park Cemetery in Forest Gate on 31 July 1894 and the *Illustrated Police News* carried two illustrations of the 'boy hero': one, a montage of Clinton performing his acts of heroism and, the other, a depiction of the graveside funeral service (see plates 9 and 10).[149] The paper also described how 'the funeral cortege consisted of a hearse and two mourning coaches, with the coffin being almost entirely hidden by wreaths, one of which bore the words "he saved me" sent by the boy who Clinton had rescued'.[150] Other floral tributes were sent by the Metropolitan Fire Brigade and teachers from the local board school. It was also reported that Clinton's schoolfellows had 'started a subscription for the purpose of erecting a tombstone to his memory, as well as a tablet to be placed in St John's Schools, Walworth where the deceased attended'.[151] It is not clear if these objectives were ever achieved and there is no evidence of a headstone having been erected at the grave. There may or may not have been a tablet at John's school, but he was, of course, later commemorated on the Watts Memorial in 1902.

In circumstances strikingly similar to those involving John Clinton, the River Thames was also the site of another of the incidents featuring children which appears on the memorial – one child losing his life while trying to save another who had got out of his depth while swimming at a notoriously dangerous spot on the river. The spot in question is a promontory of land about 11 miles downstream of London Bridge called Tripcock Point, and it was (and perhaps still is) best known as the site of the most deadly single accident in modern British history.[152] On 2 September 1878 a paddle steamer, the *Princess Alice*, was returning to London from a day-trip to Sheerness in Kent with around 800 people on board; the exact number is not known as the boat was substantially overloaded. At around 7.40 p.m. it was struck by a coal ship, the *Bywell Castle*, which had been approaching from the opposite direction and had not seen the steamer due to the bend in the river. The *Princess Alice* was cut in two and sank within four minutes with the loss of more than 650 lives. Hundreds drowned but it is believed that many were actually poisoned by the foul condition of the water because, around an hour before the collision, millions of gallons of raw sewage had been pumped into the river from the outfalls at Barking and Crossness. One would imagine that this was the last place that anyone would choose to swim but, nevertheless, people did.

Two of those people were 12-year-old James Bayne and his friend **Daniel Thomas Selves**, also 12, who lived close by the river in Plumstead. James lived at 37 Glyndon Road with his mother, Ann, his stepfather, Peter, his siblings, Ada, Lily and Rose, and his half-siblings, Emily, Julia and Peter. Peter Bayne senior was a metal turner working at the Woolwich Arsenal, where one of his workmates was a man called George Selves, which is how Peter's stepson, James, became good friends with George's son, Daniel. It also helped that the two boys were neighbours, Daniel living just around the corner at 160 Ann Street.

Daniel Selves was from a very large family; the thirteenth of fourteen children born to George Selves, a bricklayer from Woolwich, and his wife, Emma.[153] George's father, Thomas Selves, had been a licensed victualler and Emma's father, Daniel Baker, a wheelwright. The couple married at St Pancras parish chapel in Camden on 3 October 1847 and the first of their fourteen children, George junior, was born in 1848. Daniel (who appears on the Watts Memorial as David) was born on 24 October 1873 and baptised at St Mary Magdalene church in Woolwich on 16 November the same year. He was admitted to Earl Street School in Greenwich in April 1881 and did well, achieving the required standards each year. James Bayne also attended Earl Street School, so the two boys spent a lot of time together.

During the summer, some of this time was spent swimming and, despite it being a known blackspot for drowning, the boys used to frequent Tripcock Point, a short walk from their neighbourhood.[154] While swimming there on 4 September 1886, James got out of his depth and called to Daniel, who promptly swam out to help him. Moored close by was the ship *Royalist*, which served as a station for the Thames division of the Metropolitan Police, and at the time Constable William Hall was rowing nearby in the ship's cutter. Giving evidence to the coroner's inquest, held on 7 September, Hall reported that he had heard someone shouting, 'Keep it up a little longer, Jim!' and his attention had been drawn to two boys who were 'clasped in each other's arms, 30 feet from the shore in 15 feet of water'.[155] Realising the lads were in trouble, Hall rowed promptly to the spot but by the time he arrived they had gone. About an hour later, the bodies of James Bayne and Daniel Selves were pulled from the river and both were pronounced dead at the scene. The inquest jury later returned verdicts of 'accidental death' on both boys.

The parish register for St Margaret's church in Plumstead records that both Daniel and James were buried on 9 September 1886. No address is recorded for James and the entry simply reads 'found drowned in River Thames'. St Margaret's did not have a burial ground, but the vicar was responsible for the churchyard at nearby St Nicholas' so it is possible that the two boys were buried there. However, the parish register could simply indicate that the funeral service was held at St Margaret's and the burial may actually have taken place in another cemetery or churchyard in the area. Consequently, their final resting place is currently unknown.

Daniel's parents continued to live at 160 Ann Street, initially with their two youngest surviving sons, Albert and William, and then later with just Albert. Their elder son, Arthur, had already died, aged 14, in 1878. Emma Selves, Daniel's mother, died on 12 March 1907, aged 79, and her estate of £979 passed to her husband, George, who died later the same year, on 7 December; his estate of similar value was inherited by the couple's eldest son, George junior. He married Mary Ann Mellership in Woolwich in 1869 and they had at least nine children over the next thirteen years.[156] George died on 9 November 1930, at which time he was living at 140 Robert Street in Plumstead.

Of Daniel's other brothers, Richard Selves served in the British army for a short while then worked as a railway porter. He married Mary Ann Baldwin in Bromley in 1878 and by 1891 the couple had six children. Samuel Selves also served for a spell in the British army and then worked as a machinist. In 1908, he married Elizabeth Christina Kimmis and the couple do not appear to have had any children. Albert and William Selves both worked at the Woolwich Arsenal, Albert as an overlooker and William as an engineer's labourer. William married in 1898 to Edith Mary Mays and in 1907 Albert married Alice Mary Connely. William and Edith had at least three children, Edith, Phyllis and William, and Albert and Alice had at least two children, Albert Edward and Amy. Melville Selves worked as a labourer in an iron foundry and in 1889 he married Ellen Morrow, the couple going on to have two children, Melville junior and Albert. Melville and Ellen died within a few days of each other in 1930, Ellen on 18 December and her husband less than a week later. At the time they were living at 120 Robert Street in Plumstead, just a few doors along from where Melville's brother, George, had been living.

Emma, Daniel's eldest sister, worked in and around the Woolwich area as both a domestic servant and a cook. She did not marry and died at St Nicholas Hospital in Plumstead on 29 January 1933, aged 83. All of Daniel's other sisters married and had families. Caroline Selves worked at the Woolwich Arsenal sewing gunpowder bags until, in 1875, she married Thomas Redding. They had at least five children: Amy, Thomas junior, Percy, Willie and Maud. Caroline died, aged 80, in 1934. Eliza also worked as a domestic servant and on 3 October 1881 she married Ernest Ellard, a soldier, at St Margaret's church in Plumstead. They had at least four children, Albert, Thomas, Daisy and Sydney, and lived the life of a military family, moving from place to place as Ernest was posted. Frances Selves followed a similar course and married John Sweeper, a soldier, at St Margaret's church on 31 October 1881. It is not, though, entirely clear what happened to the couple after this and it is likely they were stationed outside the UK.

The River Thames was by no means the only major body of water in nineteenth-century London and the city was also home to a system of canals. Although certainly not as extensive as the wider UK canal network, the waterways still had a part to play in distributing the goods that flooded into the capital. There were four major London canals in the nineteenth century. One was the Lea Navigational, which essentially ran from the Thames in east London to Bedford. The others were three canals which linked together to provide passage from the Thames at Limehouse, all the way through to Braunston in Northamptonshire; these were the Regent's Canal, the Paddington Arm of the Grand Junction Canal and then the Grand Junction Canal itself.[157]

On its journey between the Regent's Canal and the Grand Junction Canal, the Paddington Arm weaved its way across west London, passing through Maida Vale, Kensal Green and then just north of Wormwood Scrubs, where it was crossed by a bridge, aptly named Scrubs Bridge. It was in the Grand Junction Canal, in the shadow of Scrubs Bridge, that 10-year-old **Edward Morris** and his friend Sidney Moody went swimming on 2 August 1897; a hot bank holiday Monday that had drawn lots of boys to the water. Once again, there are some striking similarities between Edward's story and other boys who feature on the memorial.

Edward Morris, who was born on 29 June 1887 and baptised the following day at St Mark's church in St John's Wood, was the son of Edward Morris senior, a pedlar and hawker, and Harriett Butler, the daughter of a cab proprietor, who had married at St Clement's church in Notting Hill on 8 May 1882. At the time of Edward's birth, the couple were living at 7 Swinbrook Road in Notting Hill, but by 1891 they had moved to 374 Portobello Road and then by 1897 they had moved again, to 79 St Ervans Road near Westbourne Park railway station. Living in the same building in 1897 was the Moody family, consisting of Richard Moody, a cab driver, his wife Ellen, a daughter Mabel and a son Sidney, who at 9 years of age was just less than a year younger than Edward Morris. The two boys became firm friends in much the same way as John Clinton and Campbell Mortimer had.

Both the boys were good swimmers and on 2 August they spent quite a long time in the water, but perhaps too long because Moody began to tire and was struggling to keep his head above the surface.[158] The water was deep and they were still some distance from the bank, so Morris swam to his friend to try and help him along. However, by the time Morris reached him, Moody was in a panic and, grabbing out at him, Moody clutched so tightly that it prevented either one of them from swimming and the two boys, grappling with one another, sank beneath the surface of the water. On the opposite side of the canal, two men were fishing and, witnessing the incident, they jumped in to try and help. The first man, James Brown, was unable to find the boys but the other, a local character, Charles Simmonds, who lived at 17 Edenham Street in Kensal Road, got hold of Morris and dragged him out. Simmonds then also located Moody and pulled him onto the bank next to Morris, where attempts were then made to revive the boys. Nothing, though, could be done and it was clear that both were dead; drowned in the Grand Junction Canal on what should have been a happy bank holiday excursion.

Two days later, on 4 August, the coroner Charles Luxmoore Drew held the inquest into the deaths of the two boys and some interesting details emerged.[159] It was reported that, at the time of the incident, there were a number of men walking along the tow path by the canal and, despite their attention being drawn to the situation, they just carried on walking. What was also remarkable about the actions of Charles Simmonds was that he was described as a 'cripple' and, although the exact nature of his disability was not made clear, it makes his actions in trying to rescue Moody and

Morris even more noteworthy. This was highlighted by the coroner who, in summing up, remarked, 'the evidence did not say much of the manhood and pluck of the men who walked away when the boys were drowning. The behaviour of Simmonds and Brown was in great contrast and they were deserving of commendation for their pluck.' The jury added a rousing 'hear hear' to this sentiment before presenting their verdicts of 'accidental death' in both cases.

After the death of their son, Edward and Harriett Morris continued to live at 79 St Ervans Road until at least 1901, but by 1911 they had moved back to Swinbrook Road in Notting Hill and were living at number 72. It seems likely that Edward junior had an older half-sister, because on the 1881 census his parents Edward and Harriett appear as a married couple, living at 10 Hurstway Street, with a 9-year-old daughter, Catherine. When they married in 1882, Edward senior was declared as a bachelor and Harriett Butler as a spinster, so Catherine was not the product of an earlier marriage for either of them. The most straightforward explanation is that Catherine was born out of wedlock and the couple lived as husband and wife until they were able to marry officially. This hypothesis is strengthened by information on the 1911 census which recorded, among other information, the number of years a couple had been married and the number of children born and still living.

Edward and Harriett were recorded as having been married for forty years, which would give a date of around 1871 and would fit with the birth of Catherine in 1872, but does not tally with their official marriage in 1882. Notably, for Edward, a figure of one child born and one child dead was recorded (which would have been Edward junior), but for Harriett it was two children born, one dead and one living, strongly suggesting that Catherine was Harriett's child, born out of wedlock to someone other than Edward, and that he unofficially adopted her as his own. Without knowing, though, what Catherine's birth name was and whether or not she stuck with her adopted name of Morris or reverted to her birth name, it is very difficult to trace her in the records and she must, for the time being at least, remain unaccounted for.

The last of the eight cases commemorating a child is, in some ways, one of the most interesting on the Watts Memorial, so it is ironic that it very nearly did not make it. In 1930, a replacement tile, correctly detailing the East Ham sewage workers, was manufactured by Doulton of Lambeth (see Chapter 2). The Doulton tablet presented such a stark visual contrast to the De Morgan tablets that it was decided not to replace it in its original position, on the De Morgan row, but instead to locate it alongside the three new Doulton records on a new row (see Chapter 10). This left a gap in the original De Morgan row, but as De Morgan tiles were no longer being manufactured, there was little choice. However, a few years later, Benjamin Norman, the treasurer of the memorial committee based at St Botolph's church, managed to secure the next best thing.

When De Morgan's Sands End pottery closed in 1907, two of De Morgan's decorators, brothers Charles and Fred Passenger, set up business in the nearby Brompton Road, manufacturing ceramics using De Morgan designs.[160] Fred went on to work at the Bushey Heath pottery, established by the artist Ida Perrin, and it was here that Norman located him and asked him if he would produce a tablet to fit with those originally created. Fred agreed and so an individual was selected from the lists of cases that G.F. Watts had collected in the late Victorian period. No details have survived as to how or why that particular case was selected, but perhaps those making the decision discovered how interesting it was and felt it deserved commemoration. In April 1931, Fred Passenger's replacement tablet was installed into the space on the De Morgan row and blended almost seamlessly; to this day, few people can tell it is a replacement until it is pointed out to them. Given what has been revealed about the individual commemorated on the replacement tablet, it is amazing to think that he almost did not feature at all.

If one were looking for the most worldly individual on the Watts Memorial, a prominent contender would certainly be **Herbert Moore McConaghey**; his parents were born in Ireland, and travelled to England and then to India where Herbert was born. He then travelled back to England where he attended school in Wimbledon in Surrey and finally died in the sea at a north Devon holiday resort; and all before the age of 14.

Herbert's father, Matthew Allen McConaghey, was born in Ireland on 6 January 1839. On 17 September 1861 in County Tyrone, he married a woman named either Martha Donnell or Martha Anderson; the surviving records are not entirely clear which. In February 1862 the couple arrived in India, Matthew having passed the entrance examinations to join the Imperial Civil Service (ICS).[161] Matthew was initially assigned to the role of assistant settlement officer, 3rd grade, at Mynpoorie and later, in 1869, he was placed in charge of the Mynpoorie settlement. A distinctly 'home from home' way of life was famously maintained by those within the British Raj and, as they would have done had they been in Britain, Matthew and Martha started a family. Their first child, Edith, was born in Mynpoorie in Bengal on 10 June 1865, followed by Herbert Moore, also born in Mynpoorie, on 29 July 1869. A second son, Francis (known as Frank), was born on 27 April 1871 in Naini Tal in Bengal, as was their second daughter, Ethel Mary, born on 4 July 1874.

It was customary for the children of imperial civil servants to be schooled in England, and as each of the children reached a suitable age, they boarded ships and sailed back to Britain. By 1881, both Edith and Ethel were pupils at a girls' boarding school run by Margaret Brook and her sisters at Cambridge Gardens in Richmond-upon-Thames in Surrey. Nineteen girls between the ages of 6 and 16 were resident at the school, seventeen of whom were born in the East Indies. Herbert and Frank were also being educated in Britain in 1881 and were resident at Elizabeth Palmer's boarding school for boys at Neilgherry House in Lansdowne Road in Wimbledon, Surrey. The cohort at the school ranged in age from 5 to 12 and consisted almost entirely of boys born in India.

In mid-July 1882, the boys from the school were taken to Croyde in Devon for a six-week summer break. Mary Ellen Hardie, one of the governesses at the school, accompanied them and they stayed with Thomas Heddon who ran a boarding house in the area. It was an opportunity for the young men to get some sea air and plenty of exercise to energise them for the school term that would begin again in September. A favourite pursuit was swimming and the beach at Croyde provided a long stretch of soft sand and something of a natural harbour that made it a relatively safe place for bathing and a popular holiday destination, as it still is today. The boys swam every day, leaving their lodgings at about 10 a.m. and returning before lunch. Within the cohort at the school, four lads were particularly close friends: Edward Cornford, aged 16, Herbert McConaghey, aged 14, George 'Havelock' McGeorge, aged 13, and Charles Binney, the youngest of the four, aged 11.

On 28 August 1882, seven of the boys, including the four friends, went out to swim at 10.15 a.m.[162] The water at Croyde was benign but just around the headland was Glover's Pool, which had a reputation for causing unusual tidal swells and strong currents. Charles Binney and Havelock McGeorge had swum out further than the others and they suddenly found themselves being pulled by the current towards the headland and out to sea. Their cries for help were heard by the others, who were close to the shore and in no danger themselves, at which point Herbert called to Edward, 'Quick, you save one boy and I'll save another!' at which point he waded into the sea and swam after his friends. Cornford followed but was unable to reach Binney and, in fear for his own life, headed back to the beach. McConaghey, however, continued to try and rescue McGeorge, but the two of them, along with Binney, were dragged out of sight and into Glover's Pool. The press was quick to report the incident and, under a headline of 'a triple bathing fatality', it was dramatically reported, 'seven went out together, but only four returned'.[163]

It took a couple of days to confirm what everyone feared and one by one the bodies were washed up along the coast; McConaghey's was the last to be recovered when a local labourer, Thomas Staddon, came across it in a deep gully further along the coast from Croyde beach. Mr Potter, the north Devon district coroner, convened an inquest into the three deaths, which was held at the King's Arms Inn in nearby Georgham on 6 September 1882.[164] Various witnesses gave evidence, but not Edward Cornford, who was too ill to attend. A solicitor representing the 'friends of the deceased' said he wished Cornford was there because he would have told them that McConaghey 'was in no danger and that he lost his life trying to save one of the deceased'. Finch also added that it was his understanding that 'the place where they [the boys] had bathed was not dangerous, but the sea took them to Glover's Pool, where they were drowned'. The jury returned verdicts of 'accidently drowned while bathing' in each case and they recommended that 'a board be placed on the sands, warning visitors to only bathe at half-tide'.

With their parents away in India, it was decided to bury the three boys locally and they were laid to rest, side by side, in the churchyard of St George's church in Georgeham. Sometime later an elegant and evocatively conceived grave memorial was designed and installed, which individually commemorated the three boys while still indicating and representing their close friendship (see plate 11). In the centre of the memorial, an upright stone cross mounted on a stepped plinth carries the words 'In loving memory of Charles Binney, Aged 11 years.' This is flanked on either side by bevelled tombstones with large carved stone crosses. One carries the inscription, 'George Havelock MacGeorge, born Nov 1868, died August 28th 1882' on the right-hand face and 'Blessed are the pure of heart' on the left. On the other tombstone the words 'Herbert Moore McConachey [sic], the beloved son of Matthew Allen & Martha McConachey, died Aug 28 1882, aged 13 years' are engraved on the right-hand face and 'Truly god is wiser than man, forever with the Lord, Amen, Let it be' on the left. The memorial touchingly remembers the three boys as individuals, but it appears as a single monument, underlying the manner in which they died – as close friends trying to save one another.

It appears that at some point in the mid-1880s, Herbert's parents, Matthew and Martha McConaghey, returned to England because on 17 August 1890 Matthew died at 15 Pelham Place in Seaford, Sussex, where he had been living. At the time Martha was living at 8 Queen's Gardens in Richmond-upon-Thames and it is not clear why the family were separated. Employment with the Imperial Civil Service offered a generous pension provision and following Matthew's death his widow and children were well provided for. Martha received a pension of £330 per annum in perpetuity, Edith and Ethel were guaranteed £100 per annum until marriage, and Frank was allocated £150 per year until he was 21, which was only two years after his father's death.

In 1891, Martha McConaghey was living at 12 'Coverdale' in Montague Road, Richmond-upon-Thames with her two daughters, Edith and Ethel, but by 1901 the three women had moved to Northam near Bideford in Devon. This was where Martha died nine years later, on 18 March 1910, and it would appear that Matthew's career in the civil service had been a lucrative one; Martha left an estate valued at £817 which passed to the couple's eldest daughter, Edith. It is not clear exactly if or how the family was specifically connected with Devon, but it is interesting that Northam is only about 10 miles from Croyde, where Herbert lost his life, and Georgeham, where he was buried.

After their mother died, Edith and Ethel's pension payments increased to £150 per annum. This, coupled with Edith's inheritance, allowed the two women to be substantially financially independent and neither of them married. In 1911, Edith was living in St Leonards near Hastings in Sussex at a school run by Louisa Brook, one of her governesses from her time at boarding school in Richmond. Edith died on 5 September 1933 in Northam in Devon and her estate of £3,603 passed to her sister, Ethel. Ethel died on 22 November 1948 in Northam in Devon and her estate of £15,558 passed to a retired lieutenant-colonel, Lennox Theobald Hay, and Evelyn Dorothy Newburgh McConaghey, Ethel's widowed sister-in-law.

Frank McConaghey, Herbert's brother, joined the Indian army and enjoyed a successful career, rising to lieutenant-colonel in the political department. Sometime before 1915, Frank married Evelyn Dorothy Newburgh Manduit and the couple had at least one daughter, Evelyn Delphine, born in Karachi, Bombay in 1915. Frank died on Christmas Day 1924 aboard the RMS *Maloja*, a P&O passenger ship which ran fortnightly sailings between Tilbury and Sydney in Australia. The official cause of death was cardiac failure resulting from a malignant intestinal obstruction; he was 53.

The biblical quotation 'greater love hath no man than this, that a man lay down his life for his friend', taken from John 15:13, was, and still is, frequently quoted in funeral services and upon headstones and memorial tablets commemorating people who lost their own life while attempting to save another. It is, undoubtedly, a fitting piece of text, and it seems particularly apt for the cases outlined in this chapter; all of the boys who died did so trying to save a friend. Childhood friends can sometimes last just a summer holiday, or perhaps through school years and even beyond, but there is often something very strong about the bonds of friendship that people form as children. Childhood may, in many ways, have been something quite different in the Victorian period, but some things do transcend time and the impulse of one friend to save another *is* something which has endured and provides an enduring connection to these 'boy heroes' of the past.

A POLICEMAN'S LOT

9

'ON DUTY'

In 1829 the Conservative home secretary, Sir Robert Peel, introduced the Metropolitan Police Act, which created a 'new police' force responsible for preventing crime on the streets of London.[165] In Parliament, Peel pressed his case for a new force by citing rising levels of criminality, but he was equally concerned with organising and reforming an outdated and increasingly ineffective system of watchmen and constables that had its origins in the thirteenth century. The burgeoning capital was, it was argued, fast becoming a breeding ground for 'an incorrigible criminal class that lurked in the rougher parts of town', and the modern city needed a modern force to combat this rising threat. Consequently, at 6 p.m. on 29 September 1829, the first constables of the new Metropolitan Police Service took to the streets in their top hats and tightly buttoned blue tunics.

There were initially around 1,000 men in the force, but this quickly rose to 3,000 within a few months, and their day-to-day activities were very different from those of their predecessors. There was no more 'calling the hour', as the watchmen had done, and the new force was mobile, with constables patrolling a designated area, or 'beat', small enough to cover in ten to fifteen minutes. Prevention of crime was key, but patrolling was also about the constable getting to know (and be known in) his local area and about setting standards for decorum and acceptable behaviour. By 1886, London was administratively portioned into twenty-one police divisions, each covering a specific area and identified by a code letter; Whitehall was 'A' division, Westminster 'B' division, St James' 'C' division and so on. This was intended to be organised and rationally policed by a 'fit for purpose' service of respectable and respected young professionals who would institute the policies and practices of reformers like Peel.

For many working-class men, skilled and unskilled, the service offered employment opportunities that few other jobs could rival. Admittedly, the work itself could be difficult and dangerous, it was physically demanding and it involved long hours and tedious and repetitive activities. But this was true of many working-class occupations and police work had the great advantage of being consistent and stable as well as providing a pension to those who completed twenty-five years' service. Despite this, staff turnover was high, especially in the early years of the force, with many recruits resigning or being dismissed after relatively short periods.

The new police were not always welcomed or appreciated by all, and the workaday duties of a constable, such as enforcing licensing hours or preventing illegal gambling, often incurred verbal and physical abuse. Furthermore, stringent codes of behaviour and conduct were expected of officers outside of working hours, and there were restrictions and caveats regarding things like marriage and lodgings. So constables were, to some extent, institutionalised into the service but, as the historian Clive Emsley has stressed, 'If Bobbies were an institution they were also men, and men with different origins and aspirations, whose careers and family lives followed different and very personal trajectories.'[166]

For many of the working-class men who joined the Victorian police force, it represented a distinct departure from the lives and lifestyles of their parents and grandparents in terms of both social and geographical mobility. **Robert Wright** was the first member of his family to join the police; his father, Robert senior, had worked as an agricultural labourer and rat catcher, and his grandfather, John Wright, had been a cordwainer who made fine soft leather shoes (see plate 4). Robert senior was born in Scredington in Lincolnshire in 1829, and in 1855 he married either Mary Chambers or Mary Holmes in Seaford in Lincolnshire. Robert junior was their fourth child and second son, born in Scredington on 21 December 1864, following on from Mary Ann, born in 1857, Maria Elizabeth, born in 1858, and John Thomas, born in 1861. Another daughter, Ellen, followed in 1867 and the family continued to live in Scredington.

By 1881, Robert junior had moved out of the family home and was a live-in farm servant working for John Leak and his wife in Helpringham, a few miles east of Scredington. Robert clearly had aspirations beyond manual labour in rural Lincolnshire, and in October 1882 he enlisted in the 2nd Battalion of the Lincolnshire Regiment of the British army. Between 1883 and 1887 he served in the East Indies and, in total, he completed seven years' service before being discharged in October 1889. Two months later Robert moved to London and, on 30 December 1889, he joined 'W' division of the Metropolitan Police, covering the area of Clapham in south-west London.[167] His admission record described him as 5ft 9in tall, weighing 11st 4lbs, with grey eyes, brown hair, a fresh complexion, and a mole on the right-hand side of his face.

In the early days of the force, police divisions tended to operate out of small clusters of old houses which were rented for the purpose. However, by the 1890s, when Wright entered the service, the Metropolitan Police had begun acquiring or constructing purpose-built police stations which included accommodation for officers. Most men were single when they joined, so either rooms were shared or beds were provided in dormitories with communal areas for dining and recreation. Some stations, especially in central divisions, could be quite large, accommodating upwards of sixty or seventy men, but the one at 83 Croydon High Street, where Robert Wright lived, was smaller and housed around ten to fifteen constables. The division's police inspector, Joseph Spencer, and his family lived next door at number 84 and this was quite a common arrangement.

This barrack accommodation was considered, by senior members of the force, not only to provide constables with lodgings, but also to foster teamwork and inculcate a sense of comradeship among officers.[168] The realities could, though, often be quite different. Sanitary conditions in the stations were not always very good, leading to sickness and disease, and men usually had to vacate their beds by lunchtime even if they had just finished a nightshift. Furthermore, associational living cultivated revelry and mischief as much as it did camaraderie, and station houses frequently became fairly noisy and rowdy places, rife with practical jokes and good-natured roughhousing. As the men matured and married they moved out of the barracks and into family quarters, which would have happened to Robert in 1892. On 19 April that year, the young constable married Bessie Backhurst, the daughter of a carpenter, at St Mary's church in West Kensington and they moved into Hingdson Terrace near Carl Street in Westminster. The couple's first child, Ada Ellen Wright, was born around the beginning of April 1893, but her father would not live to see her first birthday; within a month, PC Robert Wright was dead.

The business of an 'oil and colourman' was wide and varied, including mixing oils and pigments into paints, supplying oil and paraffin for lamps and stoves, and even selling gunpowder and other explosives. At 99 North End in Croydon, Surrey, Henry Bennett ran just such a shop, and Saturday, 29 April 1893 had been a particularly busy day. At around 10 p.m., Bennett's assistant, a 15-year-old lad called Frederick Chandler, went down into the basement of the shop and, as he did every day, turned off the gas supply at the meter.[169] Frederick then went home and, about an hour later, Mr Bennett locked up the shop and headed to the station to catch a train to Gravesend, where his wife and family were staying at the time.

Across the road from Bennett's shop was a piece of waste ground and for a few days a travelling circus had been performing there. Saturday had been the last performance and, while working late into the night dismantling the big top, one of the circus men noticed a strange glow emanating from inside the premises at about 1 a.m. Realising that there was a fire, he ran to the local police station and informed PC Thomas Bond, who was on reserve duty. Bond sent a messenger to alert the fire brigade stationed nearby at Katherine Street and then went out into the street to summon constables with his whistle. Bond was aware that Bennett's shop, containing large quantities of highly flammable and explosive material, was in a residential area and that even a minor fire on the premises could have catastrophic repercussions.

Two constables patrolling nearby, Edward Barnett and Robert Wright, responded to Bond's whistle, and after running to the station, they made their way across the road to the shop, which was quickly being engulfed by flames. Bond began waking and evacuating residents from adjoining and nearby premises, while Barnett and Wright cut through the premises of a tea merchant at 101 West End to get to the yard at the back of Bennett's shop. Here, they broke open the doors to the cellar to check for flammable material and rolled out two barrels of paraffin which they found there. Just then, Barnett thought he heard screaming and shouted to Wright, 'Quick, there is a woman in the house!' The two constables ran up the rear steps and, forcing open the door, passed through the smoke-filled parlour and then up the internal staircase. Burning oil was dripping through the ceiling and the heat was intense, but the two men managed to check the rooms and found there was not, after all, anyone in the building.

Meanwhile, in the basement a cask of petroleum, unseen by the two men, reached a critical temperature and exploded. A ball of flame burst up through the shop, the heat and fumes overpowering the two constables inside, who ran into one of the upstairs back rooms where a window overlooked the rear yard. Outside, PC Simeon Purt, who had just arrived, saw Barnett and Wright appear at an upstairs window and shouted to them that they were in terrible danger and would be burned if they did not escape quickly. Barnett climbed onto the window ledge and jumped down onto the corrugated iron roof of a shed, from which he then toppled into the yard. Purt ran to help him, but Barnett shouted, 'Go and save Wright', who had since disappeared from view at the window, which was now furiously billowing smoke. Purt ran around to the front of the shop with the intention of going in to help Wright, but as he tried to ascend the front steps he was beaten back by the flames and smoke.

It was about 1.45 a.m. before the corporation fire brigade arrived and began trying to fight the fire by dowsing it with a hosepipe. Purt called to them that a police constable was trapped upstairs at the rear of the building, so another hose was taken around to the yard and water directed upwards through the window into the room where Wright had last been seen. The building was, however, an inferno and it was impossible for anyone to enter until around an hour later when the fire was sufficiently extinguished. It was about 3 a.m. when Inspector Lemmey and Engineer Bowers from the brigade started searching the building from the cellar upwards, and when they reached one of the upstairs back rooms, they found Robert Wright on the floor just inside the window from which Barnett had jumped.

Wright appeared to be dead, he was blackened from smoke and both his hands and face were badly scorched, but when he was carried from the building a local dentist, Mr Gillemand, examined him and said he could discern signs of breathing, so Wright was given brandy and an ambulance was summoned. When Wright arrived at Croydon General Hospital he was checked by Dr Dukes, the house surgeon, who declared him dead on arrival and recorded the cause of death as suffocation rather than burns. Barnett was also conveyed to the hospital suffering from an injury to the head and shock so severe that it was feared he would not survive. A few days later he rallied and eventually made a full recovery. The shop and all ten rooms of the house at 99 North End were completely burned out and the fancy goods repository next door, owned by Mr Rensbery, was considerably damaged by smoke and water, although Rensbery and his family had escaped injury, having been evacuated by Bond earlier in the evening.

On 3 May 1893 at Croydon General Hospital, Dr Jackson, the borough coroner, opened an inquest into Wright's death and some serious accusations were levelled at the corporation fire brigade.[170] The first concerned the length of time it took them to arrive at the fire. Thomas Bond testified that at 1.10 a.m. he had sent a messenger to fetch the brigade, which was stationed 300yds down the road, but they had not arrived at the fire until 1.45 a.m. It was suggested that had Mr Bennett and his family been present in the house they might well have been burned to death in that time. Engineer Bowers answered this allegation by saying that the brigade had received the call at 1.22 a.m. and he believed they had arrived at 1.29 a.m., but he had not looked at the clock. A more serious allegation was that several of the firemen were so drunk that they were unable to perform their duties properly. Bond reported that when the brigade eventually arrived at the blazing building, one of the firemen asked him where the fire was, to which Bond had replied, 'Can you not see?' Another constable, PC Bayliss, said he had seen one of the firemen leaning heavily against the shutters of a shop adjoining the burning building, seemingly unable to get his balance.

Engineer Bowers testified that 'he had no reason to complain of the conduct of his men, all of whom worked very hard', but he had to concede that two of them were the worse for liquor; one was in the retained and the other in the volunteer brigade. He also added that 'he did not think any of the men obtained drink at the fire'. This might sound like an odd thing to say, but it was common practice, or 'unwritten law', at fires for the local police to open the nearest public house for the use of the firemen. In this case, PC Bayliss had opened the nearby Rising Sun, but he stood guard on the door and agreed with Bowers that neither of the drunken firemen had been served there. The situation was so serious that Bowers had to send one of the men home due to the state he was in, and Inspector Lemmey of the brigade also reported that he had cause to speak to several of the men after the fire about their behaviour.

In summing up, the coroner, Dr Jackson, recorded that 'they had every reason to be proud of and pleased with the conduct of the police; but they might depend upon it that the conduct of the firemen referred to would receive the attention of the Corporation'. The jury recorded a verdict of 'accidental death' and 'expressed their admiration of the services rendered by the police', and Mr Elborough, the town clerk, 'intimated that the conduct of the two firemen would receive the serious attention of the authorities'. There was no specific reference to Wright's behaviour and neither the jury nor the coroner alluded to any heroism on his part. Among the press it was predominantly *Lloyd's Weekly News* which highlighted the 'fatal heroism of a constable' and provided its readers with a drawing of the rear of the building showing the window that Barnett jumped from and a portrait of Robert Wright.[171]

Following her husband's death, Bessie Wright received a small Metropolitan Police widow's pension of £15 per annum for herself and £2 10s per annum for Ada until she was 15. Bessie also worked as a seamstress to top up her income until 3 May 1903, when she married Frederick Henry Rothen, a clerk, at St Jude's church in Southwark. Bessie and Frederick do not appear to have had any children of their own and Bessie died aged 62 in 1929. Ada Ellen Wright, Robert's daughter, lived with her mother until at least 1901, but by 1911 Bessie was living with Frederick and Ada becomes elusive in the records. There is no clear evidence of her dying or marrying prior to 1911, but she is not easily identifiable on the census for that year.

Robert Wright's body was returned to Lincolnshire where, on 11 May 1893, he was buried in the churchyard of St Mary's and St Nicholas' church in the village of Wrangle. His parents, Robert and Mary, were still living nearby in Scredington and his younger sister, Ellen, had married James Redshaw in 1889, the couple going on to have at least eight children.[172] Mary Wright, Robert's mother, died at the beginning of 1891 and Robert senior, his father, moved in with his son, John, who in 1892 had married Matilda Oram. By 1901, John and Matilda had four children and Robert was living with the family in Scredington; five more children followed over the next ten years, all of whom were born in the Sleaford area.[173] Robert Wright senior died, aged 78, in 1905.

Attempting to rescue people from a fire also cost another of the Postman's Park policemen his life, although it was six years later and on entirely the opposite side of London. In response to the inquest report, one correspondent to *The Times* wrote: 'the story told is one of heroism unsurpassed, I venture to say, even by any of our brave soldiers in South Africa. It is a case, if ever there was one, of peril faced and death incurred in the discharge of duty.'[174] It is interesting that the author of the letter drew attention to British troops engaged in an overseas conflict (the Second Boer War), as the individual who was the subject of the inquest had himself been familiar with that situation.

George Stephen Funnell was born in Clerkenwell on Boxing Day, 26 December 1868. He was the eldest child of George John Funnell, born in Norwich, and Mary Ann Bywaters, born in Ireland, who married in the autumn of 1868 when Mary Ann was heavily pregnant. In 1871, the newlyweds and their son were living at 27 Coldbatch Square off Roseberry Avenue in Clerkenwell, and George senior was working as a waiter. By 1881, the family had moved to 9 Vinegar Yard off Drury Lane and a daughter, Emily, had arrived in 1875.

Before George junior joined the Metropolitan Police, he served for seven years and 135 days in the 2nd Battalion of the Oxfordshire Light Infantry.[175] The battalion had been formed in 1881 after an amalgamation of other regiments, and Funnell had enlisted in 1885. The 2nd Battalion was deployed in India and all members were awarded the India General Service Medal with a Burma 1889–92 clasp, indicating that they had fought in that campaign. George served predominantly in the East Indies and was discharged on 16 February 1893.

A few months later, on 30 October 1893, George joined the Metropolitan Police and was assigned to 'J' division, which covered the area of Bethnal Green in Hackney.[176] George, who was at that time living at 26 St Andrews Street off the Wandsworth Road near Battersea, was described as 5ft 10in tall, weighing 11st, with blue eyes, light-brown hair, a fair complexion and a tattoo on his left forearm. In 1895, George married Jane Lilian Boulton, the daughter of an industrial engine driver, in Gravesend in Kent, and their first child, George Stephen junior, was born in Hackney in 1896. A second son, Leonard Albert, was born in 1898, by which time the family had moved to 35 Chelmer Road in Homerton and George had his regular beat, which included Wick Road in Hackney.

The Elephant and Castle pub was a familiar fixture in Wick Road, run by Mr and Mrs Fowler and staffed by a barman and two barmaids who lived above the premises. It was in the early hours of Friday, 22 December 1899 that one of those barmaids, Alice Maryon, was woken by a loud noise from downstairs and, smelling smoke, she roused the barman, William Goodridge, who went to investigate.[177] Downstairs, in an office next to the bar, Goodridge discovered that a small fire had broken out and he quickly started trying to extinguish it. At around the same time, Constable Thomas Baker was passing the pub and when he saw some smoke emanating from a side window he blew his whistle to summon assistance. This arrived in the form of Police Sergeant John Danzey, and constables Arthur Read and George Funnell, who began banging on the doors of the building to try and gain access.

Back inside, Goodridge was battling the fire which was quickly taking hold and, hearing the constables outside, he unbolted the front doors of the pub to let them in, so they could help him put out the blaze. However, as Goodridge swung open the doors, a huge draft of air was drawn into the bar, fanning the flames, which suddenly and ferociously engulfed the room. Goodridge and the police officers ran from the building, but when the barman shouted to the constables that three women were upstairs, Baker and Funnell ran back in to try and help them.

Meanwhile, Alice Maryon had woken the landlady, Mrs Fowler, and another bar-maid, Minnie Lewis, and the three women were trying to get dressed as the upstairs rooms quickly filled with smoke. Fowler and Maryon ran down the stairs into the bar, but by that time the fire, fuelled by exploding bottles of spirits, was intense and the air was filled with choking black smoke. The two barmaids feared they were trapped, but suddenly, out of the flames, a figure emerged and wrapping himself around her, George Funnell guided Mrs Fowler to the door before running back through the bar to collect Maryon, who had collapsed. Lifting the barmaid onto his shoulder, Funnell carried her through the blazing room, which meant he could not protect her from the flames, and by the time he reached the door and laid her on the pavement outside she was blistered and burned.

While Fowler and Maryon had been escaping, Minnie Lewis had returned to her room to get dressed and collect some money she kept there, so by the time she reached the bottom of the stairs into the bar, there was no way through. Funnell heard her screaming and despite the inferno he entered the burning building for a third, and final, time. When Funnell found Lewis at the base of the stairs, she told him that through the parlour at the rear of the pub there was a back door and suggested they might be able to get out through there. She watched anxiously as the constable disappeared into the smoke, but when he did not return she assumed that exit was also blocked and, suddenly spotting another route to the front door, she managed to get out. As Read and Danzey rushed to help her, she explained to them about the back door and how she had last seen Funnell heading for the back parlour.

Danzey, Read, Baker and two other constables, John Weavers and James Elrick, went around to the rear of the premises and found the back door, which they forced open. The rooms at the rear of the pub were thick with smoke and starting to smoul-der, so the five men quickly began searching for Funnell who was eventually located unconscious on the floor behind the parlour-bar counter. The constable was dragged from the building alive, but badly burned and 'insensible', so he was immediately taken to the infirmary of the Hackney Union Workhouse in Homerton High Street, which was the nearest hospital to Wick Road. Funnell was admitted and treated for burns and smoke inhalation, but he did not recover and died on 2 January 1900. Dr Hall, who treated Funnell, reported that he had been burned on his face, his neck and both arms, and recorded the cause of death as 'pneumonia following on partial suffocation and burning'.

The inquest into Funnell's death was opened by Dr Wynn Westcott at Hackney Coroner's Court on 4 January 1900 and heard evidence from Minnie Lewis, Dr Hall, the other police officers who had attended the incident and members of the fire brigade.[178] Mrs Fowler, the landlady of the Elephant and Castle, was unable to attend as she had been badly injured escaping the fire. It was reported that several of the constables had been on sick leave following the incident and that one of the officers had almost died while trying to save Funnell. The fire brigade could not ascertain the cause of the fire, as the premises had been entirely destroyed, but it confirmed that the blaze had probably started in the downstairs office. The inquest jury returned a verdict of 'accidental death' and 'commended the police for their exertions in saving life at the fire, and they also expressed sympathy with the widow and young family of the deceased officer'.

Funnell's death created both good and bad publicity for the Metropolitan Police. On the plus side, the five officers who survived the fire and tried to save Funnell were all awarded bronze medals by the Society for the Protection of Life from Fire (SPLF), which were presented to them at the North London Police Court on 22 March 1900.[179] The SPLF also presented Jane Funnell, George's widow, with an illuminated testimonial and arranged for her to receive a payment of 10s per week for one year to help her support her family. It was, though, the provision for the family which fuelled criticism of the police force. In January 1900, the art collector Henry Seymour Trower wrote to various newspapers, including *The Times*, criticising the way in which Funnell's widow was being treated after her husband's death: 'On inquiry at New Scotland Yard I learn that she will receive a pension of £15 per annum and £2 15s per annum for each child until it attains the age of 15. This pittance, although presumably as liberal as official considerations permit, is surely inadequate.'[180]

Trower suggested that 'public generosity will probably be glad to recognise more liberally its debt to a brave fellow who gave his life for humanity and for duty' and offered to receive donations on the basis that 'some further provision for the poor young widow – she is only 27 – so tragically bereaved would deservedly betoken the respect which all must feel for the manner of her husband's death'. Unfortunately, the outcome of the appeal was not publicised and so the amount collected is unknown, but on the basis of other public collections undertaken for everyday heroes, it seems likely a good sum of money was raised for Jane and the two boys.

In the short term, this money, in addition to her police pension and the sum from the SPLF, gave Jane some financial independence and she continued to live at 35 Chelmer Road with her two children until 1903 when she married Henry Arthur Blann, a tramcar driver. By 1911, Jane and Henry had three children of their own, Arthur Henry, May Lilian and Reginald Eric, and were living at 47 Tankerton Terrace, off the Mitcham Road in Croydon. Jane's two sons from her marriage to George were also living at the address and the elder of the two, George junior, was employed as an apprentice electrician. Jane Blann died, aged 85, in 1958, but her first marriage to George Funnell continued to resonate with tragedy throughout her life.

The couple's youngest son, Leonard, moved to Burnley in Lancashire, where he worked for some time as a tram conductor. In May 1916 he followed a similar course to his father and enlisted as a gunner in the Royal Field Artillery.[181] He did not, though, serve overseas and was medically discharged in 1917, suffering from pulmonary tuberculosis aggravated by military service. He was issued with a Silver War Badge (SWB), which was introduced in 1916 for men who had been honourably discharged due to wounds or sickness. The award was partly a response to movements such as the Order of the White Feather, which sought to shame men of service age not wearing military uniform by presenting them with a white feather to imply cowardice.[182] The SWB was intended to show that these men had enlisted but were unable to serve due to illness or injury. Leonard did not, however, require his badge for very long; his tuberculosis proved to be terminal and he died aged just 20 in Strood, Kent, in 1918. Six years later, George and Jane's elder son, George junior, died in Romford, aged 27, and this closed a dreadful and heart-breaking chapter in Jane's life, which had seen her lose both her sons and their father, her first husband.

Robert Wright and George Stephen Funnell were both police constables of the late Victorian period and, in terms of their commemoration on the Watts Memorial, both men were recognised as a result of G.F. Watts collecting and transcribing a press report of the incident in which they died. There are, however, other police constables whose commemoration on the memorial came about through other circumstances and whose acts of heroism occurred long after Watts had died. The stories of three of those four men are told in Chapter 10 and the tablets to them were all erected on the memorial in 1930. Eleven years prior to that, in June 1919, there had been a single tablet installed on the far left-hand side of the memorial, to recognise a police officer who had died two years earlier, during a notable event in the history of London in the First World War.

As early as 1915 Londoners experienced the realities of the war in Europe as gigantic airships, cruising at altitudes in excess of 10,000ft, unleased their payloads of bombs upon a city unfamiliar with attacks on the home front.[183] Between May and December 1915, 127 people were killed and more than 350 injured during bombing raids on the capital. Advances in radar technology and anti-aircraft guns helped to counter the German attacks and technological developments with air-craft meant that by the end of 1916 British pilots were successfully shooting down German airships.[184] As airships became less and less effective, the Germans sought other ways of attacking mainland Britain from the air and the answer came in the shape of the Gotha: a twin-engine biplane, capable of flying for five to six hours and delivering up to 1,300lbs of bombs from an altitude of 20,000ft. The first bombing raids by planes on Britain were by a squadron of twenty-seven Gotha air-craft in May 1917 and the attack on south-east England caused much alarm. Despite only two aircraft reaching their targets, the damage was greater than any airship had ever inflicted; ninety-five people were killed and 192 wounded in a single raid. It was surely only a matter of time before the docks and factories of London became a target for these deadly machines.

It was around mid-morning on 13 June 1917 when the strange and unfamiliar noise of aircraft engines was heard overhead, and before the people of London's East End had time to wonder what was happening the first explosions began to reverberate through the streets.[185] Fourteen fully laden Gothas were depositing their deadly pay-loads, and the combination of inexperienced pilots and new technology meant many of the bombs missed their strategic targets and fell into densely populated civilian areas. In Central Street, between City Road and Old Street in the Hoxton area of London, there was a large factory manufacturing clothing for the Debenhams department store in Wimpole Street; around 150 women and girls worked the machines and were super-vised by three men. As the first bombs were heard, two of the men ran out into the street to see what was happening, but one was killed and the other badly injured, leaving the manager as the only man and supervisor in the factory. Terrified by the explosions and with little experience of daylight air raids, the women began running out of the build-ing and into the street, where they were at greater risk of being caught in an explosion. The manager of the factory was trying quickly to gather up the women and get them back inside, but he was struggling to do this on his own. Just then, a local constable arrived and, seeing the women in danger, he rushed over to the factory doors to prevent any more people exiting and to help the manager get the other women back inside.

The constable was **Alfred Smith** and, as with many of the young men who swelled the ranks of the Metropolitan Police as the organisation responded to serving an ever-expanding capital, he was not actually himself a Londoner. Alfred was born in Wokingham near Reading in Berkshire on 24 May 1880, the sixth of ten children born to George and Mary Ann Smith. George was an agricultural labourer and he married Mary Ann, the daughter of William and Hannah Pursey, in Wokingham in 1868. The couple's first child, Annie Caroline, was born in 1870 and the family ini-tially moved in with Mary's father and her younger brother, Thomas. More children followed: Edith Mary (b. 1872), William George (b. 1874), Thomas (b. 1877), Ellen (b. 1878) and then Alfred. By 1881, the Smith family had moved into their own prop-erty on the London Road in Wokingham, and Thomas Pursey, Mary Ann's brother, was living with them.

As was generally the way with Victorian families, George and Mary Ann continued to have children: Sidney (b. 1882), Harry (b. 1885), Edward (b. 1887) and finally Lily Mary born in 1891. By 1901, George had moved from labouring into carting timber, Annie, Ellen and Edward had moved out, and most of the remaining children were working; William, Alfred and Harry as car men, Thomas as a bricklayer and Sidney as a general labourer. It would appear, though, that Alfred had ambitions beyond simply carrying and delivering goods, so in 1902 he moved to London and, on 10 October, he joined the Metropolitan Police. His admission papers describe him as 5ft 11in tall, weighing 13st 2lbs, with auburn hair, blue eyes and a fair complexion. Alfred was assigned to 'G' division, which covered the Finsbury area, and he probably initially lived at the police station with other constables.[186]

By 1910, Alfred had moved to 12 Noel Street, overlooking the Regent's Canal near the City Road Basin, and on 1 October that year he married May Emma Amelia Titlow, the daughter of a tile maker, at St Peter's church in Islington (see plate 12). Alfred's police records suggest that he suffered bouts of ill health and in April 1911, when the census was taken, he was a patient at St Bartholomew's (Barts) Hospital in Smithfield. In 1914, Alfred and May had their first and only child, George, and it is easy to imagine that on 13 June 1917, as the bombs rained down, Alfred Smith must have been thinking of the safety of his own family living a few streets away, as well as the women and girls in the Debenhams factory whom he was also trying to protect. While others took cover, Constable Alfred Smith undertook his duties 'indifferent to the danger he ran' and, in addition to the women from the factory, he also helped some injured war veterans get to safety. Alfred, though, was not so lucky and while bravely standing guard at the doors of the factory he was caught in the blast of an explosion which knocked him to the ground. Smith was dragged indoors and examined by a doctor, but there was nothing that could be done; PC Alfred Smith was dead, one of the 162 people killed that day in one of the deadliest air raids of the war.

As with Constable Greenoff who features in Chapter 10, Alfred Smith's death was not distinctly or overtly reported in the mainstream press and much of the coverage of the air raid on London dwelt upon the substantial loss of civilian life, including many children, the lack of warning that Londoners had received and the need for continued vigilance and stoicism following this latest attack by the enemy. Smith was, however, very much heralded as a hero within police publications, notably *The Police Review and Parade Gossip* which in one editorial declared:

> PC Smith's sacrifice is no less noble and heroic than if he had died on the battle field in the service of his country facing fearful odds … this is the tradition of the police – to do their duty regardless of personal safety, to die for others. Can anything finer or nobler be said of any body of men?[187]

Similar sentiments were displayed on the headstone erected at Smith's grave following his funeral at Abney Park Cemetery on 19 June 1917: 'In Loving Memory of Police Constable Alfred Smith, killed in the Air Raid 13th June 1917, aged 37 Years. He Gave His Life A Ransom For Many.' Alfred was given a full police funeral, which stopped en route to the cemetery for a service in St Peter's church, Stoke Newington.

Alfred Smith was also publicly honoured by his nation and his local community. In the police orders for July 1917 it was stated that on 23 June the secretary of state had granted Smith's widow, May, a pension of £88 1s per annum with an additional allowance of £6 12s per annum for her son, George. However, a few days later in the House of Commons on 28 June, the MP for Finsbury East, Allen Baker, asked the home secretary, Sir George Cave, if he was aware of Alfred Smith's 'act of bravery and self-sacrifice' and whether 'any special provision [had] been made for the widow and child of the deceased constable?'[188] Cave replied that the commissioner of police had informed him of the incident and that Smith's widow and child had been granted the highest pension that the Police Act allowed for constables killed in the execution of their duty. 'Is it not a fact,' Baker continued, 'that had he [Smith] lived one more year he would have had a larger pension?' and would that be considered and granted, to which Cave responded, 'I was not aware of that fact, but I shall certainly go to the utmost limits in my power.' It is not clear if the pension was increased but, ultimately, it was already a generous sum, equivalent to 34s a week plus the allowance for George, and the need to increase it was, in fact, lessened by some further measures that Allen Baker subsequently undertook.

Baker approached the directors of Debenhams and solicited from them a donation of 100 guineas (£105) in 'appreciation of the heroic act which saved so many of their workpeople'. A committee was then convened, chaired by Baker and including representatives from local and national government, for the purpose of increasing the initial donation through a public subscription via which everyone could demonstrate their gratitude for Smith's bravery. The fund received over a thousand donations, ranging from 6d, of which there were many, up to the substantial sum given by Debenhams. Other notable subscribers included Imperial Tobacco, Lipton's Tea, the Finsbury Distillery Co., Lyon's Teahouses, the Singer Sewing Machine Co., Coutts Bank and The Royal London Insurance Society.[189] In total, the fund raised £471 14s 2d, some of which was used to pay for and erect the tablet on the Watts Memorial, which was officially unveiled on 13 June 1919, exactly two years to the day after Alfred had been killed.

The rest of the fund was cleverly invested in war bonds which provided an additional regular income for May, rather than a lump sum, while also amplifying the patriotism and duty of Alfred's sacrifice. The Carnegie Hero Fund Trust, established by the philanthropist Andrew Carnegie in 1908 to support financially those who had been disadvantaged as a result of an act of heroism, also awarded May a pension of 10s per week.[190] The awards were made at a ceremony held at the Leysian Hall in the City Road on 11 March 1918, which was attended by various luminaries including the home secretary and the chief commissioner of police. Further commemorations followed. As with all known officers killed before 1920, Smith is recorded in the Metropolitan Police Book of Remembrance, housed in the entrance of Simpson Hall at the Peel Centre in Hendon. He is also recorded on the Carnegie Hero Roll, which is kept in Dunfermline, Scotland, on the Metropolitan Police War Roll of Honour housed at Westminster Abbey and on the National Police Officers Role of Honour.

Alfred's widow, May, did not remarry and lived in the Bermondsey area of London, at 56 Tranton Road, then 49 Storks Road, in the 1930s; she died, aged 72, in 1953. Alfred and May's son, George, married and had a son, Roy, but tracing them with the surname Smith is extremely problematic.

These three police cases, much like the ones discussed in the next chapter and the cases of firemen discussed in Chapter 16, are, in some ways, slight anomalies given the context of the memorial. Watts' intention was to commemorate and memorialise 'everyday' heroism, which, in his mind, was performed by people with no specific responsibility to do so and people who were unlikely otherwise to be recognised for their actions. Police constables do not, necessarily, appear to fit this profile. However, both Wright and Funnell died while attempting to rescue people from a fire and it is probable that Watts considered their actions to be beyond the remit of a constable and, therefore, over and above the call of duty; this was why he considered them suitable candidates for his memorial. With Smith, the case originated several years after Watts had passed away, but similar judgements appear to have been applied. At a time of war, when unprecedented circumstances were presenting themselves, the demarcation between roles became less important and, as the reports of his death emphasised, Smith's actions were seen very much as part of the war effort and beyond what would usually have been expected of a constable. Ultimately, although they all had a duty to protect the public, the three men who feature in this chapter went beyond that duty, and therefore qualified as everyday heroes.

10

THREE IN
A ROW

In October 1927, in response to an article in the press about the Watts Memorial in Postman's Park, the parish clerk of St Botolph's Aldersgate, T.H. Ellis, decided to write to Mary Watts, the widow of George Frederic Watts, to enquire about the possibility of continuing to install tablets on the monument.[191] There had been no installations since 1917 and, although the vicar and churchwardens were keen to continue the records, there was no money to support the idea. A public appeal for funds was issued in May 1929, with the hope of raising £500 to repair and restore the slightly shabby monument and provide in perpetuity for the placing of tablets.[192] Donations were forthcoming, but not to the desired extent, and in the event, a total of just over £250 was achieved. Around £30 of this was spent on the restoration of the cloister and other miscellaneous expenses, leaving £220 for the purpose of placing records – a considerable sum, but not as much as had been anticipated.[193]

With £220 in hand, the Heroic Self-Sacrifice Memorial Committee, which was based at St Botolph's and responsible for the monument, began to consider who should be chosen to feature on the new tablets. Mary Watts forwarded to the committee the volumes of records and transcripts of cases that her husband had collected, almost all of which related to the reign of Queen Victoria, and expressed her regret that she had not been able to continue the process of collecting press cuttings beyond that time. The committee reviewed the cases but decided that they were too 'Victorian' and not really in keeping with 1920s conceptions of heroism; this was, after all, a nation that was still coming to terms with the enormous losses of the First World War.[194] The committee decided instead to contact various public bodies and solicit from them suggestions for suitable cases which had occurred more recently. The British Medical Association was contacted with regard to heroic doctors and nurses, the Metropolitan Police for brave officers, and it was hoped that the Post Office would also be able to supply a suitable case, considering the park's long association with its workers.

In the end, only the Metropolitan Police responded, returning the details of three officers who had each died while performing a heroic act. At a meeting on 26 May 1930, the committee and subscribers decided that these were suitable cases and resolved to erect memorial tablets in their memory.[195] The order for the tiles was placed with Doulton of Lambeth and the committee also took the opportunity to have an additional tablet made in order to replace the De Morgan one which incorrectly recorded the details of the four workmen who died at the East Ham Sewage Works in 1895 (see Chapter 2). According to Doulton, the cost of producing the tiles had gone up considerably since the war and reportedly amounted to '£9 per tablet'.[196]

A decision was taken to install all four tablets on the upper row of the second bay of the monument, and to perform an unveiling ceremony to mark the beginning of a new era in the history of the memorial. The focus on Metropolitan Police cases provided for a grand and well-attended unveiling, which took place on 15 October 1930, with guests including twenty-one police officers in full-dress uniform and several relatives of those being honoured. Also present were Mary Watts, Hastings Lees-Smith, the Postmaster General, the Mayor and Mayoress of East Ham, the Bishop of London and several Members of Parliament, including Samuel Viant, MP for Willesden West. The Bishop of London delivered an address on 'courage' and declared that 'they did not commemorate enough or think enough of those who gave their lives in the service of their country in civil life'.[197] He commended the recent service held in St Paul's Cathedral to remember the forty-eight men who had died in the R101 airship crash, but thought that fourteen miners who had lost their lives the same week had not been sufficiently recognised.

The bishop also made reference to the three constables being commemorated and highlighted 'the excellent way in which they carried out their arduous duties and the courage and heroism subsequently displayed which so frequently passed by without any acknowledgement'. On this occasion, though, the heroism of the officers was not being passed by and they were to be honoured and remembered on the memorial. Each had given his own life while attempting to save another, and although each incident was quite different from the others, all reflected the responsibility and public duty which each man held and which each had died trying to uphold. Furthermore, they were all Metropolitan Police officers and it was fitting that they should be commemorated upon a monument which, by and large, was focused upon the heroism of Londoners or incidents which had occurred in the capital. This was not, though, as straightforward as it seemed.

Harold Frank Ricketts was a Metropolitan Police officer based in London; but he did not die in London, nor was he born there. Harold's father, Ambrose Henry Ricketts, was born near Wareham in Dorset in 1858, and in 1887 he married Ruth Burt, also born near Wareham in a hamlet called Puddleton. Ambrose Ricketts had joined the Dorset Police as a constable sometime between 1876 and 1881, and eventually rose up the ranks to be superintendent of the force. The couple had their first child, Charlotte Edith, in 1890 while they were living at 3 Camden Terrace in Wyke Regis, Dorset. They then appear to have had a set of twins, Ambrose Henry and Harold Frank, who were born in the first quarter of 1893. A second daughter, Mabel Kate, was born in 1896 and then a third son, Arthur George, in 1899.

By 1901 the family had relocated from Camden Terrace to Long Street in nearby Cerne Abbas, and then by 1911 they had moved again to 6 Poole Road in Wimborne. Two more children had arrived by then: a son, Albert Ernest, born in 1901 and a daughter, Ethel May, born in 1905. All of Ambrose and Ruth's children were still living with them and the elder three were employed in a range of occupations: Charlotte was a certified assistant teacher, Ambrose junior was an iron founder and Harold was working as his apprentice. The four younger children were all attending school. Four years later, on 15 June 1915, Ambrose senior, superintendent of Dorset Police, died aged 57. Ruth Ricketts, his wife, survived him by another thirty years and died, aged 85, in 1947.

In 1911, Harold Ricketts was an apprentice iron founder working with his twin brother in Dorset, but two years later, on 3 February 1913, he enlisted with the Metropolitan Police.[198] Given his father's position, it is relatively unsurprising that Harold joined the service, but it is interesting that he joined the Metropolitan Police rather than the Dorset constabulary. There would certainly have been more vacancies and opportunities in the Metropolitan force, but perhaps Harold also felt the need to move out from under the shadow of his father. Harold was assigned to 'F' division, covering the Covent Garden area of London, and lived, with other constables, at the police station in Kensington High Street until, on 19 August 1916, he married Kate Ellen Gilpin, a domestic servant, at St Barnabas' church in Kensington.

Kate Gilpin had been born in Teignmouth, Devon, where her father had been employed as a Trinity House pilot responsible for leading and guiding shipping into the harbour. Kate worked locally around Teignmouth as a domestic servant for a number of years, but by 1911 she was working for the Bull family in Cranford near Linsfield in Surrey. It is likely that she subsequently moved to work in Shepherd's Bush in west London, which is how she came to meet Harold Ricketts. In 1914 Kate's father, William, died but her mother, Elizabeth, continued to live at 7 Teign View Terrace in Teignmouth, the Gilpin family home since the mid-1870s. Two weeks after their wedding, Harold and Kate Ricketts decided to have something of a honeymoon and so they travelled down to Teignmouth to spend some time with Kate's mother and the rest of her family. The trip should have marked the start of a long and happy marriage for the couple, but instead it proved to be fatally tragic.

It was around 6 p.m. in the evening on 11 September 1916, and at 7 Teign View Terrace a pleasant family gathering was drawing to a close.[199] Elizabeth Gilpin had thoroughly enjoyed the day; her newlywed daughter and son-in-law, Kate and Harold, were staying with her, and her other married daughter, Florence Westlake, had travelled down for the day from nearby Bishopsteignton, bringing her 4-year-old daughter, Ethel, and her daughter's friend, Alice Hooper. Discussions turned to Florence's journey home and it was decided to take a boat upriver to Shaldon Bridge en route to Bishopsteignton. After her husband William had died, Elizabeth Gilpin had kept his large rowing boat and so the six people clambered in and, with Florence at the oars, they set off. The boat was only licensed to carry five people, but as two of the passengers, Ethel and Alice, were children, nobody really gave that much thought.

The vessel had gone a short distance and was just off Polly Steps when a figure was spotted in the water, grasping onto a moored boat and calling for help. Florence dug in with the oars and drove the boat to the spot where they found Stanley Drew, a local lad who lived in Bitton Road, clinging to an anchor chain in around 10ft of water. Florence carefully manoeuvred the boat alongside Drew, but as Harold reached out to help pull him in, the boy panicked and threw his arms around the constable's neck. Possibly because it was slightly overladen, the boat tipped heavily to one side and then overturned, spilling its six passengers into the water. Florence could swim and she grasped the two children and tried to keep them afloat, while Elizabeth and Kate managed to grab onto the boat chains. Harold, however, could not swim and Florence looked on helplessly as he struggled to reach the chains, then struggled to stay afloat and finally disappeared under the water.

Nearby in the estuary, James Fraser, the captain of the schooner *Rhoda Mary*, was heading out of the harbour when he became aware of a commotion in the water near some moored boats. Turning his craft around, he headed towards the spot and could see a woman and child in the water, although several times they appeared to sink and then resurface. He arrived just in time to rescue Florence and her daughter Ethel, who had, indeed, gone under several times, and he also located Elizabeth Gilpin and managed to get her into his boat. Florence looked around frantically for Alice but could not see the 6-year-old in the water.

Meanwhile, back on the shore, a fisherman, Frank Loosemore, heard screaming and when he was told there were people in the water he ran to the quayside and jumped in. He saw Kate Ricketts clinging to a chain, but as he swam to her she screamed, 'For God's sake save the child' and gestured to Alice Hooper, who was floating unconscious some distance away. Loosemore swam to Hooper and managed to get her to Fraser's boat, but it could not be rowed as Fraser had lost an oar while trying to save the other women. Loosemore swam, towing the boat, back to the quay, stopping en route to collect Kate, and then applied artificial respiration to Alice who, after five minutes, regained consciousness. The children were all conveyed to the

Old Quay Inn, where blankets were fetched and first-aid administered by Sergeant Bilton and Private Fursdon of the St John's Ambulance Brigade. Soon after, a local GP, Dr Johnson, arrived with a car and the children were taken to the local hospital where they were treated and made a full recovery. Elizabeth Gilpin and her two daughters were taken back to Elizabeth's home, from where they had departed just a few hours earlier, and the shock began to set in.

While Loosemore had been performing artificial respiration on Alice Hooper, a crowd of people had gathered and among them was Tom Hitchcock, 'a youthful fisherman of Brunswick Street'. He was told that everyone was apparently accounted for, but looking out into the harbour, he suddenly spotted a single figure, waving and struggling, being swept out to sea. Diving from the quay, he swam out and found Stanley Drew, the boy who had unwittingly caused the entire incident, exhausted and on the verge of drowning. Hitchcock clutched the boy to his chest and paddled his way back to the quay, where an elderly Belgian gentleman tried to help lift him out of the water with his walking stick. Drew, however, was unable to hold on and fell back in, where Hitchcock then held on to him until two other men arrived and pulled the lad out. It was a somewhat farcical ending to a dreadful accident, and as the crowd on the quayside began to disperse, several boats were launched to try and recover the body of Harold Ricketts, who was still missing and presumed drowned. It was the following day before this was confirmed, when a coast watcher, William Hitchcock, found Harold's body in 2ft of water opposite Polly Steps.

The sudden accidental death warranted an inquest, which was convened by the district coroner, Sidney Hacker, and held in the council chamber in Teignmouth on 13 September 1916.[200] The most stringent line of questioning concerned the number of people in the boat, and the coroner ordered Florence Westlake, who was rowing at the time of the incident, to produce her mother's licence for the boat. The licence was found to be four years out of date and, crucially, the boat was only intended to carry five people. 'How is it,' the coroner asked Florence, 'that six of you went in a boat when it was only licensed to carry five?', to which she replied, 'We thought the two children would make up for one grown up.' The coroner pressed the matter further: 'Didn't you know you were infringing the licence?' 'No sir,' was the reply. The coroner, however, continued this line of questioning when William Hitchcock, who recovered Harold's body and knew the family, was giving evidence. 'Was it [the boat] large enough for the party?' asked Hacker. 'Yes, if they sit still,' replied Hitchcock. 'It was a good boat, I suppose,' mused the coroner. 'Yes sir, a very good one,' was Hitchcock's response.

Ultimately, as the boat was being used for personal, rather than professional, purposes, the coroner's concerns about licensing were moot; he was, though, clearly trying to account for why the boat had seemingly capsized so easily. Concluding the inquest, Hacker suggested that the jury 'would no doubt wish to record their appreciation of the gallant and commendable conduct of Loosemore and Hitchcock;

their prompt action was worthy of commendation'. The foreman of the jury asked 'if he would be in order in suggesting that a recommendation be made to the Royal Humane Society with a view to its being recognised' and the coroner replied that it was down to them. The jury then expressed its sympathy with the widow and the relatives of the deceased before returning a verdict of accidentally drowned. They added no rider to their verdict, neither a recommendation of awards for Loosemore and Hitchcock, nor any mention of heroism on the part of Ricketts.

The day after the inquest, family and friends of Harold Ricketts gathered in Teignmouth Cemetery on Higher Buckeridge Road for his funeral.[201] The Rev. J. Veysey, vicar of St Michael's, officiated at the service, for which the Rickett and Gilpin families were the chief mourners. Members of the Teignmouth district of the Devon constabulary acted as pallbearers for a coffin of polished English elm, with oak mouldings, brass mounts and a polished brass nameplate. Floral tributes included 'in affectionate and loving remembrance of my dear husband from his heartbroken wife', 'to my dear boy, from his affectionate mother', 'Officers and men of the F division Metropolitan Police' and 'members of the Wimborne Football Club'. It seems inconceivable that a headstone was not erected at some point, but there is no evidence of this and no headstone has survived. Aside from the Watts Memorial, PC Ricketts is also commemorated in the Metropolitan Police Book of Remembrance, which is housed in the entrance of Simpson Hall at the Peel Centre in Hendon.

With little point of reference, it is difficult to trace Harold's wife, Kate, following her husband's death. The couple had only been married a matter of weeks, they had no children and, at the time of writing, there are no census returns available for 1921. It seems likely that she would have remarried, but there are numerous marriages after 1916 and as Kate had relatively few ties to any particular area, it is difficult to identify, conclusively, whether or not they relate to her. Harold's female siblings, however, prove slightly easier to track. Charlotte, Harold's eldest sister, married Percival Turner in Wimborne in 1918, but it is not clear if they had any children. Mabel, Harold's younger sister, married Henry Edward Tite, a widowed builder, on 9 April 1921 at St John's church in Wimborne. The couple do not appear to have had any children and Mabel died, aged 67, on 23 November 1967 at 6 Edward Road in Dorchester. Her rather significant estate of £20,863 passed to her brother, Ambrose, and a Robert Samuel Elliott Mitchell. The youngest girl in the Ricketts family, Ethel, married Ernest J. Riggs in 1924 and they had one child, Vera, born in 1925.

Of Harold's brothers, his twin, Ambrose, served in both the police force and the army. Between 1909 and 1912 he served in the 4th Battalion Dorset Regiment and then in the Metropolitan Police until October 1918, when he enlisted in the Training Battalion of the Machine Gun Corps. He was demobilised a year later and in 1924 he married Maud Knight in Wimborne. It is not clear if the couple had any children, but when Ambrose died on 4 April 1965 at 108 Coburg Road in Dorchester, his estate passed to Lilian Ethel Knight, one of Maud's sisters, suggesting that there were no children, or at least no surviving children. Arthur Ricketts, Harold's younger brother, married Elsie Honor White in 1924 and the couple appear to have had at least three children: Kitty (b. 1924), Eric (b. 1925) and Joan (b. 1927). Arthur died, aged 64, on 4 August 1963 at 37 Old Farm Road, Poole, and his estate of £2,571 passed to Elsie, who survived him by fifteen years and died in 1978. Harold's youngest brother, Albert, married Dorothy Forward in 1924; the couple do not appear to have had any children and Albert died, aged 71, in 1973.

Of the three officers commemorated on the Watts Memorial in 1930, only one received the prestigious King's Police Medal for Conspicuous Gallantry. The decoration was instituted in 1909, ostensibly in response to the bravery displayed by constables during the so-called 'Tottenham Outrage' in January 1909. During the incident, two armed robbers killed two people (a police officer and a 10-year-old boy) and injured scores more in a running gun battle through the streets of Walthamstow.[202] The medal was awarded to this officer posthumously on 20 June 1917 and was given in recognition of heroism displayed at the largest explosion in London's history, either before or since, which occurred on 19 January 1917.

As the First World War progressed, the demand for munitions grew and sustaining the production of high explosives became central to the war effort. The Brunner Mond chemical works at Crescent Wharf in Silvertown was ideally equipped for refining TNT, but the process was very dangerous, with a significant risk of explosion, and the works were situated in a highly residential area.[203] Despite numerous warnings, production began in 1915 and continued on the site even after the opening of a larger works in Cheshire in 1916. At full production, the plant at Silvertown could purify around 9 tons of TNT a day. In the early evening of 19 January 1917, a fire broke out in the melt-pot room and firemen from the local station were called to fight it. The firemen were, however, unable to control the blaze and in a sudden cataclysmic moment, 50 tons of stored and production TNT exploded.

The factory was utterly destroyed and the local area bore the full brunt of the blast. Chunks of burning debris were strewn for miles, crashing through the roofs of houses and causing numerous secondary fires. It was said that the explosion blew out windows in the Savoy Hotel in central London and could be heard as far afield as Norfolk and Suffolk, over 100 miles away. Sixty-nine people were killed on the night, four more died later from their injuries, and hundreds of others were injured. The death toll could, though, have been much worse; it was early evening on a Friday, so most of the workers at nearby factories and warehouses had gone home, but people had not yet gone upstairs to bed and it was the upper storeys of houses where most damage occurred. Had the explosion happened a few hours earlier or during the night, fatalities could have stretched into the hundreds.

Many stories of heroism emerged from the incident, not least the firemen who fought the initial blaze in full knowledge of the high explosives that surrounded them. There were also two plant workers, Dr Andrea Angel, the chief chemist, and George Wenborne, the leading male hand, who stayed to help fight the fire, despite being implored to leave. Angel and Wenborne were both killed but posthumously awarded the First Class Edward Medal for their actions. There was also a police constable patrolling that evening by the gates of the plant, who when he saw the fire, could easily have run for safety but, instead, ran towards the danger, intent on raising the alarm and getting people as far away as possible.

Edward George Brown Greenoff had joined 'K' division of the Metropolitan Police on 7 December 1908.[204] Edward was the eldest child of Samuel Edward Greenoff, a plumber, and Emily Sarah Brown who married in St Pancras in the early part of 1886. Emily may have been just pregnant at the wedding as Edward George was born on 20 September 1886. He was followed in 1888 by Emily Alethea, and a third child, Samuel Albert, was born in 1890. In 1891, the family was living at 1 Julia Street in Kentish Town, and soon after, in 1892, a third son, Sydney Albert, was born. After a gap of about seven years, the couple had their fifth child, another boy, Stanley William, who was born in 1899. In quick succession a second girl, Lilian Elsie, was born in 1901, at which time the family was living at 5 Trinity Road in Finchley. Two final children were born at the Finchley address, Doris Amelia in 1904 and Ernest Charles in 1908.

On Boxing Day, 26 December 1908, a few weeks after joining the Metropolitan Police, Edward Greenoff married Ada Mina Thorpe, the daughter of a shoemaker, at Holy Trinity church in Finchley. He was described at the time as a plumber, 5ft 11in tall, weighing 10st 4lbs, with black hair, brown eyes and a 'fresh complexion'. The couple went on to have three children: Edward Arthur Cecil (b. 1909), Elsie Irene M. (b. 1912) and Albert George (b. 1914). In 1917, when he was killed, Edward was living at 2 Rhea Street in north Woolwich, but it is not entirely clear how long he and his family had been living there. On 2 April 1911, when the census was taken, Ada Greenoff appears to have been a patient in the London Hospital in Whitechapel and their only son at that time, Edward, was staying with George and Emily Meyrick at 15 Auberon Street in Woolwich. This would suggest that the family was living in the Woolwich area at that time, but exactly where is difficult to discern. They were, though, definitely living at 2 Rhea Street in north Woolwich on 19 January 1917, when Edward went off to work as on any other day.

Edward's beat would certainly have taken him down the North Woolwich Road in west Silvertown and past the entrance gate of the factory; perhaps he often shared a joke or a smoke with the watchman at the gate as he passed by. However, there was no light-hearted banter on 19 January and when Edward approached the gates it was clear that a desperate situation was unfolding; flames were billowing from the factory and a fire engine was in attendance.[205] Knowing full well the likely consequences of such a serious fire at the plant, Edward realised that people needed to be evacuated from the immediate area, so he began to make his way towards the outbuildings on the site. Minutes later, the Brunner Mond chemical works were gone and Greenoff had been caught in the blast.

Writing in 1937, the author Miles Henslow gave one account of what may have happened to Greenoff after the explosion:

> He was found amongst the other injured and dead almost as soon as they arrived at the spot where the factory had stood. He was crawling along the ground, hurt and completely dazed with what he had been through. Friends took him to one of the comparatively undamaged houses, and after a while he was able to sit up in a chair. The doctor who was called to him, attended to others in the room who were, apparently, more grievously injured; but even as he spoke to his friends, complaining of a strange nausea, they saw with horror that the side of his head was dreadfully wounded. Though the doctor ordered him to hospital at once, there was no hope for him. There never had been. He died two days later.[206]

This account by Henslow suggests that Greenoff died on 21 January 1917, but other evidence suggests that he was treated in hospital until he died on 28 or 29 January 1917, and this seems more likely, not least because his funeral was held at St Marylebone Cemetery in Finchley on 3 February 1917. More than '500 police constables from all parts of London and 300 special constables, headed by the "K" division police band' were said to have attended the burial.[207]

Following the loss of her husband, Ada Greenoff found herself with three young children to support, and on 3 March 1921 she married a police constable, Herbert Colwell, at St Mary's parish church in Finchley. The couple had at least three children: Beryl M. (b. 1921), Clara Eileen (b. 1923) and Betty Mina (b. 1926). Ada Colwell, Edward Greenoff's wife, died in Barnet in 1958, aged 74. The eldest of Edward's three children, Edward Arthur Cecil, married Annie Chandler in 1931 and the couple had at least two children, Edward G. (b. 1932) and John (b. 1934). Edward Greenoff died, aged 75, in London in 1984. Edward's eldest daughter, Elsie Irene, married Edward J. Ebbage in Barnet in 1934 and the couple had at least two children, Barbara A. (b. 1935) and Lynda M. (b. 1949). Elsie Ebbage died in Surrey in 1996, aged 84. Albert George, the youngest of Edward's three children, married Irene May Bolding in Barnet in 1935 and the couple had at least one child, George, born in 1935. Albert George died, aged 50, in Barnet in 1964.

In the 1920s, the owners of Brunner Mond erected a memorial, at that time on the site of the works, to commemorate those killed in the explosion. It was, though, really more of a war memorial, as the inscriptions demonstrate. On the eastern-facing side of the memorial was engraved 'To the glorious memory of the men from these works who fell in the Great War 1914–19', followed by a list of seven names, and on the western-facing side, 'and to the memory of those who whilst serving their country by making T.N.T perished in the explosion in this works. January 19th 1917', followed by a list of eighteen names, including Andrea Angel and George Wenborne. An inscription to the memory of those who fell in the Second World War was subsequently added to the southern side. As Edward Greenoff was not an employee, his name does not feature on the memorial.

Greenoff was, however, much more fittingly commemorated in an ornate memorial plaque dedicated to 'fallen comrades' which was originally erected at the North Woolwich Police Station (see plate 13). The plaque features Greenoff and another constable from 'K' division, Sidney Thomas Newbury, who was killed in action on 16 September 1918 when his ship, the SS *Tasman*, was sunk by a submarine. The plaque contains a photograph of each man, encased in an oval glass frame, both of which are then mounted on a polished metal plate which is, in turn, mounted on a carved wooden base. The photograph of Greenoff depicts him in formal wear, rather than uniform, sporting a large white carnation in his buttonhole, so it may well have been taken on his wedding day. The plaque is a thing of beauty and gives a real sense of the esteem and respect that the two men earned from fellow officers.

The final tablet of the trio erected in 1930 features the most recent incident officially commemorated on the memorial, which took place in October 1927. Given that the vast majority of the incidents documented occurred in the late Victorian or very early Edwardian period, this later case appears really quite different; even the language on the tablet itself stands out as depicting a more modern technological age: 'voluntarily descended high tension chamber at Kensington'. Furthermore, the press reports of the incident talk of 'electric lighting' and 'cylinders of oxygen', as well as ambulances and motorised vehicles, all of which at first appear to set this incident apart from others that feature on the wall.

However, as the details of the case emerge, the circumstances and the behaviour of those involved all begin to feel strangely and regrettably familiar, echoing events which took place thirty or forty years earlier. Workmen entering a long-neglected underground space are overcome by noxious gas, and other men, who descend into that space to try and assist them, are also gassed and lose their life as a result. One of the men even ties his handkerchief over his mouth and nose to try and guard against the fumes; not exactly a hallmark of modernity. This could, in fact, be a description of the Three Mills Distillery incident or the fatalities at the East Ham Sewage Works, but it does not relate to either of those tragedies. It relates, rather, to another, equally as dreadful as those.

The passing of the Electric Lighting Act, the first legislation relating to the public supply of electricity in London, took place in 1882 and there was much initial competition to secure supply rights. The Board of Trade was in control of administering this process and it specified an operating period of twenty-one years, after which time the supply company agreed to be compulsorily purchased by the local author-ity.[208] Companies were also not permitted to form associations across supply districts, which led to problems creating a unified network and to the creation of small elec-tricity-generating stations serving particular companies. Street lighting was primarily the first application for public electricity and this could be delivered using relatively low-voltage cables. In 1888, the Notting Hill Electric Light Co. (NHELC) was formed for just this purpose, and it started supplying electricity to light the streets of the Notting Hill district from a generating station at Bulmer Place.

As the benefits of electric lighting, rather than gas, became apparent, the demand for supply soared, and in 1900 the NHELC joined forces with the Kensington and Knightsbridge Electric Lighting Company to build a new power station at nearby Wood Lane. This was the first distribution of high-voltage, three-phase electric-ity, requiring 'high tension' cables which, for safety reasons, needed to be buried underground to a depth of around 25ft; well below the level of the water mains and the sewers. In order to gain access to inspect and maintain these cables, vertical shafts about 3ft square were sunk into the ground at strategic points along the supply line, allowing engineers to climb down and enter the 'high tension chamber' at the bottom. These shafts, similar in nature to a well shaft, were then capped and sealed with manhole covers to prevent unauthorised access.

On 7 October 1927, three employees of the NHELC were dispatched to the junc-tion of Holland Park Avenue and Addison Avenue, where they were tasked with unsealing a high-tension chamber which had not been used since 1905.[209] The three men were John Samuel Brown, an assistant engineer and foreman for the job, Richard George Ball, a service layer responsible for the maintenance of the cables, and David Richard Williams, a Welsh labourer who was there to assist the other two men. When they arrived, Brown instructed Ball and Williams to unseal the manhole but not to descend down the shaft to the chamber until it had been ventilated. Brown then went to collect some equipment while Ball and Williams removed the manhole covers. After about five minutes, Ball poked his head into the shaft and said to Williams, 'It's all right, the air is sweet.' Williams reminded Ball that they had been ordered not to go down to the chamber, but the latter climbed into the shaft and started to descend, using the foot-irons that were fixed into the wall.

As Williams peered down into the dimly lit shaft, he could just make out the figure of Ball as the serviceman inched his way down. Suddenly, Williams saw Ball slump and, as his hands and feet slipped from the irons, he fell about 5ft into an inspection pit beneath the main chamber. Williams paused, waiting for a shout or a sign that Ball was all right; but he heard nothing. Looking around him, Williams found a length of chain and fixed one end to a metal bar at the entrance of the shaft and then made his way down with the other end of the chain, intending to fix it to Ball, climb back up and then pull his workmate back to the surface. Williams, however, had barely got to the bottom and was just trying to locate Ball when he too collapsed. Brown returned a few minutes later and, seeing the two men unconscious at the bottom of the shaft, he shouted for help. His calls were answered by two local police officers, Sergeant Joyner and Constable Cook, both from the nearby Notting Dale Police Station.

Percy Edwin Cook had joined the Metropolitan Police seven years earlier on 2 February 1920 and had initially been assigned to 'F' division, responsible for the Covent Garden area of London.[210] By 1927, however, he had transferred to Notting Dale, which covered the Shepherd's Bush and Notting Hill areas. Percy was by no means the first person in his family to join the police force, although he was the first to join the Metropolitan Police. His grandfather, Isaac Cook (b. 1832), was a police constable in Bedfordshire in the 1870s, and his father, Harry Cook, joined the Buckinghamshire Police Force as soon as he was old enough, probably in around 1878.

Harry Cook, Percy's father, was born in Maulden in Bedfordshire, and in 1881 he married Annie Neal in Buckingham and the couple started a family. Alice Annie was their first child, born in 1882, and she was followed by Arthur Harry (b. 1884), Frederick (b. 1885), Florence Ada (b. 1886), Ada (b. 1888) and Ambrose (b. 1890). In 1891 the family was living in a cottage in Flitcham cum Appleton in Norfolk, where Harry was working as a police constable. Children continued to arrive in steady succession: Leonard in 1891, Helena Thorpe in 1893, and then, on 10 October 1894, Percy Edwin. Harry and Annie had three more children and then in 1901 Harry died, aged 40.[211] Annie continued to live in Norfolk with her three youngest sons until at least 1911, when the family is recorded living at Roughton House, 51 Station Road in Cromer.

In 1914, duty called and so rather than follow his father into the police force, Percy enlisted in the armed forces and joined the 3rd (Reserve) Battalion of the Norfolk Regiment as a private in September of that year.[212] He was described as being 6ft 2in tall, weighing 157lbs, with a fresh complexion, brown hair and brown eyes. After completing a year of basic training in Britain with the British Expeditionary Force, during which time he was promoted to lance corporal, he transferred to the 9th Service Battalion and was posted to France in August 1915. Later that year Percy was promoted to corporal and the 9th Battalion transferred to the 6th Division, so it is likely that Percy served on the Western Front in phases of the Battle of the Somme in 1916. On 18 August 1916 he was shot in the back, and he was treated at a casualty clearing station until 10 September when he rejoined the battalion.

Following his injury, he was promoted to sergeant in September 1916, but on 24 March 1917 he was wounded again, this time sustaining gunshot wounds to both thighs. The injury was described as 'dangerous' and he was evacuated to Bevan Military Hospital in Kent before being transferred to Shorncliffe Military Hospital, also in Kent. In June 1917 he was transferred to Shoreham, where he stayed until September the same year, then returning to the 3rd (Reserve) Battalion in Norfolk.

Following his time at the front, Percy agreed to undertake a year of national service and in September 1917 he joined the King's African Rifles and sailed for East Africa. He arrived in October 1918 and served until March 1919, when he returned to the 3rd (Reserve) Battalion for the remainder of his service until September 1919.

During his military service, Percy was awarded the Military Medal for Gallantry and Devotion to Duty. The award was announced in the *London Gazette* on 11 May 1917, suggesting that it was perhaps connected with the action in which he received his serious injuries in March of that year. He also received a trio of medals awarded to British men who served in the theatre of war between 5 August 1914 and 31 December 1915: the 1914–15 Star, the British War Medal and the Victory Medal. These three medals were always awarded together and, after the war, were often referred to as the 'Pip, Squeak and Wilfred' after a cartoon of the same name in the *Daily Mirror*. Percy's elder brother, Arthur Harry Cook, also joined the armed forces and served as a lance sergeant with the 3rd Battalion Grenadier Guards. He too received the Military Medal but was killed in action on 12 July 1916 and buried in the Cité Bonjean Military Cemetery in Armentières.

Constable Cook had already behaved courageously and been seriously wounded while serving his country, so he was clearly no stranger to facing risk and danger. Seeing the men at the bottom of the shaft, Cook said, 'I will go down and rescue them', but it was clear that there was some sort of problem with the air in the chamber and so Joyner strongly advised him to wait for a respirator to arrive; 'I don't want a respirator,' replied Cook and insisted on going down the shaft. So it was, then, that 'the sergeant helped to tie a handkerchief round his mouth and nostrils and Cook, with the end of a chain twisted around his arm, the other end being held by Joyner, went down into the inspection chamber'.[213] This was the last time that he was seen alive. When he reached the bottom, Cook unwrapped the chain from his own arm and was in the process of tying it around the limp body of David Williams when the constable collapsed. Joyner hauled in the chain but it came up empty and all three men remained unconscious at the bottom of the shaft.

By this time a crowd had gathered and the fire and ambulance services had both arrived to assist. Edward Overton, a sub-officer with the London Fire Brigade, tried to get down to the men using a smoke hood, which was designed to help breathing during fires and was only of limited use in gas situations. Cylinders of oxygen had already been released into the shaft in the hope of reviving the men below, but these did not help. Neither could Overton who, having been lowered down on rope, was forced to come up empty-handed after he began to feel faint. He was taken to a nearby chemist's shop where he was treated and recovered. It was not until self-contained breathing apparatus arrived that anyone managed to get down to the men and, in the end, it was a Fireman Garner who brought them out one by one; Cook, then Williams, and then finally Ball, who, in addition to the gas, had also been found entirely immersed in water in the inspection pit.

The ambulance men tried in vain to resuscitate Ball and Williams, but after two hours it was clear that the two men were dead. Meanwhile, a local GP, Dr Webb of Parson's Green, and a police surgeon, Dr Broughton, had been working on Cook and he seemed, at one point, to be recovering, so he was given oxygen and rushed to the West London Hospital in an ambulance. Upon arrival, however, he was examined by the medical superintendent, Dr Illingworth, who pronounced him dead. Giving evidence at the coroner's inquest into the three deaths, which was held in Hammersmith on 11 October 1927, Illingworth reported that the cause of death was 'asphyxiation caused by the inhalation of gas'.[214] It was probably carbon dioxide with a small amount of carbon monoxide and inhaled in dense concentration; death was likely to have come very quickly.

Also giving evidence at the inquest was Sydney More, a representative for the Notting Hill Electric Light Co., who reported that the shaft had been sealed again but 'it was intended later to conduct experiments with the object of discovering how the gases were generated'. The coroner, in summing up, described Cook's action as 'a very gallant act' and added that 'all who were concerned in the work of rescue were to be commended for their courage and devotion to duty'. The inquest jury recorded a verdict of 'accidental death' and the jurors expressed their sympathy with the relatives of the three dead men. Ball was married and lived nearby in Mersey Street; Williams appears to have been single and was lodging in Farmer Street in west London, his parents living in the village of Gelli near Ystrad in the Rhondda Fawr valley.

Percy Edwin Cook had married Edith German in Pancras in the first quarter of 1925 and the couple do not appear to have had any children before he died in 1927. The surname Cook is very common and therefore it is very difficult, with little additional context, to track Edith Cook after her husband's death. Likewise with Percy's eleven siblings; tracing them with any degree of certainty is difficult, time consuming and, in this instance, unlikely to reveal any more about Percy. As with Ricketts and Greenoff (and the other PCs documented in the preceding chapter), Percy Cook is commemorated in the Metropolitan Police Book of Remembrance which is housed in the entrance of Simpson Hall at the Peel Centre in Hendon.

The three cases which feature in this chapter are interesting for many reasons, but in the wider context of the memorial itself they are notable because they are the only cases which were solicited, rather than being gleaned from newspaper reports or as the result of a direct approach from people connected with the deceased. Had these incidents, or incidents of a similar nature and circumstances, occurred prior to 1904, there is a good chance they might not have made it onto the memorial. This is certainly not to take anything away from the sacrifice that the men made, but it is, nonetheless, interesting to compare and contrast these cases with those that preceded them.

Given that Watts primarily employed newspaper cuttings supplied to him on the basis that they were stories in which someone had risked and lost their own life while trying to save another person, it is probable that the case of Harold Ricketts would not have come to his attention. No reports of the incident implied any heroism on the part of Ricketts, which is not to say that he was not brave or did not risk and give his life for another, but simply that the press did not regard his actions in that way at the time. The incident also occurred outside London and was not extensively reported in the metropolitan press so, again, Watts would have been less likely to have known about it.

The same might be said about the incident involving Greenoff, where press report-ing tended to focus on the enormity and the tragedy of the Silvertown explosion and the heroism and courage displayed across the board rather than dwelling on the stories of individuals. It was a time of war and it was concerted and unified efforts that were praised and promoted to bring the nation together. Again, this is not to say that Greenoff did not behave heroically or that people were not saved as a result of his brave actions, for undoubtedly they were. It is just that in the mechanism of how cases tended to reach Watts, Greenoff perhaps would not have come to the fore. Of course, ten or twenty years earlier the precise circumstances of the incident would also have been different; Brunner Mond was not manufacturing TNT prior to 1915. However, similar incidents on a smaller scale were not unknown: for example, an explosion at the Woolwich Arsenal in June 1903 which killed sixteen men. Watts, though, was very much interested in 'unsung' heroes and individuals who gained little or no recogni-tion beyond a paragraph in the press. Even if Greenoff had come to his attention, it is likely that the award of the King's Police Medal would, for Watts, have been consid-ered sufficient recognition for the constable's bravery and, as such, the artist would have discounted him.

Cook is probably the case which would most likely have still made it onto the memorial, had it occurred pre-1904. As highlighted earlier in this chapter, the inci-dent bears striking similarity to two of the other cases that feature on the memorial, and men being killed through exposure to gas and noxious fumes in wells, sewers and other enclosed spaces were relatively common in the Victorian period. What is more, the way in which Cook's actions were reported would have ensured the case reached Watts; headlines such as 'Gallant action by a policeman; attempt to save men in gas-filled shaft' and 'Three deaths by asphyxiation: policeman's sacrifice in attempted rescue', would certainly have attracted the attention of those collecting cuttings on his behalf.[215] Cook was a policeman and, to some extent, Watts would have felt that the constable was just doing his job, but for those who went over and above the call of duty, the artist was in favour of recognition and it is likely he would have seen Cook in that light. So at least one of the tablets erected in 1930 would still have made it, even if it had happened forty years earlier.

NOBLE WOMEN

11

THE STEWARDESS
OF THE STELLA

On 30 March 1899, Maundy Thursday, the SS *Stella* left Southampton bound for
St Peter Port in Guernsey. The route between Southampton and the island was the
regular route for the London and South Western steamer, but this particular voyage
was a special Easter excursion and the first daylight crossing of the season. A total
of 190 people were on board, and while the passengers relaxed in the cabin area,
the crew went about their usual duties. Later that afternoon, a dense fog came down
and the ship's captain, William Reeks, called his first and second mates alongside him
on the bridge to keep watch and to listen for the foghorn that warned ships they
were nearing the notorious Casquets Rocks. It was reported that when the warning
was eventually heard, it was too late, and as the rocks loomed out of the mist, Captain
Reeks was powerless to prevent the *Stella* from ploughing into them.[216]

The granite reef ripped an enormous gash into the hull of the vessel, which lurched
violently as it veered along the jagged rocks. As water poured in, the fate of the ship
was sealed and the captain gave the order for the lifeboats to be launched. According
to survivors, an orderly evacuation began with the women and children first to be
lowered into the boats, followed by the male passengers where space allowed. Among
the crew assisting with the evacuation were the ship's two stewardesses, who were
helping the female passengers with their lifebelts and taking them to the lifeboats.
It might be argued that none of the crew was experienced for such a dreadful situation, but the stewardesses were especially ill-equipped, given their usual duties.

The role of a stewardess was in essence that of a lady's maid or nursery nurse and many of the duties were essentially domestic in nature, such as attending to the needs of ladies in their bedrooms or in the female lounge, and washing and tending to the children. As one contemporary examination of the role of a stewardess reported, 'by far the most appreciable services they render is in attending upon and administering to the wants of lady passengers during sea sickness and other illnesses on board'.[217] Now, though, as the *Stella* pitched and rolled, throwing its passengers around like skittles, the stewardesses were wholly responsible for the lives of the women and children, rather than simply for their domestic requirements. One of the stewardesses was a young woman named Ida Preston, who had not been in the job for long. The other stewardess was an older woman, Mary Rogers, who had years of experience, and it was the story about her behaviour during the sinking of the *Stella* which captured the imagination of the public and George Frederic Watts (see plate 14).

Mary Rogers was born Mary Ann Foxwell on Valentine's Day, 14 February 1855, at Dyehouse Close Lane in Frome, Somerset.[218] Mary Ann was the third of eight children born to James Foxwell, a slaughterman, and Sophia Dredge, the daughter of a weaver, who had married in Frome in 1850. Mary's two elder siblings were William (b. 17 November 1850) and Elizabeth (b. 11 November 1852), and the two immediate youngest were Sophia junior (b. 13 August 1857) and Charles (b. 20 January 1860, d. 9 January 1863). In 1861 the Foxwell family were living in Bell Lane in Frome and this is where they had their sixth child, Emily (b. 20 January 1863). Sometime before 1865 the family moved to 19 Western Shore Road in Southampton, where James and Sophia had their final two children, Caroline (b. 21 December 1865) and Samuel (b. 7 June 1868).

By April 1871, the 16-year-old Mary had moved out of the family home, but she had not gone far and was working next door as a general servant for Charles Trubbett and his family at 17 Western Shore Road. Five years later, on 20 March 1876, Mary married Richard Rogers, a seaman, and their first child, Mary Ellen, was born on 29 December 1878. The couple's second child was conceived early in the spring of 1880, and a few weeks later Richard set sail from Southampton as second mate on the SS *Honfleur*, a cross-channel steamer operated by the London and South Western Railway Company (LSWR). Frederick Rogers was born on 4 January 1881, but he would never see his father; Richard Rogers drowned in the English Channel on 21 October 1880.[219] Mary was, it would seem, no stranger to tragedy at sea and Richard's death effectively set in motion a series of events that, ultimately, led her to a similar fate nearly twenty years later.

Although he was a seaman, Richard Rogers had been employed by the LSWR and it was common practice for railway companies to offer employment to the widows or children of deceased employees so as to avoid having to pay compensation or provide a pension. These were often roles as clerks or cleaning staff, but in Mary's case she was offered a position as a stewardess aboard the LSWR steamships which plied their trade between Southampton and the Channel Islands. Channel steward-esses reportedly received, in addition to their 15s a week wage, a 'good income' from gratuities during crossings, so it was a reasonable arrangement for Mary. The job did, however, require her to spend periods of time away at sea or in the Channel Islands awaiting return sailings, and so she moved in with her parents at 22 Albert Street in Southampton and they looked after the children while she was away. By 1891, James and Sophia Foxwell had moved to Frome Cottage, 45 Clovelly Road in Southampton, and Mary and her family moved with them. William Reeks, the captain of the *Stella*, lived a few streets away and Ida Preston was a neighbour. In fact, it is likely that the two women walked together to the quay in Southampton on the morning of 30 March 1899; the same quay where, the following day, relatives of those on board the *Stella* gathered anxiously to wait for news of their loved ones.

In the sea off the Casquets, it took just eight minutes for the *Stella* to sink, and although four of the five lifeboats were successfully launched, eighty-six pas-sengers and nineteen crew members lost their lives, including the ship's captain, who remained on the bridge and was seen to go down with the ship. In those eight minutes, it was reported that numerous acts of bravery and self-sacrifice were per-formed. One newspaper editorial commented that 'many acts of self-denial, devotion, gallantry and heroism are related and altogether would fill a large volume', while a survivor, Miss Drake, summed it up clearly and succinctly: 'the whole crew behaved like heroes'.[220]

Other witnesses were more specific, such as those who described how the master's boy declined to leave his post, although urged by the captain to do so, or those who praised the second-mate Reynolds for his heroic actions in attempting to save pas-sengers.[221] A male crew member, a stoker, was seen to ask a female passenger if she had secured a lifebelt, and when 'she said she had not, he took his off and placed it around her neck'. Another report stated that, 'in more than one instance a member of the ship's company was seen to divest himself or herself of a lifebelt to give it to a pas-senger'. Male passengers were said to have given up lifebelts to wives and daughters of other passengers and there were numerous accounts of husbands and fathers securing lifebelts for their wives and daughters rather than for themselves.[222] It was, though, the actions of Mary Rogers that caught the imagination of the press and the public; so much so that her heroic and self-sacrificial behaviour was heralded as symbolic of the bravery displayed by all on board.

Precisely what happened on the deck of the *Stella* before it listed and sank to the bottom of sea is impossible to know, not least because all the information derives from the memories and recollections of those who survived the wreck, some of which were not written or recorded until many years after the incident. With regard to Mary Rogers, almost all the accounts of her act derived from a single narrative, related to a reporter by an unnamed female survivor, and published in the *Jersey Times* of 15 April 1899:

Mrs Rogers, with great presence of mind and calmness, got all the ladies from her cabin to the side of the ship and after placing life belts on as many as were without them, she assisted them into the small boats. Then, turning around, she saw yet another young lady was without a belt, whereupon she insisted on placing her own belt upon her and led her to the fast-filling boat. The sailors called out, 'jump in, Mrs Rogers, jump in', the water being then but a few inches from the top of the boat. 'No, no!' she replied; 'if I get in I will sink the boat. Good-bye, Good-bye' and then with uplifted hands she said, 'Lord, save me' and immediately the ship sank beneath her feet.

There is, undoubtedly, a good proportion of theatrical licence in this account and it is doubtful that Mary's final moments, facing death on board a violently sinking ship, were as serene and considered as this account suggests. Nevertheless, it was, apparently, an eyewitness report, given at the time of the incident, and it is in keeping with other reports of similar behaviour on board, so the main points are probably reasonably accurate. More crucially, though, this was the narrative that came to be accepted by the general public and it was the story upon which Mary's heroism was founded. Whether it was entirely true or not quickly ceased to matter; it was what was perceived to have happened that was important and it was what motivated Watts to include Mary as one of the first four people to be recorded on his memorial.[223]

Watts was not, though, the only person to pay tribute to Mary Rogers, and one of the most striking things about the whole tragic incident is the public recognition and commemoration of her actions. James Parton, a *Stella* survivor whose account of the incident was published in 1905, described it as 'the bravest deed he ever saw', while another survivor, Greta Williams, said of it, 'Never was there put on record a nobler deed than that of Mrs Rogers, the Stewardess.'[224] In an editorial on 29 April 1899, the *Jersey Times* hailed Mary's act as 'a deed of heroism which for splendour has rarely been equalled ... It stands out in a bold relief effacing, somewhat, glorious records of other days; a deed without parallel; sublime ... It is Homeric in its majesty ... the stewardess of the *Stella* has immortalised herself in the history of England.' This was, perhaps, going a little too far but it aptly illustrates the manner in which Mary was venerated by the press and admired by the general public.

The tablet to Mary in Postman's Park is not the only public commemoration of her bravery. On 13 April 1899, a letter appeared in *The Times*, which suggested that 'a short paragraph is far from being sufficient tribute of honour to the woman whose calm devotion and self-sacrificing death were chronicled in your columns yesterday'.[225] The letter went on to argue that all honour was accorded to a captain who went down with his ship and that sufficient money should be collected to erect 'a simple monument to Mrs Rogers's memory, and for the perpetuation of the honour she deserves'. The author of the letter stated that she could not undertake such a collection, but that she would gladly contribute £25 to any fund that was established;

a considerable sum considering that a modest public monument could be erected for around £40. The letter was from Francis Power Cobbe, a significant and prominent writer and spokeswoman on a range of political and social platforms.[226]

Cobbe's plea for a memorial fund was taken up by Annie Bryans, the wife of Herbert Bryans (a noted stained-glass artist), and following an appeal in *The Times* donations began to flood in.[227] The substantial sum of £570 was raised and as this was far in excess of what was required for the planned memorial it was decided that around half the proceeds should instead be given to Mary's two children; her daughter, Mary Ellen, received £50 as a wedding gift and her son, Frederick, £200 as an income to support his apprenticeship as shipwright.[228] Cobbe, along with G.F. Watts, advised and assisted Bryans with the planning and practicalities of the project which, after bureaucratic difficulties in agreeing a site with Southampton Council, was eventually unveiled on the newly constructed Western Esplanade in Southampton on 27 July 1901. Herbert Bryans designed the monument, a canopied drinking fountain in Portland stone, and upon the central column was a brass plaque with a lengthy inscription written by Cobbe. After a brief narrative of the events of 30 April, the inscription continued:

> Actions such as these – revealing steadfast performance of duty in the face of death, ready self-sacrifice for the sake of others, reliance on God – constitute the glorious heritage of our English race. They deserve perpetual commemoration, because among the trivial pleasures and sordid strife of the world, they recall to us for ever the nobility and love-worthiness of human nature.

Although it is now surrounded by busy roads, the monument has remained in its original position on the Western Esplanade in Southampton and the inscription is still very much legible.

Another commemoration of Mary Rogers can be found in Liverpool Anglican Cathedral, where a stained-glass window on the staircase in the Lady Chapel pays tribute to 'noble women'. The Lady Chapel was consecrated on 29 June 1910 and served Liverpool as its cathedral until the completion of the chancel and transepts in 1924.[229] In 1909, while the chapel was in construction, the Liverpool branch of the Girls Friendly Society (GFS) set about collecting money to furnish the building with stained glass. The GFS had been founded in 1875 by Mary Elizabeth Townsend, the daughter of an Irish clergyman, to protect and support young, impressionable working-class girls from the country who left home to take up employment, primarily domestic service, in towns and cities. The society collected £200, which was sufficient to install windows in the ante room of the chapel and on the staircase.

After much discussion and deliberation, nine women were selected for the staircase window on the basis that each one could be considered to represent a different virtue and that they were deceased.[230] It was this second clause which effectively excluded Florence Nightingale, who, it is often said, is a notable absentee. The nine women chosen included: the missionary Louisa Stewart; the physician Alice Marval; Kitty Wilkinson, who nursed the poor of Liverpool; Grace Darling, who was well known for saving nine crew members from a shipwreck near the Farne Islands; and Mary Rogers, who was commemorated under the virtue of 'faithful servants'. The beautifully decorative window contains a head and shoulders portrait of Mary with the Casquets Lighthouse behind her (see plate 15). In a sermon inspired by the window, the Rev. William McNeill summed up the perceived martyrdom of Mary's heroism:

> Mary Ann Rogers achieved fame not by the labour of a lifetime but by one heroic deed. In the last five minutes of her life with a dying hand she grasped it, rescuing herself from oblivion. It is true of her, literally true, that nothing in her life became her like the leaving of it.[231]

Mary's heroism inspired verse as well as sermons, with poems being composed by writers great and small. The Poet Laureate wrote from the perspective of a boy asking his mother to recount her escape from the shipwreck:

> Tell me the tale again, mother, tell me the tale again!
> Of the cheery start and the joyous trip,
> And the folds of the fog, and then;
> How men may be heroes in their death,
> And women as brave as men.
>
> Yet one there was who, though faultless, still
> Sought never herself to save,
> But the last of the life belts gave away,
> Though aface with the waiting wave:
> A mother like me, with a son like you,
> But braver than the bravest brave.
>
> O Mother! The tale must be ne'er forgot,
> But be told again and again;
> And her statue stand in the market-place
> Pure white in all England's ken,
> That its sons may be heroes still in death
> And its women as brave as men![232]

Meanwhile, Joseph Gwyer, the 'Penge Poet', composed a booklet of poetry, including a poem on the *Stella* disaster, which was then sold at a penny, with all proceeds going to the Mayor of Southampton's distress fund. Although Gwyer did not mention Mary by name, one verse alluded to her actions:

The officers and crew worked well,
Our highest praise to all we tell,
To give their lives were willing found,
Our praise to them shall here abound.[233]

Finally, not one to miss out on the opportunity to lament a dreadful disaster was the Scottish poet William McGonagall. Best known for his poem 'The Tay Bridge Disaster', McGonagall also wrote verses on Grace Darling, the shipwreck of the SS *London* and the fire at the People's Variety Theatre in Aberdeen. McGonagall was often referred to as the writer of the worst poetry in the English language, something which he delighted in, as evidenced by these verses on the sinking of the *Stella*:

'Twas in the month of March and in the year of 1899,
Which will be remembered for a very long time;
The wreck of the steamer 'Stella' that was wrecked on the Casquet Rocks,
By losing her bearings in a fog, and received some terrible shocks.

And brave Captain Reeks felt rather nervous and discontent,
Because to him it soon became quite evident;
And from his long experience he plainly did see
That the fog was increasing in great density.

Still the 'Stella' sailed on at a very rapid rate,
And, oh, heaven! rushed headlong on to her fate,
And passed o'er the jagged rocks without delay,
And her side was ripped open: Oh! horror and dismay![234]

That last verse from McGonagall highlights an issue which attracted huge amounts of publicity at the time and threatened to bankrupt the LSWR if it was proven: was the *Stella* travelling too fast for the conditions? It has even been suggested that Mary's heroism was publicised and extolled to distract attention from this issue, but it certainly did not escape the attention of the official inquiry into the shipwreck.

Under the Merchant Shipping Act of 1894, a Board of Trade inquiry into the sinking of the *Stella* took place at the Guildhall in Westminster between 27 April and 10 May 1899, with the final report being published on 15 May.[235] The inquest was presided over by the judge and former cricketer Robert Henry Marsham, assisted by Henry Knox, a captain in the Royal Navy, and two assessors, A. Ronaldson and W.F. Caborne. Many of the people who died had legal representation at the inquiry, including Captain Reeks, who was represented by Warington Baden-Powell, the elder brother of Robert Baden-Powell, the founder of the Boy Scout movement. The inquiry decided that the main questions to be addressed were: had the *Stella* been properly navigated in the fog? Was proper notice taken of the foghorn sounding from the Casquets? Was the speed at which the ship was travelling excessive given the weather conditions? If the speed was excessive, why was such speed maintained? And the most controversial question of all, had the ship maintained full speed because it was engaged in a race with the Great Western Railway steamer which was scheduled to arrive at the same time? Usually, the GWR and LSWR ships sailed at different times, but as both lines had decided to run the same Easter excursion at the same time, rumours began to circulate that the captains of the ships had agreed a wager upon who would be first to arrive. This, it was argued, was why Captain Reeks had maintained full speed when it was unsafe to do so, and the *Stella* had been wrecked because he was trying to win a race with another ship and a bet with another captain.

In many ways, the answers obtained were damning for the LSWR, and especially Captain Reeks. It was concluded that, although the correct course had been set and the *Stella* had all the necessary equipment to check its progress, the means to do so had not been employed and 'the vessel was not navigated with proper and seamanlike care'. The foghorn had not been heard, it was argued, because the density of the fog had deadened the sound and also because the ship's steam-whistle had been sounding at similar intervals. In terms of speeding, it was ascertained that, although the speed of the vessel had been slightly reduced when the fog first appeared, it was not adjusted any further, and when conditions worsened, 'the speed of the vessel should have been reduced and soundings taken', which had not been done. The final judgment of the court was that:

> the cause of the stranding and the subsequent loss of the vessel was that she had not made good the course set and that the master continued at full speed in thick weather when he must have known that his vessel was in the immediate neighbourhood of the Casquets, without taking any steps to verify his position.

Why, though, had the captain been speeding?

During the course of the inquiry, this question was addressed to Captain Lewis, the LSWR's assistant marine superintendent based at Southampton. The court asked Lewis if he was aware of reports in the press that the boats had been racing. 'No sir,' replied Lewis. 'Please think, Captain Lewis,' pressed the inquiry. 'I am quite certain,' he maintained. Had Lewis ever heard anyone suggest anything of that kind? 'I have heard people suppose such a thing,' mused Lewis. Had it ever occurred to him to take notice of what people supposed? 'Certainly not!' was the indignant retort. When questioned as to why the two rival lines had unusually scheduled their excursions for the same time on that day, Lewis denied any knowledge that such a thing had been done, which seems inconceivable given his positon. The court assured Lewis that the services had been run at the same time and accused him of knowing full well that the two lines were in competition with one another, to which Lewis replied, 'I know nothing of the sort, sir.' 'You will swear to that?' asked the inquiry. 'Yes, I think I can,' declared the captain.

In the end, the inquiry placed much of the blame on Captain Reeks and concluded that a combination of reckless speed and poor navigation had led to the sinking. Despite the weight of evidence, the inquiry sidestepped the matter of racing and made no explicit judgment, although no other explanation was provided as to why Reeks had needlessly maintained full speed. The inquiry did highlight that it was natural for rivalry to exist when two lines competed to serve the same route, and it recommended that, in future, services should always be staggered and arrival times at St Peter Port should not coincide. This seems strong evidence that the inquiry believed that racing had played a part in the tragedy, but it stopped short of actually saying so. The judgment that Reeks was responsible did, however, pave the way for legal action against the LSWR, and forty bereaved families brought compensation claims against the company.

Many of these claims were highly contested, including one instance in which a passenger had taken out £2,000 worth of insurance just before boarding the boat-train at Waterloo, but the LSWR refused to pay out because the widow could not produce the documents; they had been in her husband's pocket when he went down with the ship. Many of the claims were, nevertheless, settled and the costs to the company were substantial. So much so, in fact, that within months the LSWR was forced to pool its resources with its rival, the GWR, and the two lines shared the cross-channel route. It is a pity that such an arrangement had not been brokered earlier, as perhaps then the *Stella* would not have been racing across the Channel and the 105 victims of the shipwreck, including Mary Ann Rogers, would not have lost their lives.

Along with Alice Ayres, Mary Rogers was one of the most publicised and recognised figures commemorated on the Watts Memorial, and one where the notional construction of her heroic act became, in many ways, far more important and relevant than what actually happened. It was a similar case with Grace Darling, who, it is argued, was more or less harassed to death as a result of her perceived heroism.[236] What is more, the incident featuring Mary Rogers is particularly interesting in relation to ideas about women and heroism discussed elsewhere in this book and in other studies.[237] Generally speaking, shipwrecks tend to conjure up the impression of 'women and children first', and it is often argued that women were mostly considered to be either 'hysterical obstacles to evacuation' or 'passive inanimate objects, reliant on men to save them'. This was due to the general perception, in the latter half of the nineteenth century, that 'feminine characteristics of hysteria, physical weakness and weakness of character meant that women could not successfully occupy the "male sphere" of the ship at sea'.[238]

Mary Rogers, though, provides a very different example of how a woman could behave at sea and how differently from that 'traditional' image she was treated on board the ship. Acknowledging Mary's professionalism and dedication to duty, a *Derby Mercury* editorial contended that 'she appeared, from all accounts, to regard herself as part and parcel of the ship, nor did she move from her post until all the passengers, the women especially, were supplied with lifebelts; she persistently refused to accept one for herself saying that she must stick to the ship'.[239] Furthermore, in the narrative of Mary's last minutes on board, no man attempted to force her into a boat, as was the case with the female passengers. In the accounts, the male passengers and crew already in the lifeboat reportedly implored the stewardess to get in, and yet when she refused because it was overcrowded, none of them offered up their seat for her, as they would undoubtedly have been expected to do for a female passenger.[240] It would appear that those on board the *Stella* viewed Mary Rogers more as a member of the crew than as a woman, and as such she transcended the gap between the male and female spheres that is supposed to have predominated. Furthermore, in choosing to undertake her professional duty and stay with the ship, rather than exercising her accepted priority for escape accorded on the basis of her gender, it would appear that Mary also, in this respect, viewed herself as a stewardess first and a woman second.

It took almost 100 years for any official memorial to the *Stella* disaster to appear in the Channel Islands, and this was rectified in 1997 when a bronze plaque was erected on the harbour wall at St Peter Port in Guernsey. The inscription reads: 'In memory of those who perished on the SS *Stella*, March 30th 1899, particularly stewardess Mary Rogers who sacrificed her life to save another.' There was also a set of postage stamps produced in 1999 to mark the centenary of the incident, and one of those featured an image of Mary taken from her stained-glass window in Liverpool Cathedral. Mary's body was one of many which were never recovered and so she was, effectively, buried at sea. Her parents were buried in Hill Lane Cemetery in Southampton, now commonly known as Southampton Old Cemetery, and a dedication to Mary was included on their headstone. It is still, though, on the Watts Memorial where Mary Rogers is perhaps most notably commemorated, her tablet being among the first four installed, and it is beautifully decorated with one of William De Morgan's trademark ship designs. When Mary was implored by one passenger to get into a lifeboat, she apparently replied, 'No, my place is here', and the very same thing can now be aptly said of her commemoration in Postman's Park.

12

'OUR ALICE'

It happened at night – the night of Thursday April 23rd 1885; never to be forgotten in the annals of the neighbourhood. The police gave the alarm, and messengers were despatched in hot haste in search of fire-escapes and firemen; but the flames spread with fearful rapidity and the neighbours were awakened by the sound of the explosion of a barrel of gunpowder which 'went off like a cannon'. The sight that greeted their horrified eyes is destined to live in their memories to the hour of their death.[241]

Witnesses to the terrible fire that engulfed the shop premises and house of the Chandler family, at 194 Union St, Borough, in April 1885 spoke of how a young female figure, clad only in her nightdress and carrying a small, crying child, appeared suddenly at an upper-storey window. Having successfully thrown a feather bed out of the window to help cushion the fall, the young woman carefully dropped the small child down to the waiting crowd, who then implored her to save herself. When she disappeared back into the smoke, the crowd presumably feared the worse, but the girl appeared with a second child, whom she also deposited into the waiting arms of the crowd. Once more she disappeared and once again reappeared clutching yet another child, whom she also dropped from the window to the crowd below. This time she heeded the calls to save herself, but apparently overcome by smoke and exhaustion, she fell limply from the window and, striking part of the shopfront in her fall, hit the pavement below. Conveyed to Guy's Hospital with severe spinal injuries, the young woman's condition deteriorated and two days later she died.[242]

The woman in question was **Alice Ayres** and her case is particularly interesting and noteworthy for a number of reasons. Firstly, Alice was by far the most publically celebrated and recognised individual to be commemorated on the Watts Memorial. Although she did not achieve the fame of Grace Darling, the story of her heroism spread around the country and she became the subject of monuments, memorials, artworks, sermons, poems and books; even a road near to where she died was later renamed in her honour. A second reason why Alice is especially interesting is that when G.F. Watts wrote to *The Times* in 1887 he cited her case, which had occurred two years earlier, as an example of exactly the type of person whom he wished to honour.[243] It was another fifteen years before her tablet appeared on the memorial, but for Watts, Ayres epitomised the idea of everyday heroism. Finally, Alice is notable as a conduit through which many people find and visit the monument, thanks to the work of the playwright Patrick Marber. In his 1997 play *Closer*, Marber set several pivotal scenes around the monument, including one in which a principal character adopts the pseudonym of Alice Ayres after spotting the name on a memorial tablet.[244] The play was later adapted into a motion picture, with Natalie Portman playing 'Alice', and it is through the film that many people learn about, and become intrigued by, the memorial. There are certainly no 'celebrities' on the Watts Memorial, but Alice Ayres is probably the closest to being one.

Alice was born in Isleworth on 12 September 1859, the seventh of ten children of John Ayres, a labourer, and his wife, Mary-Ann Harris, who married in Brentford, Middlesex, in 1848. The couple's first child, Mary Ann junior, was born in 1848, followed closely by John junior in 1849, and in 1851 the family were living in a cottage in the Railshead area of Isleworth, close to where the River Crane flowed into the Thames. By the end of 1861, six more children, including Alice, had arrived in quick succession and the family had moved to a larger cottage nearby.[245] By 1871, John Ayres and his family had moved, yet again, to Magdala Road, where members of the family would live for at least the next twenty years.[246] Some of them had, though, already moved out, including their two eldest daughters, Mary Ann and Emily.

Emily Ayres found work as a kitchen maid for Charles Mingaye, a GP living in Twickenham, but in 1874 she married Frederick Chandler, a butcher's assistant from Charing Cross, and the couple moved to 9 Devonshire Street in Holborn. Meanwhile, Mary Ann Ayres had also found work as a domestic servant, but it must have caused her some health problems because in 1871 she was a patient at the Invalid Asylum for Respectable Females at 187 Stoke Newington High Street. This was essentially a care home, established in 1825 by the Quaker Mary Lister, to 'afford a temporary asylum to respectable females, employed in shops and in other dependent situations, and servants, obliged by illness to quit their places'.[247] A certificate of sound moral conduct was required for admittance and patients were subject to strict discipline and regular daily routines. It is not clear how long Mary Ann spent in the asylum, but in 1877 she was well enough to marry Henry Chandler, Frederick's cousin, in Westminster.

By 1881, Mary Ann and Henry had moved to 26 Rosomon Street in Clerkenwell, where Henry started running a business selling oil, paint and paraffin. The couple had three children, Henry (b. 1879), Edith (b. 1880) and Ellen (b. 1881), and Mary Ann's younger brother, David, was living with them and working as an assistant to Henry.

Meanwhile, Mary Ann's younger sister, Alice Ayres, had also moved into the city from Isleworth and was working as a housemaid for Dr Edward Woakes, a Harley Street physician. When Mary Ann fell pregnant with her fourth child, Elizabeth (b. 1882), Henry moved his business to 194 Union Street in Southwark, where he ran a shop on the ground floor and the family lived in rooms above. Mary Ann needed extra help with the children and a sensible solution was for Alice to move in with them and essentially work for her sister as a nursemaid. So it was, in April 1885, that Alice came to be living above the oil and paint shop in Union Street, where she cared for her sister's four children (see plate 16).

When the fire broke out in the shop in the early hours of Friday, 24 April 1885, Mary Ann Chandler and her husband, Henry, were sleeping in one bedroom with their 6-year-old son, Henry, while Alice slept in a room across the landing with the other children: Edith, aged 5; Ellen, aged 4; and Elizabeth, aged 3. From her hospital bed Alice related how she had been woken by a fearful explosion and, looking downwards out of the window, she saw that the front of the shop had been blown out and flames were arching upwards towards the rooms above. Alice recalled how she had attempted to reach her sister, but fearing there would not be time, she set about rescuing the children. The first two who were dropped, Edith and Ellen, the latter of whom clung to her aunt and begged not to be released, were safely caught by the crowd below. Elizabeth, however, suffered terrible burns to her legs and, although she too was caught and transported to hospital, she died a few days later. The quantities of stored paint and oil fuelled a ferocious blaze, and when the firemen eventually managed to extinguish it and enter the house, they discovered a dreadful scene. The badly charred body of Mary Ann was found near to a first-floor window, with her young son Henry dead by her side. The body of her husband, also badly burnt, was lying on the staircase with a locked money box clutched in his hand; apparently he died trying to save the family's financial security, while his wife and sister-in-law perished in attempting to save the family.

As per usual in the case of sudden and unexplained fatality, inquests were held into the deaths of the five victims: one for Mr and Mrs Chandler and their son Henry on 27 April, one for Elizabeth Chandler on 28 April and, finally, one for Alice Ayres on Wednesday, 29 April.[248] However, even something as relatively routine as an inquest was unusual in the case of Alice Ayres. It was reported that 'there was a very crowded attendance and it was remarked that the coffin in which the deceased was placed was covered with flowers as a mark of respect and appreciation of her bravery'.[249] This public outpouring of affection at an inquest was unusual and just the beginning of the adulation that would build in the weeks and months that followed. Having heard evidence from various witnesses, including relatives of Alice who had spoken to her in hospital before she died, the coroner summed up the case and the jury returned a verdict of 'accidental death'. The coroner then made a short statement which, again, was unusually reverential:

In the hurry and excitement of the fire there were few who had the presence
of mind to act as she has done, or would have run the risks she did in order to
save others. He deeply regretted that so valuable life, offered so generously, had
not been spared.[250]

Bearing in mind that Alice was a relatively poor and lowly working-class nursemaid
whose death, in ordinary circumstances, would have gone largely unnoticed, it is
interesting to note the extent to which perceptions of heroism could influence and
overcome other attitudes.

Henry and Mary Ann Chandler were buried, along with their two children,
Henry and Elizabeth, at Lambeth Cemetery in Tooting on 30 April 1885.[251] A few
days later, on 4 May, the funeral of Alice Ayres took place amidst remarkable scenes
for an otherwise ordinary individual. The funeral was a very public affair and the
cortège left the family home at Magdala Road at 2.30 p.m. for the mile or so
journey to Isleworth Cemetery, where Alice was to be buried.[252] The procession
covered the whole distance on foot and the coffin was carried by sixteen firemen
in full-dress uniform, who worked in shifts of four along the route, which was lined
several deep with crowds of people. Sadly, Mary Ann Ayres, Alice's mother, was
bedridden and unable to attend the ceremony. A 'very impressive' service was held
in the cemetery chapel and there were plans for twenty girls from the local school,
dressed entirely in white, to sing at the graveside as the coffin was lowered into the
ground. However, a sudden and torrid hailstorm began just as the proceedings were
concluding and so the idea was abandoned. Despite the inclement weather, hundreds of people crowded around the grave to witness Alice being laid to rest and
the scores of wreaths that covered the lid of the coffin.

Shortly after Alice's death, it was announced through the press that a subscription fund was being established to fund a monument or gravestone in recognition
of the nursemaid's actions. Donations poured in from numerous sources and many
collections were taken up among working-class neighbourhoods in Southwark.
Some sense of both the strength of feeling and the economic status of those
giving can be gleaned from a memorial service for Alice, held at St Saviour's
church (Southwark Cathedral), which was so over-attended that people were
turned away for lack of standing room. The collection at that service was a little
over £7 but was comprised of 951 coins, so a great many people must have given
a little, rather than there being large donations from wealthy benefactors.[253] By
the end of July 1885 the fund had raised just over £100, and on 15 August 1885 it
was reported that a decision had been made: 'The committee have decided upon
a red granite "needle monument" after the fashion of Cleopatra's needle on the
Thames embankment. It will stand 14 feet high and the epitaph lettering will be
of lead sunk in the stone to last for 100 years.' This imposing public monument,
carved from red granite, still adorns the grave in Isleworth Cemetery, towering

above most other headstones, and, as promised, the leaded inscription is still easily legible. Facing the grave are the words:

> Sacred to the memory of Alice Ayres aged 26 years who met her death through a fire which occurred in Union Street, Borough the 24th day of April 1885 A.D. Amidst the sudden terrors of the conflagration with true courage and clear judgement she heroically rescued the children committed to her charge. To save them she three times braved the flames; at last leaping from the burning house, she sustained injuries from the effects of which she died on April 26th 1885. This memorial was erected by public subscription to commemorate a noble act of unselfish courage; 'be thou faithful unto death, and I will give thee a crown of life.'

The gravestone memorial and the tablet in Postman's Park were not the only public commemorations to Alice, and one of the others was particularly poignant as it was located in Southwark, very close to where the fire had taken place. Sandwiched between White Cross Street and Red Cross Street, opposite the Stanhope and Mowbray model dwellings, was the Red Cross Hall: a 'parish parlour' community centre founded by the social reformer Octavia Hill in 1888.[254] Prior to the opening of the hall, Mrs Emilie Barrington, an acquaintance of both Hill and G. F. Watts, commissioned the artist and illustrator Walter Crane to design a series of nine large-scale murals for the interior of the hall, each dramatically depicting an act of everyday heroism.

The first design undertaken by Crane was for the mural commemorating Alice Ayres and it was erected in the hall in 1890. In the finished panel, Ayres is depicted standing on the ledge of the open window, wearing a long flowing gown or nightdress and holding a small child in her arms while another cowers behind her. In the foreground, two figures have ascended a ladder to assist Ayres, one being a fireman and the other a seaman. The fireman, depicted in vivid and well-crafted detail by Crane, holds his arms wide to receive Ayres and the child, while the seaman is shown cradling a third child. A single arm is shown reaching up from below so as to suggest the presence of further assistance below. The expression on Ayres' face suggests that she is calm and collected as she waits to be drawn into the arms of her gallant rescuers. The facts of the case were, of course, greatly different and far more tragic, but Crane's illustration was not intended to be documentary; it was much more of a carefully idealised and highly symbolic image, designed, in many ways, to pay tribute to the overall idea of working-class heroism rather than the specific act undertaken by Ayres.

Nevertheless, the mural did have a significant impact on people in the local area, many of whom had witnessed the fire or known Alice. After one particular visit to the hall in 1893, its founder Octavia Hill recalled a conversation she had with some members of the audience:

The other Sunday a gentleman recited a beautiful ballad about a heroic rescue from fire. The hall was hushed in breathless attention while the words re-ech-oed through it. As I passed down among the audience just afterwards I was twice stopped. One man said 'did you see how every eye was turned to her' pointing to the Alice Ayres. A woman said 'I couldn't but think of Alice Ayres'. 'Did you know her?' I asked. 'Yes, I always dealt there' she said 'and I was glad when they put up the panel there'.[255]

Even the site of the incident in Southwark became a catalyst that fuelled Alice's heroic rep-utation. Mrs Barrington described how she visited the house in 1890 and found, despite it being a burnt-out ruin, 'the atmosphere about it still vibrating with memories'.[256] Such was the power of Alice's heroism and her reputation that it was able, even five years after the event, to conjure up vivid and evocative images in the mind of the observer.

Another person who captured the strength of local feeling was the writer Laura Lane, who visited the area around Union Street where the fire took place to speak to people about Alice for her book, *Heroes of Every-day Life* (1888). Lane was best known as an author of semi-didactic advice novels for girls, but she was also an interesting figure who had, among other things, run a charity school and spent time collecting evidence about women in sweated labour on behalf of feminist organisations.[257] Lane's account of her visit was littered with quotations apparently taken directly from the working-class inhabitants of Southwark and, unsurprisingly, nobody had a bad word to say about Ayres. However, Lane also highlighted the emotion that the incident had provoked in people and the manner in which it had touched them: 'I have seen the cheeks and lips of strong men grow pale as ashes; I have heard rough voices falter; I have seen tears spring to hard eyes, as the story of Alice Ayres' magnificent daring was poured into my ears.' Lane was not herself from the working classes and her desire to recount heroic actions was, to some extent, influenced by the genre of sensationalist and voyeuristic journalism and literature about working-class life which was popular at the time.[258] Nevertheless, allowing for the middle-class mediation and the dramatic licence liberally employed by Lane, it is clear throughout her account that the everyday heroism of Ayres was significantly admired by those within the community and that it had a profound and moving effect upon them.

Lane was not the only writer to take Alice as her muse and the heroine was cele-brated in several other collections of heroic narratives and numerous poems published in newspapers, periodicals and books. The poet and civil servant Sir Francis Doyle contributed his composition to the *Pall Mall Gazette*, and among the nine stanzas was a particularly evocative verse:

The heavens are clear and calm, when lo!
A sudden voice rings through the night;
Men gather, hurrying to and fro,
With quivering lips and faces white;

A small mean house burst forth in flame,
Within crash down the burning stairs;
And, like a picture in her frame,
Stands at the window, Alice Ayres.[259]

The author and political activist Laura Ormiston Chant was another writer who published verse on the subject, and her poem, extolling Alice's 'glorious womanhood', was appositely published in *The Englishwoman's Review*:

Alice, this deed of thine, doth place,
Thy sweet pathetic story,
Upon the page of saintly lives,
And saintly deaths of glory.

And men who hitherto have deemed,
A woman's arm too weakly,
For anything but ill paid toil,
And thankless tasks done meekly,

Shall own the majesty of soul,
That renders thee immortal,
By glorious womanhood that led,
To fame through such dark portal.[260]

Finally, somewhat in the spirit of William McGonagall was Canon Hardwicke Rawnsley, a clergyman and conservationist who wrote a volume of poetry, entitled *Ballads of Brave Deeds*, on various examples of everyday heroism, including Alice Ayres:

Alice Ayres,
On the stairs,
Do you hear the horses come?
God grant that we may see,
Your mantle falling free,
When you soul is caught up home.

'Alice! Leap!
We will keep
Safe from Harm!' the great crowd calls;
Half in swoon, faint for breath,
From a fiery doom to death,
Shattered fearfully, she falls.[261]

There was also prolific newspaper reporting of the Union Street fire and, be it daily or weekly, national or local, the story and its tragic aftermath were reported in vivid detail. Initial reports were followed days later with news of Alice's death, then details of her funeral the following week and finally monthly publication of the subscription lists for the public memorial fund. The saga of Alice Ayres unfolded like the instalments of a grand Dickensian narrative and her heroic reputation gained ground at every turn. Even her dying words as she lay broken-backed in her hospital bed, reported to have been 'I tried my best and could try no more', signalled heroic characteristics to contemporary readers and contributed to the creation of the heroine's reputation.[262]

As with the incident involving the stewardess Mary Rogers, which is discussed in the previous chapter, it is interesting to consider the case of Alice Ayres in relation to prevalent ideas about women and heroism, particularly in relation to the Victorian concept of domestic ideology. Heroism was generally regarded as being the domain of men, so when a woman undertook a heroic act, some mechanism was required so as to acknowledge and celebrate that heroism without allowing it to challenge or devalue the dominant position of men. One way to achieve this was to ensure that the woman involved, or the act of heroism that she undertook, was intrinsically linked in some way with the domestic sphere. In this way, any potential challenge to the perceptions of men could be diffused via the safety-valve of domestic ideology.[263]

Acts of heroism involving female servants, such as Alice Ayres and to a great extent Mary Rogers, had the distinct advantage of usually taking place within a domestic space. A striking example of how this assisted in characterising female heroism is presented by a fire, astonishingly similar to that in which Ayres perished, which occurred above a tailor's shop in Dorking, Surrey, three years after the fire in Union Street. In the early hours of 10 September 1888, a gas explosion ripped through the building, engulfing it in flames and smoke, and trapping Mr and Mrs Inglis, their three children and a 15-year-old maidservant, Minnie Murrell.[264] Murrell, having raised the alarm, turned her attention to the children in her care. The baby had already been accounted for, but the 3- and 5-year-olds were trapped on the first floor and Minnie ran to their assistance. Opening the window, she called to the crowd below 'Catch the children' and then dropped each one safely from the window to the people beneath. At this point in the account, Mr Inglis reappeared, having forced his way through the flames to be of assistance to Minnie, and it would appear just as well that he did. For as the report continues:

> And now, having been hitherto as cool as a salamander and as gallant as a fireman, Minnie promptly regained the privileges of her sex, and was on the point of making a fool of herself by shrieking and jumping out of the window. She had at this crisis a sort of hysterical or fluttering fit, and would have leaped headforemost to probable death, had not her master caught hold of her in time and lowered her carefully to the enthusiastic arms below.

This quotation clearly and succinctly illustrates the gendered stereotyping of heroines along the lines of 'separate spheres' ideology. Minnie was a maidservant and as such was employed in what was considered to be fitting employment for a young woman. According to the construction in the narrative, her duty of care for the children provided her with the strength and courage required to undertake her heroic act, but when that was completed she 'regained the privileges of her sex' and consequently became hysterical. At this point, Mr Inglis, not only a man but her 'master', stepped in and rescued her from probable death, brought about by her irrational, yet distinctively female, behaviour, which needed to be checked or controlled by a man. In a nutshell, this, or slight variances upon it, was the most common type of narrative with regard to acts of female heroism and it situated the women firmly within the feminine role, as prescribed by the 'cult of domesticity'.

In some ways, the narrative of Alice's death was different from this and it might be argued that she acted autonomously and without the assistance of a man. Nevertheless, there were still many elements of her behaviour which conformed to the gendered separation of Victorian social attitudes. Alice was responsible for saving the children, rather than other adults, and female children rather than boys. Her innate mothering instinct gave her the strength and resilience to throw the mattress out of the window and to withstand the heat and smoke of the fire for as long as required to save the children in her care. Once they were safe, however, she became weak and faint and fell limply from the window. In other cases, the signs and indicators of domesticity were far more subtle, but nonetheless important. In press reports of the Union Street fire, it was reported that Mr Chandler, the man of the house, father of the children and proprietor of the shop below, was found dead at the bottom of the staircase with the money-box from the shop clasped in his arms.[265] It is easy and tempting to regard the reporting of this information as a criticism of Mr Chandler, who appears to have prioritised saving his money over saving the lives of his family. However, from a gendered perspective, it could be argued that, in seeking to secure financial provision for his family in the event of their surviving the fire, Henry Chandler was actually being shown as performing his allocated role. Meanwhile, the women of the house, the perceived custodians of the domestic and the nursery, performed their gender-allocated role by attempting to save the children.

What, then, of the children who were saved, Edith, aged 5, and Ellen, aged 4; what became of them? In June 1885, a solicitor, Alfred Eves, who was acting as the receiver for the estate of Henry Chandler, wrote to *The Times* highlighting that once all the claims from creditors had been settled, there would be no money remaining to support the children. He continued that the Chandler family were not able to support the children financially but that they greatly wished for them to be taken care of and educated.[266] In his letter, Eves reported that if the sum of £365 could be raised, the Orphan Working School at Kentish Town would accept the children and accommodate them until they were both 14 and, technically, able to support themselves.

Along with around 400 other children they would receive board and education, which for girls was training for domestic service – following in the footsteps of their mother and aunts.[267] Eves' letter was intended to solicit donations and, as with the memorial fund, they arrived in abundance.

In March 1886, Eves wrote again to *The Times* to report that the fund had raised well in excess of the required amount, thanks largely to the work of George Chance, the magistrate of the Lambeth Police Court, and an anonymous female donor who had given £250.[268] Chance had undertaken numerous collections in and around the Lambeth and Southwark areas, in the police courts, pubs and other venues, to collect batches of money which he then sent to Eves. The letter stated that Edith and Ellen Chandler were, at that time, residing at the Alexandra Orphanage in Hornsey Rise but that the money raised had more than covered the £365 required for entry into the Orphan Working School, and the two girls were recorded as resident there on the 1891 census. The surplus from the fund was sufficient to purchase the Chandler burial plot in Lambeth Cemetery and erect a headstone, which left £4 4s to invest in a lump sum for the girls when they left the school. While they were not exactly living in the most auspicious of circumstances, the girls were lucky to be alive and they owed that to the heroism of their aunt, Alice Ayres.

With the focus on Alice, it is easy to forget that her parents, John and Mary Ann, lost two daughters and two grandchildren in the fire, which must have taken a heavy toll on them. John Ayres, Alice's father, died in 1889 at the age of 69, and shortly afterwards, Mary Ann moved in with her daughter Ada, leaving the family home at 33 Magdala Road to her youngest son, Alfred, and his family. Mary Ann Ayres, Alice's mother, died in 1895 at the age of 73. John Ayres, Alice's eldest brother, worked as a brass finisher and later as a gas fitter. He married Mahala Harrison on 16 July 1876 and the couple had two children, Charles Frederick (b. 1879) and Hugh Stanley (b. 1889). The family lived in and around the Kilburn area and John died in Willesden in 1912, aged 63. Mahala survived him by nineteen years and died, aged 83, in Bromley in 1931.

Lydia Ayres married James Cooper, a grocer, in 1883 and the couple had one child, Herbert John, born in 1890. The family moved to Norfolk and then Cambridgeshire before James died in 1893 at the age of 32. Lydia took over the grocery business based in Outwell in Cambridgeshire and eventually ended up running the local post office. Lydia died, aged 58, in 1918. Ada Ayres married Harry David Harfield, a publican, in Richmond-upon-Thames on 31 May 1887. By 1891, the couple were living in Kingston-upon-Thames with their three children, Harry, Frederick and John, and Ada's mother, Mary Ann Ayres. By 1901, the couple had two more children, Frank and Victor, and had moved out to Reading in Berkshire, where they lived until their deaths: Harry in 1929, aged 70, and Ada in 1944, aged 83. Having married Frederick Chandler in 1874, Alice's sister, Emily Ayres, lived in and around the Islington area, where she and Frederick raised a family. Emily died in 1925 at the age of 71.

After working as an assistant for Henry Chandler, Alice's brother, David Ayres, became a house painter and, on 6 September 1887, just a few months after the Union Street fire, he married Emma Draper in Turnham Green. They settled in the Chiswick area and raised a family of six. Emma Ayres died in December 1923 at the age of 59 and, eight months later, David committed suicide in the River Thames near Kew; he was 61 when he died.

Today 194 Union Street no longer exists and a large office building, Union House, occupies the corner of Union Street and Great Suffolk Street where the paint and oil shop once stood. However, there are still reminders of Alice in the local area. In 1936, in an act both demonstrating and compounding the endurance of her legacy, White Cross Street in Southwark, about half a mile along Union Street from the site of the fire, was renamed Ayres Street in recognition of Alice.[269] Adjacent to Ayres Street is Redcross Way, where the Red Cross Hall and cottages built by Octavia Hill still stand, situated in the beautifully restored Red Cross Gardens. The mural to Alice Ayres in the hall has long since been painted over, but the gardens offer a tranquil place to sit and consider her legacy. Some described her as 'the maid of all work' and others as 'a household drudge', but through her self-sacrificial act of bravery Alice transcended both her lowly occupation and her poor background to become a household name in the late nineteenth century. It is important, though, to remember that, beneath the exemplified and extolled heroic reputation, there was an otherwise ordinary working-class girl from a small village on the outskirts of London, a devoted daughter, a supportive sister and a loving aunt, who gave up her own life to save the lives of her loved ones; very much a heroine of daily life long before she became an everyday hero of Postman's Park.

TRAINS AND RAILWAYS

13

'HEROISM ON THE ENGINE'

Men who but a few years since scarcely crossed the precincts of the country in which they were born, and knew as little of the general features of the land of their birth as they did the topography of the moon, now unhesitatingly avail themselves of the means of communication that are afforded.[270]

There can be little doubt that the arrival of the railways in the 1830s marked a key moment in British history; as the transport historian Christian Wolmar has highlighted, 'the railways turned the Industrial Revolution into a social revolution that had an impact far beyond the routes where the tracks took the trains'.[271] The point that Wolmar is making is that the railways not only changed the geographical, physical, economic and political landscape of Britain, but also changed the lives of its people. From the speculative businessmen who made millions, through to the masses whose leisure habits were changed for ever, and then down to the tens of thousands of households displaced by the infrastructure or forced to live in its shadowy hinterlands; there were very few people not caught up in the 'railway mania' of the nineteenth century.

The influence and impact of the railways upon the everyday lives of 'ordinary' people in that period can be clearly seen in the stories recorded on the Watts

Memorial. Six of the individuals commemorated died in railway incidents, and in many of the other cases, such as Brown, Cambridge, McConaghey, Strange, Tomlinson, Ricketts and Rogers, the railways were key elements in the circumstances leading up to their death. Five of the six killed on the railways were employees and this serves as a reminder of the way in which the transport boom stimulated employment opportunities for the working classes. Some idea of the volume and range of work can be gained from the journalist Henry Mayhew, writing in the 1850s.

Mayhew cited the London and North Western Railway (LNWR) as the largest employer, with 6,194 workers ranging from inspectors, managers and clerks down to engine drivers, porters and labourers.[272] Combining the employees for the twelve leading railway companies, he arrived at a total figure of 35,735 workers (almost exclusively men), which, he concluded, meant that 122,940 people were maintained by that employment.[273] However, when all passenger-carrying railways were included, the figure for employees rose to 159,784 which, by Mayhew's calculations, suggested that around 739,000 people relied upon income from employment with railway companies. What is more, for manual workers they were relatively good jobs, which generally paid more than industrial labour, and substantially more than agricultural labour, and the work tended to be stable, regular and preferable to working in a foundry, factory, mine or pit.

There were, of course, downsides, the least of which were the long and often antisocial hours, the punitive system of fines for a multitude of misdemeanours, and a convoluted rotational system for promotion known as Buggins' Turn. Of paramount concern, though, for those who worked on the trains and tracks were the risks and dangers, which were high and severe. Between 1873 and 1878, the railways killed an average of 682 workers every year, twenty times the number of passenger deaths which tended to grab the headlines. Statistically, the railways were the third most dangerous occupation after mining and the Merchant Navy.[274] Dangers came in all shapes and sizes, and all workers were exposed: labourers and platelayers risked being struck by trains, porters and station staff had to contend with people on the tracks, guards and inspectors might be involved in derailments, and the elite men on the footplate, the drivers and firemen, spent their working hours perched above a raging inferno and gallons of pressurised boiling water. The potential for disaster was, literally, inches away, and when things went wrong, it was the workers who most often paid the price.

In Kensal Green Cemetery in west London, nestled among the graves of luminaries including the engineer Isambard Kingdom Brunel, the novelist Wilkie Collins and the explorer Sir John Ross, there is a large headstone commemorating two men whose achievements were less notable, but who, nevertheless, were sufficiently respected to warrant recognition (see plate 17).[275] At the top of the ornately carved grave marker, a more recent piece of slate, etched with an image of a steam locomotive, has replaced the original brass plaque which carried a similar design, and the inscription on the face of the stone has been re-leaded to ensure it remains legible; this is clearly a monument which is still maintained and cared for. The inscription on the headstone reads:

> To the memory of Walter Peart who is interred here and of Henry J. L. Dean, his fireman, who is interred at Dawlish, Devon, who lost their lives in the execution of their duty through an accident to their engine (no. 238) near Acton whilst running the Windsor Express to Paddington on the 18th July 1898.

At the base of the headstone, it is revealed that it was 'Erected by members of the Amalgamated Society of Railway Servants', a trade union for railway workers founded in 1871.

About 200 miles south-west of Kensal Green Cemetery, on Oak Hill in Dawlish, Devon, there is another cemetery and another headstone, equally ornate but with no clue of the dramatic circumstances that led to the death (see plate 17). The inscription on that headstone simply reads, 'In Loving Memory of Henry J. L. Dean who died July 19th 1898 aged 25 years. Sleep on, beloved, sleep, and take thy rest. Lay down thy head upon thy saviour's breast. We love thee well but Jesus loves thee best. Good Night.' The two burials may be separated by hundreds of miles and the methods of remembrance different, but on the Watts Memorial, as on the Kensal Green monument, the two men share a tablet in much the same way as they shared a footplate, and shared an unnecessary and untimely demise.

Walter Peart, the engine driver, was born in Islington but his family roots were further north and east in Norfolk and Suffolk (see plate 4). His father, James Peart, was born in the parish of Witton in Norfolk and worked as an agricultural labourer. Walter's mother was almost certainly Mary Norman, born in Suffolk, who was listed as James' wife on the 1861 census, although there is no evidence of the couple marrying.[276] Mary was certainly recorded as a 'Peart' on the birth certificate for the couple's first child, Robert, who was born towards the end of 1853. Walter was their second child, born in 1857, and again 'Mary Peart' was recorded as the mother. In 1861, James Peart was working as an omnibus driver and the family was living at 1 Shaftsbury Road in Islington. By 1871, the Peart family had moved to 7a Hethpool Street in Paddington, just off Maida Vale, and both Robert and Walter were working as labourers. Mary 'Peart', Walter's mother, died in 1883, and in 1884 James married Eliza Bowden. James Peart, Walter's father, then died in 1901.

It was in the early part of 1872 that Walter Peart started working for the Great Western Railway Company (GWR), but it was many years before he reached the level of engine driver. For the first three years and five months he worked at Paddington as a cleaner and then, in November 1875, he was promoted to a fireman working on goods trains.[277] He continued at Paddington at this level until August 1882 when he was promoted to first-class fireman, and in 1883 he was transferred from Paddington to Aylesbury. After four years working at Aylesbury, Walter was finally appointed to the position of engineman in October 1887, and he worked for three years moving trains around the railway yard in Wolverhampton before being promoted to a third-class engineman and transferred to Didcot. His final promotion was to second-class engineman in April 1897, and later that year, in November, he moved back to Paddington Station.

During his twenty-five years working for the GWR, Walter was officially reprimanded on just three occasions. In February 1891, he was fined 2s for mismanaging his engine and allowing it to run short of steam. In April 1896, while working on the line between Newbury and Didcot, he was reported for 'not uncoupling engine after failure and working train on with one engine resulting in empty miles being run', for which he was fined 5s. Finally, in August 1897 he was cautioned, but not fined, for allowing some nuts on his engine to work loose and cause damage. Interestingly, before being promoted to second-class engineman, Walter had to pass both eyesight and colour vision tests, providing some indication of the importance and responsibility for safety that engine drivers held at that time.

While he was progressing through the ranks of the GWR, Walter was also enjoying a prosperous and fruitful personal life. On 29 December 1881 he married Ada Jane Scadding, the daughter of James Scadding, an engine driver, at St James' church in Paddington. At the time of their marriage, both Walter and Ada were recorded as living with Ada's parents at 77 Waverley Road in Paddington, although their first child, James Ernest, was born in the Chelsea area of London in 1882. In 1883, Walter's promotion to first-class fireman based at Aylesbury meant the family had to move. The couple's next two children, Emily Lydia (b. 1884) and Walter Norman (b. 1887), were both born in Aylesbury and the family lived for some time at 7 Brook Street. Another promotion in 1887 took the Pearts to Wolverhampton and this is where their fourth child, Sidney Robert, was born in 1888.

A second daughter, Daisy Alice Ada, was born in 1890 in Didcot, Walter having been transferred there following his promotion to engineman, and this is where the family were recorded as living in 1891. In 1897 Walter was moved back to Paddington, and in 1898 they were all living in the Kensal Green area of west London. Walter was employed as a 'spare man', which meant he covered shifts for other drivers or drove special additional services as required, but since the beginning of 1898, he had been regularly working with a keen young fireman from the West Country who had joined the GWR eight years earlier.

Henry Dean, the fireman, was living and working in London but he was originally from Dawlish in Devon (see plate 4). His father, also Henry, was born in Kenton, Devon, and undertook an apprenticeship to become a cabinet maker. In 1871, Henry senior was living with his parents, Richard and Mary Ann, and younger brother, James, at 9 Beach Street in Dawlish. The following year, he met and married Mary Lancey, also from Devon, who had been working nearby as a domestic cook.

Henry junior was the couple's first child, born on 11 January 1873, and his full name was Henry John Lancey Dean, following the popular custom of using the mother's family name as a middle name for the child. Two more children followed: Gertrude Alice (b. 1877) and Elsie Olive (b. 1883). By 1881, the family were living at 13 West Cliff in Dawlish, a property they would inhabit for at least twenty years. Henry senior must have earned a good wage as a cabinet maker because the family was able to employ a general servant. Mary Ann Dean, Henry senior's mother, died in 1891 and his father Richard, a basket maker, moved in and lived with them until his death in 1896.

Henry junior initially followed his father into the carpentry trade, but in July 1890 he joined the Great Western Railway as a cleaner based at Paddington Station. In July 1891 he was promoted to a shunting fireman and would have been responsible for stoking the engines used when moving trains around the yard.[278] At this point, he was advised that, in order to gain further promotion, he would need to 'improve himself in writing from dictation'. On 23 January 1892, Henry was unable to work for two days after crushing the top of one of his fingers when he caught it in the rim of an engine firebox door. Finally, in October 1893, he passed his examination in writing from dictation and was promoted to a third-class fireman based at Exeter Station, where he worked until July 1897.

Around the same time in 1897, Henry married Elizabeth Blackmore in St Thomas' church in Devon while also passing inspection for promotion to first-class fireman. Shortly after this the couple moved to Paddington, where Henry took up his post working on express trains. In January 1898, Henry was suspended for eight days without pay after the locomotive he was working on took a wrong signal and ran onto a section of line where a passenger train was approaching. The engineman was also suspended for eight days. Despite this, Henry was happy in the job, which paid well and, although hard work, gave him the opportunity to work in an exciting and fast-paced environment. It was also an exciting time for Henry because Elizabeth was expecting their first child. For about six months, Dean had been working alongside an older engine driver, Walter Peart, and on 18 July 1898 the two men were scheduled to work the passenger service back and forth between Paddington and Windsor. Both men left their families early that morning as usual, but tragically, the day would be anything but routine and neither of them would return home.

For the staff and passengers aboard the 4.15 p.m. Windsor to London train, the journey had been uneventful and the service was due to arrive on time at Paddington at around 4.40 p.m.[279] On the engine, Dean was keeping the firebox fuelled while Peart held the locomotive at a steady 45mph. Back in the nine carriages which followed, William Jarrett, the guard, was chatting with the passengers, answering queries and keeping a watch on the timetable. The train was approaching Acton Station and had just passed the signal box when Jarrett suddenly noticed a huge amount of steam and smoke pouring past the windows. Leaning out to try and see what the problem was, he felt an intense heat and could hear a crackling sound, so he ran to the rear of the train to activate the automatic vacuum brake. Finding that it had already been applied, Jarrett could do nothing but anxiously wait as the train screeched and slid for about 600yds, passing through Acton Station before finally grinding to a shuddering halt. Jumping from the rear carriage, Jarrett started to run towards the engine, but he met a platelayer, Edward Mears, coming the other way, who shouted to him, 'They are both gone', which the guard took to mean that neither the driver nor the fireman was on the engine. Jarrett's main responsibility was to the passengers and so he returned to the train to calm people and prevent them from leaving the train.

At Acton Station, Fred Webster, the stationmaster, was attending to some paper-work in his office, which overlooked the main line to London, when he suddenly saw the stricken train, enveloped in clouds of steam and smoke, careering through the station. Hurrying down to the platform, Webster sent a porter with a stretcher to the front of the train, where he thought the crew would almost certainly require help, and then sent a messenger to fetch a doctor. Webster found Jarrett on one of the coaches and the guard told him that, apparently, both the driver and the fireman had fallen from the engine some way back, so the stationmaster sent several men back down the line to look for them. He then examined the engine and, finding it to be dead and posing no further danger, he went to assist with the search for Peart and Dean. Meanwhile, Edward Mears, the platelayer, and another ganger, John Hodges, who was working nearby, had joined up with the stretcher party and the group soon found the driver and fireman lying by the side of the tracks.

By the time Webster arrived at the scene, Peart had been placed on the stretcher and Dean on the grass embankment; both men were conscious but very badly scalded and the prognosis did not look good. Webster arranged for a passing train to London to be stopped and Peart and Dean were carried back to the station and lifted into one of the carriages, which then conveyed them to St Mary's Hospital in Paddington. During the journey, Peart stirred and asked Hodges, 'Where are we?' to which the platelayer replied, 'Acton'; 'I thought so,' continued Peart, before enquiring, 'Is my face cut?' Hodges surveyed Peart's badly scalded appearance and offered, 'Yes, a bit.' 'Never mind,' mused Peart. 'I stopped my train. I put the brake on. I've got no broken bones.' Peart then looked around him. 'Where is my poor mate?' he asked anxiously, and as Hodges explained that he was alive but in another part of the carriage, Peart sighed and closed his eyes.

The two men were admitted to the hospital and settled in beds, where their burns were treated and bandaged. Edward Baker, a foreman at Paddington Station, was watching over the two men and asked Henry Dean what had happened. 'I am so cold,' replied Dean. 'Can I have some brandy?' Baker then asked Peart the same question, and the driver gave him a slightly fuller answer: 'I stopped my engine,' he said. 'Didn't you jump off?' queried Baker. 'No,' replied Peart, so the foreman pressed him further. 'What did you do? How did you get burned like this?' Peart explained:

When it first happened, I got back out of the way and I thought to myself the train is running as fast as ever. I thought I would get back to the fire and put the vacuum brake on. I did it, and as I got out from the fire and the smoke I couldn't see and when I was by the side of the engine my leg was struck by the connecting-rod which was broken.

Baker then asked the driver one more time if he jumped off and Peart declared, 'No; I stopped my engine.' Baker left the two men to sleep but when he returned the next day he was informed that Peart had died at around 6 a.m. and Dean about three hours later.

As usual in cases of sudden and unnatural death, an inquest was held, which took place at Marylebone Coroner's Court on 22 July 1898.[280] The coroner, George Danford-Thomas, and the jury heard evidence from various witnesses and it emerged that George Goschen, First Lord of the Admiralty, was a passenger on the train, returning from a government meeting in Windsor. It was announced that Goschen had written to the railway company expressing his admiration for the heroism of the driver and the fireman, and that he had opened a subscription for the families which he was urging fellow passengers to contribute to. Some technical information was presented by railway engineers, but this was kept to a minimum in the knowledge that a Board of Trade inquiry was to be held and the inquest was primarily concerned with establishing the circumstances related to the deaths of the two men.

After lengthy deliberations, the inquest jury returned verdicts of 'accidental death' in both cases and placed on record its 'high appreciation of the conduct of the two deceased men in applying the brake and in keeping at their posts, thus averting a very serious catastrophe which would have endangered the lives of the passengers of the train'. The jury also added that, in its opinion and from the limited evidence heard, 'the engine was not a fit and proper one for drawing an express train', but that was something for the Board of Trade inquiry to investigate.

The inquiry was undertaken by Colonel Francis Arthur Mandarin, who was the Senior Inspector of Railways for the Board of Trade, and it reported on 7 August 1898, with the findings being sent to the NWR on 27 August. In total, ten people were called to give evidence.[281] The guard, William Jarrett, the stationmaster, Fred Webster, and the platelayer, Edward Mears, all spoke about the events of the day and the roles they had played. Alfred Rogers and James Barfield, both engine fitters for the GWR, gave technical evidence about work they had previously done on the engine. Alfred Attwood, a chief locomotive foreman, and John Webb, an assistant foreman, recounted the events of the day and the movements of the engine between London and Windsor before the incident.

A lengthy and highly technical report was given by John Armstrong, a divisional locomotive superintendent, regarding the manufacturing of components within the engine, the maintenance regime for the engine, and the damage to the engine and the engine parts after the incident. Armstrong was, certainly, the most assertive and defensive of those who gave evidence, and seemed keen to show that there was no negligence on the part of the railway company. Finally, John Philpin, who had driven the engine the previous day, and John Donovan, who had cleaned it on the day of the incident, told the inquiry that 'the engine was in perfect working order' when they finished with it.

The inquiry was fastidiously detailed and its findings were elaborately technical in nature, as would be expected from the Board of Trade. Essentially, though, it was ascertained that the right-hand connecting road, attached at one end to the piston and at the other to one of the drive wheels, had snapped. A short section of the rod, still attached to the wheel, had flailed around and punctured through both the firebox and the boiler, causing 'a sudden and violent rush of steam and scalding water out on to the footplate that no man could possibly stand up against'. The inquiry did not seem entirely to share Peart's interpretation of his actions and suggested that he 'was probably running with his hand on the vacuum brake handle', which he then pulled or pushed over as he tried to escape the boiling water. Peart, it was stated, deserved the greatest credit for applying the brake, but the inquiry noted, on several occasions, that the steam had not been shut off, which would, it was argued, have stopped the train quicker. That said, based on marks on the ground and the location of the two men when they were found, the enquiry conceded that Peart and Dean could have done no more and that they 'had little or no warning and had therefore no chance of saving themselves, being no doubt terribly injured, before they knew what was happening'.

Having ascertained the cause of the accident, the inquiry then set out to determine what had caused the connecting rod to break. It transpired that engine number 238, which Peart and Dean were running, was a six-wheeled goods engine rather than one intended for pulling passenger trains; it had only been employed on 18 July because another passenger locomotive had broken down. The engine had been built in 1867, rebuilt in 1885, and substantially repaired in Swindon in October 1897, just nine months before the incident; since then it had done 25,916 miles. The possibility that the age of the engine, or its maintenance, or the fact that it was being overloaded, or that it was being run at an unsuitable speed, were contributory factors to its failure were thoroughly examined and not considered responsible.

Rather, following close inspection of the broken parts, it was suggested there had been some sort of internal manufacturing flaw in the connecting rod itself, probably a hairline crack in the iron when it was cast, and this was the most likely explanation for the fracture. The superintendent, Armstrong, said he had been at the Paddington depot for fifteen years and only knew of two other instances of broken rods. He also added that the hairline fault would not have been visible, hence it had not been identified when the engine was rebuilt or during routine maintenance. On that basis, Colonel Mandarin reached the conclusion that 'the accident was one which could not have been prevented, and there is no reason to impute blame to anyone'. Apart from giving credit to Peart for applying the brake, the inquiry made very little comment about the behaviour or conduct of the driver and fireman, and there was certainly no suggestion that either had behaved heroically or done any more than their duty.

The press, however, was quick to lionise the two men and praise them for their behaviour. The *Pall Mall Gazette* paid its tribute, 'Stokers and drivers carry their lives in their hands every day, but they make no fuss about it, and when danger comes they meet it with the quiet heroism of poor Walter Peart and Henry Dean', while the *Illustrated Police News* wrote of how 'fire and steam were blown with great force from the fire-box, and the two men were seriously burnt and scalded. Notwithstanding this, they stood manfully to their posts and did their utmost to bring the train to a standstill.'[282] A particularly dramatic homage was delivered by the *Penny Illustrated Paper* which, under a headline of 'The Bravest of the Brave', printed a dramatic illustration of the incident and published a lengthy poem by its resident laureate, Kate Bishop, or 'Kay Bee' as she was known to regular readers.[283] The last two verses of the poem read:

> Steam and fire, dread and anguish, yet the Britons 'must' and 'will',
> Rising over all triumphant, nerved them to be faithful still,
> Through the 'vale of death' they thundered,
> At the 'mouth of hell' they stood,
> Till had passed the hour of danger and was stemmed the fiery flood.
>
> Then and only then the heroes left their pose and never yet,
> In our crown of heroism brighter jewel e'er was set;
> Ay, in spite of days commercial and the love of golden gain,
> In Briton's blood undaunted runs the old heroic strain.

It was also reported that the *Daily Telegraph* had opened a subscription fund for the 'brave martyrs' and that there had already been a 'warm hearted response to the appeal'.[284] The newspaper was quick to state how both 'the Duchess of Rutland' and 'a poor governess' had both contributed sums, thus highlighting the breadth of feeling for the gallant railway servants. Contrary to what had been said at the inquest, George Goschen did not actually start the fund, or contribute to it, but he did send an undisclosed sum directly to both Ada Peart and Elizabeth Dean to help them support their families following the death of the breadwinners; and there most certainly were families to support.

Following her husband's death, Ada and four of the five children moved back into 77 Waverley Road, while her parents, James and Mary Scadding, moved into rooms at 44 Alfred Street, just around the corner. Two lodgers were also living at the address, John James Scott, a railway engine stoker, and Frederick Meredith, a sorter for the General Post Office.

As some of her children married, Ada moved to 21 Myrtle Gardens in Hanwell, Middlesex, where, in 1911, she was living with her two sons, Walter and Sidney. It would appear that while he was lodging with the family at 77 Waverley Road, John Scott became more than just a tenant and on 18 September 1912 he and Ada Peart married at St Mellitus' church in Hanwell, Middlesex. Ada was 49 and the couple did not have any children. Ada died, aged 77, in 1940.

It was customary for the widows and children of men who died while working for railway companies to be offered jobs within the company in lieu of a pension and it seems that this is what happened with the Peart family. Walter and Ada's eldest son, James, began working for the GWR in December 1898, just a few months after his father's death. Walter junior joined the company, aged 14, in October 1901 and finally Sidney, also aged 14, started in January 1903. All three lads worked as clerks, starting on an annual salary of £20, which then more or less rose by £10 a year during their service.

James Peart married Lillian Alice Rouse, the daughter of an engine driver, on 26 March 1910 at St Mary's church in Hanwell, Middlesex, and the couple had at least one child, Eric Ernest, born in 1914. James enlisted in the London Regiment of the British army in September 1914 and served, as a sergeant major, at Gallipoli in 1915. In November that year, during a blizzard, he became trapped up to his waist in water and snow in a flooded trench and he suffered frostbite in both feet and his left hand. As a result of this, he had problems walking and was medically discharged from the army, with a pension, in 1917. James died, at the age of 69, on 30 December 1951 while living at 33 Woodstock Terrace in West Ealing. His estate of £2,270 passed to his widow, Lillian.

Walter and Ada's second son, Walter junior, did not marry until he was in his mid-fifties, when he tied the knot with Alice Gray in Uxbridge in 1942. The couple do not seem to have had any children and Walter died, aged 69, on 30 March 1956 at 11 Kinsley Avenue in Southall. Sidney, the youngest of Walter and Ada's children, appears to have moved to Cornwall, probably through his employment with the GWR. In 1914 he married Gertrude Hocking in Penzance and the couple had at least three children: Gertrude P. (b. 1915), Marjorie D. (b. 1917) and Sidney M. (b. 1921). It is possible they also had a fourth child, Gerald E.W., in 1927. Sidney died in Penzance in 1962 at the age of 73.

Of Walter and Ada's daughters, Emily married her first cousin, Robert Peart, on 16 December 1912 at St John's church in Ealing. It is not clear if the couple had any children and Emily died, aged 56, on 10 September 1940 while living at 50 Trinity Road in Southall, Middlesex. Daisy Peart married Frank Herbert Sorrell, a railway clerk and son of a police superintendent, at Holy Trinity church in Southall on 21 April 1915, and the couple had at least two children, Keith Hydra (b. 1916) and Maureen (b. 1919). Daisy and Frank both died as a result of an air raid on 22 November 1940 which destroyed their house at 6 Cambridge Road in Southall; Daisy was 50 and Frank was 56.

As Elizabeth Dean was heavily pregnant when Henry died, the GWR made a payment of £40 in compensation for her husband's death and she would have received a share of the *Telegraph* subscription fund. Elizabeth must have travelled to either her family or Henry's in Devon to have the baby as, in late 1898, Lancey Elsie G.D.E.T.G. Dean (six middle names) was born in Dawlish. In late 1900, Elizabeth married John Vickery in Cardiff and by 1901 the married couple and Elizabeth's daughter (going by the name Vickery) were living in Roath in east Cardiff. John Vickery appears to have died, aged 50, in Cardiff in 1924. In 1920 Lancey Dean married Tom W.E. Grant in Cardiff and at least two children followed: Edgar J., born in 1921, and Vera E., born in 1922. Tom died in Carlisle in 1957, aged 59, and Lancey died in Penrith in 1998, aged 100.

Henry's sister, Gertrude, married Thomas Huxham Jarvis, a marble mason, at St Philip's church in Lambeth on 5 December 1899. Their first child, Thomas Frederick Lancey, was born in Lambeth in 1901. The couple then appear to have moved back to Devon where they had two further children: Evelyn Gertrude and Cecil Jackman, both born in 1907. In 1911, the family was living in Dawlish in Devon with Gertrude's widowed father and two visitors from the USA, Margaret Johnson and Mary Tyles Johnson. Shortly after this, in 1913, the family emigrated to the USA and in 1930 was resident in Rockleigh, New Jersey. Thomas Jarvis died in New Jersey on 5 November 1949 and his wife Gertrude followed a few weeks later on 23 December. Henry's other sister, Elsie, lived with her parents in Devon, where she was recorded on the 1901 census. However, by 1911 she had moved to Cardiff and was living at 180 Carlisle Street with her sister-in-law Elizabeth Vickery and Elizabeth's family, which included Elsie's niece, Lancey. Elsie appears not to have married and at some point she moved back to Devon where she died, aged 53, in 1936.

The implied heroism of engine drivers and stokers endured for many years and a good example is John Axon, who died in 1957 in very similar circumstances to Peart and Dean.[285] Axon was crossing the Peak District en route to Stockport when a steam pipe fractured and, despite being terribly scalded, he clung on to the side of the cab and managed to raise the alarm so that another passenger train could be moved, thus preventing a terrible collision. Axon's train eventually crashed into an empty freight wagon and John was killed, but he received a posthumous George Cross for his bravery and his story was also immortalised in one of the *Radio Ballads* composed by Ewan MacColl and Peggy Seeger.[286]

In many ways, it was relatively straightforward for people to glorify and exemplify the actions of individuals like Axon, Dean and Peart because the men could be portrayed somewhat as gallant knights on horseback; except, of course, that it was an iron horse they were riding. Locomotive drivers and firemen were held in high esteem by the railway-travelling public and considered to be both fearless and responsible in equal measure. They were also seen as public servants, conveying passengers quickly but safely from place to place and helping to build a prosperous and successful Britain by connecting people and businesses. Those at the sharp end of the train were certainly at the top of their profession and therefore relatively unproblematic in terms of heroic recognition; but what of those at the bottom of the business, the people who laid and maintained the tracks?

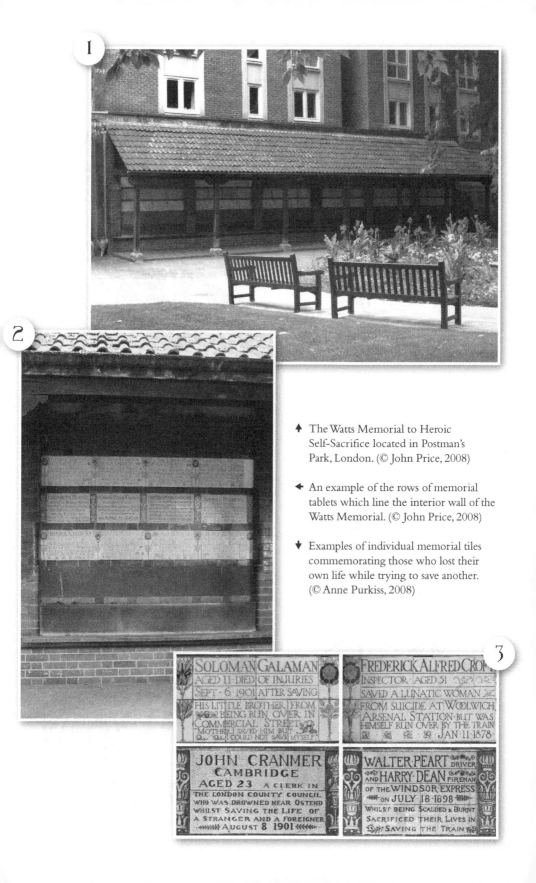

▲ The Watts Memorial to Heroic Self-Sacrifice located in Postman's Park, London. (© John Price, 2008)

◀ An example of the rows of memorial tablets which line the interior wall of the Watts Memorial. (© John Price, 2008)

▼ Examples of individual memorial tiles commemorating those who lost their own life while trying to save another. (© Anne Purkiss, 2008)

SOLOMAN GALAMAN
AGED 11 DIED OF INJURIES
SEPT · 6 · 1901 AFTER SAVING
HIS LITTLE BROTHER FROM
BEING RUN OVER IN
COMMERCIAL STREET
MOTHER I SAVED HIM BUT
I COULD NOT SAVE MYSELF

FREDERICK ALFRED CROFT
INSPECTOR · AGED 31
SAVED A LUNATIC WOMAN
FROM SUICIDE AT WOOLWICH
ARSENAL STATION BUT WAS
HIMSELF RUN OVER BY THE TRAIN
· JAN · 11 · 1878 ·

JOHN CRANMER
CAMBRIDGE
AGED 23 A CLERK IN
THE LONDON COUNTY COUNCIL
WHO WAS DROWNED NEAR OSTEND
WHILST SAVING THE LIFE OF
A STRANGER AND A FOREIGNER
AUGUST 8 1901

WALTER PEART DRIVER
AND HARRY DEAN FIREMAN
OF THE WINDSOR EXPRESS
ON JULY 18 1898
WHILST BEING SCALDED & BURNT
SACRIFICED THEIR LIVES IN
SAVING THE TRAIN

 Newspaper portraits of (clockwise from top left):
Henry Dean, Walter Peart, Robert Wright and Thomas Griffin.
(*City Press*, 1898; *Lloyd's Weekly* 1893; *Lloyd's Weekly*, 1899)

⬆ Newspaper portrait of Samuel Rabbeth and a photograph of his grave in Old Barnes Cemetery, SW13. (*Illustrated London News*, 1884: © John Price, 2013)

➡ The memorial to men who died at the Three Mills Distillery, located on Three Mills Green, Newham, E3. (© John Price, 2013)

⬇ The memorial plaque commemorating four of the five men who died at the East Ham Sewage Works in 1895. (Newham Heritage Services)

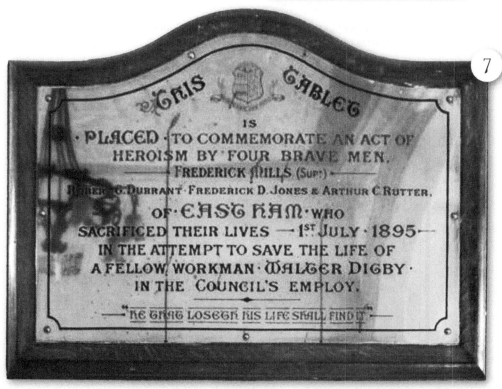

THIS TABLET IS PLACED TO COMMEMORATE AN ACT OF HEROISM BY FOUR BRAVE MEN, FREDERICK MILLS (Supt) HERBERT G DURRANT FREDERICK D JONES & ARTHUR C RUTTER, OF EAST HAM WHO SACRIFICED THEIR LIVES — 1ST JULY 1895 — IN THE ATTEMPT TO SAVE THE LIFE OF A FELLOW WORKMAN WALTER DIGBY IN THE COUNCIL'S EMPLOY. "HE THAT LOSETH HIS LIFE SHALL FIND IT"

▲ The grave of William Freer Lucas in the churchyard of Christ Church, Shamley Green, Surrey. (© John Price, 2013)

▲ Newspaper illustration depicting two heroic acts undertaken by John Clinton. (*Illustrated Police News*, 1894)

▼ Newspaper illustration of the funeral of John Clinton. (*Illustrated Police News*, 1894)

⬆ The graves of Herbert McConaghey, Havelock McGeorge and Charles Binney in the churchyard of St George's church in Georgeham, Devon. (© John Price, 2013)

➡ Police Constable Alfred Smith and his wife May. (© Robert Jeffries, reproduced with permission)

⬆ Memorial plaque commemorating police constables George Greenoff and Sidney Newbury. (Newham Heritage and Archives, Godfrey Collection)

▲ Newspaper illustration of the sinking of the SS *Stella* and (inset) the stewardess Mary Rogers. (*Illustrated London News*, 1900)

✦ A stained-glass window, located in the Lady chapel of Liverpool Anglican Cathedral, depicting the stewardess Mary Rogers. (© John Price, 2009)

✦ Newspaper portrait of Alice Ayres. (*Illustrated London News*, 1885)

▼ On the left, the grave of Walter Peart in Kensal Green Cemetery, W10 and on the right, the grave of Henry Dean in Dawlish Cemetery in Devon. (© John Price, 2013)

FUNERAL OF FORD THE HEROIC FIREMAN

↑ Newspaper illustration of the funeral of fireman Joseph Ford. (*Illustrated Police News*, 1871)

→ The memorial drinking fountain commemorating Alice Denman and Arthur Regelous located in Museum Gardens, Bethnal Green, E2. (© John Price, 2008)

↓ Memorial plaque commemorating John Cambridge located in the English church in Ostend, Belgium. (© Helen Simpson, reproduced with permission)

IN·LOVING·MEMORY·OF
JOHN·CRANMER·CAMBRIDGE
AGED·23·WHO·WAS·DROWNED
AT·OSTEND·AUG·8·1901·WHILE
RESCUING·A·STRANGER

BLESSED·ARE·THE·PURE·IN·HEART
FOR·THEY·SHALL·SEE·GOD

PLATELAYERS AND FLAGMEN

If engine drivers and firemen were, metaphorically, the high-profile 'jockeys' of the iron horse, then railway labourers, platelayers and engineers were akin to grooms, blacksmiths and stable hands; the backroom staff who kept the beast fed and watered, as well as ensuring its safe passage from A to B. These men were absolutely essential to the running of the railways but, as with all supporting roles, the railway-travelling public seldom had cause to acknowledge or recognise the contributions of the labourers, despite often seeing them working beside the tracks. The manual workers of the railways were very much the unsung heroes of the transport system; or at least they were until they did something perceived to be genuinely heroic.

The two railway labourers who feature on the Watts Memorial were both in their sixties when they died and both had spent much of their working lives as unskilled labourers across a range of industries. Neither of them was a born-and-bred Londoner and both came to the capital from rural backgrounds where agriculture had traditionally been the largest employer of men. The railway companies, looking to build a steadfast and effective manual workforce, tended to recruit from both the armed forces, where men were accustomed to strict discipline, and agricultural labour, where strength and physical fitness were paramount. Furthermore, as various factors including industrialisation and urbanisation pushed and pulled increasing numbers of people from the countryside to the towns, there was a ready supply of men eager to swap their low-paid jobs in the fields for better-paid employment as 'public servants' on the railways.

One such man was **William Goodrum**, the son of James and Frances Goodrum, who was born in the village of Saham Toney near Thetford in Norfolk in around 1820. William was the first of the couple's eight children and not a great deal can be discovered about his childhood.[287] James Goodrum was an agricultural labourer and so family life would have very much followed the seasons: periods of high employment and good income in the spring and autumn, but little work and meagre earnings through the winter months. Aside from the low pay, the seasonality of agricultural labour was another drawback, but for many there was little alternative.

Consequently, by 1841 the 20-year-old William was, like his father, working as an agricultural labourer and he had moved out of the overcrowded family home to lodge with John Grass and his family in the nearby village of Stanford. On 15 December 1844, William married Caroline Corston, the daughter of Charles and Ann Corston, in Swaffham in Norfolk, and by 1851 the couple were living in the 'Steward's Lodge' in Langford with their first child, Elijah, born in 1845. The couple had a second child, Deborah, in 1851 while still living in Langford, but with extra mouths to feed and increasingly limited opportunities for work, the family decided to leave Norfolk for a new and hopefully more prosperous life in London.

They initially settled at 9 Warrington Place in Poplar, and William quickly found work as a coal labourer. By the mid-1860s, four more children had arrived and so the family moved to larger accommodation at 4a Lion Street in Poplar.[288] In 1874, tragedy struck the Goodrum family when Deborah, aged just 22, died and it was shortly after this that William joined the North London Railway Company. He was employed as a labourer, but by that time he was in his mid-fifties so there was a limit to the physical work he could undertake. His age, though, put him at some advantage and his maturity equipped him for more responsible jobs involving supervision and safety. A typical role for William was 'flagman', which involved working alongside groups of labourers and keeping watch for approaching trains so that the men could be warned and, if necessary, move out of the way. It was not a physical job, but it was a necessary and crucial one as the flagman was responsible for keeping the men safe in what was a very dangerous environment.

When William arrived for work on Saturday, 28 February 1880, he was instructed to take a group of labourers up to the iron bridge that crossed the Kingsland Road in Hackney and act as flagman for them while they cleaned the gutters.[289] The men trudged to their destination and, as they began work, William surveyed the four lines that passed over the bridge. At about 1.30 p.m., William saw, in the distance, an approaching train that was on the same tracks as the men and so he signalled to them to clear out of the way. Most of the men clambered into the safety of the '6ft way', the space between the lines, but one, his head down and intent on his work, did not see the signal and remained on the tracks.

As the train sped on and rattled towards the labourer, William ran towards him, shouting and waving his arms to attract the attention of both the worker and the engine driver, who might be able to apply his brakes. The labourer remained oblivious until Goodrum was almost upon him and then, suddenly realising his predicament, he scrambled to his feet and threw himself out of the path of the train; William, though, being older and slower, was unable to get clear. Although the driver was braking, he could not stop the engine in time and watched in horror as one of the front buffers ploughed into the flagman, knocking him to the ground beside the tracks. As the train ground to a halt, several labourers ran over to Goodrum, but it was immediately clear from his injuries that the blow had been a fatal one. William Goodrum was dead; struck by a train while warning another man that his life was in danger.

The inquest into Goodrum's death was held at the Lord Truro pub in Dalston Lane, Hackney, on 2 March 1880 and the inquest jury recorded a verdict of 'accidental death'.[290] Very little was said of Goodrum's actions and there was certainly no inference that he had performed heroically. Unlike the case of Peart and Dean, nobody wrote poetry about Goodrum, or raised a subscription for his widow and, until his name appeared on the Watts Memorial in 1905, he passed by as just another worker among hundreds who was killed on the railways that year. It is possible that William's employers, the North London Railway Company, awarded a pension to his widow, Caroline, as she did not remarry and in 1891 she was living alone at 20 Cobden Street in Bromley, where she was described as an 'annuitant', suggesting that she was in receipt of some sort of financial support. Caroline died in Streatham in 1910 aged 87, but how and why she came to be living there is unclear.

William and Caroline's eldest son, Elijah, initially worked as a dock labourer and then as an engineer. On 24 June 1866 he married Jane Daven at St Mary's in Bromley and the couple had their first child, Jane junior, in 1867. Over the next fifteen years the couple had five more children and lived in the Lambeth area, where Elijah began working as a steam-engine driver on a tugboat.[291] By 1901, Elijah and his family had moved to 9 Nelson Street in Bromley, a few houses down the road from the home of his brother George, where his mother was also living. Elijah and Jane both died in Poplar; Jane, aged 84, in 1926 and Elijah, aged 88, in 1933.

The rest of William and Caroline's children all went on to enjoy relatively full lives and lived to good ages. Their son, William Edward, worked as a steam tugboat engine driver with his brother Elijah and in 1884 he married Emmeline Salisbury. The couple had seven children and lived in the Southwark area until 1903 when Emmeline died at the age of 41.[292] William remarried to a widow, Alice Susan Gaze, in 1904 and the couple had at least three children of their own. Alice and William both died in Southwark; Alice, aged 60, in 1929 and William, aged 81, in 1940.

The couple's youngest son, Charles, found work as a shop boy before joining 'E' division of the Metropolitan Police in 1884. On 10 March 1899 at St John's church in Poplar, Charles married Alice Jane Broan, the daughter of a tradesman, and in 1901 they were living at 14 Ravenscroft Buildings in Bethnal Green. The couple did not have any children and Alice died in 1909. On 5 June 1910 Charles then married Florence Gertrude Price, the daughter of an engine driver, at St Matthews in Stepney. At around the same time, Charles retired from the Metropolitan Police and his service of twenty-five years entitled him to a pension. Charles and Florence did not have any children and in 1911 they were living alone at 48 Hind Street in Poplar. Florence Goodrum died, aged 52, in Hackney in 1931 and Charles followed fifteen years later in 1946, aged 79.

Caroline Goodrum junior worked as a domestic servant and, in 1871, was employed by Charles Willis, a coffee house owner, at 311 Poplar High Street. On Christmas Day 1875, Caroline married James Barnett, the son of a labourer, at the church of St John the Evangelist in Lambeth. The couple raised a family of six, during which time they lived in Lambeth, Bromley and West Ham.[293] Caroline Barnett died, aged 75, in West Ham in 1930. Charlotte Goodrum married George Durdant Pead, a lighterman, in West Ham in 1875 and the couple had two children, George William (b. 1876) and Robert Edward (b. 1878). In 1881, the family was living at 2 Emily Terrace in Ford Street West Ham. By 1891 they had moved to 17 Windsor Road in East Ham, and by 1901 to 146 New Barn Street in Canning Town. Charlotte died, aged 87, in Essex in 1946.

One of the many remarkable things about the Watts Memorial is that it represents a portal into the past and provides opportunities to discover more about the everyday lives of otherwise ordinary people. Each memorial tablet records the sudden and dramatic death of the individual, but it also alludes to the life they led, often providing information about how old they were, where they lived and what they did for a living. It is these narrative elements which really give the memorial its innate charm and stand it apart from the more straightforward monuments which just record dates of birth and death. All that said, there is a great deal about the individuals that the tablets do not document and, as the studies in this book demonstrate, the lives they led were not always straightforward or conventional.

A really good example of this is **Daniel Pemberton**, who is remembered on the memorial for hurling his mate out of the path of an oncoming train. The tablet records that Daniel was a 61-year-old foreman, working for the London and South Western Railway Company (LSWR), and that he died on 17 January 1903. But there was much more to Daniel Pemberton than this and there had been quite a lot of twists and turns in his life that are not revealed in Watts' short narrative about him.

Daniel was born in South Stoke in Oxfordshire and was the son of Stephen and Fanny Pemberton. Daniel's father was an agricultural labourer and he married Fanny Cooper in 1833. Their first child, James, was born soon after and he was followed by George (b. 1834, d. 1845), Vincent (b. 1837) and Stephen (b. 1839). Daniel was born in 1842 and then Alfred (b. 1844) and another George (b. 1849). The couple certainly had other children, including Samuel (b. 1854), but it is difficult to trace all of Daniel's siblings. Stephen and Fanny lived in and around South Stoke for their entire lives; Fanny died, aged 63, in 1880, while Stephen lived to the remarkable age of 96 and died in 1907.

By 1871, Daniel had moved to Whitton in Middlesex, where he was working as a railway porter. He was lodging with a widow, Jane Green, and her five children, including her 10-year-old daughter, Alice, and her 5-year-old son, George.[294] Romance, or at least something akin to it, must have blossomed between Daniel and Jane and they married in Windsor in 1873, Jane being 15 years older than her new husband. Daniel effectively adopted Jane's youngest son, George, and by 1881 the three of them were living together on the Whitton Road with Daniel working as a railway labourer and George doing some labouring work to contribute to the household economy.

Daniel then suffered two dreadful losses in a relatively short space of time. In 1887, George died aged just 21 and three years later the age gap between Jane and Daniel caught up with them when Jane died at the age of 66. Suddenly, Daniel went from being a happily married family man to being a widower living alone at Holly Bush Corner in Whitton.

Meanwhile, Jane's only daughter, Alice, had been working as a domestic servant in and around Ealing and Hounslow. She was, effectively, Daniel's stepdaughter, but something more must have developed between them following her mother's death and in 1893 the couple married in Brentford. This time the age gap was reversed, with Daniel being nineteen years older than Alice, but despite this, the couple started a family with Ada being born in 1893 and then twins Alice junior and Daniel junior in 1895. Alice junior, however, did not survive infancy and died the following year. In 1901, the family was living at 8 Railway Cottages in Whitton, which was the last home that Daniel Pemberton would know before his death in 1903.

It was 17 January 1903, to be precise, and on that Saturday Daniel and another labourer, Thomas Harwood, had been dispatched to a stretch of the line near the west Twickenham signal box to gauge the tracks.[295] This involved carefully measuring the '3ft way' between the two rails and making adjustments where necessary to ensure that everything was correctly aligned. It was a relatively commonplace maintenance task, but one which required a certain amount of concentration, close observation and attention to detail. Pemberton was measuring while Hudson adjusted, but there were some trains shunting nearby, making a lot of noise, so the two men were working closely together and having to shout their instructions.

All of a sudden, Thomas was aware of Daniel quickly jumping to his feet and, before Harwood knew what was happening, Pemberton had pushed him heavily and sharply on the chest, sending him toppling off the tracks and into the '6ft way' beside the lines. Before Harwood could catch his breath, there was the deafening noise of an approaching train, which thundered at high speed along the very tracks that, seconds earlier, the two men had been measuring. As the clouds of smoke and steam slowly cleared, Thomas got to his feet and looked around for Daniel, who was nowhere to be seen. Cautiously walking back to where they had been working, Hudson spotted Pemberton lying face down on the opposite side of the tracks, so he ran to him and rolled him over.

A few minutes earlier, Inspector Batten of the LSWR had been making his way along the trackside to the signals when he had noticed Hudson and Pemberton working on the line. Batten thought little of it and, as he had a nasty cold, he hurried on to get into the warmth of the signal box. He had walked on for about 30 or 40yds when, in the distance, he noticed an approaching express train and realised with panic that it was on the same line as the men. The inspector turned back and tried to shout a warning to Hudson and Pemberton, but he was hoarse from his cold and could not make himself heard. Batten began waving frantically and he saw Pemberton get up and push Hudson out of the way of the approaching locomotive. At that point, Batten was enveloped in the steam from the passing train and did not see exactly what happened to Daniel.

When Hudson reached him, Pemberton appeared to be dead; he had a large gash on his shoulder as well as a raw crimson welt on the side and back of his head. Hudson called for help and some of the men who were shunting the trains came over. Batten soon arrived and more help was summoned, but everyone agreed it seemed a hopeless cause as no signs of life could be detected. Hudson explained to Batten that he had not heard the approaching train whistle, although it may well have done and the noise from the shunting masked it. He said he had also not heard the inspector calling and the first he knew of the approaching train was when Pemberton pushed him out of the way. Within an hour, a Constable Brown arrived and, examining the body, agreed that Pemberton was dead and made arrangements to have the body removed to the mortuary to await an inquest.

It was Reginald Kemp, the deputy coroner for west Middlesex, who convened the inquest, which was held at the Wesleyan Schools on Queen's Road in Whitton on 20 January 1903.[296] Various witnesses gave evidence, including Batten, Hudson, Brown and the engine driver of the train, whose surname was Stone. Stone told the court that he had not seen the men at all and the first he knew of the incident was when he arrived at Waterloo and was informed by station staff. He reported that, according to regulations, he had blown his whistle as he passed the Twickenham signal box and that there was a lot of smoke and steam at the time, which was probably why he had not seen the men. He had examined the front of the engine and found no marks, but concluded that Pemberton could not anyway have been hit head-on by it, as 'they were travelling at nearly forty miles an hour and he would in that case have been knocked to pieces'. It was more likely that Pemberton had been part of the way off the tracks and had been struck a glancing blow, which would account for the wounds on his head and shoulder.

After hearing all the evidence, the inquest jury returned a verdict of 'accidental death' and added that 'great credit was due to [the] deceased for his action'. They also expressed their sympathy with Alice Pemberton, Daniel's widow, and the coroner formally released the body for burial before closing proceedings. Four days later, on 24 January 1903, Daniel was buried in a family plot in Twickenham Cemetery,

Whitton, along with his first wife, Jane, his stepson, George, and his infant daughter from his second marriage, Alice. There is no evidence that a headstone was ever erected and, if one was, it has not survived as the grave is unmarked. As with Goodrum, there was little fanfare over the death of Pemberton and no recognition of his actions until 1908 when his tablet was installed on the Watts Memorial.

By 1911, Daniel's wife Alice and their two children had moved to 97 Wellington Road in Hounslow; Daniel junior, aged 15, was working as a house boy and Ada, aged 17, as a general servant. It is interesting that neither of the children took up employment with the LSWR, as would have been the case in years before. The practice of avoiding responsibility for dead and injured workers in that manner had been largely prevented through legislation such as the 1880 Employer's Liability Act and the Workmen's Compensation Act of 1897. Alice Pemberton, Daniel's second wife, died in 1920, aged 59. Neither of the couple's children appear to have married or had families of their own; their daughter, Ada, died in Hounslow in 1986, aged 92, and their son, Daniel junior, also died in Hounslow in 1976 at the age of 80.

In the hierarchy of railway employees, the 'aristocracy of labour' were very much the engine drivers and firemen, with labourers, platelayers and engineers coming far lower down the pecking order, despite the industry being built and maintained by their efforts. These gradations also appear to have carried through to the manner in which people were recognised and commemorated for heroism, with some workers being accorded a higher level of respect and admiration than others. It is interesting that even the Amalgamated Society of Railway Servants appears to have subscribed to that position, being quick to memorialise the heroism of Peart and Dean but not the actions of Goodrum or Pemberton.

All four men were railway servants and all four faced dangers on a day-to-day basis, so they should arguably have been accorded the same level of respect and admiration for their actions. It could even be argued that both Goodrum and Pemberton directly saved a man's life, whereas the evidence suggests that the train driven by Peart would have coasted safely to a halt whether the brake had been applied or not, and there is not really any evidence that Dean acted in an especially heroic manner. Both men died in the course of doing their jobs, which was terrible and lamentable, but it was the manner in which their deaths were exemplified by the press and the public, on the basis of their roles rather than their actions, which made them into 'heroes'. Fortunately, the incidents featuring Goodrum and Pemberton found their way to Watts, the two men gained the recognition they deserved on his memorial and, from that, we can gain some insight into their lives as well as their deaths.

15

ONE
UNDER

As the previous two chapters have demonstrated, working on trains and maintaining the tracks upon which they ran were dangerous occupations and hundreds of employees were killed each year. Railways, though, presented a range of hazards to all of those who came into contact with them, and it should be remembered that, up until the late nineteenth century, steam locomotion was relatively new technology that people did not always fully understand or appreciate. Vehicles travelling at speeds of between 40 and 60mph were a revelation, but they were also unfamiliar and often people could not judge the speed and distance of an approaching train or just did not comprehend how the system worked. Stories of mishaps included a man who had been trying to impress his friends by walking on a rail like a tightrope and had failed to notice a train approaching from behind, and the three passengers who had impatiently walked up the track to find out where their train was and were hit by a service coming the other way. People often tried to get on or off trains while they were still moving, and trespassing on the tracks, both criminal and unintentional, was a frequent occurrence.[297]

In terms of maintaining safety on the railways, all employees were seen as being accountable and this extended from the labourers who repaired the rails up to the drivers who conveyed the passengers and everyone in between; they were all railway 'servants' and they should all do their utmost to protect the passengers they served. This, of course, had some bearing on notions of heroism, and quite often members of railway staff were denied or refused decorations or awards for life-risking bravery because they were deemed to have been responsible for the life they had saved. In such cases, reasons including 'he was a railway servant and not an ordinary member of the public' and 'in removing the passenger in question he was merely carrying out his duty' were common reasons for refusal.[298] These judgements were often levelled at the men who worked at the stations, such as porters, signalmen, booking office staff or ticket inspectors, as they were the ones called upon to go onto the tracks to help people who had fallen from the platforms. In the case of these men, if they were to be recognised or commemorated for their bravery, they had to go over and above what were deemed to be the usual responsibilities of the job; they literally had to put their life on the line.

The individual recorded on the Watts Memorial as Frederick Croft was actually **Frederick Alfred Craft**, who was born in Enfield in Middlesex in 1848. Frederick's father, also Frederick, was a farmer who worked 16 acres in the Scotland Green area of Ponders End. Frederick senior married a widow, Elizabeth Kent (formerly Newman), in Edmonton in 1841 and the couple's first child, Thomas George, was born in 1843. Frederick Alfred arrived in 1848 and was followed by Henry Jennings (b. 1850) and Daniel Newman (b. 1854). By 1861, the family had left the farm and moved to Westenhanger in Kent where Frederick senior was working as a railway porter. When Frederick died in Elham in Kent in 1884 aged 66, Elizabeth moved in with her son, Thomas, at 8 Croft Road in Ashford in Kent; she died fourteen years later in 1898 at the age of 85.

Frederick Alfred Craft left the family home in his teens and, in 1871, was lodging with Mr and Mrs Betten at Eltham Lodge House in Lewisham. Frederick entered the employment of the South Eastern Railway Company and initially worked as a guard on the north Kent line. Around the same time, he met Elizabeth Jarret Phillips and the two were married in Southwark in 1872. Their first child, Frederick Thomas, was born in 1873 and their second, William Harry, in 1875. Both boys were baptised at St Mary Magdalene church in Woolwich, as the family was living nearby at Warwick Street. They were still living at the same address in January 1878, by which time Frederick senior had been promoted to an inspector and was based at Woolwich Arsenal Station. It was a good step up for Frederick and a well-paid job that would allow him to look after his family; the irony was that, had he remained a guard, he would probably have lived to see his family grow up.

Eliza Newman, a widow whose husband had worked at the Woolwich Arsenal, had resided in and around Woolwich for many years and was a well-known figure in the area. Although she suffered from delusions, Eliza was considered to be 'a perfectly harmless lunatic' and was generally allowed to live outside of an institution. On 9 January 1878, Eliza was found wandering the streets of Woolwich, despite the fact that she was supposed to be living in Worthing at the time, and so she was taken to the Union Workhouse in Tewson Road.[299] Upon admission, Eliza's delusional behaviour was noted and so a poor-law relieving officer named Joseph Moore took her to the workhouse infirmary to be examined by Dr Thomas Baker. However, Baker said he could find no indications of insanity and declined to take Newman to the police court to have her committed. Moore, unhappy with this diagnosis, said that *he* would take Eliza to the court but that he would require two female nurses to accompany him; a request that Baker denied. However, a matron in the infirmary, Sarah Wilkinson, volunteered to go with Moore and so arrangements were made to attend court on 11 January.

Proceedings at the court were swift and the police physician, Dr Sharp, concluding that Newman was 'of unsound mind, though neither suicidal nor dangerous to others', licensed her to be immediately committed to the Kent County Asylum at Barming Heath near Maidstone. Moore and Wilkinson were assigned responsibility for transporting Newman to the asylum and so they got a Hackney carriage to Woolwich Arsenal, arriving at the station just before 5 p.m. When transporting mental patients or prisoners by train, it was common practice, for the safety of the other passengers, for the party to travel in a single locked compartment. Thus, on arrival at Woolwich, Moore went to look for the stationmaster to make the arrangements and purchase the tickets, while Wilkinson stayed with Newman.

There was no waiting room at the station, so the two women stood on the platform and Wilkinson discreetly kept hold of Eliza's coat to stop her from walking around. Around 5.30 p.m., just as the train to Plumstead was approaching the station, the patient suddenly pulled away from the matron with a wrench so violent that it tore Eliza's coat, and as Wilkinson stared blankly at the torn piece of material in her hand, Newman leapt from the platform onto the rails and into the path of the oncoming engine. Frederick Craft, who was on the platform, saw Newman on the tracks and, with the train bearing down on her, he too jumped down onto the permanent way with the intention of grabbing the woman before she was struck.

In the cab of the engine, the fireman, William Healy, saw a dark shape or object fall from the platform, and just as he realised it was a woman, he heard the engine driver, Thomas Rowell, exclaim 'Whoah!' as he reached for the whistle and the brake. The object then continued across the rails and into the 6ft way between the two tracks, so Healy called back, 'It's ok; she's out of our way.' Just at that moment, another figure, this time a man, appeared about 5yds in front of the engine and tried to cross the track, but before Rowell could do anything, the offside buffer of the train struck the gentleman, knocking him to the ground beneath the train. 'We've caught the inspector!' cried Rowell, who immediately applied the brake and slammed the engine into reverse, which quickly halted the vehicle. The driver and fireman then climbed down from the cab and walked back along the train, looking underneath for the man they had hit. Healy could hear moaning and, peering between a pair of wheels, he saw Craft lying on the ground and close by, but detached, a lower portion of the inspector's leg and foot. While Healy tried to help Craft and Rowell went to fetch help, Eliza Newman watched on from her position of safety between the tracks.

When Craft was eventually extricated from under the train, he was laid on a makeshift stretcher and lifted up onto the platform. A Dr Small, the Principal Medical

Officer at the nearby Woolwich Garrison, happened to be at the station and he assessed the extent of Frederick's injuries; both of his legs had been severed, one above the knee and the other below, his left arm was 'crushed to pieces from top to bottom' and he had many cuts to his face and head. Small quietly told the stationmaster that Craft's injuries were undoubtedly fatal, but that they should get him to the nearest hospital where he could, at least, be made comfortable and receive something for the pain. Craft was taken by train to Plumstead and then conveyed to the Woolwich Union Infirmary, from which, just hours earlier, Eliza Newman had left for her court appearance. Thomas Baker, the doctor who had judged her to be of sound mind, was the attending physician when Craft arrived and, as Dr Small had suspected, there was nothing that could be done to save the inspector. At around 9.30 p.m. on 11 January 1878, Frederick Craft died as a result of blood loss and shock to the system.

The Lord Derby pub in Woolwich was the venue for the inquest into Craft's death and it was convened on 15 January amidst much interest and with capacity attendance.[300] Charles Carttar, the coroner for Kent, presided over the lengthy proceedings and heard evidence from many witnesses. Charles Batholomew, the stationmaster, told the court that the train was formed of sixteen carriages, about twelve of which had passed over the inspector before it came to a halt. Healy, the fireman, confirmed this but added that there was no way the train could have been stopped any quicker. Sarah Wilkinson told the jury that she had hold of Newman's coat but the patient broke free so violently that the matron was left with a torn piece of fabric in her hand. Wilkinson added that she did then try to grab Eliza with her other hand but a lad on the platform had got in her way. Dr Small, who accompanied Frederick on the train journey to the infirmary, said that Craft was perfectly sober at the time and appeared to be a steady, respectable man. When Small visited Frederick at about 7 p.m., he found him to be 'quite sensible, talking about his wife, children and parents as well as the accident, stating that he jumped off to save the woman, but did not know the train was so near'.

Joseph Moore gave an account of his actions at the time of the incident and then told the court that he, Wilkinson and Newman had continued by train to the asylum at Barming Heath after Craft had been taken to hospital. On the journey, Newman had told him that 'she was very sorry she had jumped too far because she wanted the train to go over her body; she only wished it had been her instead of the man'. Moore told the jury that, in his opinion, Newman's intention had been to commit suicide and 'being a very light woman she had jumped too far and cleared the line in one bound'.

Thomas Baker was firmly questioned by the jury about his role in failing to correctly diagnose Newman's insanity and his refusal to provide Moore with sufficient attendants for the journey. Baker was rather dismissive in his responses, maintaining that Newman had been 'rational and gave clear answers' during his assessment of her and that he had seen nothing to warrant certifying her as insane. He also added that, as the decision to transfer the patient to the asylum had been made outside the infirmary, it was not his responsibility to provide attendants, and as 'Mr Moore brought her and took her away, he did not consider her [Newman] to be under his [Baker's] care at all'. Baker gruffly concluded his testimony by saying that Moore often took lunatics to Maidstone and was in the habit of finding his own attendants.

In summing up, the coroner stated that 'it was manifest that the deceased had lost his life through his courage, boldness and good feeling in endeavouring to save another' and that, although Moore should have been firmer about the number of attendants, neither he nor Wilkinson could be held criminally responsible for the incident. The inquest jury returned a verdict of 'killed in attempting to save the life of a lunatic who had thrown herself on the line' and the foreman added that, in future, it was hoped that 'the most careful preparations would be made for removing lunatics'. The jury also encouraged the public to recognise the gallantry of the deceased by providing for his widow and children through the subscription fund that Bartholomew the stationmaster had opened. The fund had already received donations to the value of £24 2s, including £20 from the South Eastern Railway Company, and the jurors all agreed to donate their fee, which came to £3 8s. With that, the coroner thanked everyone for their time and the inquest closed.

Frederick Craft was laid to rest in the churchyard of St Thomas' church on Woodland Terrace in Woolwich on 19 January 1878. One report described how, 'A large concourse of people, including many railway servants, attended the funeral last Saturday afternoon.' At the conclusion of the ceremony, the Rev. A. Morris, rector, delivered an address at the grave, 'speaking of the circumstances under which the deceased lost his life in the action of saving a fellow creature and of the lesson to be learnt from his example and his sudden death'.[301] Craft was the first to be buried in the purchased plot, intended to serve his whole family, and an impressive headstone was erected and inscribed 'in loving memory of Frederick A. Craft whose life was taken by saving another on January 11th 1878 aged 31 years'. Around twenty-four years later, the body of Frederick's wife was also interred in the grave and the following inscription added to the headstone, 'Also of Elizabeth Rastin, wife of the above, who died August 5th 1902 aged 52 years. Until the day break and the shadows flee away'.

Following Frederick's sudden and untimely death, Elizabeth Craft found herself alone with two small children and no means of support beyond the subscription fund that had been collected in honour of her husband's conduct. Consequently, Elizabeth married Charles Rastin, a railway clerk, on 17 July 1880 at All Saints church in Rotherhithe. In 1881, Charles, Elizabeth and Frederick's two sons, Frederick junior and William, were living at Bangor House in Charlton with Charles' parents, Robert and Mary Rastin. The children were recorded as Robert's grandsons and with the surname Rastin. However, in 1891, when the family had moved to 3 The Pavement on the main road in Mottingham in Kent, Frederick and William were recorded with the surname Craft and listed as Charles' stepsons.

By this time, Charles Rastin had left the railway company to run a tobacconist and the couple had two children of their own, Mary Elizabeth (b. 1883) and Charles (b. 1886). Charles Rastin senior died in 1896 at the age of just 49 and Elizabeth once again found herself widowed with two reasonably young children. Five years later, the family of three were living at 5 Devonshire Road in Mottingham with 18-year-old Mary working as a laundry maid and 15-year-old Charles employed as a builder's clerk, both supporting their mother. A little more than a year later, in August 1902, Elizabeth died at the age of 53. Although she had subsequently remarried, Elizabeth was buried with Frederick in the churchyard of St Thomas' in Woolwich, presumably because of a prior arrangement when they were married.

Frederick and Elizabeth's eldest son, Frederick junior, initially followed his father and his stepfather into employment on the railways, working as a clerk in his late teens and early twenties. He was probably offered the post in lieu of compensation for his father's death, as was common practice with railway companies. Frederick then moved to the north-west of England and in 1900 he married Mary Ann Matilda Haworth in Carlisle. Shortly after this, the couple moved to Wigton (in what was then Cumberland) and Frederick was recorded working as a teacher of wood carving; something of a departure from a career on the railways. Their first child, Mabel, was born in 1901, but her birth was registered in Bromley rather than Wigton, which suggests the couple may have been staying with family at the time; the birth of their second child, Dorothy Mary, in 1905 was registered back in Wigton.

In 1911, Frederick and Mary Ann were recorded as living with their two children at 10 Victoria Road in Whitehaven, and Frederick was working as a 'superintendent of manual instruction'. The couple appear to have had at least three more children and then Mary Ann died in the Carlisle area in 1928.[302] In 1946, in his early seventies, Frederick appears to have married Janet Marion Macfarlane, who was in her early forties, and the couple enjoyed seventeen years together before Frederick died, aged 90, at 12 Strawberry Terrace in Edentown near Carlisle on 24 July 1963. His estate of £1,275 passed to his widow, Janet.

William Harry, Frederick's younger son, appears to have travelled quite extensively outside the UK. In October 1907 he left Scotland on the SS *Grampian* and on 3 November the same year he arrived at Quebec in Canada. In 1913, he departed from New Brunswick in Canada and sailed on the *Empress of Ireland* to Liverpool, arriving on 8 May 1913. On 3 January 1914 he sailed for New York on the ill-fated SS *Lusitania*, arriving later the same month. In 1925 he arrived back in the UK aboard the SS *Intaba*, which had sailed from the West Indies. He lived in Scotland for some years before, in 1937, travelling to Canada and back upon the SS *Ausonia*. He also appears to have travelled to the West Indies again in 1940. He was still alive in 1968, living at Spylaw Bank Road in Monklaw, Midlothian, but after that the trail goes cold, so he may, once again, have left Britain and then died overseas.

With railways being so heavily used by the public, it stands to reason that passengers were also exposed to some of the risks faced by employees; although, of course, ticket-holders were precious cargo and companies strove to keep customer casualties to an absolute minimum. There was, it must be said, a rather macabre irony that the opening of the world's first steam-pulled twin-tracked railway on 15 September 1830 was also the occasion of the first official passenger fatality, when the hapless MP William Huskisson was run over by George Stephenson's engine *Rocket*.[303] Generally speaking, though, trains were a relatively safe form of transport, particularly for those who used them sensibly and soberly; which was not, however, always the case.

It was just gone 11 p.m. on Monday, 23 September 1878 and at Richmond Old Station in Surrey a number of people waiting on the concourse for their train to arrive were watching in amusement as a drunken man wandered aimlessly and unsteadily back and forth along the platform.[304] Taking one step back for every two steps forward, the man, John Charles Jepson, was clearly much the worse for drink and when he stopped to ask Thomas Darnill for a match to light a cigarette, he admitted to being 'a little tipsy'. Darnill, who was waiting for the 11.25 p.m. train to arrive, had been watching Jepson for about ten minutes but neither he, nor anyone else on the platform, apparently saw the potential danger that the drunken man was placing himself in.

In a cacophony of noise, smoke and steam, the 11.25 p.m. train began to approach the station and, as it drew level with the refreshment room at the far end of the platform, the driver began to ease back the power and started slowing the train to a halt. At that moment, Jepson, who was still staggering around the station, lost his balance and his bearings, and with a reeling motion he put a foot over the edge of the platform and toppled down onto the track in front of the approaching train. The driver, suddenly spotting the hazard, increased the reverse power he was already applying and jammed on the emergency brakes, but as the train gratingly screeched onwards it was clear that it was going to hit Jepson. At that moment, a man on the platform, who had also been watching the drunken antics, ran forward, jumped down to where Jepson was lying and started struggling to try and move him off the tracks. There was, though, no time and no space; the train ploughed on and, to the horror of the bystanders, it rolled over the two men as they tussled on the rails.

The man who jumped onto the rails was **James Hewins**, who was recorded on the Watts Memorial as James Hewers, and there are some things which can be clarified about him. He was reported to be a gardener and on 1 April 1875 he married Susan Smith, the daughter of William Smith, a shoe and boot maker, at St Matthew's church in Kensington. It was William Smith who identified James' body at Richmond Infirmary. James and Susan had a daughter, Emma, born in 1876, and in 1878 they were reported to be living at 2 Derby Villas in East Sheen. James' wedding certificate recorded his age as 31 and his father as being James Hewins, who was also employed as a gardener. Beyond those few facts, it is difficult to say anything absolutely conclusive about James Hewins. The surname 'Hewins' has many variants, including Hewens,

Hewers, Hewings, Ewans, Ewins, Ewings, Yewens and Yewins, so locating the correct individual in the available records is not straightforward. Also, with the incident taking place in 1878, the nearest census was seven years earlier and, with James unmarried at that time, there is little context beyond his father's name to work from.

Although there are some anomalies which are difficult to explain, the most likely candidate is a James Hewins who was born in Alstone in Gloucestershire in 1844. His father was another James Hewins, an agricultural labourer, and his mother was Mary Sorrell, who married in 1842. James was the couple's second child, his elder brother, Charles, having been born in 1843. Two more children followed, John (b. 1847) and Ann (b. 1849), and the family was living in the village in 1851. The next appearance of James Hewins junior, aged 26, was in 1871 when he was recorded as living in Spilsby in Lincolnshire, where he worked as a gardener. If this is indeed the correct James Hewins, which seems likely, it is not entirely clear how or why he came to be living in London in 1875 when he married Susan in Kensington. She and her family were from Hampton in Middlesex, so that would explain the connections with Richmond. Furthermore, if, as reported, James and Susan were living in East Sheen in 1878, it would have made sense for James to be on the platform at Richmond Old Station on 23 September, waiting for a train to take him to either North Sheen or Mortlake Station, which were both within walking distance of his home. The train arrived at Richmond on time, but it was very late leaving again, and James Hewins tragically ended up under it, rather than aboard it.

When the train finally stopped, the driver and several men in the station clambered underneath and found Jepson and Hewins alive, but dreadfully injured. In due course, several constables arrived and, one by one, the wounded men were carefully eased out from beneath the train and taken straight to the nearby Richmond Infirmary in Kew Foot Road. Jepson, who was just 20 years old, arrived at about 11.45 p.m. and when examined by the house surgeon, Dr Ward, he was found to be insensible from drink, part of his left hand had been cut off, and he had sustained a compound fracture of the skull. Hewins arrived at the hospital about twenty minutes after Jepson and was found to be much more seriously injured; he had a broken pelvis, fractures in both thighs, a mangled left leg and several large wounds on his scalp and back. There was little that Dr Ward could do for either man apart from treating the pain and making them as comfortable as possible; James Hewins died at around 3 a.m. on Tuesday, 24 September, and later the same day, John Jepson also passed away from his injuries.

The inquest into the two deaths opened on 27 September at Richmond Infirmary and, in summing up, the coroner remarked that 'all honour was due to the poor man Hewens [*sic*], who, in endeavouring to save the life of a fellow creature, lost his own'.[305] Having heard evidence from numerous witnesses, including Thomas Darnill and Dr Ward, the court concluded that no blame could be attached to anyone and the jury returned verdicts of 'accidental death' in both cases. The bodies were formally released for burial and both men were interred at Mortlake Cemetery; Hewins on

28 September and Jepson two days later. Both appear to have been buried in common ground at the expense of the parish and there is no evidence of a headstone being erected for Hewins. At the conclusion of the inquest, the coroner told the court that 'Hewens [*sic*] had left a widow, and he wished that there were some fund out of which something could be given to her.' There is no evidence, however, that any subscription fund was established.

James Hewins left not only a widow, Susan, but also a 2-year-old daughter, Emma, and after his sudden death they moved in with Susan's parents, William and Mary Smith, who were living at 46 Faraday Street in Southwark. In 1881, Susan and her daughter were both recorded under her maiden name of Smith, and Emma Hewins was described as the 'adopted' daughter of William and Mary. It is not clear if Emma retained the surname Smith, which if she did would make her very difficult to trace, or if she reverted to any of the various different spellings of her birth name. Whichever is the case, she did not continue to live with her mother or her grandparents and, after 1881, she becomes elusive in the records. Susan Hewins did not remarry and by 1891 she was living in Peckham and supporting three children belonging to her sister Sarah, who in 1855 had married John Henry Davey Anthony. By 1901, Susan had moved again and was living in Romford in Essex with Charles Harvey, her half-brother from her mother's first marriage, and his wife, Ann. Another move took Susan back to Peckham where, in 1911, she was living with her sister, Sarah Anthony, who had been widowed in 1894. Susan Hewins lived to the age of 83 and died, a widow, in Camberwell in 1926.

Although the deaths of both Craft and Hewins were recorded as 'accidental', there was certainly a degree of misadventure in the circumstances; both were killed trying to save people who, arguably, should have been prevented from getting onto the railway lines. Had Joseph Moore been given the correct number of attendants, it is likely that Eliza Newman would have been safely conveyed to Barming Heath without incident and Frederick Craft would not have been killed. Likewise, if bystanders had recognised the danger that the drunken John Jepson posed and the possibility that he might fall onto the tracks, perhaps someone would have kept hold of him or at least tried to keep him away from the edge of the platform. It also appears, though, that once Newman and Jepson were on the tracks, the potential for tragedy was exacerbated by both Craft and Hewins being unable to judge the speed of the train and the amount of time before it arrived. It is plausible that they would still have attempted the rescue even if they had known there was high risk of being struck (many people in similar situations did) and the consequences would have been the same. Conversely, with more knowledge and experience of fast-moving transport, they may have been better able to judge the situation and may have realised, particularly in the case of Hewins, that there was little they could do to help, and they would then have become just two more bystanders at railway accidents, rather than everyday heroes.

LONDON'S BURNING

16

FIREMEN OF THE BRIGADE

There cannot be many Londoners who do not recognise the striking red livery and distinctive wailing siren of an engine from the London Fire Brigade (LFB) as it carves its way through the crowded streets of the capital, or the reassuring figure of the skilled and professional firefighter, equipped with the very latest technology and strategically stationed throughout the metropolis to protect and rescue its inhabitants from the threat and danger of fire. The LFB is a single, unified and state-funded body, but the background to its creation reveals a much more complex and haphazard history of fire-fighting provision in London.

Following the Great Fire in 1666, the City and Liberties of London were divided into four areas, each of which was charged with maintaining fifty ladders and 800 leather buckets for the purposes of preventing similar disasters in the future.[306] More effective, though, were the fire brigades established by large insurance companies, including the Alliance, the Globe, the Imperial, the Phoenix and the Sun, which were keen to limit payouts by protecting the increasing number of properties they were insuring against fire.[307] Wall plaques attached to the outside of buildings indicated which company insured them, and in the event of a fire, the brigade belonging to that particular insurer would be dispatched to extinguish it. Although there was some co-operation, perhaps when life was at risk, brigades were largely instructed only to fight fires at their own properties and to leave the others to burn.

These unsavoury standoffs ceased in 1833 when the ten principal companies combined their brigades to form the London Fire Engine Establishment (LFEE). James Braidwood, who had previously been the Firemaster of Edinburgh, was appointed as superintendent and he took charge of around seventy-five men and all of the equipment from the various amalgamated brigades, including fourteen horse-drawn manual pumps and one floating engine for fighting fires at wharfs and docksides.[308] One such fire, at Cotton's Wharf near Tooley Street in June 1861, was particularly disastrous and Braidwood was killed, along with one of his officers, when a wall collapsed on him while he was directing his men. The incident marked something of a turning point in the history of fire prevention, as it pressurised the government into taking control of the service. In 1865, the Metropolitan Fire Brigade Act was passed and the Metropolitan Board of Works took responsibility for a new publicly funded Metropolitan Fire Brigade (MFB), which was established on 1 January 1866.

This new brigade was predominantly comprised of the personnel and equipment from the LFEE, but in 1867 it absorbed another organisation which had been working alongside the LFEE since 1833.[309] The Society for the Protection of Life from Fire (SPLF) was a subscription-funded charity which had established a network of fire escapes across the capital; while the LFEE was occupied with saving property, the SPLF concerned itself with saving life. By 1867, the SPLF had eighty-five 'fire escapes' stationed around central London, which operated at night and were manned by conductors, who then employed the escape once it was pulled to the site of the fire. Between 1844 and 1867 the SPLF was recorded as having saved 1,150 lives and attended 9,304 fires, so it made sense to incorporate it, and its fire escapes, into the new MFB rather than have it continue working alongside.

Both of the firemen commemorated on the Watts Memorial died while operating fire escapes, so it is useful to understand exactly what these machines were and how they worked. The primary function of a fire escape was to evacuate people from upper floors of buildings and this was achieved in two ways. The escape consisted of a long ladder, around 35ft in length, which was fixed at one end to a carriage with two large wheels that effectively allowed the ladder to be pivoted vertically into the air, where it could then be positioned at an angle against the wall of a building. The fireman, or conductor, would then ascend the ladder and either gain access to the building through a window or assist people already at windows to get onto the escape. Strung beneath the full length of the ladder was a canvas trough or tube, reinforced with a mesh of copper wire, which formed a chute into which people could be dropped and quickly slide down to the ground, rather than needing to descend the ladder. Evacuation via the chute was neither elegant nor entirely without hazard, but these SPLF escapes undoubtedly saved lives and that is why they were adopted by the MFB.

London now had its first publicly funded fire brigade, responsible for saving life as well as protecting property, and the chief constable and chief officer of the Belfast Fire Brigade, Captain Eyre Massey Shaw, was appointed as its chief officer. In addition to central London, the brigade now had to cover the whole area of the Metropolitan Board of Works and so the parish vestry engines, which had previously covered outlying areas, were also commandeered into the MFB. By 1875 twenty-nine purpose-built stations had been constructed to extend the service outwards to much of greater London. By this time the MFB was responsible for a population of around 3.5 million Londoners across 120 square miles, and these were protected by a network of forty-nine fire engine stations, 107 fire escape stations and four floating stations, all of which were manned by a total of 400 trained firemen, who were fast becoming recognisable and respected figures on the streets of the city.

Shortly after taking command of the MFB, Captain Shaw replaced the firemen's outdated leather headgear with a striking peaked helmet, fashioned entirely in brass, and he introduced a navy-blue double-breasted tunic with brass buttons to replace the jumble of different uniforms which had persisted in the LFEE. What was generally required in a fireman was physical strength, stamina, dexterity, good judgement and discipline, but characteristics like teamwork, punctuality, honour and good conduct when not on duty were also important, as was the ability to cope with the long antisocial hours and the inherent risks of the job. Ex-seamen of various types were, by far, the most common recruits to the service in its first hundred years; in 1905, only ninety-four of the 1,351 men employed by the brigade did not have a seafaring background.[310] Manual workers, mostly from skilled trades, made up the rest of the rank and file, an added bonus being that those men could fabricate pieces of equipment and help to maintain fire stations.

In fact, all kinds of station work took up a considerable amount of a fireman's time on duty; cleaning the watch-rooms, offices and toilets, maintaining and testing equipment, feeding and mucking out the horses and various administrative tasks were undertaken on top of any call-outs actually to fight fires. It is unsurprising, then, that long hours were one of the main complaints raised by firemen, many of whom were working sixty to seventy hours a week when comparable industrial workers were doing around fifty-six. Generally speaking, firemen were on continuous duty, which meant they could be called out at any time, even when technically 'off duty'. All that said, firemen were well remunerated for the work: a weekly wage of between 24s and 35s, a uniform allowance, subsidised accommodation, one week's annual leave and a pension, discretionary upon a long and clean service record. The package was slightly better than that offered by the Metropolitan Police, but it was said that the regime was tougher and discipline more strictly enforced. There was, though, another 'perk' that placed employment in the fire service above being a Bobby and that was the popular image of the fireman as hero.

A Metropolitan Fire Brigade engine being pulled through the streets by four brigade horses was not an uncommon sight, but on 14 October 1871 thousands of people lined the streets of London to see just that.[311] The engine was, though, heavily draped in black crêpe and was carrying the coffin of a brigade fireman who had lost his life a week earlier while attempting to rescue people from a blazing building (see plate 18). The band from 'E' division of the brigade played the 'Dead March' from *Saul* as it led the cortège, followed by the family of the dead fireman and two divisions of Metropolitan Police officers. Behind them followed 'nearly the whole of the fire-engines of the brigade, fully manned, each of the men wearing a band of crêpe on his left arm'. The procession left Holborn fire station and as it passed across the viaduct its ranks were swelled by officers and constables from the City of London Police, who followed the coffin to Abney Park Cemetery where the internment took place. Great honour was accorded to the dead fireman, who was laid to rest alongside the most famous firefighter London had known, Superintendent James Braidwood.

The funeral was for **Joseph Andrew Ford**, who had joined the brigade five years earlier in March 1866. As with so many firemen at that time, Joseph's background was distinctly nautical. Joseph Andrew was the eldest child of Joseph Ford, a coastguard, and Jane Winter, both from Essex, who married on 21 June 1837 at St Mary's church in Littlehampton, Sussex. Joseph Andrew was born on 26 February 1840 and christened at St Mary's on 22 March that year. At the time, Joseph senior and Jane were living at West Street in Worthing and at least five more children followed while the family was living in the town: Alfred (b. 1841), William John (b. 1843), Louisa (b. 1845), Caroline (b. 1847) and Henry (b. 1849). In around 1850, the family moved to Quakers Square in Grays, Essex, where Jane junior was born in 1851 (d. 1856), followed by the couple's last child, George Albert (b. 1854).

Joseph junior followed his father into the seafaring profession and in 1861 he was employed as a seaman aboard the *Look Out*, a schooner involved in the coal trade moored off Orfordness on the Suffolk coast. Joseph spent several years working at sea before joining the Metropolitan Fire Brigade in 1866. He started at the bottom and worked his way up through the ranks, his last promotion being to second-class fireman in July 1867. During his employment with the brigade, Ford undertook several special duties alongside his regular service, including working at the Queen's Theatre in London.

On 6 December 1868, Joseph Andrew Ford married Emmeline Eliza Harland, the daughter of a pensioned cavalryman, at the church of St John the Evangelist in Limehouse in east London. Later the same year, Joseph was appointed to Holborn Fire Station at 254 High Holborn in St Giles, and this is where he and his wife were living in 1869 when they had their first child, Emmeline Louisa. They were still living there in 1871, and Emmeline senior's mother, Anne Harland, and Joseph's second cousin, Ernest Godfry, were also residing with them. The couple had their second child, Frederick George, in the early part of 1871, just months before his father's tragic and untimely death.

It was around 2 a.m. on 7 October 1871 and PC Morris Elms from 'G' division was patrolling along the Gray's Inn Road when he spotted smoke pouring from number 98, the chemist shop belonging to William Brown.[312] Elms raised the alarm and at the nearby Holborn Fire Station, Joseph Ford rolled out fire escape number 22 and headed to the scene. Upon arrival, Elms helped Ford to raise the ladder of the escape and position it against the house, then watched as the fireman scaled the ladder and climbed into the building through a third-floor window. Inside the house, William Brown was sleeping in a room on the first floor and, having been awoken by the alarm being sounded and realising that the shop below was on fire, he ran upstairs to help the four elderly women who lived on the third floor. Just as Brown was assembling the women by one of the windows in their room, he heard a clatter as the escape was leant against the wall and, shortly after, fireman Ford appeared at the window. Brown helped Ford to lift the eldest of the three women onto the escape and the fireman climbed down the ladder, carrying her on his shoulder. When Ford returned a few minutes later, it was decided that the other women would be able to use the chute and, one by one, they cascaded down the canvas tube, followed lastly by Mr Brown and then Ford, who descended the ladder.

The fireman had little time to catch his breath and, hearing reports that there were further people trapped on the third floor, he set off once more up the ladder of the escape. For a few minutes, the flames which were grasping out of the windows of the building had been licking around the chute of the escape, and as Ford reached the top of the ladder, the canvas began to smoulder and then caught alight. Three floors below, PC Elms and Mr Brown lost sight of Ford as the smoke from the fire obscured their view and they anxiously waited for the fireman to reappear. Suddenly they saw a figure plummeting out of the smoke and could only watch in horror as Ford crashed to the pavement beside the fire escape. Rushing to his aid, they found him badly burned and heavily disorientated with a large wound to his head. Fearing the burning escape would collapse, they dragged Ford out of the way before assisting others to wheel the contraption away from the burning building. Another escape in attendance managed to bring down a woman from the third floor and the men from the brigade continued to battle the blaze. Meanwhile, Joseph Andrew Ford was placed in an ambulance and conveyed to the nearby Royal Free Hospital.

Four days after the fire, on 11 October 1871, Dr Edwin Lankester opened an inquest into the death of Joseph Ford, who had perished from his injuries on the evening of Saturday, 7 October.[313] Andrew Thomas, the house surgeon who treated Joseph, gave evidence that the fireman was insensible when admitted to the Royal Free and remained that way until his death. He had been burned on his face, arms and thighs, he had a broken rib and a collapsed lung, and there was a large star-shaped wound on the right side of his head. Thomas concluded that 'concussion of the brain and shock from the extensive burns' was the cause of death. The coroner reminded the jury that their task was not to question how the fire had started, but rather how Ford had met his death and whether there was anything that could be done to make fire escapes better for preserving the life of firemen. The reason this line of questioning had arisen was due to a letter the court had received from G. W. Cooke, a committee member for the SPLF.

In his letter, Cooke claimed that when the SPLF transferred its escapes to the Metropolitan Board of Works, the canvas chutes had been reinforced with copper gauze to strengthen them and help them to retain their structure in the event of their catching alight, which was not an infrequent occurrence. Cooke alleged that, since the MFB had been using the escapes, the expensive copper gauze had been replaced with an inferior wire netting, which was much cheaper but could not withstand the same amount of heat or flames. In Cooke's opinion, 'the life of the deceased would not have been lost if the escape had been fitted with copper gauze'. The court then heard evidence from the chief officer, Captain Shaw, who opened his testimony by stating that Ford was 'an able fireman and a steady well-conducted man'. As far as Shaw was concerned, he had investigated the matter and 'found that there was no blame attached to any person'. He had also examined the escape, which was in good condition, although the canvas had been burnt and there was a hole in the wire netting through which, he imagined, the deceased had fallen while trying to descend.

Shaw was then questioned as to why the brigade did not treat the canvas to make it non-flammable and why it had switched to using wire netting rather than copper gauze. The chief officer replied that treating the cloth with a solution of alum had been tested and was not found to be a suitable method of fireproofing the material, but the brigade would continue trying to find something that was both effective and sustainable. In relation to the netting, he reported that it was most certainly not an issue of cost and that the wire had been found to be stronger than copper; in addition, many firemen preferred netting to gauze, although the latter was still in use on some escapes. At that point in the proceedings, members of the jury informed the coroner that they wanted to examine the escape themselves and so it was decided to adjourn the inquest for six days to allow that to happen. The original inquest did, however, hear medical evidence so that Ford's body could be released for burial.

Great interest and excitement greeted the resumption of the inquest on 18 October, not least because in the period since it was adjourned there had been much consternation in the press about the manner in which Ford appeared to have died. 'Why should Captain Shaw, the brave Captain of the Fire Brigade, be sensitive because a searching inquiry is being made into the death of Joseph Andrew Ford, the brave fireman?' asked *The Era*, before continuing: 'it is impossible to read the evidence before the Coroner's jury without noticing a querulousness on the part of those who represent the Fire Brigade and the Board of Works'.[314] Firemen were also taking advantage of the publicity surrounding Ford to highlight that their lot was not necessarily a happy one. 'Sir, I beg through the medium of your widely-spread paper to let the public know how the men of the Metropolitan Fire Brigade are overworked, underpaid, and otherwise badly treated', wrote one anonymous correspondent who signed himself 'a fireman'.[315] His letter to *The Times* highlighted long hours, back-to-back shifts, poor rates of pay and little or no compensation for men who were injured on the job or the families of men who were killed. The writer was in no doubt as to where the blame lay: 'Since the Board of Works have taken over everything has gone wrong. They want everything as cheap as possible regardless of quality.' So, as the coroner and jury reconvened, people were keen to see what further evidence had emerged and whether anyone would be held to account.

The testimony of a police constable, George Carter, revealed more clearly what had happened to Ford. Carter saw the fireman try to get into the chute, which was by that time on fire, but he appeared to get tangled in the wire netting, which trapped him against the flames, where he received his burns. As part of the chute gave way, Ford was left hanging upside down, supported by the wire, but as that burned through Ford was released and plunged to the ground. The coroner said it was now 'beyond doubt' that the fireman had fallen through the wire, but the question was whether the escape was faulty. George Clarke, a manufacturer of fire escapes, stated that he had always used copper gauze for SPLF escapes but recently, at the request of the Board of Works, he had switched to wire netting, which was cheaper to buy and install. Clarke also spoke about the fireproofing he applied to the canvas, which was a solution of his own invention and worked well, but needed to be reapplied once a year. It did not add to the initial cost of the escape and he saw no reason why the material should not be made non-flammable. Clarke concluded his evidence by stating that, in his opinion, if the escape had been fitted with copper gauze rather than wire netting, Ford would have escaped.

Clarke's evidence appeared damning, but the MFB and the Board of Works put up a strong defence, including testimony from several firemen. William Maidment, head fireman at Stepney Station, suggested that netting was preferable to gauze because it lasted longer and the gauze tended to crack. Alfred Trimming, sub-engineer from the Watling Street Station, said that netting was lighter, which in turn made the escapes lighter, and this meant they could get to fires quicker; he estimated it could save five minutes on a half-mile journey. Finally, Henry Douglas, a former fire-escape conductor, testified that he had seen canvas catch light through gauze as easily as through netting and he preferred the latter for that reason. The coroner questioned each man, but when it became clear that their testimony was based purely on opinion rather than on any experiments or tests, he stated that it was 'useless to ask them any further questions' and more or less rejected their evidence. Thus it fell to Captain Shaw to defend the brigade's position.

Shaw was adamant that the wire netting was vastly superior to copper gauze, not because it was cheaper, but because it was stronger and lighter, did not catch the wind and was preferred by the men themselves. As Shaw delivered his evidence it became clear that, actually, the two products were used in quite different ways: 'the gauze is to prevent the direct action of the fire on the canvas; the netting is to support a man coming down when the canvas is burned away'. Essentially, the copper was directly attached to the canvas chute as a kind of heat shield, which strengthened the material and helped protect it from catching fire, while with the wire netting it was more a case of hanging it under the chute as a sort of safety net to catch people if and when the canvas burned through. The coroner, however, spotted a flaw in the argument: 'in point of fact, the netting serves one purpose while the gauze serves two', to which the jury added, 'Exactly, sir. We don't want to hear any more after that.'

Ultimately, the inquest jury had no direct powers and so all they could do was give their judgment and hope that others acted upon it. They returned a verdict of 'accidental death' but added a crucial rider which they knew would be widely reported:

> We are of the opinion that the fire escape, by falling from which the deceased met with his death, was not constructed in the most efficient manner and are of the opinion that had the shoot [*sic*] of the escape been covered with copper gauze instead of wire netting and the canvas rendered uninflammable, the death of the deceased would have been avoided.

Shaw remarked that 'he hoped it would not go forth that there was any neglect in his department' and to some extent there was not; most of the blame was directed at the Board of Works who, it was perceived, had sacrificed the life of a brave and heroic fireman for the sake of a few shillings. In the short term, escapes continued to use a combination of gauze and netting, but it was not long before telescopic metal ladders began to replace the outdated wooden escapes and the matter slipped out of public interest.

Controversy around Ford's death continued, however, to pursue the Board of Works beyond the conclusion of the inquest and it came under fire for not properly supporting his widow, Emmeline, and his two children, Emmeline junior and Frederick. When the brigade was constituted in 1865, a resolution was passed which stated: 'in the event of an officer or fireman being killed in the discharge of his duty, his widow be provided for by an annuity which shall continue during the pleasure of the Board'.[316] Ford was the first married fireman of the MFB to die on active duty and so the Board of Works had no precedent for actually implementing its resolution. A figure of £1 a week was decided upon, which considering Ford had been paid £1 8s a week represented less than his wage, and it was decided initially to award the sum for just six months and then revisit the situation. Meanwhile, a subscription fund had also been established, which was rapidly accumulating donations from a grateful public, moved by the reporting of Ford's bravery. In the end the fund raised around £1,000, at which point the Board of Works withdrew its pension provision, stating that '[the fund] brought to the widow an actually larger income than the pay her husband received when he was living'.[317] This was, though, hardly the point and it distinctly gave the impression that the board was trying to avoid its responsibilities.

In addition, following Joseph's death, his wife and children were required to vacate the fire station, and by 1881 Emmeline and her daughter were living at 50 Dixon Road in Stepney with Emmeline's younger brother, Ernest Harland. Joseph and Emmeline's son, Frederick, was living at 2 Dinah Terrace in Orsett near Grays in Essex with his grandparents, Joseph and Jane. By 1891, the family was reunited and Emmeline was living at 73 Stamford Road in East Ham with her two children. Emmeline Ford died, aged 56, in West Ham in 1896. Emmeline Louisa Ford, Joseph and Emmeline's daughter, lived with her mother until at least 1891, and in 1899 she married Reuben William Pressman, a clerk, in West Ham. In 1901, the couple were living at 158 Plashet Grove in East Ham with their daughter, Winifred Emmeline (b. 1900) and Reuben's sister Elizabeth. A second child, Irene Elizabeth, was born in 1906 and by 1911 the couple had moved to 56 Ingleby Road in Ilford. A son, Arthur P.R. Ford, was born in 1917. Emmeline died in Ilford in 1940, aged 71, and Reuben died, also in Ilford, seven years later in 1947, aged 77. Frederick Ford, Joseph's son, lived with his grandparents, Joseph and Jane, for some years and then with his mother until her death in 1896.

As the historian Shane Ewan has argued, the decision to municipalise the fire service meant that the heroism of firemen was also aligned with local government, and it needed to be sensitive to the public exaltation accorded to those men if they died heroically while on duty; the Board of Works could not reap the benefits of its association with brave fireman without stumping up to support their families if those men died.[318] There was undoubtedly exaltation for Joseph Andrew Ford, as these lines from a poem written by Arthur Locker and published in *The Graphic* demonstrate:

My fireman comes with his quaint machine,
a burning house is a nightly scene
to him, so he's not perplexed;
He climbs for the bees of this smoking hive,
he clutches them – one, two, three, four, five!
he has saved all these unhurt and alive!
and now he mounts for the next.

Horror! an envious tongue of fire
darts, like a snake, through the netting wire
the canvas is all aflame!
He falls! he falls! is there none to save?
Ah! cruel, to think that one so brave
who snatched five souls from a fiery grave
should perish by the same.[319]

The press were in no doubt that Ford had lost his life attempting to save another while in the employment of the Metropolitan Board of Works, and that the corporation had reneged on its duty not only to protect firemen on the job, but also to support their families if the worst should happen. This was certainly no way to treat a hero.

Captain Shaw, who gave evidence at the inquest into Joseph Ford's death, was still the chief officer of the Metropolitan Fire Brigade in 1876 when another fireman died in very similar circumstances. On this second occasion, however, Shaw declared that 'after a very long experience he believed this was the greatest act of bravery ever shown by any fireman in the world'.[320] Shaw also summed up the incident in a manner that would have been very appealing to G.F. Watts: 'The cool, dauntless bravery displayed by the deceased was a thousand times more noble than the valour of a soldier on a battlefield, where martial music and all the other accessories of strife were an incentive to bravery.' Watts was a great believer that civilians were every bit as capable of bravery as their military counterparts and that everyday heroism deserved to be recognised and commemorated to the same extent as military heroism. Watts was particularly interested in the unsung and those who had no official responsibility to save life, although individuals who were doing their duty could qualify for recognition on his monument if they went over and above the call of that duty. Lifeboat men were one example of this, as were policemen and, of course, firemen.

The subject of Captain Shaw's enormous admiration was **George Lee**, a fourth-class escape attendant who had joined the brigade in 1873 and who is the second of the two firemen who feature on the Watts Memorial. George was undoubtedly from a large family, but with such a common surname and relatively little context it is not straightforward to discover the exact details. His father was certainly Joseph Lee, a shoemaker and then a cabinet maker, who was born in London around 1816. Joseph married Sarah Perry at St John's church in Hoxton on 17 June 1839 and she was described on the wedding banns as being a minor, so probably under the age of 18. The marriage would have still been legal with the consent of her father, John. The 1841 census suggests that Joseph and Sarah had their first child, John, in late 1840 or early 1841.

The next window into the life of the Lee family occurs in 1851 and at that time they were living at 28 Playhouse Yard near Clerkenwell. The census for that year listed seven children for Joseph and Sarah, although the eldest recorded, Joseph, aged 15, does not seem particularly plausible. The others make slightly more sense, although it is still difficult to discern accurately the year of birth: Maria (aged 7), Thomas (aged 7), Emma (aged 5), Edward (aged 3), George (aged 1) and Emily (aged 1 month). Moving on a further ten years to 1861, the family had moved to another house in a street nearby and neither Maria nor Emma was listed on the census, although two further children had appeared: Caroline Ann (aged 6) and Sarah (aged 3). A further ten years on, in 1871, just Emily and Sarah were recorded as living with their parents at 12 Hamilton Road in Bethnal Green, the rest of the family having moved out to make their way in the world.

George Lee and his elder brother Thomas both appear to have initially followed their father into the cabinet-making trade. On 27 November 1863, Thomas married Amelia Emma Hathorn, the daughter of a block printer, at St Mary's church in Haggerston, and by 1871 they were living at 24 Reeves Place with their three children: Emma, Martha and Louisa. George was also living with them and still described as a cabinet maker. It was not until October 1873 that George entered the Metropolitan Fire Brigade, initially being stationed at Grand Junction Wharf near the City Road in Hoxton, where he underwent drill training and examinations. His service record described him as a seaman when he entered the service, so he must have become a mariner sometime after 1871. In January 1876, George was assigned to the St Luke's Fire Engine Station in Whitecross Street as an escape attendant, and it was from there, on 26 July 1876, that he was dispatched to a fire nearby in St John Street.

It was shortly after 8 p.m. and John Smith, a milliner and owner of the hat shop at 97 St John Street in Clerkenwell, was in the process of serving a customer when he suddenly noticed plumes of dense black smoke swirling upwards from the stairs that led down to the basement.[321] Smith knew that there were lodgers upstairs, but the fire had spread quickly and already cut off access to the upper floors, so he had no choice but to follow his customers out of the shop and raise the alarm. The fire escape at nearby Goswell Road was summoned and two escape attendants manning it that evening, James William Pelley and George Lee, dragged it through the streets to the site of the fire. Just as they pulled up, two women were spotted at a second-floor window and so the ladder was raised and the escape positioned against the wall adjacent to the window. However, the first floor of the building was ablaze and, as the flames burst out through the windows, they engulfed the lower portion of the escape and ladder.

It looked impossible to ascend but 'amidst the cheers of a tremendous crowd' George Lee rushed forward and, leaping as high up the ladder as he could to avoid the worst of the flames, he quickly climbed to the second floor and disappeared through the open window. Upstairs in the building were three members of the same family, 46-year-old Elizabeth Mary Francombe and her two children, 17-year-old Walter and 15-year-old Mary Anne. As Lee entered the room, he shouted to Walter to get down the escape, which the lad promptly did; he dived headfirst down the canvas chute where, at the bottom, he was pulled clear of the flames by Pelley. Walter told Pelly that his mother and sister were still in the house with the other fireman and Pelley fought his way through the flames at the base of the escape and set off upwards to try and assist Lee. Meanwhile, Lee was struggling to save the women in the room above.

When interviewed in hospital, just before he died, George Lee recounted his actions in the house:

I saw a girl on the floor and crept to her and taking her in my arms tried to make for the window. The heat overpowered me and I fell. I picked her up again and again fell some five or six times. I never lost my hold of her from first to last. I managed to put her into the chute of the escape and threw myself on the ladder. She stuck and I did my best to get her loose but the flames were playing all round us.[322]

Pelley was outside on the ladder of the escape and could see Lee and the girl, Mary Anne Francombe, trapped in the burning canvas chute, so he began stretching down to try and free them. Meanwhile, on the ground, the crowd of spectators who had gathered could see the three people on the escape being engulfed by the flames and decided to try and move the contraption away from the burning building. The chocks were removed from the wheels, but as the escape was dragged back from the wall, the blazing ladder was unable to support its own weight and snapped into several pieces. Francombe, Pelley and Lee came crashing to the ground amongst the remnants of burning wood and canvas.

Mary Anne Francombe was pulled from the wreckage and taken to Dr Franklin's on the opposite side of the road, where she was initially treated for burns before being transferred to St Batholomew's Hospital. Pelley and Lee were also conveyed there and Lee's condition was judged to be so serious that he was immediately admitted. The house surgeon who examined him reported that he was very much burned and that the fireman's death, on 7 August, had been caused by lockjaw resulting from those burns. Pelley recovered from his injuries, as did Walter Francombe, but Mary Anne Francombe was not as fortunate and she died from the burns and injuries she received at the fire. Mary's mother, Elizabeth Francombe, had remained trapped in the burning building after the escape collapsed and it was not until several hours later, when the fire was finally extinguished, that her badly charred remains were discovered. Smith's hat shop and the premises above it were utterly destroyed, but the milliner had been lucky to escape a terrible fire which had claimed three lives.

The inquest into George Lee's death, which was opened by the coroner, Mr Payne, at St Batholomew's Hospital on 9 August 1871, revealed something interesting about how the brigade wanted their heroic fireman to be remembered.[323] Giving evidence, Captain Shaw described Lee as being 'of exemplary character and although he had only been 18 months in the Brigade [he] had been promoted to first class', which, according to Lee's service records, was not the case; he had been with the brigade for nearly three years and was a fourth-class escape attendant. Shaw's embellishment of Lee's career helped to increase the fireman's posthumous reputation by portraying him as a driven and hard-working man as well as one who was prepared to give his life trying to save another. Lee's deathbed narrative of his attempt to save Mary Anne Francombe was also recounted in full by Shaw, adding a good degree of mournful pathos to the proceedings. In summing up, the coroner declared that 'it was another instance of pure and unhesitating self-sacrifice at the call of duty', sentiments which were endorsed by the jury, who returned a verdict of accidental death and donated their fees to George's sister.

As with Joseph Ford, George Lee's funeral was the epitome of the late-Victorian 'celebration of death', with his heroism adding an extra layer of public excitement and adulation.[324] The cortège took three hours, at a slow march, to complete its journey and the whole route was said to be lined by crowds of spectators; Barbican, Long Lane, the central avenue of Smithfield Market, St John Street, Wilderness Row, Old Street, Kingsland Road, then along Stoke Newington High Street and through the gates of Abney Park Cemetery.[325] A fire engine drawn by four horses carried the coffin, which was draped in a union flag, and resting upon it were the fireman's distinctive brass helmet and his scorched and blackened uniform. At the head of the procession following the engine was a single mourning coach containing three women: George's sisters Emily and Sarah and his fiancée, whom unfortunately the press did not name. The rest of the cortège was a roll-call of public servants: Captain Shaw, 150 retained firemen, volunteer firemen of the auxiliary brigade, seven fire engines, 200 Metropolitan Police constables, the Metropolitan Police band and members of the City of London Police.

George Lee was laid to rest close to the graves of James Braidwood and Joseph Ford in an area that was developing into something of a 'fireman's corner'. The *Daily News* published a long account of the proceedings and described the committal thus:

> The concourse at the interment was immense, while hundreds vainly endeavoured to get near the spot. Many men and boys climbed some of the larger trees in the vicinity to obtain a better view of the burial place and the mourning relatives. The latter consisted of a brother and two sisters of the deceased and a young woman to whom he was engaged to be married. The three women cried bitterly, and their sobs broke the respectful silence which was carefully maintained under great difficulties owing to the pressure of the crowd. All remained uncovered to the last; none were indecorous. Never was such universal sympathy more unmistakably evinced on such an occasion.[326]

At the close of the ceremony, George's relatives threw wreaths onto the coffin and after they had left there was a large rush by the crowd to catch a glimpse of the open grave before the earth was shovelled in. Everyone was keen to catch one last glimpse of the fireman who had died so bravely, trying to save the lives of others. A few months later a memorial stone was placed over the grave and George Lee was also publicly memorialised with a brass tablet fixed to the wall of the appliance room at Whitecross Street Fire Station, where he was based.

In some ways, it is odd that two firemen were commemorated on the Watts Memorial, given G.F. Watts' preference for recognising unsung heroes and those who had no duty or responsibility to save life. Joseph Ford and George Lee were not, on the surface, archetypes of the 'everyday' heroes whom the artist had in mind when he conceived his monument. However, Watts was very much a subscriber to prominent Victorian ideas such as character, altruism, perseverance and determination, all of which contributed to and informed his thinking on the nature of heroism. Consequently, those with a duty to save life were not necessarily heroic in the same way as 'everyday' heroes who stepped up when there was not requirement to do so, but overstepping one's duty and going over and above in the quest to save life, as the firemen had done, was, for Watts, indicative of the heroism he was looking for in his subjects.

FRIENDS AND NEIGHBOURS

> Connected with the subject of chimney sweeping is one which attracts far less of the attention of the legislature and the public than its importance would seem to demand: I mean the fires in the metropolis, with their long train of calamities such as the loss of life and of property. These calamities, too, especially as regards the loss of property, are almost all endured by the poor, the destruction of whose furniture is often the destruction of their whole property, as insurances are rarely effected by them.[327]

These were the sentiments of the journalist Henry Mayhew who in the 1850s, as part of his wider study into *London Labour and the London Poor*, investigated the subject of fires in London. As the previous chapter outlined, by the time Mayhew was writing, London was on the brink of establishing its first publicly funded fire brigade, responsible for saving life and protecting property. It was, furthermore, a brigade which was very much needed. Using statistics compiled by W. Baddeley, a manufacturer of fire-fighting equipment, Mayhew calculated that in the seventeen years between 1833 and 1850 there had been an average of 665 fires per year and he broke the causes of those fires down into broad categories.

Top of the list was 'various accidents with candles', then defective flues and chimneys, stoves overheating, linen drying and airing, and other unavoidable domestic accidents. Fires connected with manufacturing in domestic premises were also common, as were fires arising from children playing with fire, tobacco smoking, discarded matches and fires kindled in unsuitable hearths. 'Wilful' and 'suspicious' were listed as causes, as were 'drunkenness' and 'smoking in bed', but these all came relatively low on the list. Surprisingly, higher than all four of those reasons was 'spontaneous combustion', which, according to Mayhew, accounted for an average of thirteen fires per year.

Whatever the causes, the main issue for Londoners, above all else, was preventing people from dying in fires. Mayhew cited average times for horse-drawn fire engines

arriving at fires as being twenty-eight minutes for incidents within a mile of a fire station and twenty minutes for those within half a mile. The figures were based upon the
time it took a messenger, on foot, to get from the fire to the station and then the time
it took the engine to reach the fire at a speed of 10mph, or 'best Royal Mail pace' as it
was referred to. There had been, it was stated, complaints that engines travelling faster
than this were being 'reckless' and so it was not thought desirable to push the horses any
harder. These response times were actually fairly good; the problem was that, on average,
properties tended to be more like 2 miles from a station and this could mean waiting up
to an hour for an engine to arrive and start extinguishing the fire.

Fire escapes, the sole purpose of which was to evacuate people from burning buildings rather than fighting the fire itself, offered another option but, again, time and
resources were key issues. For an escape to be effective for saving life, it was estimated
that it needed to reach the fire within five minutes of the alarm being raised. From
this, it was calculated that escapes needed to be stationed within a quarter of a mile
of each other and this all added up to a requirement of around 250 manned escapes.
In 1867, when it was incorporated into the Metropolitan Fire Brigade, the Society
for the Protection of Life from Fire had amassed a total of eighty-five escapes, which
shows the enormous shortfall between necessity and provision.

The reality, then, was that domestic fires in Victorian London were common and
often unavoidable, through combinations of poverty, overcrowding and cottage
industry, or brought about by carelessness or lack of attention. Once a fire was discovered and the alarm had been raised, time was of the essence and getting an engine or
an escape to the scene as quickly as possible was imperative if lives were to be saved.
This was, though, often easier said than done, and it could often be up to an hour
before professional help from the brigade arrived. Thus it was that the responsibility
for helping to fight fires and, when required, trying to save people who were trapped
by them, often fell to those living nearby and members of the local community. These
people were certainly not firemen (and often not men at all), but they displayed
similar levels of courage and bravery and, as with Joseph Ford and George Lee, they
sometimes lost their own lives while attempting to save others.

The person commemorated on the Watts Memorial as George Frederick Simonds
was actually **Frederick George Simons**, the second son of Richard Henry Simons,
a carman and timber porter, and his wife Eliza. Richard married Eliza Oakley at
St Philip's church in Bethnal Green on 21 July 1845, although their first son, William
Richard, had been illegitimately born two years earlier on 29 June 1843. Consequently,
Frederick George was the couple's first legitimate child, born on 21 November 1845
and baptised, along with William, at St Botolph's-without-Bishopsgate on
11 January 1846. At that time the couple were living in 26 Primrose Street above the

main lines into Liverpool Street Station, and this is where their third son, James, was born on 1 January 1848. Presumably on account of their growing family, Richard and Eliza moved slightly eastwards to 5 Blossom Street where their two daughters were born, Emily in 1850 and Sarah Maria in 1852. Both girls were baptised at St Mary's Spital Square on 27 May 1855.

Frederick Simons lived with his parents until around 1865 and then on 19 July 1868 he married Eliza Pinckney, the daughter of Joseph Pinckney, a cotton weaver, at St Matthew's church in Bethnal Green. On the wedding banns, Frederick is described as a 'soda water maker', but that does not appear to have been profitable because by 1871 he was working as a porter in a toy warehouse. At that time, Frederick and Eliza were living at 4 Beckford Square in Bethnal Green and had three children; their eldest son, Frederick George junior, was born on 18 August 1868 (Eliza must have been heavily pregnant at her wedding), their second son, James, arrived in 1869 and then their daughter, Eliza junior, was born in 1871.

By 1876, when their eldest son was admitted to St Matthew's School in Islington, Frederick and Eliza had moved the family to 14 Rheidol Terrace, off Prebend Street in Islington, and around that time Frederick senior was working as a confectioner, perhaps related in some way to his earlier occupation as a soda water manufacturer. It is easy to imagine Frederick Simons as something of an entrepreneur and by 1886 he had moved on from confectionery and was buying and selling toys and fancy goods. The family was still living at Rheidol Terrace, near its junction with St Peter Street, and Frederick got to know Elizabeth Corke, a widow who lived with her three sons at number 61 St Peter Street. The three boys were all engravers and Elizabeth's lodger, David Jones, was a jeweller, so it is likely that Frederick was acquainted with the family through his fancy goods business.

House fires were not uncommon in the area, so when, on the afternoon of 1 December 1886, Frederick heard that smoke had been seen emanating from a nearby property he was not, at first, overly concerned.[328] However, gossip about the fire quickly rattled through the neighbourhood; it was in St Peter Street, possibly number 61, and the old lady who lived there with her three sons was unaccounted for. Suddenly realising that his friend Elizabeth Corke could be trapped in the building, Frederick ran around the corner and, pushing his way through the crowd that had gathered, he was horrified to see smoke and flames billowing from the ground-floor windows. People were saying that a runner had been sent to fetch the brigade, but who knew how long the engine or escape would take to arrive and what would become of the inhabitants of the house in the meantime? At this point, Frederick decided to take matters into his own hands and he ran into the burning building to try and rescue Elizabeth.

Inside, Frederick darted past the downstairs rooms, which were quickly being consumed by the fire, and stumbled his way through the thick smoke to the staircase, which he climbed to the second floor. There was, however, no sign of Elizabeth

Corke or her sons, and so Frederick descended to the first floor and checked there, but the house appeared to be empty. On the ground floor, the fire had spread to the staircase, blocking Frederick's escape, so he ran back up to the second-floor landing and pushed open a window to shout for help. On the pavement outside, the crowd suddenly saw Frederick at the window and some people shouted to him to jump, but the height was considerable and there was nothing to break his fall. There was still no sign of the brigade, so Frederick made his way back down to the first floor and found a staircase window, which he forced open.

The distance to the ground was about 20ft, but about 6ft down from the window there was a water cistern fixed to the wall. Frederick climbed out of the window and, holding onto the ledge, he lowered himself down to the cistern with the intention of then jumping down to the street from there. However, as he released his grasp of the window ledge and dropped onto the cistern, he lost his footing and fell around 14ft, hitting the pavement headfirst with a heavy thud. Frederick was discovered a few minutes later and when people recognised him they carried him back to his home in Prebend Street. A local GP, Dr Harle, was summoned, who examined Frederick and found him 'insensible' and suffering from a fractured skull and broken ribs as well as other cuts and bruises. Plans were being made to convey Frederick to the hospital when his condition deteriorated, and around two hours after he was brought back to his house, he died.

Back in St Peter Street, the fire engine arrived and set to work extinguishing the blaze. The ground floor of the building was burnt out and the staircases and upper floors damaged by fire, smoke and water. Elizabeth Corke had, after all, escaped the blaze and later explained that she was in the downstairs back room when a spark from the fireplace set fire to a rug. Unable to stem the spreading flames, Elizabeth escaped via a back door and was safely in the backstreets behind the buildings when Frederick Simons was inside trying to find her. Initial press reports of the incident suggested that Simons was in the house when the fire broke out and that he jumped from a second-storey window to escape the blaze. This account was corrected by a correspondent who wrote to *The Standard* explaining that Simons had fallen from the cistern while trying to get out through the landing window, having entered the house to try and rescue Corke.[329] This account was substantiated by witnesses who gave evidence at the inquest, held at the Islington Coroner's Court on 4 December 1886, and the jury returned a verdict of 'accidental death'.[330]

In the years following her husband's death, Eliza Simons and the three children moved to 3 Phillip Passage, off Phillip Street in Haggerston. The three children all worked to support the household: Frederick junior as an electrician, James as an assistant to a local butcher and Eliza junior, continuing what appears to have been something of a family trade, earning her living by bottling mineral water. On 22 August 1893, Eliza junior married Richard Henry Chaloner, a stoker, at St Thomas' church in Bethnal Green, at which time she was still working as a water bottler. The couple had at least five children: Ernest Albert (b. 1896), Grace (b. 1897),

Lucy Constance (b. 1899), Richard Henry (b. 1906) and Rose (b. 1911). Eliza Chaloner, Frederick Simons' daughter, died in 1948, aged 77.

Frederick's youngest son, James, progressed from an assistant butcher to being a butcher himself and on 16 February 1895 he married Emily Lester, the daughter of a greengrocer, at Christ Church in Hoxton. The couple settled in the Clerkenwell area and had at least two children, Edith Emily (b. 1897) and James Victor (b. 1899). James senior, Frederick's son, died at the age of 48 in 1918. The variable recording of the surname 'Simons' makes tracking the family especially tricky and, unfortunately, it is not entirely clear what happened to Frederick's wife or his eldest son after 1891.

Ultimately, Frederick Simons gave his life in vain because the object of his bravery, Elizabeth Corke, had already escaped the blaze. This does not, however, diminish the intent behind his behaviour and his motivation to save life, even at the risk of his own. Miscommunications and misunderstandings were frequent problems during the commotion that accompanied fires, and it was often unclear if people had escaped from buildings or were still trapped inside. Frederick was certainly not the only person to rush into a burning building to try and effect a rescue without really knowing if there were people inside, and another case of a similar nature is commemorated on the Watts Memorial.

The fire which raged in the Bow Road on the evening of Monday, 14 October 1901, was described as 'one of the largest and most destructive conflagrations which have occurred in this part of London for some considerable time … the shops and houses of 14 rooms were alight from top to bottom and the interior of the structure resembled a veritable furnace'.[331] Thousands of people watched on in 'terrible excitement' as 'great bursts of flames enveloped the staircases and rapidly involved the entire building'. Engines from four stations were called and firemen from Bow, Hackney, Bethnal Green and Mile End discharged huge volumes of water onto the fire, but 'the combustible character of the materials stored within rendered the efforts of the firemen fruitless'. The blaze was engulfing the premises of Emery and Sons, a well-known drapery business which occupied three adjacent buildings at 127–9 Bow Road, and there were fears that it could also spread to the Little Driver pub next door.

There was 'anxious anxiety' among the crowd as to the whereabouts of those who worked in the shop and lived above it, and stories circulated about 'narrow escapes' on the part of those inside. As the fire was brought under control, people started to be accounted for and by the time the worst of the flames were finally extinguished at about 7 p.m. it was concluded that everyone had escaped the dreadful catastrophe. The building, though, was completely gutted: 'the roof had been destroyed, the front of the premises entirely burned away, while within all was a mass of falling and burning timber'. As night closed in, the firemen continued to damp down the smouldering wreckage and the crowd dispersed back to their homes, thankful that the fire had not cost any lives.

As Tuesday morning dawned, a different picture began to emerge and it started to appear that perhaps not everyone had escaped the blaze after all. When the alarm was first raised, one of the shop's window dressers, Henry Newman Ludlow, had gone down into the basement of the shop to collect his coat, but then later he was reportedly seen crossing the road outside, so it was supposed he had escaped. However, when enquiries were made at his lodgings, it transpired that he had not returned home on Monday night and so firemen began the sorrowful task of searching through the sodden piles of rubble for a body.

Down a small staircase and towards the rear of the premises, by some barred windows, they made their grim discovery, the charred and blackened body of Henry Ludlow, but close by there was another body in a similar state. Everyone from the drapers and the rooms above was now accounted for, so speculation began to spread as to who the other body might be. Meanwhile, across the road, the staff at Bussey's Auction Rooms were opening up for the day and it was noted that one of the employees had not turned in for work that morning; in fact, he had not actually been seen by anyone since the previous evening.

That missing employee was **James Charles Akhurst Bannister**, who worked at the auction rooms as a painter and general labourer. James was born in Bromley-by-Bow on 2 April 1868. His father, Charles Akhurst Bannister, was a farrier who married Susan Squire at All Saints church in Poplar on 21 January 1849. The couple went on to have five children: Charlotte Ann (b. 1850), Susannah Elizabeth (b. 1852), Emma (b. 1860), Mary Ann (b. 1864) and then finally James (b. 1868). Shortly after they married, Charles and Susan moved into 18 Gloucester Street in Mile End, which they shared with two other families, before later moving to slightly larger lodgings at 9 Upper Mary Street in Bromley, as their family grew.

By 1871, the three older girls had moved out of the family home and James, aged 3, was living at 7 Priory Street, Bromley, with his parents and his elder sister. In February 1878, the family was living at 1 Sheffield Road and James was admitted to the Dalgleish Street School in Tower Hamlets. It is not clear how long he was a pupil at the school, but in 1881, when the family was living at 3 Seaton Street in West Ham, he is described on the census as a 'scholar', suggesting he was still in formal education.

By 1891, James was working as a house decorator and was boarding with the Hatfull family at 782 Old Ford Road in Bow. Henry Hatfull, the head of the household, was a house decorator, as was William Wells who also lodged with the family. It was around that time that James met Mary Ann Driscoll, a carpenter's daughter, and the two were married at St Leonard and St Mary church in Bromley on 30 August 1891. Over the next ten years, James and Mary Ann raised a family of four: Mary Ann Emily (b. 1892), James Richard (b. 1894), Ernest Albert (b. 1896) and May Eleanor (born in 1901, just months before her father's untimely death). Mary Ann and James junior both attended the Bow High Street School, Mary being admitted in January 1892 and James in June 1899. The family settled in and around the Bow area and was living at 14 Brewery Yard in 1898 and then 9 Brewery Yard in 1901. Their lodgings were literally around the corner from the auction rooms and Mary must have known about the terrible fire at Emery's, but could not have guessed that it would have such dreadful consequences for her and her family.

On 22 October 1901, Mr Wynne Baxter, the coroner for east London, resumed the inquest into the deaths of James Bannister and Henry Ludlow.[332] Baxter had previously opened and adjourned the inquest on 16 October, but on that occasion the jury had only heard evidence of a formal nature. At the second sitting, numerous witnesses were called and their evidence allowed the full story of the dramatic and tragic events of 14 October to emerge. Frederick Taylor, a salesman's assistant, looked gaunt and pale as he gave his evidence. He had just finished lighting the gas lamps in the shop window and was walking back through the shop when he heard someone calling that the window display was on fire. Turning back around, he saw that a curtain acting as a divider had caught light and had set fire to numerous items in the window. Taylor conceded that he must have caught the curtain with the lighted taper but had not noticed at the time. He then told the inquest that he pulled down the curtain and began stamping out the flames, at which point a police constable came into the shop and started throwing flaming items out of the window into the shop, which spread the fire.

Constable Goodchild from 'K' division was passing the shop when he noticed a commotion in the window and, seeing flames and smoke near the door, hurried in. Contrary to Taylor's testimony, Goodchild told the inquest that the salesman's assistant was standing in the shop with a lighter taper in his hand and staring dumbstruck at the blazing window. The constable shouted at him three or four times to move before pulling down the curtain himself. According to Goodchild, merchandise was piled high on the shelves and this drew the flames up to the ceiling, at which point he realised that evacuation was the only option. 'All clear out,' he shouted three or four times and was alarmed to see men and women still milling around in the shop despite the flames and smoke.

Two women employees ran upstairs, where they were able to climb out of a window and escape across the roof of the pub next door. Others were just about able to get out through the front door, but the exit was quickly being cut off by the fire. Goodchild spotted George Emery, the owner of the drapers, and another man, an assistant named Septimus Dane, trying to work the shop's fire extinguisher, but he bellowed at them, 'It's too late now, you must all clear out', at which point the men left the appliance and followed the constable through the front door. As they did, the frontage of the shop collapsed, making it impossible to get out that way.

George Emery gave lengthy and detailed evidence to the inquest, telling them that it was around 5 p.m. and he was behind the counter in the centre of the shop when he was told that there was a fire in the front window. He sent two assistants to find out what the problem was, but soon realised that the shop was ablaze and so, having secured his books and cash, he shouted to Septimus Dane to get to work with the fire extinguisher which was kept on the premises. When it became clear that they could not fight the fire, Emery ordered everyone to evacuate and, looking around, he believed he was the last to leave the shop.

Under questioning from the jury, Emery admitted that, although the property consisted of three shops, there was just one front door and the only other exits were windows at the front and rear of the property, but these were barred. He said that Ludlow would have known he could not get out through the rear windows and Emery had been told that the window dresser had been seen going home, so he thought he was safe. Emery also defensively stated that the windows were dressed as usual, with nothing hanging down and nothing around the gas lights.

In terms of fighting the fire, the assistant Dane testified that Emery had put him in charge of the shop's extinguisher, but that he did not really know how to use it. 'Did it work?' asked the coroner. 'No,' replied Dane. 'I hurt my hand trying to make it work.' Station officer Jones from Bow Fire Station gave evidence and said that a steam-driven pump had arrived within three minutes of being summoned and in total eight engines working from two hydrants had tackled the blaze, which was, eventually, extinguished with great difficulty. The next day his men searched the building and found two bodies, lying more or less head to head and within 4ft of each other. 'Neither of the bodies were much burnt,' reported Jones, so he surmised that death had resulted from suffocation.

Evidence regarding Bannister's involvement in the fire was presented to the jury by William Cubitt, who worked at Bussey's. He told them that 'he [Bannister] was seen to rush into the building, presumably to render assistance, and was never seen again', but why this did not come to light at the time of the fire remained unclear. Emery told the inquest that he knew nothing about Bannister and none of the witnesses reported seeing him in the shop or outside. The local press picked up on rumours that the position of the two bodies suggested that Bannister had been attempting to rescue Ludlow when the two men perished, but station officer Jones made no mention of that in his evidence.

It is possible that Bannister was in the drapers when he should actually have been across the road working and that Cubitt's evidence was covering for him, but that seems improbable given the circumstances. It is most likely that James Bannister was, indeed, across the road at the time and entered the burning building to help those inside. As the front of the building collapsed, Bannister became trapped and in the process of trying to rescue Henry Ludlow the two men suffocated from smoke inhalation. The only mystery that remains is why Cubitt or someone else did not tell the brigade firemen that Bannister had entered the building, so they might then have had at least a slim chance of going around to the windows at the rear of the shops and getting the two men out before they perished.

As the inquest drew to a close, the coroner made a point of placing on record two serious accusations which were implied rather than boldly stated. The first was a concern that 'these big buildings, each 90ft long and 40ft wide and filled with flammable materials, had only one exit in spite of the fact that many people lived in the place and that it was used by a good many customers'. The coroner also remarked upon 'the existence of only one fire extinguisher which no one knew how to use'. In the case of both Bannister and Ludlow, the jury returned a verdict of 'accidental death' and 'added a rider commending Constable Goodchild for his prompt conduct in connection with the fire', inferring that they had believed his testimony rather than Taylor's. Undoubtedly, the initial minor fire in the window had been caused by Taylor but, beyond that, a number of other factors escalated it and led to the two fatalities, which could perhaps have been avoided if there had been more exits and if the shop's extinguisher had been working. All of this rhetoric, though, was of little use to Mary Ann Bannister, James' widow, or the family of Henry Ludlow.

The scale of the fire, the level of destruction and the loss of life caused much interest and consternation in the local area, and two committees were quickly formed to offer support to those who had incurred losses at the fire. Immediately after the fire, a 'meeting of influential gentlemen' was convened at the Black Swan pub on the Bow Road 'for the purpose of raising a fund to alleviate any suffering resulting to the employees by their being thrown out of work, to assist them in their loss of clothes and belongings, and to aid the widows and orphans of those who met their deaths at the fire'.[333] It would appear, though, that this fund took some time to organise and collect the money. Three weeks later, on 25 October, a meeting of the Mile End Philanthropic Society at the Royal Hotel in Mile End voted to pay £5 immediately to Mary Ann Bannister 'for immediate necessities pending the expected realisation of assistance by the local committee'.[334] Given that James Bannister was probably earning something in the region of 25–30s a week, this would have provided the family with income for around four or five weeks, by which time, it was hoped, the main fund would be able to pay out. Unfortunately, the total amount collected by the main fund was not publicly reported, so the exact level of financial support provided is not known. However, in similar cases, funds often raised hundreds of pounds, so it is likely that Mary Ann and the family were well looked after by the people around them.

The money was not, though, used by Mary Ann for long and she died as a widow in Poplar in the autumn of 1910 at the age of 41. James and Mary's eldest daughter, Mary Ann Elizabeth, married Leonard Christopher Harker at St Mary Magdalen church in St Pancras in June 1908. In 1911, the couple were living at 18 Gorringe Park Avenue in Mitcham, Surrey, where Leonard was working as a foreman for a mineral water company. James Richard, the eldest of the two boys, appears to have taken custody of his youngest sister and in 1911 he and May were listed as lodgers with a wheelwright named James Brown and his family at 16 Egleton Road, Bow; James was at that time employed as a general labourer. In the autumn of 1929, May Bannister married Henry Veares in Poplar and the couple had at least two children, Iris M. (b. 1931) and Henry junior (b. 1933). It is not entirely clear what happened to 4-year-old Ernest Albert after the death of his parents, but evidence suggests that by

1911 he had entered the Poplar Training School in Hutton near Brentwood in Essex. The school, housing around 700 poor and destitute children from the East End of London, opened in 1907 and it is likely that Ernest would have been learning a trade such as tailoring, carpentry or boot making. So, much like his father, Ernest would probably have gone on to earn his living in a manual trade.

When Henry Mayhew compiled his statistics on the causes of fires in London between 1833 and 1850, he concluded that, on average, stoves and lamps overheating accounted for around thirty-seven fires per year and drunkenness was responsible for around five. Consequently, a combination of those two factors was likely to be a potent and dangerous mixture, as it certainly was for one household in Stepney in the early hours of Boxing Day, 26 December 1902.

The Christmas of 1902 was a particularly poignant one for **John Slade**, as he was reunited with his family after two years of military service in South Africa. John was an infantryman in the Royal Fusiliers and served in both the 2nd and the 4th battalions.[335] He was awarded both the Queen's South Africa Medal (QSA) and the King's South Africa Medal (KSA), and as the KSA was only awarded to troops who fought in 1902, but who had also completed at least eighteen months' service prior to the end of the war on 1 June, John must have joined the Royal Fusiliers sometime before December 1900. Just before he left to fight in the Boer War, John Slade got married, tying the knot with Mary Elizabeth Deboeck at St Dunstan and All Saints church in Stepney on 3 July 1900. Mary was the daughter of George Thomas Deboeck, who was described on the wedding banns as a 'traveller'. Soon after the wedding, John left for South Africa and did not return until sometime in 1902.

For John's parents it must have been a rewarding period to see their son married and serving his country, not least because they had already experienced more than their share of loss and tragedy with their other children. Thomas Slade, John's father, was a brush maker and he married Ellen Nash, the daughter of a shoe maker, at St Mary's church in Lambeth on 21 July 1862. Ellen must have been quite heavily pregnant at the time as their son, Thomas John, was born on 19 September that year. Their first daughter, Jemima, arrived just over a year later on 15 November 1865, and then a second daughter, Rose, was born in the first quarter of 1868. Later that year, Thomas and Ellen experienced their first loss when their eldest son, Thomas, died at the age of 5. At the end of 1870, another son was born and named Thomas, perhaps in memory of his elder brother, but this was something of an ill omen as he died less than a year later.

Around this time the couple moved from the Southwark area, where they had lived since they married, to Bethnal Green and this is where their third son, John, was born in 1873 and baptised at St Phillip's church on 17 September that year. If Thomas and Ellen thought they had left their ill fortune behind them, they were much mistaken and in 1875 their 7-year-old daughter Rose died. Another son, Walter, was born in Bethnal Green in 1877 and then the family moved back to Southwark, where they had another daughter, Sarah Ann, in 1881. Both John and Walter Slade initially followed their father into the trade of brush making, but John then decided to enlist in the British army and joined the Royal Fusiliers.

When John returned from South Africa, he and his wife moved into 99 Whitehorse Street in Stepney, and it is easy to imagine the relief felt by Mary when her husband returned safely from the war. As the end of 1902 approached, the couple were perhaps looking ahead to the New Year and the prospect of starting a family. They certainly had a full house for Christmas that year; John had invited Herbert Baxter, a friend and fellow Royal Fusilier, to stay with them, Mary's brother was visiting and there were also some other lodgers or friends, which meant that people were sleeping in various rooms all over the house. After a fairly boisterous Christmas Day, John and Herbert decided to walk into nearby Woolwich and have a few drinks at a local pub. It was about midnight when they returned, and as John headed upstairs to bed, Herbert Baxter lit a paraffin lamp and took it into the front parlour, where he then stretched out on the couch and fell asleep.

It was about three hours later when John was stirred by a clattering noise from downstairs, but with so many people in the house he thought little of it.[336] A few minutes later, however, he began to smell burning, and when he opened the bedroom door he found the upstairs landing filling with thick black smoke, which was flooding up from below. John immediately roused Mary and then raised the alarm, shouting to everyone else upstairs to get out as quickly as they could. By the time John and Mary got downstairs, they realised the smoke was coming from the front parlour and as they pushed open the door they saw Herbert Baxter lying on the floor with flames raging around him. Crawling across the floor, John managed to reach Herbert and drag him out of the blazing parlour, after which he and Mary carried the unconscious infantryman into the street. Looking around him, John could not see any of the other inhabitants of the house and, presuming they were still trapped inside, he ran back into the burning building to try and help them.

News of the fire spread quickly and a neighbour hurried off to fetch the brigade. Meanwhile, two police officers arrived, constables Bouillancy and Edwards, who tried to get in through the front door but were beaten back by the flames. Undeterred, the two constables passed through another house in Whitehorse Street and managed to get into the garden behind number 99, where they used some old tin baths to climb up to the windows and pull people out. At the front of the house, there was still no sign of John Slade, but Mary spotted her brother at an upstairs window and screamed in horror as he fell into the street, suffering serious injuries. During the commotion to help him, the brigade arrived and several firemen began pumping water onto the fire, while others went around to the rear of the house to help the constables.

A back door was forced open and when the firemen entered they found Slade and another man, William Flynn, overcome by heat and smoke and both quite badly burned. Stretchers were fetched and the men were carried out to a waiting ambulance, which conveyed them to the nearby London Hospital on the Whitechapel Road. Flynn recovered but Slade was more extensively burned and his condition deteriorated over the next couple of days. Slade's burial record states that he died, sometime between 27 and 31 December 1902, at Cambridge Barracks in Woolwich, which by that time was being used as a headquarters for the Royal Artillery; the young fusilier must have been taken there from the hospital, as the house in Whitehorse Street was completely destroyed in the fire. Everyone else appears to have escaped the blaze, although Herbert Baxter, Flynn and Mary's brother all received serious burns and other injuries.

Wynne Baxter, the east London coroner, held the inquest into John's death at the London Hospital on 1 January 1903.[337] The lines of inquiry primarily concerned the paraffin lamp which had apparently started the fire and the sobriety of Baxter and Slade. When questioned by a London County Council inspector about the quality of the oil in the lamp, Mary Slade replied that she had paid 8*d* a gallon for the oil and she estimated that there was around 3 pints in the lamp when she extinguished it before going to bed that night. This seemed to satisfy the inspector and nothing more was said about the lamp being faulty or overfilled. When Herbert Baxter was questioned he said, 'the only thing he could remember was the deceased [Slade] pulling him out of the room and saying "the place is on fire"'; Herbert also 'denied that he was the worse for drink'. Evidence was also given by the constables and members of the fire brigade, who spoke about how they had rescued people from the back of the house and then extinguished the blaze.

In summing up, the coroner remarked that 'the deceased had lost his life through trying to save his friend and relatives. His conduct was heroic and the result was to be deplored; at the same time it was impossible to doubt that both deceased and [Herbert] Baxter were the worse for drink.' The jury returned a verdict of 'accidental death' and 'highly commended PCs Bouillancy and Edwards for their bravery and prompt and judicious conduct'. Straight after the inquest, Slade's body was legally released for burial and was taken to Greenwich Cemetery, where he was laid to rest in a common grave at the expense of the local council. There is no evidence that a headstone was ever erected and the site has subsequently become overgrown.

It is not entirely clear what happened to John's wife, Mary, after his death; she is not easily identifiable on the 1911 census and with no children and little contextual information it is difficult to identify any remarriage. John's younger sister, Sarah Ann, married George Edward Notman in 1905 and they had at least three children: Sarah Ann junior (b. 1910), George junior (b. 1911) and Emily (b. 1913). In 1911 they were living at 32 Burgess Road in Stratford, east London, and Sarah's father, Thomas, was living with them, having been widowed in 1899. Thomas Slade, John's father, died in 1918.

John's elder sister, Jemima, also seems to have married at least one, and possibly two, members of the Notman family. A Jemima Slade married Henry George Notman in 1885 but he died ten years later, and then, in 1896, a Jemima Slade married James Notman, who may have been Henry's brother. On one hand, it seems improbable that this second marriage was the same Jemima, as she should have had the surname Notman rather than Slade. That said, it also seems hugely coincidental that two different Jemima Slades would marry two members of the Notman family, particularly considering the consecutive nature of the marriages.

Given the frequency and ferocity of domestic fires in Victorian London, it is perhaps surprising that relatively few of the incidents commemorated on the Watts Memorial occurred under those circumstances. Of course, fires did not always involve the rescue of people, if they did, those rescues might not necessarily be 'heroic' and, even if they were, the rescuer might not have lost their life in the process; so a lot of factors needed to add up in order to produce a case that would have come to the attention of Watts. Perhaps more interesting, though, is that the majority of fire-related incidents which were commemorated on the memorial were undertaken by women, and seven out of the nine women are commemorated as a result of a fire. Three of those women were single and three were married, and their stories are revealed in the two chapters that follow.

18

THE 'CULT OF DOMESTICITY'

There are, in total, nine women commemorated on the Watts Memorial in Postman's Park and this, in itself, is somewhat noteworthy. Generally speaking, the Victorians had relatively fixed and compartmentalised ideas about the roles of men and women in society, which has been described as a 'separate spheres' way of thinking. Essentially, by the middle of the nineteenth century a dominant 'cult of domesticity' was effectively confining women to the 'private' sphere of the home and consequently limiting them to the roles of wives and mothers.[338] This ideology most obviously manifested itself through a physical separation of the sexes, men in the public world of paid work, business and politics, and women in the private domestic world of the house or nursery.

Of course, it is important to recognise that this strict separation of spheres between men and women was often far more of a prescriptive ideal than a descriptive reality.[339] For many women, especially those in working-class families, paid work in the 'public' sphere was a reality and a financial necessity. Nevertheless, it is clear that the idea of separate spheres, even though it was predominantly a middle-class prescriptive ideology, still represented a pervasive and influential set of ideas in Victorian society. For many it was how they lived, for many more it was how they would have been happy to live had it been financially or practically viable, and for the vast majority it was a set of ideas with which they would have been familiar, even if it had little or no direct influence on their particular lives.

In addition to the social and cultural implications, the 'cult of domesticity' also created and reinforced differences and stereotypes of a more biological and emotional nature. Not only were women perceived as being physically weaker than men, but their biology also determined for them the innate and natural role of motherhood. Emotionally, women were considered timid and unassuming, unable to act decisively, and dependent on men to lead and take charge. Women *were* regarded as the ethical compass in society and the custodians of religious and moral standards, thus equipping them for roles like teaching, but they were still considered, more generally, subordinate to men in most areas.

All of this had important repercussions for the way in which Victorian society tended to understand the heroism of women and, more often than not, it was overlooked or certainly not extolled. Women were seen as weaker than men and subordinate to them, and so their heroism was regarded in the same manner. Women could certainly be considered heroic, but they were never considered to be as heroic as men, and a particular concern about championing heroic women was that they would lower the overall standard and drag men down from the pinnacle of excellence. There were, of course, a few exceptions to this: women whose stoicism and commitment were interpreted as heroic, such as Florence Nightingale; women who undertook public or political roles, such as Elizabeth Fry and Josephine Butler; and occasionally women who undertook a single act, the most notable being Grace Darling.[340] However, the 'heroism' of these women tended to be derived from their life, character or reputation rather than a single act of life-risking bravery, even in the case of Grace Darling.

So, G.F. Watts' decision to include otherwise ordinary working-class civilian women on his memorial was a bold move and not entirely in keeping with prevailing ideas on heroism at the time. In the latter half of the nineteenth century, 'establishment' models of heroism had tended to privilege military and imperial examples as a means to encourage citizenship and loyalty to the nation.[341] As civilian heroism became more widely reported and in the light of political reforms which were enfranchising large swathes of the working classes, there were attempts to encompass civilian heroism within existing establishment models, such as decorations for gallantry.[342]

However, individuals like Watts were part of a wider network of liberally minded reformers, philanthropists, artists and writers who sought to promote and champion civilian 'everyday' heroes and to do so through alternative methods, such as art and architecture.[343] Watts' Memorial to Heroic Self-Sacrifice represented a radical departure from the usual methods of selecting and publicly recognising civilian heroism and it is just as well that it did; the incidents involving heroic women are arguably some of the most interesting and dramatic that feature on the wall.

Leading actors and actresses assuming a pseudonym, rather than using their given name, became a familiar practice in the twentieth century. However, it was also a common phenomenon in the Victorian era and, surprisingly, a custom adopted by minor performers as well as leads. The pantomime artist commemorated on the Watts Memorial is a prime example of this and the young ballet dancer who performed under the name of **Sarah Smith** was known to her friends and family as Sarah Gibson.

Sarah appears to have been the first and only child of Andrew Gibson, a boilermaker, and his wife, Sarah, who married on 1 December 1844. Sarah senior was the daughter of William Everett Smith, a coachman, and Sarah junior took her mother's maiden name as her stage name when she entered the entertainment business. Sarah junior was born in the latter half of 1845 in the Greenwich area and it is plausible that her father was working in one of the shipyards, making boilers for steamers. This employment could have taken Andrew out of the country, which may explain why he was not apparently accounted for on the 1851 census; Sarah senior and her daughter *were* recorded, living with Sarah's parents at 1 Lovegrove Street in Camberwell. By 1861 the family was reunited and living at 44 Oakley Street, just off Westminster Bridge Road in Lambeth. Andrew Gibson, Sarah's father, was around twelve years older than his wife and he died, aged 59, in Greenwich in 1875. His wife, Sarah, does not appear to have remarried and also died in Greenwich, in 1908 at the age of 80.

In 1844, four years after it had opened, the Princess' Theatre on Oxford Street was described as:

> an elegant structure ... the audience part consists of four tiers of boxes, exclusive of the stage boxes, and a pit. It is constructed upon the plan of the best Italian theatres of the horse-shoe form. The grand Concert Room of this establishment, elegantly decorated, is one of the largest in London, and the saloon, or minor Concert Room, though not so extensive, is nevertheless of noble proportions. The Theatre and Concert Rooms are calculated to contain about 3000 persons.[344]

Performances at the Princess' tended to be English versions of foreign operas as well as farces, burlesque and ballets. Admission prices ranged from a little over a guinea for a private box down to a shilling for a seat in the gallery, so the theatre was not the preserve of the poorer classes but well within the reach of many in the working and middle classes. Doors opened at 6.30 p.m. and the curtain went up at 7 p.m.

At 7 p.m. on Friday, 23 January 1863, the curtain at the Princess' rose on the evening performance of a ballet based upon Charles Perrault's French fairy-tale pantomime, *Riquet with the Tuft*.[345] It was a large production, staged across Christmas and the New Year, and requiring a substantial cast, so a number of extra ballet girls had been employed for the duration of the run. Three of these dancers, Ada Eddison, Sarah Gibson (Smith) and Anne Perkins (who performed under her maiden name of Hunt), were performing that night and they charmed the audience as they whirled and pirouetted around the stage in their colourful and flamboyant dresses. As one of the key scenes approached, eight special-effect lights, consisting of fire-pans burning mixtures of chemicals to produce coloured illuminations, were lit and positioned on stands above the stage while the performers danced beneath. The fire-pans hissed and crackled as the fuses burned down and the chemicals sparkled red and green like fireworks.

Suddenly and without warning, Anne Perkins' dress burst into flames and a horri-fied gasp rang through the audience as the stricken performer screamed and flailed while trying to extinguish the fire. Seeing her friend and fellow performer ablaze, Sarah Gibson ran to her aid and tried to smother the burning garment but, as she did so, her own dress caught fire and, within seconds, both girls were desperately and frantically trying to put themselves out by rolling around the floor. Other perform-ers, fearful that they would be engulfed, scattered from the stage and members of the audience cried out for someone to do something and save the women. At that point, a man bolted on stage from the wings, threw a large, heavy cape over Anne Perkins and then took off his jacket to smother Sarah Gibson. As the flames were snuffed out and thick smoke hung in the air, some members of the audience sobbed and a call went out for a doctor.

Both women were badly burned and so they were taken to the female accident ward of the nearby Middlesex Hospital in Mortimer Street. Gibson's condition was critical and one newspaper reported, 'her appearance while lying in a half sensi-ble state at the hospital was most shocking. It was hardly credible that life could be sustained in a frame burnt and charred to blackness, her features being almost undistinguishable.' Despite her terrible injuries, Sarah Gibson survived in the hospital for five days, but mid-afternoon on Wednesday, 28 January, she became increasingly delirious and she died at around 6 p.m. that evening.

In the very next bed, the woman she had tried to save, Anne Perkins, was making a good recovery and, 'though much depressed by the sight of the empty bed beside her, the poor girl declared herself much relieved from bodily pain'. She was not entirely out of the woods and the burns on the upper part of her body and especially her arms were severe to the point that splints were applied to prevent muscular contractions as the flesh healed. It was also said that Perkins would be 'maimed and scarred for life', and it was doubtful that she would ever perform again. She was, however, alive and that possibly owed something to the actions of Sarah Gibson, who had not been as fortunate.

The Middlesex Hospital had seldom seen such crowds of people as those who arrived on 31 January for the inquest into Gibson's death.[346] Dr Lankester, the coro-ner for central Middlesex, opened the inquest and there was much excitement as one by one each witness gave their evidence. Sarah's mother was first and, dressed in full mourning dress, she told the court that she had spoken to her daughter in the hos-pital before she died, but the young dancer did not know exactly how the incident had occurred. She did, however, tell her mother that if there had been fire rugs in the theatre she would have been saved, something which would occupy much of the dis-cussion at the inquest. Next to testify was Edward Morgan, the house surgeon at the Middlesex Hospital, who spoke graphically about Gibson's injuries and how 'a third of the whole surface of her body was burnt'. He had recorded the cause of death as 'exhaustion from burns'.

Much of the testimony presented at the inquest came from staff and management at the theatre, including William Harris, the 'supermaster', and Robert Roxby, the stage manager. It was Roxby who had run onto the stage to extinguish the two girls using his inverness cape and his jacket, and, completely unprompted, he stated that, in his opinion, the outcome would not have been any different even if wet blankets or fire rugs had been available. A juror commented that blankets had always been available under the previous management of the theatre, at which point the coroner intervened and excused Roxby, reminding the jury that the stage manager had received severe burns while rendering assistance to the women.

Two members of the technical staff spoke about the lighting employed on the night. William Randle, the firework artist, explained at length about how the fire-pans worked, what chemicals were used and the method of igniting and fuelling the special-effect lighting. Randle said that the chemicals did not sputter but that occasionally the match or fuse within the light could throw out a spark, although he had not seen that happen on the night and had never known sparks to cause such a fire in thirty years of working stage lights. Randle's assistant, William Aitken, who was also operating the lights that evening, concluded that if it were a spark, it could only have come from one of the effect lights, rather than the gas lights. However, he maintained that the fire-pans were designed to catch sparks and embers, so he could not say, conclusively, that it was the lights he was operating which had caused the fire.

Ada Ellison, one of the dancers on stage, confirmed for the court that dresses could not really be ignited by the gas lights on stage and therefore it must have been one of the fire-pan lights which had caused the fire. Ellison also said that, from what she saw, it was not Perkins' skirt that had caught fire first, but the drape around her shoulders, and the flames had spread from there. One of the jurors suggested that the best person to explain what had happened was surely Perkins herself, and asked if she could be called before them. Edward Morgan told the jury that Perkins was too weak to attend the court, but that she might be able to answer a question at her bedside, and so, amidst much excited murmuring from the audience, the coroner left the court and went up to the ward to question the recovering dancer.

When Lankester returned, he read an unsworn statement from Perkins which declared:

The pans were held above the heads of the ballet girls when they were being turned to the audience and she felt the flames on the upper part of her body ... she thought it came from the light held by the man at the third entrance [William Aitken] ... she did not know whether anyone was to blame for the accident but she had performed in other theatres and in every theatre, large or small, except the Princess' wet rugs or blankets were kept to put out flames in case any of the dresses should catch fire. Her own life had been saved at the Surrey Theatre on one occasion by means of such blankets.

It appeared to be quite damning evidence and pointed the finger towards both the lighting and the fire prevention measures taken by the theatre management.

Finally, the witness whom everyone had been waiting for was called to give evidence and Henry William Lindus, the leaseholder and manager of the theatre, strode in and took his seat. He then proceeded to give a performance worthy of any member of his company of actors. When asked if the skirts supplied to the dancers were fireproofed, Lindus flippantly quipped 'that from what had occurred on Friday he presumed they were not and that the witness who had stated his belief that they were, was mistaken'. A juror then asked why a guard was not provided between the stage and the lights, to which Lindus snapped back, 'because the ballet girls had no business to go near the footlights and were constantly cautioned not to do so'. Surely, countered the juror, 'it was the business of the management to prevent them from doing so', to which Lindus patronisingly replied that 'he could assure the juror that if *he* had the management of a theatre for three months *he* would find it very difficult to make the employees take care of themselves'. Lindus also took issue with an earlier suggestion made by a juror that he had discontinued his predecessor's use of wet blankets; they had not, he claimed, been in use when he took over and so he had never used them, although since the incident they had been available at every performance. The jury asked no further questions and Lindus left the court.

Having heard all the evidence, the coroner began the long process of summarising all the key points and making the jury aware of certain implications. The evidence, said Lankester, suggested that all possible precautions had been taken by those operating the lights and that, as the men had been doing their jobs within the law and in a careful and cautious manner, he did not think that any criminality could be attached to them. There were, however, two wider questions, 'in which the public were much interested and to which he thought it desirable to call to the attention of the jury'. First was the question of fire precautions and the coroner suggested that they might like to make a recommendation along the lines that 'wet blankets were simple and inexpensive and every stage ought to be provided with them'. The second, and more important, question related to the fireproofing of dancers' dresses which, Lankester suggested, had implications beyond the world of the theatre.

During his time as a coroner, Lankester told the court, he had held 601 inquests, twenty-three of which were cases of burning and eighteen of those were caused by clothing catching fire. In his opinion, at least two-thirds of those deaths would have been prevented through the use of uninflammable materials. Supply was not an issue and, just that day, there had been a letter in *The Times* from a firm in Oxford Street saying that, if there were a demand for uninflammable materials, they could certainly meet it; 'there seemed no reason', declared the coroner, 'why an inflammable nightdress should be put on any child in the kingdom'. In terms of ballet dresses, there was the matter of cost, the responsibility for bearing the cost, and the maintenance of the fireproofing in the long term, but these were all issues which could and should be discussed and dealt with in a satisfactory manner. Lankester concluded by saying 'he did not know how many women would be required to be burnt to death before any of the fair sex would give up wearing an article of fashion, but if there was no chance of getting rid of the dress itself then there were means of rendering it uninflammable'.

Inquest juries had no powers to bring about actual changes to law or legislation, but they were able to make recommendations which, in high-profile cases, could put pressure on those in positons of responsibility. In the case of Sarah Gibson, the verdict returned was 'accidental death' but with a resolution that 'the jury wishes to express their opinion that sufficient precautions were not taken at the Princess' Theatre to extinguish any accidental catching fire of the clothing of the *corps de ballet*. They strongly urge the necessity of rendering articles of linen clothing fire proof by manufacturers and laundresses.' This brought the inquest to a close and Gibson's body was released for burial. She was laid to rest in Nunhead Cemetery in southeast London on 4 February 1863, where there was 'some demonstration of sympathy on the part of the theatrical fraternity as well as the general public'.[347] The funeral expenses were paid in full by Henry Lindus, perhaps as a genuine act of kindness but probably more for the purposes of salvaging some public credibility and, perhaps, to try and subdue a slightly guilty conscience.

Whereas the ideology of separate spheres prescribed that men should be the breadwinners while women remained at home, running the household and raising the children, the reality for many working-class families was very different. Low rates of pay, reduced hours, seasonal or irregular employment and periods of unemployment due to illness or injury could all reduce a man's wages, and therefore undertaking paid work was often a financial necessity for many working-class women. This did not, though, necessarily mean that they broke with convention, and paid work for women was often 'outwork' undertaken within the domestic sphere and in addition to all the usual household responsibilities. At the lower end of the scale, women might undertake 'piece work', such as making matchboxes or assembling toys, and the clothing trades employed thousands of women to stitch garments through a system of middlemen, which came to be known as 'sweating'.[348]

Laundry was another avenue of domestic-orientated employment for women, and as prosperous middle-class consumerism boomed, the demand for laundry services grew, and many women progressed from simply washing clothes to running large and successful laundries, often based within their own homes. These businesses served several purposes: they provided income, they gave the woman some autonomy while still allowing her to fulfil her family duties, and they provided employment for the children of the family, particularly the daughters. In the 1881 census, 287,000 women were officially listed as employed in laundry services, which accounted for 8.5 per cent of all working women, and this did not include women who took in washing on a more informal basis.[349] The slightly derogatory label of 'washerwoman' was increasingly replaced by the more respectable title of 'laundress' and in neighbourhoods across the country large-scale laundries based in domestic premises became an increasingly common sight.

In 1871, in Edwards Lane in Stoke Newington, just such an establishment was being run from numbers 1 and 2, which were joined together by an internal door and corridor. The ground floors of the houses were used as a laundry and the family lived in the rooms above. The business was run by 61-year-old Elizabeth Kennedy and she lived there with her husband George and four of her five children. Elizabeth's maiden name was Skelton and she married George Edward Kennedy, a carpenter, at St Marylebone church in Westminster on 19 November 1837. The couple's first child, Elizabeth Frances, was born on 11 May 1842 and three more followed at regular intervals: George Edward junior (b. 1844), John Wiston (b. 1846) and Frederick George (b. 1848). By 1851, the family had moved into 4 Edwards Lane, the first of several properties they would own in the road, and Frances' niece, Eliza Skelton, had moved down from Leicestershire to board with them.

Amelia Kennedy, the last of George and Elizabeth's children, was born in 1852 and by 1861 the family had moved to 2 Edwards Lane, where they had also been joined by Harriet Skelton, Eliza's sister. George Kennedy suffered from epilepsy and was often unable to work, so Elizabeth had fallen back on her previous experience and started taking in washing to supplement the household income. Over time, the business grew and the family acquired the property next door so as to keep pace with demand. In 1861 Amelia's cousin, Eliza Skelton, who had been lodging with the family, married Henry Rout and by 1871 the couple were living in the lodge attached to The Rookery, a large house in Putney Park in Roehampton, Surrey. Amelia was staying with her cousin on the night of 2 April 1871 and she was recorded as a visitor on the census, although it seems likely that her permanent residence was still in Edwards Lane, as this is where she was living on 18 October 1871 when tragedy befell the Kennedy family.

As per usual, George and Elizabeth Kennedy were sleeping upstairs in number 1 Edwards Lane, with their two sons, John and Frederick, in the adjacent room.[350] George Kennedy junior, the eldest of the five children, had moved out of the family home and lived nearby at 3 Elizabeth Terrace. Meanwhile, upstairs at number 2 Edwards Lane, Elizabeth and Amelia Kennedy shared one bedroom while two female servants slept in another. The ground floor was given over to laundry and directly beneath the girl's bedrooms was the drying and ironing room containing a large cast-iron stove which, during the wetter months, was kept running throughout the night. In the early hours of 18 October, while everyone slept, some linen in the room fell onto the hot stove and began to smoulder.

It was around 3 a.m. when Elizabeth Kennedy was woken by the sound of crack-ling wood and a strange choking sensation which she soon realised was due to the smoke that was filtering upwards through the floorboards. As Elizabeth roused Amelia, she was shocked to see the tips of flames flickering through gaps in the floor and both girls could feel the terrible heat rising from the room below. Amelia quickly woke the two servants and then called to Elizabeth that she was going next door to raise the alarm and wake her parents and brothers. Elizabeth saw Amelia disappear down the stairs, but before she could follow her, flames broke through the wall and she was forced back up into the bedroom. Realising that escape through the house was no longer possible, Elizabeth opened one of the bedroom windows and she and the servants were able to climb out and crawl across the roof of a washhouse next door, which then allowed them to drop down into the yard behind the lane.

Around the corner at 3 Elizabeth Terrace, George Kennedy was woken by shouts of 'fire' from the street outside, and when he got downstairs he was met by his two younger brothers, who told him that the laundry was on fire. As they hurried back to Edwards Lane, John Kennedy related to his elder brother how the family had been woken by Amelia and they had initially tried to fight the fire but were forced out by the flames and smoke. The three boys arrived to find their parents in the street but no sign of Amelia. John told them that she had expressed concerns about the well-being of her sister and he had last seen 'Milly' running through the house in the direction of the back door, although she may have gone back into number 2 to find Elizabeth. The fire was raging through the front of the building, so George made his way around to the rear of the property, where he tried to force open the back door, but something was blocking it.

Peering in through the gap between the door and the jamb, George could just make out a body lying face down on the floor behind the door and realised, with dismay, that it was his sister Amelia. The heat was intense and with flames darting out from inside, George was forced to concede that his sister was probably dead. A few minutes later George's two younger brothers arrived and one tried to crawl in through the gap, but he could not reach his sister and was driven back by the choking black smoke. It had been nearly an hour since the alarm had been raised and, at the front of the house, the fire brigade finally started to pump water, but by that time the interior was an inferno and much of the property destroyed. The firemen had been told there was nobody trapped, but when the Kennedy brothers appeared and explained that they had seen their sister in the back kitchen, all efforts were focused on getting her out. It was, though, a futile endeavour and when the brigade eventually managed to get into the kitchen, they were shocked to find the body of 19-year-old Amelia Kennedy almost entirely consumed by fire and nothing but cinders from the waist down.

The buildings in Edwards Lane were still smouldering two days later when, on 20 October, an inquest into the death of Amelia Kennedy was opened a few streets away at the Rose and Crown pub in Church Street.[351] George Kennedy, Amelia's father, had suffered several fits since the blaze and was unable to give evidence, but three of the four children related the terrible events to the jury. The court then heard from fireman George Bailey and some worrying details emerged about the brigade's ability to fight the fire. Bailey explained that the horses for the engine were stabled about 500yds from the fire station and it took about eleven minutes to fetch them and yoke them to the carriage. Despite this, Bailey estimated that the appliance had reached Edwards Lane about eleven minutes after the alarm was raised and that was when serious problems were encountered. The roadway had recently been paved and when the firemen located the fire-plugs (water hydrants) they found them choked with gravel and could not get them to work. Different plugs were tried but on both occasions the supply of water failed, and it was at least forty minutes before they were able to start extinguishing the blaze; 'it was no fault of his,' Bailey told the jury, 'the parish authorities or the water company were to blame'. With all the evidence presented, the jury returned a verdict of 'accidental death' with a recommendation that 'the horses should be kept at the fire station and the plugs should be constantly visited to see that they were in proper working order'. Perhaps if they had been, Amelia Kennedy would have survived the dreadful conflagration that consumed her family's home and laundry business.

Testament to the income that laundry could generate, the Kennedy family were able to buy a large burial plot in nearby Abney Park Cemetery and erect a substantial headstone to the memory of Amelia, who was buried there on 24 October 1871. In the years that followed, the grave became the final resting place for several other members of the family. The physical damage to the properties in Edwards Lane was slowly repaired, and in 1881 George and Elizabeth were living there along with their eldest daughter, Elizabeth, their son, John, a domestic servant, Sarah Milliner, and three lodgers. Elizabeth was helping with the laundry business while John was working as a commercial clerk for a furrier. George Kennedy died, aged 70, on 14 June 1883 and his estate of £3,238 passed to his wife, Elizabeth, who died three years later at the age of 76; both were buried in the plot in Abney Park Cemetery.

The couple's daughter, Elizabeth, continued to live in the property but she did not marry or have any children, and when she died, aged 45, on 27 March 1888 she too was buried in Abney Park and her estate of £1,062 passed to her brother, John Wiston Kennedy. John married Ellen Esther Hensey in Hackney in 1881 and the couple moved into 1 Mount Pleasant Lane in Clapton. They were still there in 1891, but by 1901 had moved a few doors along to number 9, where they stayed until at least 1911. The couple do not appear to have had any children and John died in 1921, aged 75. His wife died four years later, aged 74.

Amelia's elder brother, George Edward junior, not only had his father's name but his life quite remarkably followed a similar course. He became a carpenter and on 5 February 1871 in St John the Baptist church in Warwick he married Elizabeth Skelton, the daughter of a pipe maker, Ralph Skelton. It is not clear exactly what relation George junior's wife was to his mother or what his in-law relationship was to his new wife, but there was undoubtedly a family connection. Initially the couple moved into a cottage on Avenue Road in west Hackney, but by the end of 1871 they were back living at 3 Elizabeth Terrace and by 1881 at 144 Church Street in Stoke Newington. The family continued to expand and, following the death of his parents and his elder sister in the 1880s, George moved his substantial family into the property at 2 Edwards Lane.[352] They were living there in 1891, but George must have felt that the property was jinxed when his eldest son, George junior, died in 1900 at the age of just 21. Shortly after this, the family moved to 14 Lordship Lane and by 1911 they were living at 12 Lordship Terrace. George Kennedy, Amelia's elder brother, died in 1930, aged 86; his wife lived to 97 and died in 1943.

Amelia's brother, Frederick, found work as a commercial clerk and lived with his parents until 1878 when he married Jane Thompson in Biggleswade. The couple moved into 8 Crescent Terrace, off St Anns Road in Edmonton, where their first child, Alice Margaret, was born in 1879. Another two daughters followed, Kate Thompson (b. 1880) and Annie (b. 1881), then a son, Frank Harry (b. 1882) and finally another daughter Florence Mary (b. 1885). In 1891 they were living at 79 Hawkslea Road in Stoke Newington, but by 1901 they had moved a few streets away to 12 Grayling Road. Frederick died, aged 61, in 1910 and Jane initially stayed at 12 Grayling Road with her three daughters, Alice, Annie and Florence. Jane appears to have died in Hackney in 1927, aged 71.

In terms of employment opportunities for women, there was one occupation which hugely predominated and that was domestic service. For working-class women, it was, by far, the most available type of work and was overall the largest employer; on average, between 1851 and 1901, 43 per cent of working women were employed in domestic service.[353] The job was usually nothing more than a financially necessary hardship for working-class women and their families, but it was perceived by middle-class observers as the most fitting occupation for single working-class women because it provided an environment and opportunity for both social control and the inculcation of middle-class morals and standards.[354]

Towards the latter half of the nineteenth century, increased educational provision led to greater opportunities for women from the more prosperous working classes to move into teaching, nursing and, eventually, secretarial work with employers like the Post Office, all of which were viewed as good, stable and, most importantly, respectable occupations. Nevertheless, domestic service persisted and it was still the largest employer of women in all censuses from 1901 until well past the Second World War.

Elizabeth Coghlan entered domestic service at the age of around 12 or 13 and in 1891 she was working for a German traveller, Philip Boss, and his family at 73 St Thomas Road, near Victoria Park in Hackney. Elizabeth was born in south Hackney in 1878, but it is tricky to build a clear picture of her extended family from records like the census because of the variant spelling of her surname. Her father, Dennis Coghlan, was born in Ireland and her mother, Ann Taylor, was born in Surrey; the couple married at St John the Baptist church in Kentish Town on 1 November 1864. Unusually, they do not appear to have started a family straight away or, if they did, the children do not appear to have survived because, in 1871, the couple were recorded as living alone at 5 Mildmay Avenue near the Balls Pond Road in Islington.

Dennis and Ann's first recorded child, Annie, was born in 1872, their second, Dennis, in 1875 and then Elizabeth in 1878. In 1881 the family was living at 29 Abney Gardens in Hackney, and in 1885 another daughter, Emily Amelia, arrived. By 1891, most of the Coghlan family had moved to 6 George Place in Hackney and Elizabeth was working nearby for the Boss family. Ten years later, in March 1901, Elizabeth had changed employer and was working as a live-in general domestic servant for the Brien family at 2 Albion Cottages in Church Path, Stoke Newington. Robert Brien was a house painter and he lived with his wife, Amy, his two sons, William aged 12 and Stanley aged 4, and Amy's father Thomas Starling, a retired porter. As a general servant, Elizabeth would have been responsible for cleaning and maintaining the house, helping in the kitchen, sewing and repairing clothes, and looking after the children. It would have been a relentless living with very little time off or time to herself.

This even extended to occasions such as New Year's Eve and on 31 December 1901, while the rest of the family went out to welcome in 1902, Elizabeth stayed at home to mind the children and busy herself around the house.[355] One of her tasks was making sure the house was warm and lit for when her employers returned, and so she set about stoking the fires with coal and filling the lamps with oil. Later that evening, Thomas Starling turned the corner into Church Path and as he walked towards Albion Cottages he became increasingly alarmed as he realised there was a crowd outside his house and numerous constables and firemen were going in and out.

Anxiously pushing his way through the throng of neighbours, he hurried into the house and was shocked to see the servant girl, Elizabeth Coghlan, laid out on the kitchen floor, seemingly unconscious and apparently badly burned. Starling urgently enquired about his grandchildren and was told that they were safe upstairs in their beds. A doctor had been summoned and recommended that Coghlan be taken as quickly as possible to the nearest infirmary, so she was taken to the German Hospital on Ritson Road. A Dr Paravicini examined Coghlan and found her to be suffering from shock due to burns, so she was admitted straight away and treated. The young woman was, though, quite badly burned and she only survived a few hours in the hospital before dying on the morning of Wednesday, 1 January 1902. It was an immensely unhappy New Year for the Coghlan family.

There was much interest in the coroner's inquest, held at Hackney Coroner's Court on 2 January 1903, as people were keen to find out what had happened to the poor girl and how she had met her death.[356] Dennis Coghlan confirmed some basic information about his daughter and Thomas Starling told the court what he knew about the incident, which was very little. More was revealed by his next-door neighbour Eliza Taylor, who explained that she had suddenly seen Elizabeth, enveloped in a ball of flames, lying in the back garden of number 2. She grabbed a hearth rug and, while shouting for help, climbed over the dividing fence between the two gardens and tried to smother the flames. Taylor's shouts attracted the attention of James Barnes, a railwayman who was walking along Church Path, and he ran through Taylor's house, vaulted the fence and assisted with putting out the fire. Barnes and Taylor then carried Elizabeth back into the house and another neighbour went to fetch a constable.

Both Taylor and Barnes testified that Elizabeth Coghlan had managed to speak to them before she passed out and she told them that 'she had been filling the lamp and whilst putting the oil can on the shelf it fell off on to the lamp which was alight. She then became alarmed and ran out into the garden.' Evidence along these lines was also presented by a London County Council inspector, Alfred Butler, who reported that he had visited the premises and concluded that:

the vapour from the oil probably came into contact with the light ... the oil in the reservoir would have caught fire and caused a considerable flame. The woman [Coghlan] must have run out into the garden with the lamp and dropped it, her clothes in the meantime having caught fire.

Press reports emphasised that William and Stanley Brien were asleep upstairs during the episode, but there had been no fire in the house and neither boy was injured. It was also reported that 'Before she died, Miss Coghlan said there were children asleep in the house and she rushed into the yard in order to prevent the house taking fire and endangering their lives', an account from which the incident derived its element of heroism.[357] Several newspapers mistakenly reported that William and Stanley were Coghlan's children, under headlines including 'A Mother's Devotion' and 'Brave Mother's Death'.[358] The jury, having heard all the available evidence, returned a verdict of 'accidental death' and 'commended the witnesses Eliza Taylor and James Barnes for their prompt action in attending to the deceased woman'.

The problems with variant spelling of the name Coghlan continue to make it difficult to trace Elizabeth's family after her death. Annie Coghlan, Elizabeth's eldest sister, married Henry Day, a labourer, at St James the Great church in Bethnal Green on 6 June 1892. They were recorded as living at 17 Florida Street at the time. Evidence suggests that the couple had already had their first child, William Henry, who was born on 19 June 1891 and that Annie was pregnant with their second, Edward Charles, who was born on 27 November 1892. Both boys were baptised at St John's church in Stamford Hill on 2 August 1893. Two further boys followed, Arthur (b. 1899) and Dennis junior (b. 1901), and in 1901 the family was living at 72 Mill Road in Lewisham. They were still at this address in 1911, but the ranks had been swelled by four more children: Florence (b. 1903), Leonard (b. 1905), Violet (b. 1907) and Elsie (b. 1910).

Amelia's sister, Emily, worked for a spell as a domestic servant and then in a factory before she married Frederick William Keeling, a labourer living at 8 Henrietta Road, at St John's church in Stamford Hill on 15 December 1907. They had their first child, George, in 1908, and in 1911 they were living at 7 Catherine Road, in Edmonton, and Emily's mother, Ann, was living with them. At least four more children followed: George Frederick (b. 1908), Edward C. (b. 1915), Frederick W. (b. 1917) and Leonard A. (b. 1919, d. 1921). Frederick died, aged 64, in Edmonton in 1947. Emily died on 15 January 1962 at 44 Weir Hall Avenue in Edmonton. She left an estate valued at £257 which passed to her eldest son, George Frederick Keeling.

In many ways, the Watts Memorial is highly unusual among Victorian monuments commemorating heroism because it features women and children. Watts, and a wider circle of associates and acquaintances, were undoubtedly radical in their approach and challenged many of the preconceived ideas about the types of people and acts that should be considered heroic. However, when placed firmly into its wider historical context, it is clear that there was still a limit to that radical streak and that the memorial, while breaking with some conventions, firmly accorded with others. It is interesting that almost all of the women who feature lost their lives in distinctly domestic settings or environments which were considered to be within the 'female' sphere of society, the only exception to this, arguably, being Sarah Gibson (Smith). It would appear that Watts was more than willing to recognise the heroism and sacrifices made by women, but only within the fairly tight constraints of domestic ideology. This is not to say that it was a deliberate or intentional decision, but it does indicate the dominance and influence, certainly among the middle classes and in prescriptive literature, of those ideas at the time.

19

HER LIFE FOR
HER CHILDREN

One striking and consistent element that manifests itself in newspaper reports and semi-fictional narratives of acts of heroism undertaken by women is the suggestion that the act itself, and in particular the level of bravery, is all the more remarkable because of the fact that it has been undertaken by a woman. Just one of many examples can be found in *Heroines of Daily Life* by Frank Mundell, where he recounted the story of a young woman who dived from Southampton Pier to attempt a rescue of three people who had overturned their pleasure boat. In remarking upon this act, Mundell concluded that 'it was a feat of which the best male swimmer would have every right to feel proud, and executed as it was by a young lady, was almost without precedent'.[359] Generally speaking, women were portrayed as unusual candidates for heroism and this was partly linked, as might be expected under the influence of Victorian ideas of gender, to their perceived fragility and weakness.

Furthermore, if women *did* display physical strength and fortitude, it was usually considered to be a one-off and stemming from a particularly female characteristic. This sentiment is suitably exemplified by a comment in *The Englishwoman's Domestic Magazine*: 'notwithstanding the physical weakness of her constitution, there is an internal energy of character and strength of endurance fed from the deep and solemn sources of affection, that render women capable of performing the most heroic and glorious acts'.[360] An example of this is a Mrs Walker, who while searching for her two children during a snowstorm in the High Peaks area of Derbyshire, 'tore the cold snow-clods asunder with the miraculous strength that comes to mothers when their children are in peril' after discovering her son buried in a snowdrift.[361] More often than not, when women undertook acts of heroism the ability to do so was seen as being intrinsically linked to a duty of care or the nurturing and mothering tendencies that were considered to be innate in the female sex. This would extend to nursemaids saving their charges, teachers saving pupils, nurses saving the elderly or those in their care, and, of course, mothers saving their children or the children of others.

It was a few minutes past midnight in the early hours of Sunday, 20 April 1902, and Ernest Rogers was finishing work for the week and shutting up his ticket-writing shop at 423 Hackney Road.[362] Two brass oil lamps hung from the ceiling and, with the intention of extinguishing them, Rogers climbed onto a box and reached up for one of the lamps. However, as he tipped it and unhooked it from its mounting, some oil spilled out and suddenly the whole lamp was engulfed in flames. In alarm, Rogers dropped it, but as the lamp hit the carpet, more oil gushed out and within seconds much of the shop floor was ablaze. Realising he could not extinguish the flames, Rogers' thoughts turned to the tenants who lived about the premises and, in particular, the family with young children whom he knew would be upstairs at that time. He managed to reach the back parlour, but when he started to ascend the staircase he looked back and, as flames licked at the steps behind him, he knew that he, and the people upstairs, would have to find another way out.

The family who lived above the shop at 423 Hackney Road were the Denmans, consisting of Charles Denman, his wife and their six children. Charles had been born in Shoreditch on 23 February 1867. His father, William Denman, was a costermonger and general dealer who had married Elizabeth Thornton, the daughter of a labourer, at St Matthias' church in Bethnal Green on 28 November 1853. The couple moved into 2 Bernales Buildings in Shoreditch and started a family, Charles being the sixth of the eleven children whom the couple went on to have.[363] In 1876, Charles' father William died at the age of 44, and Elizabeth, Charles' mother, took over the family business. Charles continued to live with his mother and siblings, and started buying and selling cheese to earn a living. The family moved to 67 Huntingdon Road, just off the Kingsland Road in Bethnal Green, but sometime between 1891 and 1893, Charles moved out and into lodgings at 362 Hackney Road. Across the road and a few houses away lived Owen Murrell and his family, whom Charles became friendly with, and soon started courting Owen's youngest daughter, Alice.

Alice Maud Murrell was born in Bethnal Green in 1875. Her father, Owen, was a cabinet maker and he married Mary Ann Hunt on 12 March 1850 at Christ Church in Spitalfields. The couple moved into a room at 50 Wards Row in Bethnal Green and a family quickly followed. Their first child, Mary Ann junior, was born in 1852, followed in 1854 by Owen junior, then Samuel in 1856. By 1857, when Marie Jane arrived, the family was living at 50 Bethnal Green Road, but a year later, in 1858, George Murrell was born at 60 Edward Street in Bethnal Green. The couple's sixth child, Alfred, was born in 1861, followed by Louisa in 1864, Frank Charles in 1868 and William in 1870. Prior to the birth of their tenth child, Henry Charles, in 1872 the family moved to 464 Bethnal Green Road and this is probably where their final child, Alice Maud, was born in 1875. Between 1875 and 1881, the family moved yet again to 423 Hackney Road. It would appear that this last move was to allow Owen to expand from cabinet making into timber production, and he started a family business with his sons assisting him as wood sawyers and turners. Alice Maud continued living with her parents and entered the hat-making trade until, on 12 March 1893, she married Charles Denman at St Peter's church in Bethnal Green.

After the couple were married they moved in with Alice's parents at 423 Hackney Road and Alice must have been heavily pregnant at the wedding as their first child, Alice Maud junior, was born on 12 June 1893. A second child, Lillian May, followed soon after on 18 October 1894, and then a third child, Charles George, born on 25 March 1896. By this time, Charles had moved from selling cheese to meat and was trading as a butcher and provision merchant at premises nearby. The couple had three further children: Ethel Mary (b. 1898), Percival Owen (b. 10 November 1899) and Winifred Daisy (b. 2 January 1902). Alice Maud and Lillian were admitted to Teesdale Street School in September 1898, followed in May 1900 by their younger brother, Charles. Ethel Mary was admitted to the school on 14 April 1902, less than a week before the fire that would claim her life, and her name is poignantly crossed through in the admissions register. Alice's mother, Mary Ann, died at the beginning of 1898 and the following year, on 14 April, her father, Owen, passed away. Owen's estate was valued at £7,456 which passed to his eldest son, William. However, it would appear that Alice retained the use of 423 Hackney Road because she and her family continued to live there after the death of her parents. The shop was no longer needed for selling Owen's furniture and so Charles Denman let it to a ticket writer named Ernest Rogers; a seemingly innocuous transaction, but one that would bring tragedy to the family.

At around the same time that Alice Denman smelt burning, she also heard the heavy footsteps of Ernest Rogers on the staircase, and by the time he burst into the room she had already realised that there must be a fire in the shop; something which the terrified look on his face confirmed. Gesturing upstairs, Alice screamed, 'My children! Help me save my children!' and Rogers followed her as she rushed up to the top floor of the building. The rooms were in darkness and smoke was already beginning to fill the air, but stumbling around, Ernest managed to find 2-year-old Percival Denman. Rogers scooped the child into his arms and, climbing out of a window, he was able to carefully negotiate the roof-leads of a neighbouring shop and pass the child through a window into a neighbouring building, occupied by Mr and Mrs Arnold and their family.

Heading back across the roof and into the smoke-filled house, Rogers went into another room, picked up 7-year-old Lillian and was on his way back to the window when he felt Alice Denman push past him with a child in her arms. He lost sight of her, so he climbed out of the window and was heading across the shop roof when a skylight exploded in front of him, sending a huge plume of smoke and flames soaring into the air. With difficulty, Ernest Rogers negotiated the shattered skylight and handed the girl through the window to Mr Arnold, but as he turned to make his way back to see if he could help Alice Denman, he felt faint and collapsed. When he came round a few minutes later, he realised he had been lifted through the window into the neighbouring building and was relieved to be told that, apparently, everyone else in the Denman house had escaped. Sadly, that was not the case at all.

A few streets away, Lily Riley, the Denmans' housemaid, was on an errand to buy biscuits for supper, and as she passed by the butchers, she waved at Charles Denman, who was busily tying up packages of meat in preparation for closing the shop. Having purchased the biscuits, Lily was on her way back to the house when someone called out to her, 'Lil, get home quickly, the place is all on fire!' and so she hurried anxiously through the back alleys, hoping that the situation was not too serious. As she turned the corner, though, Lily was horrified to see the ticket shop and the rooms above completely ablaze, and realising she could not get in at the front, she ran around to a side entrance, but that was also blocked by flames.

Hearing a scream, the housemaid looked up and at a landing window she could just make out Alice Denman with the baby, Winifred, clasped to her chest. 'Lil, come to me quickly and help,' cried Alice, 'or my dear children will be burned to death. Come, Lil, there's a good girl, or I shall lose them.' Lily tried to get through the door but was pushed back by the heat and with tears streaming down her cheeks she shouted up to Alice, 'Oh Mrs Denman! I cannot come through the fire! My dear mistress, what shall we do?' At that point, Lily watched helplessly as Alice turned away from the window and disappeared back into the smoke. The housemaid may have been the last person to see Alice alive, but there was someone else in the house who might have seen her after that, just before both of them perished in the flames.

Next door to 423 Hackney Road there was a carting business owned by a Mr Stevens and he employed a number of carmen who were familiar figures in the area and knew its inhabitants well. They especially knew the Denman family who lived next door and were used to seeing the 'fair-haired Denman children' playing in the street or on their way back and forth from the house. Several of the men were tending to their carts in the yard at the back of Stevens' property when they heard the cries of 'Fire!' and a few minutes later they saw Ernest Rogers walking across a roof at the back of the house with a child in his arms. A number of the men ran around to the side of the house and managed to climb up onto the roof just as Rogers appeared with a second child. When he collapsed, some of them helped to lift him in through the window of the neighbouring building, but one carman was intent on seeing if there were still people trapped in the house. He clambered across the roof-leads and, with his arm shielding his face from the heat, he disappeared through the plumes of smoke into the blazing house.

The man who entered the building was **Arthur William Regelous**, better known to many residents in and around Hackney as 'little Peter', although few could recall where the nickname had come from. Arthur had been born in 1877 and baptised at the parish church of St John of Jerusalem in Hackney on 11 November that year. His father, George Regelous, was said to have Italian heritage, but he was born in Saffron Walden in Essex in 1850, as was his father, William, so if there were European roots they originated further back than two generations. By 1871, George had moved to Mile End and was working as a cashier in a bank. However, by 1873 he had changed his profession to carman, and moved house to 31 Sale Street in Bethnal Green.

On 19 February 1873, George Regelous married Rose Pearmain, the daughter of a greengrocer, at St Peter's church in Bethnal Green. Children soon followed with Rose Emma, born in 1873, and Frederick, born in 1875. Arthur William was the couple's third child and his first home was at 38 Vyner Street, next to the Regent's Canal in Hackney. Within a few months of his birth, however, the family moved to 10 Weston Place in Hackney, where a fourth child, George Robert, was born in 1879.

The family appear to have been perpetually on the move as, by 1881, they were living at 18 Brunswick Street in Hackney, in 1883 at 51 Tower Street in Hackney, and then in 1891 back in Vyner Street but this time at number 36. During this time, four more children arrived: Florence Mary (b. 1881), Henry Charles (b. 1882), Ernest Alfred (b. 1889) and Edith (b. 1890). Just three years after the birth of Edith, Rose Regelous died at the age of 43, and two years after that the 49-year-old George Regelous followed, leaving several young and dependent children as orphans. The youngest, Edith, went to live with her sister, Rose, while Ernest was sent to the Hackney Union Training School in Brentwood.[364]

After the death of his parents, Arthur Regelous lived with local relatives for a couple of years and did whatever jobs he could find to make ends meet. Over time, he got to know some of the carmen who had worked with his father and eventually he started working on and off for Mr Stevens on the Hackney Road. Around 1901, Arthur contracted some sort of illness that confined him to the local infirmary, and for some time it appeared that he would not recover. However, people in the area talked of how 'his pluck had pulled him through' and before too long he was back with his cart on the streets of Hackney; an easily recognisable figure, 'undersized, with close cropped hair and numerous scars on his scalp'. In 1902 he was living at 400 Hackney Road and was said to 'live a happy, rough and tumble life, earning a slender livelihood', so it is easy to picture him as a rather colourful and well-known local character.

Harry Lewis, one of the carmen who worked with Regelous, had helped lift Ernest Rogers in through the window of the neighbouring building and, looking around for Arthur, he realised that his workmate must have gone to try and rescue people from the fire. Flames were now bursting forth from most of the windows, but Lewis suddenly saw Regelous appear briefly at one of them with a handkerchief to his mouth and calling for help. There was, though, no way for anyone to get in and, shortly after, Arthur disappeared as flames engulfed the window at which he had been standing. Lewis climbed down from the roof and ran around to the front of the building where the brigade had arrived and were fighting the fire. He told the firemen about Regelous, but the building was, by then, described as being 'like a furnace' and all that could be done was to try and extinguish the flames as quickly as possible; there might then be chance to get in, but it would probably be too late.

Charles Denman was just pulling down the shutters on the butchers when the housemaid, Lily Riley, ran up to him in a dreadful state of anguish and distress, crying that, 'The shop is on fire at home.' Denman dashed through the streets and, finding the house ablaze, he desperately sought news about his family. Erroneously informed that everyone in the house had got out alive, he set off around the neighbourhood to various friends and acquaintances, trying to find his wife and children. By the time he returned, perplexed that he could not locate them, the fire was more or less out, but when he was stopped from entering the building, he told the constable, 'My name is Denman, this is my house.' 'If you are Mr Denman,' the constable replied, 'will you come and see if you can identify any of these bodies.' The sight that met Charles Denman was too much for him and two constables had to lead him away, as they feared he would collapse. Laid out on the pavement were seven canvas sacks, three of which were stretched over forms the size and shape of adult bodies, but also four that were barely full and clearly contained the bodies of children.

When the firemen had eventually extinguished the intense blaze and dampened down the smouldering remains of the building, they had gone inside the burnt-out shell to search for the body of Arthur Regelous, who had last been seen by Harry Lewis at an upstairs window. They had been dismayed to find not one body, but three – two women and a man, all of whom were then placed into canvas sacks and taken outside, where they were laid in a side alley. As the search continued, the true horror and tragedy of the disaster slowly unfolded as, one by one, the firemen discovered the bodies of four children, one boy and three girls, the smallest of whom was just a baby. Each was carefully and solemnly placed into a canvas sack which was then wrapped around them, and they were taken outside and placed in the alley with the adults. Eventually, witnesses were found who could identify the bodies and, as suspected, Arthur Regelous and Alice Maud Denman were two of the three adults. The four children were Alice Maud junior, aged 8, Charles junior, who had just turned 6, Ethel, aged 3, and Winifred, just 3 months old. The third adult body was Alice Biggs, a female lodger who lived with the Denman family and had been in bed in the house when the fire started.

Alice Isabella Biggs was born on 11 October 1875 and she came to reside at 423 Hackney Road through a series of family bereavements. Her father, Frederick William, worked as a bookbinder for his family's stationery manufacturing business and on 20 February 1875 he married Alice Rebecca Dean at the parish church of St John of Jerusalem in Hackney. Alice Isabella was the first of their children to be born (Alice Rebecca was possibly already pregnant at the wedding) followed by George Frederick on 13 December 1877 and then Frederick John on 4 February 1880. During this period, the family lived at a number of addresses in the Hackney area, including 35 Paul Street and 20 Lenthall Road. However, sometime after 1881, Frederick appears to have become the landlord of the Victory pub at 153 Goldsmiths Row on the Hackney Road, but it was there, on 29 January 1885, that he died aged just 32.

His widow, Alice Rebecca, remarried to Thomas Collings Hyne, a shoemaker and son of a blacksmith, on 11 July 1887 at St Peter's church in Bethnal Green. The family, consisting of Thomas and Alice Hyne and Alice's three children, continued to live at the Victory with Thomas taking over as the landlord. Alice Rebecca died at the beginning of 1898, aged 42, and on 10 December the same year Thomas remarried to Henrietta Ann Dean, who appears to have been Alice's cousin. Thomas and Henrietta continued to reside at the Victory, with George and Frederick Biggs, while Alice moved out and sought alternative accommodation. She found employment as a button-hole machinist and this allowed her to rent a room with the Denman family at 423 Hackney Road. It would appear that Alice was more than just a lodger, as she acted as a witness at Winifred's baptism in 1902, just weeks before the fire that would kill them both.

The inquest into all seven deaths was opened at Bethnal Green Coroner's Court in Calvert Avenue on 22 April 1902 and a senior coroner of high standing, Dr William Westcott, assumed the unenviable task of presiding over the sorrowful proceedings.[365] Ernest Rogers confirmed to the court that he had inadvertently started the fire while taking the lamp down to extinguish it. When questioned by a juror as to why he needed to take the lamps down, Rogers replied that they could only be extinguished by blowing down the chimney, to which the juror sardonically replied, 'Just the way to cause an accident, I would think.' The court also heard evidence from Thomas Nunan, a petroleum inspector for the London County Council (LCC), who reported that he had tested the 'Russian Czarolen' oil that Mr Rogers had been using in the lamp and found it to have a dangerously low flashpoint of 88 degrees, which had, in his opinion, contributed to the lamp catching fire.

Superintendent Charles Gerton from the Metropolitan Fire Brigade informed the court that the alarm call had reached the Green Street Fire Station at 12.10 a.m. and a horse-drawn fire escape had arrived at the scene of the fire within four minutes, followed shortly after by two steam-driven pump engines. Two escape attendants had tried to use the apparatus to enter the building, but the fire was already too severe by the time they arrived. In total, more than fifty firemen had fought the blaze, using eight steam-driven pumps and other appliances; within twenty minutes of it starting, the house was an inferno that nobody could enter or escape from. Gerton also expressed an opinion that 'the building was a very bad one and a very serious risk; all the back was enclosed and it would have been very difficult for anyone to escape that way. No fire insurance office would take such a building.' Charles Denman confirmed that the building was not insured.

Summarising all the evidence, the coroner stated that, 'Regelous lost his life in attempting to save others and nothing was known about what happened to the unfortunate lodger except that she was burnt to death.' With regard to the cause of the fire, he concluded that 'it was quite clear the paraffin lamp was at the bottom of it and everyone knew that these low flash oils were a serious and continual danger'. Having retired to discuss the case, the jury returned verdicts of 'accidental death' in all seven cases, adding that 'they hoped Mr Rogers would be more careful when extinguishing a lamp in future and that the LCC would promote legislation in connection with the low flash oil imported into the country'. The court expressed its admiration of the conduct of Regelous, the police and the firemen, and announced that the Mayor of Bethnal Green intended to open a subscription fund for the benefit of those who had suffered by the fire.

Reporting on the incident, the local press praised the actions of Alice Denman, saying that 'Had Mrs Denman rushed through the fire into the street when she first came to the landing she would have been living now, but she gave her life for her children and only a beautiful memory of the deed remains.' On 28 April 1902, the streets from Hackney Road to Stamford Hill were crowded with people and it was reported that several thousand mourners were present at Abney Park Cemetery in Stoke Newington when the funeral cortège for Alice Maud Denman and her four children arrived at the cemetery.[366] All five were buried in the same plot and a stone erected recording their names. Abney Park Cemetery has since become overgrown and reaching the grave is problematic.

Similar scenes of mourning had been witnessed two days earlier for the funeral of Arthur Regelous, which took place on 26 April 1902.[367] Arthur was described as 'as good a little fellow as you could meet' and 'a general favourite with working lads and girls'. Many floral tributes were received, including one 'made by the girls at Nardi's factory, to the memory of a brave man' and another sent by the 'Choir girls of the Ashley Mission; may God bless the memory of a brave man'. The funeral costs were paid by a Mr Merrett and the polished oak coffin was mounted with brass fittings and a brass nameplate. The funeral cortège, consisting of a horse-drawn hearse and two mourning coaches, began its solemn journey from 43 Pott Street in Bethnal Green, the home of Arthur's paternal uncle, John Regelous. The procession, flanked by a patrol of mounted police, wove its way through the crowded streets of Hackney where blinds were drawn as a mark of respect, while many other people went directly by train to Chingford Cemetery to see the coffin lowered into the grave.

Over the course of the following weeks, donations to the mayor's relief fund flooded in, bolstered by contributions of £10 from the Princess of Wales and £7 from Mancherjee Bhownagree, the MP for Bethnal Green North.[368] It was, though, the people of Hackney who swelled the coffers with their shillings and pennies. A concert at the Olive Branch pub in Hackney Road raised £5 5s, collections at church services garnered about the same, various workplaces and the Borough of Hackney Club on Haggerston Road gave generously and G. Candler and Co., tobacconists, donated a penny for every cigar sold during the collection period. By the time it closed, the fund had raised over £130 and it was decided to give £30 to Ernest Rogers, to invest around £80 for the benefit of Lillian and Percival Denman, and to set aside a small sum 'to provide some memento of the bravery displayed by those who entered the burning building to try and save life'.

A drinking fountain, serving the local community, was considered to be a fitting combination of subscribers' money and council support, and the small public gardens beside the Bethnal Green Museum on Cambridge Heath Road was selected as the location (see plate 19). The ornate granite fountain, standing more than 8ft tall, was unveiled in 1903 and it carried a bronze plaque with the following inscription: 'Memorial to Alice Maud Denman and Peter Regelous who lost their lives in attempting to save others at a fire at 423, Hackney Road, on the 20th April, 1902. Erected by public subscription, C.E. Fox, Mayor, R.Voss Junr, Town Clerk.' It is interesting that Arthur Regelous was recorded as Peter, implying perhaps that he was far better known in the area by his nickname than by his given name. The fountain was welcomed and abundantly enjoyed by local residents, but for many there must have been a twinge of melancholy every time they used it and recalled the awful tragedy that had led to its creation.[369]

Arthur's bravery in attempting to save people from the fire was honoured by the Royal Humane Society and on 16 October 1902, during a ceremony at the council hall, it awarded a posthumous medal and presented an 'in memoriam' certificate to his brother.[370] Ernest Rogers' efforts in saving two of the Denman children were also recognised with a Royal Humane Society medal, in addition to the £30 he received from the relief fund. Rogers did not attend the ceremony due to illness and the medal was accepted by his son, but it seems plausible that the unfortunate man may have been uncomfortable accepting awards and plaudits for heroism, when it was, arguably, his carelessness which had led to the dreadful events of that night. It was a heavy burden that Rogers had to carry, and no amount of money or medals was going to lighten the load.

Following his wife's death and the loss of his home, Charles Denman sought work as a general labourer and moved to 12 York Row in Pearson Street off the Kingsland Road. In 1911 he was living there with his daughter, Lillian, employed as a cigar maker, his son, Percival, and his widowed mother, Elizabeth. Elizabeth Denman had remarried to Frederick Henry Thackway at St John the Baptist church in Islington on 26 November 1881, but Frederick died less than three years later at King's College Hospital on 14 March 1884. Elizabeth initially moved back to Huntingdon Road, occupying rooms at number 33 with her son Frederick, and then moved in with Charles. Charles Denman, Alice's husband, died aged 51 in Hackney in 1916 and his mother died three years later, aged 79.

Of the two Denman children who were saved from the fire, Lillian May Denman married Alexander George Morton, an engineer and son of a French polisher, at St Mark's church in Tower Hamlets on 24 February 1917. Children soon followed: Lillian R., born in 1918, and Ethel, born in 1922. Lillian May died in Hackney in 1954 at the aged of 59. Percival Owen Denman enlisted in the 7th Service Battalion of the Royal Dublin Fusiliers in September 1914 (despite being 14 at the time) and served until June 1916 when his real age was discovered. He then married Daisy

Hockley in Whitechapel in 1917. The birth of their first child, Leslie H., in 1917 was registered in Basford in Nottinghamshire, but their second child, Daisy Alice, was recorded in Hackney in 1918, suggesting that the family may have been visiting relatives outside London when Leslie arrived. Percival re-enlisted in the Royal Fusiliers in June 1919 and served for just over a year, being discharged with a pension at the end of August 1920. Percival died, aged 72, in Croydon in 1971; the last survivor of the Hackney Road fire of April 1902.

Up until the middle of the nineteenth century, a married woman was legally the property of her husband and had very few rights of her own; the couple were considered to be 'as one' and that 'one' was the man. Legislation including the Divorce Act (1857) and the Married Women's Property Act (1870) began to erode the legal basis of this, but socially and culturally the idea persisted; it is still not uncommon for people to address a letter to a married couple using just the man's forename or initials. Although it now has little meaning beyond the envelope, this practice still alludes to a time when married women were considered to be little more than extensions of their husbands. This can even be seen on the Watts Memorial, where one case in particular stands out because, although it is a woman who is being honoured, she is only identified in relation to her husband and as his property. The tablet refers to this woman as 'Mrs Yarman, wife of George Yarman, Labourer', but she was, of course, far more than that and very much a person in her own right.

Mary Bloomfield, who would become Mrs Mary Jarman through marriage, was born in Ireland and so tracing her lineage is not straightforward. She was probably born around 1847, her father was Thomas Bloomfield and she had at least one sister, Margaret, who was about three years younger than her. Margaret Bloomfield must have arrived in England before 1867 because in that year she married James Mahoney in Bermondsey. By 1871, Mary and her father had travelled to England and were living with Margaret and her family in south London.

Mary worked as a dressmaker and then a milliner, and in Southwark in 1871 she married George Thomas Jarman, a warehouseman. George Jarman was born in Suffolk in 1847 and was the son of John Jarman, an agricultural labourer, and Elizabeth Ward, who married in 1843. The couple had three children, Ellen, George and Matilda, the youngest being born in 1850. It is not entirely clear what then happened between John and Elizabeth, and there is evidence to suggest he died in 1856, which would explain why no more children were born. However, when Elizabeth appeared in the 1861 census, living in Bermondsey with her three children and her brother, James, she was recorded as being married rather than widowed, suggesting that John was still alive but that the couple were estranged.

The plot continues to thicken because in 1871 Elizabeth Jarman was living as the 'wife' of George James Eyre at 2 Dock Head Street in Southwark, and her three children were living with her but all going under the surname of Jarman. The reason this is particularly notable is because Elizabeth and George did not actually marry until 1890. It was not rare for couples to live as husband and wife despite not being legally married and the census was a notoriously fallible document. Nevertheless, it does beg the question why, as they had been living together since at least 1871, they left it so long to marry, and why in 1890.

One explanation might be derived from the fact that George Eyre died less than a year after the wedding and it is possible that he was ill and, aware of his impending demise, wanted to ensure that Elizabeth was his legal heir. Another possibility is that Elizabeth was, indeed, estranged from her first husband and his death around that time then allowed her to marry George, and it was simply ill fortune that George died so soon afterwards. Whichever the case, the death of her second husband early in 1891 left Elizabeth Eyre on her own and so later that year she moved in with her son, George Jarman, and his wife, Mary.

Mary and George do not appear to have had any children and in 1881 the couple were living alone at 7 Perseverance Street in Bermondsey, close to the docks and wharfs where George worked. By 1891, they had moved next door to 6 Perseverance Street, where Elizabeth moved in with them, and then the family of three moved a very short distance to 34 Druid Street, which was adjacent to Perseverance Street. George carried on working at the docks, while Mary earned a living as a seamstress and, between them, they supported the household and George's mother; a way of life that continued until March 1900 when tragedy struck.

It was around 11.30 p.m. on Thursday, 22 March 1900, when George arrived home and, finding that his wife Mary and his mother Elizabeth had already retired for the night, he extinguished the oil lamp as usual and went upstairs to bed.[371] About three hours later, in the early hours of Friday, 23 March, he was urgently woken by Mary, who told him that she could smell burning, so he headed back downstairs, assuming that it was just some smouldering embers in the hearth. However, opening the staircase door, he found the ground floor full of smoke and, peering through, he was alarmed to see a ferocious blaze in the kitchen. He shouted upstairs to Mary that they were all in danger and told her to wake his mother and help get her down the stairs while he tried to tackle the fire. Reaching the kitchen, George tried to dowse the flames with water, but they had already scaled the walls and burned through the ceiling into the room above; the room where his mother was sleeping.

As the upstairs rooms filled with smoke, Mary hurried along the corridor to Elizabeth's bedroom but discovered a horrific scene when she opened the door. The flames from the kitchen below had burst through the floor, setting fire to the bedclothes, then the bed, and then the unfortunate Mrs Eyre who was sleeping in it. The poor woman was frantically trying to stem the flames and Mary crawled across the room and started trying to pull her mother-in-law off the bed and onto the floor. Mary struggled to get to Elizabeth, but the fire was relentless and Jarman was forced to concede when it became clear that the elderly woman was beyond help. Badly burned on her face and arms, and choked by the smoke, Mary staggered out into the corridor and collapsed at the top of the stairs.

Quickly realising that he could not fight the fire, but with the ground-floor exit blocked, George was forced back up the staircase, where he found Mary slumped on the floor. George opened the landing window and, down below, a crowd had gathered who implored him to jump, but he told them that his wife was unconscious and he needed to drop her to the ground. People started making a pile of coats beneath the window and neighbours fetched mats and blankets to add to the heap, while George pulled Mary up onto the window ledge. Holding her as tightly as he could by her badly burned hands, he managed to lower her about 5ft from the window and then drop her onto the bundle of materials, where the crowd lifted her and took her into a neighbouring house. George looked back along the corridor to his mother's room in the hope that he might be able to reach it, but the flames were billowing up the stairs and there was no way through. Reluctantly, but knowing there was no other option, George Jarman clambered onto the window ledge and jumped into the street below.

Three days later, on 26 March 1900, Samuel Langham, the district coroner, opened an inquest at Guy's Hospital into the deaths of Elizabeth Eyre and Mary Jarman.[372] The court heard that Mary's neighbours had wrapped her hands and arms in wet blankets and then taken her to nearby Guy's Hospital, where she was admitted and treated. Her burns, though, were extensive, spreading up her arms, across her chest and all over her face and head. She survived precariously for about forty-eight hours but died on Sunday, 25 March. When firemen had extinguished the blaze and entered the building, they had found the badly charred remains of Elizabeth Eyre in the back bedroom on the first floor of the burnt-out shell of the house. They wrapped the body in a canvas sack and it was taken to the mortuary at Bermondsey. George Jarman testified that all appeared well when he arrived home and he had no idea how the fire had started. The inquest jury returned verdicts of 'accidental death' in both cases.

In a single terrible night, George Jarman lost both his wife and his mother in dreadful circumstances and one can imagine that putting his life back together following that would have been difficult. He was not, however, to suffer for long. George worked as a warehouseman for importers, Hicks, Nash and Co., at their premises on Pickle Herring Wharf, just off Tooley Street in Bermondsey. On the morning of 23 July 1900 he was tasked with checking off bales of animal hides which had been imported from China.[373] The following day, George went to see a doctor, complaining of a swelling in his throat, but he was told it was not a dangerous condition and was sent home. Later the same day, George had a seizure or fit and the doctor ordered him to be taken to Guy's Hospital for treatment. George, however, did not recover and died the following day. The circumstances and symptoms of George's death strongly suggest anthrax poisoning, contracted from the imported hides he had been handling. It is sobering to think that at the beginning of March 1900, George, his wife and his mother had all been happily going about their daily business and yet within three months they were all dead, having lost their lives in unusual and dramatic circumstances.

All of the newspapers that carried the story of the fire reported that Mary Jarman had perished while attempting to save her mother, Elizabeth Eyre. It is easy to see how this mistake arose, as the press would have assumed that Eyre was Mary's maiden name and thus Elizabeth was her mother, not George's. This does, though, reflect the casual and somewhat disinterested level of inquiry that was made and, despite it being clearly stated at the inquest that Eyre was Mary's mother-in-law, the error predominated in the media coverage. Furthermore, somebody was equally lax in their attention to detail when recording the information on the memorial tablet and, for some inexplicable reason, the surname was incorrectly spelt Yarman, rather than Jarman. All of the press coverage contained the correct spelling and Watts transcribed it accurately in his volume of cases, so the mistake probably originated at some point in De Morgan's manufacturing of the tiles. As with others, like Edwin Clack and Frederick Craft, it is regrettable that Mary's surname was not correctly recorded and, more so, that her first name was omitted, giving the impression that she was no more than her husband's wife.

At the back of Drury Lane – on the left as you come from New Oxford Street – there run courts and streets as densely inhabited as any of the most crowded and filthy parts of the metropolis, and compared with which Drury Lane is respectability itself. As I went my way, past rag-shops and cow-houses, I found myself in an exclusively Irish population … the larger number of whom were drinking at one or other of the public-houses of the district. In about half an hour there were three fights, one of them between women, which were watched with breathless interest by a swarming crowd, and which ended in one of the combatants, a yellow-haired female, being led to the neighbouring hospital.[374]

Although not as well known or notorious as the rookeries around Seven Dials, the network of courts and streets between Drury Lane and Lincoln's Inn Fields were still regarded as among the poorest and most overcrowded neighbourhoods in London. The properties were sub-divided or sub-let and it was not unusual for families of seven or eight to live in a single room. On one visit to the area, the journalist James Ritchie described the dwellings: 'The houses seem as if they never had been cleaned since they were built, yet each house is full of people – the number of families is according to the number of rooms. I should say four-and-sixpence a week is the average rent for these tumble-down and truly repulsive apartments.'[375] One of the courts in this area was Lincoln Court, sandwiched between Orange Court and Princes Street. According to the district sanitary inspector, Lincoln Court contained twenty-one houses in which 270 adults and 96 children resided; a total of 366 people living in twenty-one houses.[376] On the 1871 census those twenty-one properties accommodated around 130 separate 'households'; an average of around six families living in each house.

If Ritchie is to be believed, Lincoln Court would have been a grim and unpleasant place to live:

> Children play in the middle of the street, amidst the dirt and refuse; costermongers, who are the capitalists of the district, live here with their donkeys; across the courts is hung the family linen to dry. You sicken at every step. Men stand leaning gloomily against the sides of the houses; women, with unlovely faces, glare at you sullenly as you pass by.

It is important to recognise that Ritchie was an outsider and a journalist, writing to excite and appal his readers in equal measure, so his description was likely to exaggerate conditions for lurid effect. It is equally important, though, not to sway to the other extreme and over-sentimentalise what was, essentially, a difficult and brutal hand-to-mouth existence. The reality was probably somewhere between the two and, as illustrated to good effect in Arthur Morrison's social realist novel *A Child of the Jago*, there was a strong sense of community in these poor working-class districts.[377] It was, undoubtedly, a rather unorthodox form of community even by contemporary standards, but people looked out for one another and shared many of the same values.

The houses in Lincoln Court were poorly built, consisting almost entirely of wood with walls constructed on a lath-and-plaster basis using mud and clay. As such, they were highly susceptible to catching fire and, once alight, they burned with alarming speed and fury; which is exactly what happened on 28 July 1873. The most consistent account of the fire is that a woman named Cowan had gone out and, in her locked room, she had left some washing to dry which subsequently caught alight.[378] At number 8 Lincoln Court were David and Mary Hussey, who lived in one room with their five children, while five other families occupied the rest of the house. When they heard shouts of 'Fire!', David and Mary Hussey gathered up their children and got them safely down the stairs and out of the building, before going back in to bring out two other children who lived in the house. By that time the fire was very much taking hold and they were lucky not to get trapped in the small passages and stairways of the cramped and overcrowded building.

House fires, although very common, were still an exciting spectacle and within minutes a large and anxious crowd had gathered, many asking if everyone was out and whether the various families who lived in the building were accounted for. Around that time, another woman who lived at number 8, having been told the building was on fire, came hurrying into the court and pushed her way through the throng. She was trying to find news of her neighbours and was asking bystanders 'if the poor brats were out', referring to the children whom she shared the house with. Nobody seemed able to tell her that they were and so the woman ran into the building and up the stairs to the first floor. Having checked all the rooms, she then ran to the top floor and, finding that empty, realised that the children must have already got out and so turned her attentions to her own escape.

The hungry blaze was quickly devouring the building and the flames had engulfed much of the lower floors, including the staircase. With her escape blocked, the woman began screaming for help, but there was no way that anyone could get in through the ground floor. By this time, a fire escape had arrived, but due to the narrowness of the court and the construction of the houses, the operators were unable to manoeuvre it or place it against the side of the building. Using a short ladder, one of the firemen tried to reach the woman by smashing a first-floor window with his axe, but the sudden rush of air caused the fire to flare up and the fireman was showered with shards of glass and flaming debris. As he was forced back by the heat and smoke, the fireman could still hear the woman screaming, but shortly afterwards she stopped and a few minutes later the roof of the building collapsed in on itself. The gossip among the crowd became quieter and more subdued at the realisation that the poor woman, who had seemingly gone back into the building to try and save some children, had perished in the terrible blaze.

According to the tablet on the Watts Memorial, that woman was **Ellen Donovan** and the newspaper account from which the narrative was derived was published in *The Times* on 1 August 1873. The story, headlined 'The Fatal Fire in St Giles', was a brief account of a coroner's inquest held the previous day by Dr William Harwicke at the King's Head pub in Broad Street, Bloomsbury. *The Times* reported that Donovan was 37 years old, but it did not give any other personal details about her. Other newspapers which reported on the inquest also named the victim as Ellen Donovan, but many of those who simply reported the incident, and presumably obtained their details from speaking to local people, named her as Ann Donovan.[379] One possible explanation for this is that the woman may have been Ann Ellen Donovan, as it was not uncommon for people to be known by their middle name rather than their forename. Another alternative is that there had just been some mistake or misunderstanding in naming or identifying the woman, which would be understandable given the vast number of people crowded into the houses in Lincoln Court and the relatively high turnover of residents. Who, then, was the woman who died in the fire on 28 July 1873?

The most likely scenario is that she was Ann Donovan, a short-haired Irish widow, who was around 40 years old and worked locally as a street hawker or 'basket woman'. In 1871, she was listed on the census as living at 8 Lincoln Court with her husband, John, also born in Ireland, and her three children, Mary Ann (b. 1853), Johanna (b. 1854) and James (b. 1860). Mary Ann was born in Ireland, but Johanna in St Giles, so John and Ann must have married in Ireland shortly before having their first child and then travelled to

London just before having their second. At the inquest into Ann's death in 1873, her neighbour, who lived at number 10 Lincoln Court, told the jury that Ann had lived at number 8 for about two years, which would place her there in 1871.[380] John and Ann must have been living in and around the St Giles and Holborn area in 1861, but they are elusive on the census. In 1872, John Donovan died at the age of 51, and Ellen must have remained at Lincoln Court until her death in 1873.

Intriguingly, in 1861 number 8 Lincoln Court was occupied by a Daniel Donovan, his wife, Ellen, and their two children, John and Ellen. By 1871, Daniel and his family had moved to Bermondsey and John and Ann Donovan had moved into number 8. It is not clear what the connection was, but it seems implausible that there was no relationship between the two families. It is also possible that, in the aftermath of the fire when asked the name of the woman who died, some local people might have mistakenly thought that Ellen still lived in the property and that was where some of the subsequent confusion arose. Ultimately, based on the information provided in the newspapers coupled with the census returns, it is not possible to say, conclusively, that the Ann Donovan living at number 8 Lincoln Court in 1871 was the woman who died in the fire. Much of the evidence, though, suggests that she was and there are no Ellen Donovans recorded on the 1871 census who fit the bill to the same extent that Ann does.

There was also some confusion in the reporting of the fire and particularly of Ann's involvement in it. One early account of the blaze stated that a woman named Donovan, who had been in the house when the fire broke out, locked herself in a cupboard or wardrobe and was burnt to death. Later reports modified this and several newspapers, including *Reynolds's News*, told of how:

> a poor hard-working woman named Ann Donovan, locked herself in one of the rooms of the house when the fire commenced. The neighbours did their best by knocking and shouting to rouse her to a sense of her danger, but all to no purpose. She stayed there until she was suffocated.[381]

It is hard to reconcile these detailed descriptions with later reports of Ann's brave and selfless attempt to save her neighbour's children. However, the most definitive and authentic account was likely to arise from the inquest, at which Mary Hussey, among others, gave evidence and confirmed that Ann Donovan had entered the building out of concern for two children whom she believed were trapped inside. The inquest concluded that the cause of death had been suffocation and the jury returned a verdict of 'accidental death'.

The ferocious nature of the fire and the close proximity of other properties meant that three houses, numbers 7, 8 and 9, were completely destroyed in the blaze. According to George Stanton, the vicar of nearby Holy Trinity church, 'no fewer than twenty-four families packed themselves into those three houses; the fire has burned their few "things" and driven them into the court utterly destitute'.[382] In a short letter to *The Times*, Stanton appealed for assistance on behalf of the families and contributions were quickly forthcoming. Just the following day, Stanton was able to write again with a list of donations which totalled more than £50 and it can be imagined that a good sum was eventually raised. The families were not, however, able to move back into their previous homes as the burnt-out remains of the three houses were pulled down.

This demolition had some interesting repercussions and was blamed for an outbreak of typhus in the area. In his 1873 report, Dr George Ross, the medical officer of health for the St Giles district, wrote:

> At the commencement of September, I was informed of the occurrence of six cases of Typhus Fever – four of these in Lincoln Court, and two in Great Wild Street. This outbreak was so unexpected that further inquiries were immediately instituted, with the view to ascertain the cause. The localisation of the fever led me to believe that the disturbance of filth in the basements of three houses that had been destroyed by fire in Lincoln Court – a disturbance caused by the removal of the old foundations preparatory to rebuilding – had set free poisonous gases which generated the fever. All the sufferers in Lincoln Court lived in close proximity to the ruins of these houses.[383]

Typhus is not an airborne disease (it is mostly spread by fleas), so it was certainly not the release of gases from the basements of the properties which caused the outbreak. A much more likely release was rats, and the demolition of the properties probably disturbed vermin living in the basements which then sought new homes in other houses, thus spreading the disease. In the four months following the demolition of the houses, there were fifteen deaths from typhus in the St Giles area when there had been only two in the preceding eight months. It seems likely, then, that the Lincoln Court fire continued to kill people long after the flames had been extinguished.

DEATH BY
MISADVENTURE

20

'KICKED BY
A HORSE'

Horses and horse-drawn vehicles are an uncommon sight on the busy roads of twenty-first-century London and any appearance tends to attract attention and comment. Mounted police probably account for most sightings, especially in areas around football grounds on match days, but the occasional brewer's dray or classic horse-drawn Victorian hearse sometimes make an appearance. It is quite difficult, now, to imagine a city where real horsepower from real horses was the motive force behind most modes of transport, from single-seat carriages through to double-decker omnibuses. That was, though, very much the case in the first half of the nineteenth century and being around horses was a routine part of day-to-day living for the majority of people.

In the 1850s, the journalist Henry Mayhew turned his attentions to horses in the capital and commented that, 'Strangers coming from the country frequently describe the streets of London as smelling like a stable-yard.'[384] Much of this smell, of course, originated from the dung, rather than the horse, and Mayhew estimated that the gross weight of horse dung deposited upon the streets of London every year was 36,662 tons. This mountain of manure was, Mayhew calculated, produced by the 24,214 horses which trotted about in London every day. That equated to roughly one horse for every

130 people in the city, a remarkable figure and one that indicates the staggering prevalence of the animals.

These were large, powerful beasts, but they could also be unpredictable creatures prone to skittishness, and in crowded streets or when harnessed to passenger-carrying vehicles, this was a dangerous and potentially fatal combination. Of the sixty-two individuals commemorated on the Watts Memorial, five were killed as a result of an incident involving horses: Solomon Gellman and William Fisher were both knocked down by a horse-drawn vehicle, Alexander Brown was recuperating from a carriage accident, and the two people who feature in this chapter were both fatally injured trying to stop horses that were out of control. The nineteenth century was not necessarily an especially heroic time, but it seems there were always plenty of potential opportunities for life-risking acts of intervention.

Neither of the individuals who died as a result of trying to stop runaway horses was killed outright during the act itself; both passed away later as a result of the injuries they had sustained. This might say as much about the quality of health care at the time as it does about the severity of the injuries, and this is especially relevant in one of the two cases.

Elizabeth Boxall, aged 17, died at her home, 27 Tagg Street in Bethnal Green, on 20 June 1888, surrounded by her friends and family. Her death was the culmination of a dreadful year of hospitalisation and operations, all of which stemmed from a selfless act she had undertaken in July 1887. It was said that Elizabeth had been in a street near to her home in Hackney when a carthorse suddenly bolted and ran out of control in the direction of some children who were playing nearby. As the playmates scattered, one was about to run into the path of the horse, but Elizabeth intervened and snatched the child out of the way. Unfortunately, as she did, the horse kicked out and struck Elizabeth in the leg, knocking her to the ground. After the horse had been subdued, people helped Elizabeth home and her family tended to her leg.[385]

The Boxalls were a large family. Elizabeth, born in 1871, was the seventh of nine children of Joseph Boxall, the son of a fishmonger, and Jane Roper, a tailoress. Joseph and Jane married at St Jude's church in Whitechapel on 8 March 1857 and appear to have moved in with Jane's family, sharing rooms at 14 Wagners Buildings in Whitechapel. A steady stream of children followed in quick succession, nine in the space of nineteen years, although two, Louisa and Amelia, both died before the age of 10.[386] To accommodate their increased numbers, Joseph and Jane moved their family into a bigger property at 27 Tagg Street sometime between 1881 and 1887.

In the months following her encounter with the horse, Elizabeth's injury worsened and, although she was just about able to get around with the use of a crutch, there was a great deal of pain and her leg remained swollen and blackened with bruising.

On 9 October 1887, Elizabeth had a fall in which she further injured the leg and so her father finally took her to the nearby London Hospital on Whitechapel Road to be examined.[387] The attending physician discovered that Elizabeth's thigh was badly contused, the thigh bone was broken and the swelling was full of blood, so she was admitted for treatment. Further examination of the injury revealed the presence of a 'previously unsuspected cancerous disease' which was destroying the bone and at risk of spreading to the rest of the leg. It was decided that an immediate amputation midway above the knee was the only way to tackle the disease and, against hospital policy, the operation was performed without first obtaining the consent of Elizabeth or her father.

The operation initially appeared to be a success and Elizabeth began to recover, so her family and friends overlooked the lack of consent. However, by the end of January 1888, examinations suggested that the cancer had recurred and it was decided to amputate the remaining portion of the leg from the hip down. This time, permission was sought and the family reluctantly consented to the operation. Once again, in the weeks immediately following the procedure, Elizabeth responded well to the treatment and, once she was out of danger, the local Samaritan Society arranged for her to stay at a convalescence home in Folkestone. She arrived on 24 May, but by 11 June she was discharged and sent home to Hackney on account of the cancer having apparently spread to her lungs and the home being an unsuitable place to treat her condition. Joseph Boxall, Elizabeth's father, managed to procure some painkillers from the hospital and Elizabeth remained at home, but her condition continued to deteriorate.

At the request of the local poor-law relieving officer, a GP, Dr Edward Berdoe, visited the Boxall family on 14 June 1888 and diagnosed 'shock resulting from the amputation of her leg'. Berdoe advised Elizabeth to go to the infirmary, but Boxhall refused, 'on the grounds that she had a horror of going into any more public institutions'. Over the next few days Elizabeth's health worsened and there seemed to be little that anyone could do to lessen her pain. On 19 June her spirits sank and she passed away the following day. Berdoe reported that when he visited Elizabeth's family, they 'seemed much embittered at what they considered the bad treatment she had received at the London Hospital' and this anger boiled over at the coroner's inquest.

The inquest was held at the Bishop Bonner pub in Bethnal Green on 23 June 1888, with Dr Roderick MacDonald, coroner for north-east London and former MP for Ross and Cromarty, presiding over the inquiry.[388] Joseph Boxall was first to give evidence and he recounted the series of events leading up to the death of his daughter. At the conclusion of his testimony, Boxall exclaimed, 'They regularly butchered her in that hospital!' to which the coroner replied, 'We cannot go into that matter.' 'I shall speak my mind,' contended Boxall and MacDonald concluded the conversation by remarking, 'Certainly; this is a free country,' before calling the next witness. After a short discussion, the jury returned a verdict 'in accordance with the medical evidence', which was that Elizabeth's death had been caused by the shock of the second amputation. Nobody from the London Hospital was present to give evidence and the jury refused to adjourn the inquest so that the hospital could be consulted. The jurors were very much of the opinion that the second operation had been the cause of death and that consent should have been sought for the first operation. The coroner thanked the jury for their service and closed the inquiry.

Just over a week after the inquest, a letter signed by William J. Nixon, the house governor at the London Hospital, was published in *Lloyd's Weekly*.[389] Nixon wrote that 'had any intimation of the coming inquest reached us, the hospital would have been represented' and then a full account of Elizabeth's medical treatment could have been presented to the jury. Had this occurred, Nixon angrily contended:

> the jury would have been able to form a clear opinion whether there was any ground for imputations of ill treatment in the hospital, and whether a verdict of 'death from shock' after an operation performed upwards of four months previously, and followed by a comparative convalescence, could possibly be a correct verdict.

Nixon's argument may well have been sound, but it came through a letter to the press a week after the inquest and, as such, it lacked the emotion and conviction of Joseph Boxall's personal and heartfelt outburst. It can be imagined that people in the local area continued to hold the hospital responsible for 'butchering' a poor young girl whose initial injury had been received so gallantly.

Elizabeth's mother and father both died in Bethnal Green; Joseph in 1899 and Jane in 1912. Elizabeth's eldest brother, Charles, lived with his parents until his father's death in 1899 and then with his mother until her death in 1912. He was employed throughout his adult life as an umbrella maker and did not marry. He died, aged 83, in Poplar in 1941. Another of Elizabeth's older brothers, Joseph James, worked as a porter and as a dealer in earthenware, but seems to have done a range of odd jobs to earn a living. In 1881 he married Eliza Bradford on Christmas Day at St Jude's in Bethnal Green and they moved to Stepney, where they raised a family.[390] Interestingly, in May 1888 Joseph was convicted of 'cruelly treating a donkey' and was fined 30s plus 10s 6d vet's costs.[391] Eliza appears to have died in 1895, but Joseph lived until he was 72 and died in Stepney in 1929.

Of Elizabeth's other brothers, Edward became a wheelwright and lived with his parents in Tagg Street until 1892, when he married Elizabeth Kemp in Bethnal Green. The couple went on to have at least three children.[392] James Boxall lived with his parents until his father's death in 1899 and then with his mother until 1907, when he married Eliza Jane Merrick in Bethnal Green. In his younger years he appears to have worked mostly as a general labourer and after the marriage he worked as a dockside porter, unloading from barges. The couple moved to 6 Hunslett Street in Bethnal Green where, after a short while, they started a family.[393] James and his wife both died in Hendon in 1952; she appears to have died at the start of the year, aged

68, and he died towards the end, aged 79. John Boxall took up work as a coachman
and lived with his parents until 1899, when he married Eliza Cuss in Bethnal Green.
Shortly after, the couple moved into rooms at 19 Bandon Road in Bethnal Green and
a family soon followed.[394] John died in Hackney in 1949, aged 74, and Eliza appears
to have followed in 1957.

Elizabeth's only surviving sister, Sarah Ann, followed her mother into the clothing
trade and in 1881 was working as a tailoress. She continued living with her parents
in Tagg Street but started a relationship with a neighbouring cabman, William South,
and in 1894 they had their first child, William. Sarah was heavily pregnant with their
second child, Sarah, when the couple married in Bethnal Green on 7 July 1895 and
they then went on to have at least four more children.[395]

Out of all the people commemorated on the Watts Memorial, Elizabeth Boxall had
the longest gap between her life-risking act and her death; far longer, in fact, than any
of the others. There can be little doubt that her injury, received while preventing a child
from being hit by a runaway horse, led to her death and, therefore, it can be argued
that her inclusion on the memorial was entirely valid; she did, ultimately, give her life
to save the life of another. However, the case is rather different from all the others and,
to some extent, it does lack the immediacy and drama which tended to accompany the
self-sacrificial acts that Watts collected and commemorated; it is surprising, in fact, that
it even came to his attention because most of the press reporting was overshadowed
by the controversy over Elizabeth's treatment. It was a similar situation with the other
case of runaway horses that featured on the memorial, although in that case it was the
identity of the person who was saved that caught the attention of the press.

Therese Titiens was a German-born opera singer who lived and performed chiefly
in London, where she was regarded as one of the finest sopranos of her day.[396]
In April 1869, she was performing in Bellini's opera, *Norma*, at Her Majesty's Theatre
in London and spent her days enjoying London life to the full. On the afternoon of
2 April she was travelling, with another lady, through Hyde Park in her brougham,
a four-wheeled, horse-drawn carriage, when a wagonette suddenly swerved in front
of them and her driver had to pull up sharply.[397] As he did, one of the carriage poles
harnessing the horses snapped and the animals reared out of control, dragging the
carriage with them. Titiens and her companion screamed in alarm and a constable,
PC Wright, ran over to help the driver of the coach as he fought to control the
startled animals. The two men managed to subdue the horses but, in the process,
the carriage driver was knocked down and received a severe kick to his right knee.

The man driving Therese Titiens' carriage that day was **William Drake**,
a 57-year-old coachman, who lived nearby with his wife, Mary. William had been
born in Kempsey in Worcestershire in 1811 and was the second of eight children

of Edward Drake and Sarah Davis, who married in 1808.[398] Little is known about William's childhood and early life, but by 1841 he had moved to London and was living in Mayfair. In 1844 William married Mary Weston and by 1851 the couple were living at 4 Chapel Place north near South Audley Street in Mayfair, with William earning his living as a grocer and cheesemonger. William and Mary did not have any children and by 1861 they had moved to 2 Chapel Place. William had switched from selling provisions to driving coaches; a decision which eight years later would have tragic consequences.

In the days following the Hyde Park incident, William's leg became increasingly swollen and discoloured, but he also began to experience shortness of breath and bouts of fever interspersed with chills. On 7 April, Drake went to St George's Hospital on Hyde Park Corner, where he was examined by George Bishopp, a house surgeon, who diagnosed advanced pyaemia, a type of septicaemia which had been caused by the injury to Drake's leg. William was admitted, but there was little that could be done to treat the infection and he died in the hospital on 8 April 1869.

The inquest into Drake's death took place at St George's Hospital the following day and a crowd gathered to see 'the distinguished artist' Therese Titiens arrive and solemnly enter the building, where it was expected that she would be called as a witness.[399] John St Clare Bedford presided over the inquest and first to give evidence was Francis Tagart, who lived at 31 Craven Hill Gardens, which overlooked the park. Describing how the horses had become unmanageable due to the breaking of the carriage pole, Tagart declared that, had it not been for the 'heroic efforts of the poor man [Drake] to stop the horses ... the consequences would have been most serious to the two ladies that were in the brougham'. Evidence was also heard from PC Wright and Dr Bishopp, but Titiens did not testify and after a short deliberation the jury returned a verdict of 'accidental death'. Before concluding the proceedings, the court heard from a spokesman for the opera singer, who said that 'those dependent on the deceased would be amply cared for by Mddle. Titiens', after which the coroner closed the case and released the body for burial.

It would appear that Titiens' generosity did not extend to the funeral and William Drake was buried, at the expense of the parish, in a common grave in Brompton Cemetery on Fulham Road on 13 April 1869. The particular area of the cemetery has subsequently become overgrown and the exact location of the grave is difficult to ascertain, but there is no evidence that a headstone was ever erected. It seems likely, though, that Therese Titiens did support William's widow. In 1871, Mary Drake was still living in the Belgravia area, lodging with the Ellis family at 21 Berwick Street, and she was described as an 'annuitant', suggesting that she was in receipt of some kind of pension or regular payment. The arrangement did not, however, have to last for long as Mary Drake died, aged 68, in 1875. Two years later, Therese Titiens, the performer whose life had arguably been saved by William Drake, died of cancer at the age of just 46 and she was buried in Kensal Green Cemetery.

It is interesting that the narratives on the tablets for Boxall and Drake do not make reference to the exact circumstances of the individual's death and both imply that the person died during the performance of a life-saving act, and as a direct result of it, rather than some time later from infection or injury. With Boxall, there was nearly a year between her act and her death, and communicating what had happened would have been difficult due to the brevity of the tablet narrative. Also, though, it would not perhaps have appeared to be quite such a heroic act or, at least, the connection between the act and the death would not have appeared sufficiently self-sacrificial alongside the other cases. With Drake, the time gap was shorter and so the description bears more resemblance to the actual incident, but it is notable that the person he saved was not identified on the tablet. Therese Titiens had been dead for over twenty-five years when the tablet was installed and so her fame would have been somewhat diminished by then. However, mentioning her on the tablet would, nevertheless, have drawn attention away from Drake and his actions, while also reducing the 'everyday' character of the people and incidents that Watts was so keen to convey through his memorial.

21

SKATING
ON THIN ICE

It is a day of hard frost, about the middle of February, and the hour is near noon.
We find the banks of the lake thronged with spectators of both sexes, and all ages
and classes; among which, however, greatly predominate the boys and the hobble-
dehoys, who make up so important a part of the London population. The surface
of the ice looks anything but tempting to a person not enamoured of its glittering
aspect. It is starred with huge cracks, stretching sheer across the basin, and in some
parts is flooded with water, welling up from broad holes; but in spite of that, it is
crowded with occupants eager in the pursuit of pleasure or of business, and all
making the most of the few short hours of light afforded by the winter's day.[400]

Ice skating has been a popular London pastime for centuries and descriptions of
people strapping animal bones to their feet as makeshift skates date back to the
twelfth century. At the famous seventeenth-century frost fairs, the diarist John Evelyn
wrote about people 'sliding with skeetes' on the frozen River Thames, and in 1853
Charles Manby Smith commented upon seeing 'new skates curiously crossed with
virgin straps and dangling from the hands of gentlemen about town'.[401] As early as
1841 Victorian inventors were experimenting with various chemicals to try and create
artificial ice rinks so that people could skate all year round.[402]

However, it was not until 1876 that Professor John Gamgee opened the first water-
based artificial rink, the Glaciarium, in the King's Road in Chelsea. A mixture of ether,
glycerine and water was circulated through pipes beneath a 2–3in deep pool of water
and the chemical reactions produced an intense cold which turned the water to ice.
One journalist from the *Penny Illustrated Paper* who visited the rink extolled the virtues of
artificial ice: 'for figure-skaters, the smoothness, hardness, and perfect level assured by artificial freezing afford everything that can possibly be desired'.[403] For many, though, the 1s
entry fee and 6d for skate hire was beyond their means and they had to wait until winter,
when lakes and ponds across the capital froze over, before they could enjoy the pastime.

Skating on lakes and ponds was not without its risks, the most prominent of which was falling through the ice into the water below, and precautions were certainly taken at some of the larger and most popular central London venues. At the Serpentine in Hyde Park, uniformed employees of the Royal Humane Society (RHS) patrolled the banks with ropes, drags and ladders, and their efforts were undoubtedly successful. In 1845 it was estimated that a total of 186,500 people had taken to the ice during the winter season and that the RHS had saved all 127 who had fallen through.[404] Another method employed at some venues was to lay long ropes across the width of the pond, and in the event of a breakage, people at each end of the rope would pull it tight and then walk along each bank, sweeping the rope across the surface so that those in the water could grab on and be pulled out. There were, however, myriad bodies of water in London upon which people could skate, and the majority of them had little or no safety equipment or provision for helping people who fell in. On most occasions, it was simply down to other skaters or people passing by to try and help, and such rescues did not always have successful outcomes, as illustrated by two of the cases which feature on the Watts Memorial.

G. F. Watts' methodology of identifying and commemorating episodes of everyday heroism based upon information in newspaper reports was effective and ingenious, but it was not without its problems. The press tended to seize upon dramatic incidents and acted swiftly to report the initial event as a news story. However, in the immediate aftermath, information was usually supplied by witnesses or locals and could often be inaccurate or incorrect, particularly in relation to the specific identities of the people involved. Sometimes very little was initially known about the victims, but more detailed and accurate information was usually revealed at the coroner's inquest, which the press tended to report in reasonable detail.

However, despite the official nature of the inquest, some mistakes and inaccuracies persisted, which were then disseminated through the newspapers, and this is how they found their way to Watts and onto his memorial. In other instances, the press reporting of the inquest was largely accurate, but the inquest itself revealed relatively little about the individual who had died, particularly if no close family existed or were known. While this was sufficient for Watts to be able to commemorate individuals on his memorial, it can make it very difficult, over 100 years later, to confidently identify exactly who they were. In terms of posterity, Watts was concerned less with recording the specific identity of the person than with the exemplary model that their deed represented.

This was certainly the case with **Thomas Simpson**, whose tablet in Postman's Park states that he 'died of exhaustion after saving many lives from the breaking of ice at Highgate Ponds' on 25 January 1885. The press, reporting on the inquest, stated that Simpson was 45 years old, that he was an occasional labourer who did odd jobs in the Highgate area, and that he worked on a nearby farm belonging to Mr Ward. That was all the information given; no address, no reference to next of kin, no names of witnesses and very little contextual information to work with. Generally, if the person was married with a family, then some mention was made of the spouse, even if just the recording of the jury's condolences. No family was mentioned at Simpson's inquest, so it seems probable that he was unmarried.

The most likely candidate recorded on the 1881 census was a 40-year-old, unmarried agricultural labourer named Thomas Simpson, who was lodging at 3 Grafton Road in Kentish Town with Wilfred Broad and Broad's two sons, Thomas and Harry. Grafton Road was about 2 or 3 miles from the Highgate area, where Simpson was reported to have worked, and the ponds on Hampstead Heath, where he lost his life, so this reinforces the probability that it was the same person. The inquest report and the death certificate both suggested that Simpson was 45, which fits with the Simpson on the 1881 census and provides a birth year of 1840. The census also stated that Simpson was born in the St Pancras area of London, so some attempt can be made to trace his family.

The most probable scenario is that Thomas Simpson was the eldest son of Thomas Simpson senior, a labourer, and Maria Cope, who married at St Pancras parish chapel on 21 July 1839. Thomas junior was born in the last quarter of 1840 and by 1841 the family was living at Hope Place between the Holloway Road and the Caledonian Road in Islington. More children followed, with all the births being registered in the Islington area, and by 1851 the family moved west of the Caledonian Road to 15 Clayton Street where, over the next ten years, two more daughters arrived.[405] During this ten-year period, the four elder children moved out and by 1861 Thomas senior, Maria and their three youngest children were living in a brickmaker's cottage on land attached to Hampstead Lodge in Highgate.

The Simpson family remained in and around the Islington and Highgate areas, which again strengthens the hypothesis that this was Thomas Simpson's family. In 1871 the two youngest girls were living with their parents at 1 Boston Terrace, off Breacknock Road in Islington. It seems likely that Thomas Simpson senior died, aged 65, in 1875 and by 1881 his widow, Maria, was lodging with the English family at 16 Fortess Grove in Kentish Town. Maria Simpson, Thomas junior's mother, died at the age of 63 in 1884.

After Thomas Simpson junior moved out from the parental home, probably sometime between 1856 and 1861, it becomes very difficult to track him in the limited range of available historical records. On the 1861 and 1871 censuses, there are no clear contenders living in the area, and as Thomas does not appear to have married or had children, there is little ancillary information available for him until he resurfaces on the 1881 census. Given the proximity of his family and his address in 1881, it is likely he remained in and around the Islington, Hampstead and Highgate areas, and would most likely have worked as labourer or agricultural labourer. He was certainly a well-known and much liked figure, as one newspaper reported: 'when the news of his death became known, there were many expressions of regret among those in the neighbourhood who had grown familiar with his good-natured face'.[406]

Thomas Simpson lost his life on 25 January 1885 when a large section of ice on the number 2 pond on Hampstead Heath gave way and numerous people were plunged into the icy water.[407] It was estimated that around 200 people were on the ice at the time, numbers having thinned down from around 500 earlier in the afternoon as many had gone home for tea. It is surprising that there was not more caution as just three days earlier a 12-year-old boy, Edward James Banks, had drowned in the same lake after falling through the ice. Locals were saying the ice was too patchy to be safe, but this did not seem to put people off. Although sudden and dramatic, the collapse of the ice was limited to a large hole at one end of the pond and the majority of the skaters were able to flee to the safety of the bank. Six or seven people had, though, fallen through and were now struggling to stay afloat in the freezing water and unable to get out due to the slipperiness of the ice.

One by one a few people gingerly edged back onto the ice and quickly, but cautiously, made their way to the hole, where they started trying to help people out. First to arrive was a boy, Thomas Burke, who took off his coat and used it as a rope to pull one man out of the water.[408] Other skaters had located the ropes which were left by the pond for lifesaving purposes, but when they were unfurled they were found to be rotten and of no use. Brave onlookers, including Police Constable Webb and a local swimming teacher, Professor White, went into the water to help people, managing to get some out but also getting themselves into difficulties. Likewise with Thomas Simpson, who appears to have been an onlooker rather than a skater; he was seen to plunge into the water and bring out a young man named Annett, who had jumped in to try and save his brother, Francis Annett.[409] Simpson then slid back in to try and help others, but the temperature of the water and the exertion started to take their toll and Frank Pullen, standing on the nearby bank, spotted him sinking. Pullen ran across the ice, slid up to the hole and disappeared headfirst into the freezing water. Resurfacing, Pullen grabbed hold of Simpson and managed, with great difficulty, to get him out onto the ice and then drag him up onto the bank.

Slowly but surely, with a combination of makeshift ropes, human chains, and some ropes and drags fetched from the local police station, everyone visible in the water was pulled out and a local GP, Dr Pepper, went from person to person checking their condition and vital signs.[410] Pepper was called to examine Simpson and, despite various enthusiastic efforts to resuscitate him, the 45-year-old labourer was discovered to be 'insensible' and the doctor pronounced him dead at the scene. An ambulance truck arrived and Simpson's body was taken to the St Pancras Mortuary to await a coroner's inquest. Annett, the lad whom Simpson had rescued, was seen to be extremely agitated and on several occasions he had to be prevented from re-entering the water. It was not until the following day that the body of his brother Francis was pulled from the pond; a second victim of a winter afternoon's recreation which had ended in tragedy.

Three days after the incident, on 28 January 1885, Dr George Danford-Thomas opened an inquest at Crowndale Hall in St Pancras into three deaths which had occurred at the number 2 pond the previous week: Edward James Banks, who had drowned on 22 January, and Francis Annett and Thomas Simpson, who had died on 25 January.[411] Giving his evidence, Professor White, who taught swimming at Paddington Baths, said that 'everyone present behaved bravely and evinced the greatest anxiety to save life', although on several occasions, 'he had much difficulty in keeping several persons from losing their own life in their anxiety to save the lives of others'. Details were presented about the accessibility of the ponds and Police Inspector Goodwin implied that more could be done to keep people from going on the ice. The ponds were situated, he told the jury, 'on the estate of the Ecclesiastical Commissioners and, although the place was private, the public constantly resorted to it without let or hindrance, especially when the ponds were covered in ice'.

Inspector Goodwin also revealed that an officer from the Royal Humane Society used to patrol the ponds when there was ice but this practice had ceased. Likewise, there used to be a set of drags kept at the ponds, but through a misunderstanding with the society these had been removed and there were also no lifebelts. Having adjourned to consider the evidence, the jury returned verdicts of 'death from misadventure' in all three cases and, as juries often did in cases where there appeared to be negligence, they added a rider, stating:

> The jurors, having heard in evidence that the Highgate Ponds are practically open to the public, would recommend that the Royal Humane Society be respectfully requested to consider the subject with the view to establish at these ponds life-saving apparatus and drags and that some authorised person should be stationed there to protect the public when ice covers the water.

As the statistics from the Serpentine demonstrate, Royal Humane Society patrols were highly effective for preventing death from drowning in frozen ponds and, had there been an officer on duty on 25 January 1885, the lives of Thomas Simpson and Francis Annett may well have been saved.

Thomas Simpson was buried on 3 February 1885 at St Pancras Cemetery in east Finchley, in a third-class common grave. There is no evidence that a headstone was erected and the area has subsequently become overgrown. The burial register records Simpson's abode as 6 York Place in St Pancras, which was a short distance from Grafton Road, where he was recorded living in 1881. On Simpson's death certificate, the cause of death was recorded as 'Found dead, suffocation by drowning whilst attempting to rescue another person in the water, accidental' and the death was registered by the coroner, George Danford-Thomas, adding further evidence to the suggestion that Thomas was not married and his parents were deceased.

As discussed earlier in this chapter, G.F. Watts obtained his information about heroic individuals through the reports of incidents which appeared in the press, and this had both advantages and disadvantages. One of the downsides was that these reports were not always accurate and, as Watts generally tended to obtain the earliest accounts that were printed, he often missed later revisions or corrections which amended mistakes. He also tended to just work from one cutting and did not always cross-reference one account with others in different newspapers. These issues with using newspaper cuttings were further complicated because the memorial tablets were being made between 1899 and 1908 but the incidents being recorded had occurred many years earlier and, essentially, all there was to work with were Watts' transcriptions of the cuttings. All of this meant there was quite a high propensity for error and, indeed, many of the tablets contain mistakes and inaccuracies because of misreporting in the press and the manner in which Watts worked.

That said, most of the individuals commemorated on the memorial were, up until their death, relatively 'ordinary' and unremarkable people, often from the working classes, who did not tend to feature in many official documents and who themselves had little need of accuracy or formality in terms of how they were known or addressed in their everyday life. For example, people might be commonly known to friends and family by a middle name, but be recorded on the census or another official document by their first name. Furthermore, despite advances in reading and writing, most working-class people in nineteenth-century London still existed, on a day-to-day basis, in a very oral environment where, if things needed to be written down, they might be spelt phonetically. Consequently, it is easy to see how, when reporting on incidents of everyday heroism featuring otherwise unremarkable people, journalists might acquire or be given incorrect or inaccurate information, and therefore how that information might subsequently filter through to Watts.

Visitors to the Watts Memorial in Postman's Park will find a tablet commemorating 'Edward Blake', who 'drowned while skating at the Welsh Harp Waters, Hendon, in the attempt to rescue two unknown girls, February 5 1895', because Watts obtained the details of the incident from the *Lloyd's Weekly* newspaper on 10 February 1895.[412] However, had Watts cross-referenced this account with other newspapers that day, he would have found that, in *The Observer*, the person who had died at the Welsh Harp Waters was reported to be Edward Charles Clark.[413] Things would, though, have become more complicated for Watts if he had cross-referenced these two accounts with the one that appeared in the *Daily News* on 11 February 1895, because that report claimed that the individual concerned was Charles Edward Clack.[414] Who, then, died at the Welsh Harp Waters on 5 February 1895; Edward Blake, Edward Charles Clark or Charles Edward Clack?

Actually, it was none of these, although the last is the closest to being correct as the full name of the person who died that day was **Edwin Charles Clack**. Edwin was born in 1868 and baptised on 18 October at St Saviour's church in Paddington. His father was William Henry Clack, a plumber, who had married Maria Emily Stockman, the daughter of a plumber, in Kensal Green in January 1865. Edwin was William and Maria's second child; their first, William Henry junior, had been born very shortly after the couple were married and was baptised on 12 February 1865. William and Maria had a further four children: Nathaniel (b. 1870), Walter (b. 1874), Arthur (b. 1877) and Ernest (b. 1881).

Edwin Clack followed his father into the plumbing profession and continued living with his parents at 11 Douglas Road in Kilburn. Adjacent to Douglas Road was Tennyson Road and number 32 was home to George Quest, a retired police-man, and his family, including his daughter, Amy Florence. Edwin and Amy began courting and were married on 14 November 1892 at Holy Trinity church in Kilburn. At the time of the wedding, the couple were recorded as living at 'Elm Villa' in Tennyson Road, close to Amy's parents, and this is presumably where the newlyweds set up their home. At the beginning of 1894, the couple had their first child, Edwin Charles Clack junior, and, almost immediately, Amy fell pregnant with their second child. In the early weeks of 1895, Edwin and his wife must have been busying them-selves for their new arrival, but tragically it was a child he would not live to see.

The Kingsbury Reservoir, located at Brent Bridge on the Edgware Road near Hendon, was created in 1835 to supply water to the Regent's Canal.[415] By dam-ming the River Brent and the Silk Stream, 69 acres of farmland near Old Kingsbury church were flooded and a vast lake was created. Nearby, there was a long-established coaching inn called the Old Welsh Harp Tavern and the reservoir became com-monly known as the 'Welsh Harp'; a nickname assisted by the fact that the reservoir was vaguely harp shaped. In the coldest of the winter months, the reservoir would freeze over and the winter of 1894–5 had been a particularly severe one; so severe, in fact, that a man had been able to cross the River Thames on the ice floes that had formed.[416] In spite of the inconvenience and hardships that such weather induced, it also provided opportunities for recreation and it was reported that 'London skaters have not for many years had such opportunities of disporting themselves. Save on the Serpentine, every open piece of water in the metropolis was crowded.'[417]

At the Welsh Harp, a young woman, Lizzie Jones, was sliding on the ice when suddenly, without warning, it gave way and she fell through into the freezing water below.[418] Her cries for help attracted the attention of Edwin Clack who was walking nearby and, spotting Lizzie in the water, he hurried to help her. The Welsh Harp was private property but Clack managed to squeeze through a gap in some railings and slid down the embankment to the edge of the lake. Cautiously, Edwin crept onto the ice, which crazed and crackled ominously beneath him, and he began to ease his way towards Lizzie, who was frantically struggling in the water. He got within a few yards of her, but the weakened ice could not support his weight and with a startled cry he fell through and disappeared into the inky black water of the reservoir. A few seconds later Edwin resurfaced, coughing and spluttering, but he could not support his weight in the water and Lizzie watched on in dismay as her would-be saviour sank from view.

Meanwhile, other passers-by had seen the commotion on the ice and, while some went to fetch help, the rest made their way down to the lake. One of them, a young man named Sidney Coke, despite having seen Clack perish, went out onto the ice and into the water to assist Jones. She was exhausted, semi-conscious and suffering severely from the cold, but Coke managed to keep her afloat until further help arrived a few minutes later. A ladder was found and pushed across the ice for Coke to grab hold of, and then he and Jones were pulled out of the water and back to the bank. Coke then used the ladder to go back into the water to try and find Clack, but within a short time he had to abandon his efforts as the water was just too cold.

In the hours that followed, constables and firemen arrived and with the use of ladders and drags they eventually located Edwin's body and pulled it from the water. There were some naive hopes that the freezing temperature might have helped to slow the suffocation process and resuscitation was vigorously attempted, but to no avail; Edwin Clack was very much dead. Lizzie Jones and Sidney Coke were also suffering from the effects of the cold and both were taken away for treatment, after which they both made full recoveries. Later in the year, the Royal Humane Society awarded Coke a bronze medal in recognition of his actions in saving Jones and attempting to save Clack. The RHS knew only too well the perils of breaking ice and the terrible costs to human life that could be caused if people, like Clack and Coke, did not act quickly and courageously.

On 9 February 1895 at the council offices in Hendon, George Danford-Thomas opened the inquest into Edwin Clack's death. Evidence was heard from various witnesses, including Sidney Coke, and the drama of the event was conveyed to the jury, who returned a verdict of 'accidental death'. As in many similar cases and incidents of drowning, the jury recommended that signs should be put up at the Welsh Harp to warn about the dangers of thin ice and of swimming in deep water. With the inquest complete, the body was released and Edwin Clack was laid to rest in a common grave in the 'new section' of the burial ground attached to St Mary's parish church in Willesden.[419] There is no evidence that a headstone was ever erected and, if one was, it has not survived to the present day.

Just a few weeks after her father's tragic and untimely death, Ivy Florence Clack was born and she was baptised, along with Edwin junior, at Holy Trinity church in Kilburn on 14 April 1895. At the time of Edwin's death, the couple had been living at 40 Tennyson Road in Kilburn. By 1898, however, Amy appears to have been working as a live-in housekeeper for William Robert Stone, and on 29 May that year, the couple married at St Paul's church in Kilburn. Amy's two children moved in, although they retained their father's surname, and in 1901 the family was living together at 109 Willesden Lane with Amy working as a grocery shopkeeper. It appears that William Stone died in 1907 and by 1911 Amy and her two children were living with her father, George Quest, at 137 Malvern Road, Kilburn. All three of them were working to support the household: Amy as a charwoman, Ivy as a dressmaker and Edwin as a ship's porter. Ivy Clack married Enoch Drayne in Willesden in 1913 and the couple had one child, Cynthia, later that year. Edwin married Edith Howlett in Willesden in 1915, but it is not clear if they had any children.

It is disappointing that Edwin Charles Clack was not properly honoured on the Watts Memorial and that his descendants may now be unaware that the Edward Blake who features was actually their ancestor. Other mistakes with surnames include Frederick Croft, who was actually Craft, Mrs Yarman, who was Mary Jarman, and Herbert Maconoghu who was McConaghey, and there are lots of other errors with names, date and details. To Watts, though, precise information was not especially important and the fact that a person reportedly performed a particular act on a given day and died in the process was sufficient for him; it was, to a large extent, the act itself and the motives behind it that the artist was championing. For Watts, the monument was less of a memorial to individual people and far more of a testament to a heroic age, and this is another reason why it did not matter that the individuals he was commemorating had died many years earlier.

The Watts Memorial was never intended to be a 'living' memorial or a place where relatives of those commemorated could come to grieve and mourn their loved ones; in many cases, parents and siblings were dead before the memorial tablet was even erected. It was designed to be a place for contemplation, inspiration, aspiration and celebration, and, to some extent, to encourage emulation. This is not to say that Watts wanted people to actively seek out opportunities for heroic self-sacrifice, but he did want them to aspire to the character, the motivations, the morals and the humanity of the people who featured, and, in many ways, the memorial has continued to serve that purpose ever since. Surviving descendants and researchers trying to establish the genealogy of those commemorated on the memorial may lament and despair at Watts' offhand attention to detail, but for most visitors it makes little difference if it was Blake, Clark or Clack who performed the act because it is the drama and tragedy of the act itself which moves them. It is, nonetheless, satisfying to be able to set the records straight and to reveal the real people behind Watts' abstract models of exemplarity.

BEYOND THE STREETS OF LONDON

22

'A DESPERATE VENTURE'

When G. F. Watts wrote to *The Times* in 1887 and put forward his suggestion for a monument recording the names of 'likely to be forgotten heroes', it represented the first 'public' declaration of his idea.[420] He had, though, been pondering and planning the scheme for many years before. In an August 1866 letter to his patron Charles Rickards, the artist expressed his desire to erect, in Hyde Park, a colossal bronze figure dedicated to commemorating 'unknown worth'. Watts explained to Rickards that he had been experimenting in his studio with creating a life-sized figure and was now ready to scale it up, but if the letter was intended to solicit financial support from the artist's benefactor it failed and the Hyde Park 'Colossus' remained unfinanced and unrealised.

Watts' 1887 suggestion for a monument to everyday heroism was also not taken up, but the essence of the project remained an enduring passion in the life and thought of the artist. In a letter to James Smith in 1893, Watts wrote: 'I do not care who carries it out or who may have the credit of the scheme but I am only anxious some justice should be done to such splendid examples of human sympathy and self-sacrifice.'[421] Watts and his second wife, Mary, were, in fact, so passionate about constructing a monument that they had their wills redrafted so as to leave the greatest part of their estate to the purpose, and considered selling their London property, New Little Holland House, to fund it.[422]

Throughout the various aborted incarnations of the idea, the design, the building materials and the location of the monument all altered, but there were some
things which stayed absolutely consistent. The memorial would only recognise civilians, those civilians must have lost their own life while attempting to save another,
and they should not have had any duty to save life, or if they did, they must have
been acting substantially over and above that duty when they died. There was, though,
a slightly less obvious, but no less important, proviso for Watts, which was that, ideally,
the incident in which the person gave their life should have occurred in London or,
if not, the person giving their life should have been a Londoner.

Watts' motivation for this was that he believed his monument would simply be the first
of many, in towns and cities throughout the country, each of which would commemorate
heroic self-sacrifice within that specific community. The Watts Memorial in Postman's
Park, commemorating heroic Londoners in a London setting, was really intended to
act as a catalyst and inspiration for a larger nationwide project, and that was why it
predominantly featured people from the capital city. There are, however, several tablets
among the majority which stand out because the incident did not occur in London and
the connection to the metropolis appears obtuse or unexplained. Most obvious amongst
these are the cases of Herbert McConaghey, who appears in Chapter 8, John Cambridge,
who features in the following chapter along with Alexander Brown, and two seemingly
unconnected young men who lost their lives on a beach in Lincolnshire.

Mark Tomlinson was employed as an assistant at the Borough of Nottingham
Lunatic Asylum on Porchester Road in the Mapperley area of Nottingham and had
been living and working there since around 1897. The asylum, which later became
better known as the pioneering Mapperley Hospital, was opened in 1880 to house
around 300 mentally ill patients, but by the early twentieth century two new wings
had been built to keep pace with the growing population of the city.[423] In April 1901,
Mark was one of twenty-three male attendants who, along with twenty-eight female
nurses, three surgeons and twenty-two domestic staff, were responsible for around 350
female and 300 male patients, ranging in age from children to pensioners. The asylum
was designed as a separate, and to some extent self-sufficient, community outside
of the city, and it was bordered by high walls to limit contact between patients and
the general public. Inside, there was medical and nursing care, but patients were also
expected to work and there was recreation in the form of sport, reading, music and
dancing. Despite its austere and foreboding outward appearance, the Nottingham
asylum was more of a therapeutic community than a Victorian 'madhouse'.

In late August 1902, Mark travelled from Nottingham to Kirton Holme in Lincolnshire
to spend a short holiday with his parents. Mark's father, Jabez Tomlinson, was a yeoman
farmer born and bred in Lincolnshire, who in 1867 married Charlotte Gash, the daughter

of an agricultural labourer. Mary Tomlinson, Jabez's mother, had died in 1848 and so the newlywed couple and their first child, Elizabeth (b. 1868), moved in with Samuel Tomlinson, Jabez's father, at his home in Kirton Holme. Two more daughters arrived, Clara (b. 1870) and Charlotte junior (b. 1872), then five sons, Alfred (b. 1874), George (b. 1875), Mark (b. 1877), James (b. 1880) and finally Fred (b. 1882). The family moved to a larger property at Drain Side in Kirton and Samuel lived with them until his death in 1889.

While Mark was staying in Kirton Holme in 1902, he was pleasantly surprised to see his cousin, Ada Mumford. Mark's father, Jabez Tomlinson, was the brother of Ada's mother, Hannah Tomlinson, who in the mid-1860s had moved to south London and in 1869 married John Mumford. Ada had been born in Peckham in 1882 and lived in London all her life, but she kept in close contact with her relations in Lincolnshire and in August 1902 she too was on holiday in the village with her fiancé. At that time, Ada was working as a cook for Robert Whur and his family at 42 Elgin Avenue in Paddington, and she had recently got engaged to a young man who lived and worked nearby in the Bayswater area.

Ada's fiancé was **Arthur David Strange**, who was born in Paddington on 28 May 1878. Arthur was the eldest son of John Strange, a coachman, and Fanny Hunt, the daughter of a coachman, who married at St Michael and All Angels church in Paddington on 30 March 1875. It was John's second marriage; he had previously wed Ann Hewett, the daughter of a maltster, at St Marylebone church in Westminster on 2 October 1865. John and Ann did not have had any children and Ann died, aged 26, in 1868. John and Fanny had their first child, Gertrude Mary, in 1876 and then Arthur David in 1878, but in 1881 John's second wife Fanny died in giving birth to a third child, Fanny junior, who also then died in 1883.

With two young children to raise, John remarried soon after Fanny's death: on 29 October 1882 he tied the knot with Maria Alsop, the daughter of a sailor, at St James' church in Paddington. John was working as a coachman at the time and the address given for both him and Maria was 45 Porchester Square. John and Maria then had several children of their own: Ellen Mabel (b. 1883), William John (b. 1885) and Cecily Mary Janet (b. 1889). At some point between 1882 and 1888 the family moved to 10 Amberley Mews in Paddington, and in May 1891 Maria gave birth to triplets: Dorothy Charity, May Faith and Olive Hope, who were baptised together at St Peter's church in Paddington on 14 June the same year. Only one of the triplets, Olive, survived infancy; Dorothy died soon after birth and May a few months later. John Strange died eight years later and the couple do not appear to have had any further children in the intervening years.

John's son, Arthur Strange, grew up in and around the Paddington area and attended Holy Trinity with St Paul's School. After school he followed his father into the transport business and by 1901 he was working as a carman, delivering milk for the department store Whiteleys of Bayswater. Whiteleys was founded as a single drapery shop opened by William Whiteley at 31 Westbourne Grove in 1863, but by

1867 it had grown to a row of shops comprising seventeen different departments.[424] In 1887, the original premises were devastated by fire, but the business kept on trading and a luxurious new building, still in use today, opened in 1911.

For many years, Whiteleys staff lived in company-owned dormitories, but this practice was dying out and, in 1901, Arthur was boarding with another milkman, Arthur Parsons, and Arthur's brother, William Parsons, at 26 Woodfield Crescent, literally around the corner from Elgin Avenue, where Ada Mumford was working. Arthur and Ada began courting and after they got engaged Ada suggested that they could have a holiday in Lincolnshire, so that Arthur could meet her extended family. This is why Arthur Strange and Ada Mumford, two Londoners with no apparent connection to East Anglia, were in a small Lincolnshire village in August 1902.

The village of Kirton was not far from Sheldyke, where the River Welland ran out into the sea, and the sandy marshlands on the north bank of the estuary were a very popular spot with holidaymakers. On 25 August 1902, the Tomlinson family, consisting of Jabez, Charlotte and Mark, decided to spend some time at the beach and they invited their young housekeeper Ida Clayton to joint them.[425] Ida was around the same age as Mark and it is possible that the two were courting or fond of one another, which would explain why Ida joined the family on their trip. The Tomlinsons also invited Ada and Arthur as well as a neighbour, 16-year-old Edith Goodman, and the group of seven reached Sheldyke sands in the early afternoon.

A few hours later, Ada and Ida decided to go into the water and they spent some time paddling up and down the shoreline as the tide turned and the sea began to flood back in. As the rest of the group sat and talked on the beach, Edith Goodman was suddenly aware that Ada and Ida were calling out for help, and as she looked over to them, she saw that they were up to their armpits in the water and waving furiously. Edith alerted Arthur who, seeing his fiancée in danger, immediately ran into the water to help and was soon followed by Mark, who realised that both girls were at risk of drowning. Tomlinson was not very far out when he disappeared under the water; Strange managed to reach Ada and Ida, but was unable to free them from the shifting sand into which they had sunk. As the tidal waters relentlessly swirled around them, the three youngsters struggled to keep their heads above the surface.

Back on the shore, Edith Goodman went for help while Jabez and Charlotte both waded out into the water, but they were soon up to their necks and still some way from Ada, Arthur and Ida. Powerless to do any more, Jabez and Charlotte were forced to watch helplessly as one by one each of the three holidaymakers was swept beneath the waves and out into the river. Eventually, assistance arrived and Mark's mother and father were helped out of the water, but there was no sign whatsoever of their son or his three companions. Several hours later, boats searching the estuary recovered the bodies of Ada, Ida and Mark, but it was two days before the body of Arthur Strange was pulled from the sea. All four of them had drowned; Ada and Ida while innocently paddling and Arthur and Mark while trying to save them.

The district coroner, a local man named Dr Arthur Tuxford, conducted two inquests: the first, held on Wednesday, 27 August, into the deaths of Ada Mumford, Ida Clayton and Mark Tomlinson, and then a second, convened on Friday, 29 August, into the death of Arthur Strange.[426] As evidence was given, it emerged that, although it was a popular spot for bathing, the area around Sheldyke Sands was quite isolated and known locally to be quite hazardous for strong tides, pockets of deep water and quicksand. In summing up, Tuxford paid tribute to Strange and Tomlinson, saying, 'the conduct of the young men was very heroic. They did all that men could to save their companions. They did a most noble duty and died a noble death.' The jury returned verdicts of 'accidently drowned' in each case and, at the first inquest, they made a recommendation that notice boards should be put up at the beach to warn people against bathing or paddling in the channel. It was hoped that this would prevent similar tragedies, but it was, of course, too late for Mark Tomlinson and Arthur Strange, both of whom had lost their lives; Arthur while trying to rescue his sweetheart, Ada Mumford, and Mark while trying to help his family's housekeeper (and possibly his sweetheart), Ida Clayton.

Jabez Tomlinson, Mark's father, died at the age of 78 on 23 June 1914 and his estate of £863 passed to his wife, Charlotte, who died, aged 77, on 31 July 1920. Her estate of £212 was inherited by their eldest daughter, Elizabeth, who in 1889 had married John Bradley, and the couple went on to have at least eight children.[427] Mark's two elder brothers both followed similar courses in life. Alfred worked in and around Kirton as a domestic servant, then an agricultural labourer, and finally a farmer, while George found employment as a farm labourer. In 1906 Alfred married Miriam Wade Faulkner and the couple appear to have had at least thirteen children.[428] Meanwhile, George married Ada West in 1905 and they had at least six children.[429]

Mark's two younger brothers experienced mixed fortunes. James worked for several years as a labourer and a domestic servant, but died, aged 31, in 1911. Fred worked as a wagoner on local farms, but then, probably taking his lead from Mark, he moved to Nottingham where, in 1911, he was one of twenty-six male labour masters in the Nottingham parish workhouse and infirmary. The census, in April 1911, recorded the range and scope of people in the institution at that time. Of the 1,040 men, 528 were listed as healthy, 305 sick and 126 imbecilic; 743 women were resident, 220 of whom were healthy, 311 sick and 104 imbecilic. There were also 54 men in the casual ward, who would have come and gone on a daily basis, and 105 female officials, the majority of whom were nurses in the infirmary. It is not clear if Fred married or had a family, but it seems likely that he did.

Arthur Strange's mother, Fanny, had died in 1881 and his father, John, died in 1899. Gertrude Strange, Arthur's only full sibling, married Henry John Shelvey, a fireman, at Emmanuel church in Paddington on 6 August 1906. The couple had at least one child, Henry Arthur John (b. 1908), and in 1911 they were living at 95 Walerton Road in Paddington. Gertrude died in Paddington in 1945 at the age of 69.

Arthur's stepmother, Maria Strange, moved to Norwood in Middlesex, where her sister-in-law, Cicely (John Strange's sister), was living, having married William Powell in 1876. In 1901, Maria and three of her four children, Ellen, William and Olive, were residing at 6 Clifton Terrace in Norwood, while Maria's daughter, also called Cecily, was lodging nearby with her paternal aunt and uncle, Cicely and William Powell. William Strange, Arthur's half-brother, joined the Great Western Railway Company (GWR) as an engine cleaner in August 1902 and applied for promotion to shunting fireman in August 1903. His application was initially rejected 'on account of decaying teeth', but shortly afterwards he was 'passed satisfactory after an operation'.[430] After all that, William only remained with the GWR until April 1904 when he 'resigned to support his mother'. Olive Strange, Arthur's half-sister, became an Anglican nun and entered the Sisterhood of St John Baptist in Clewer near Windsor in Berkshire. The sisterhood had been founded in 1852 specifically as a home for prostitutes, but by the late nineteenth century its remit had widened to encompass any 'fallen woman' in need of refuge.[431] Olive did not marry and appears to have died, aged 77, in Dorset in 1968.

It is remarkable how the strangest twists of fate can sometimes situate people in seemingly inexplicable circumstances and change the course of lives for better or worse. Such were the circumstances that placed Mark Tomlinson, an attendant at the Borough of Nottingham Lunatic Asylum, and Arthur Strange, a carman for Whiteleys of Bayswater, on a Lincolnshire beach in August 1902. The two women whom they died trying to save, and who died in the incident, were also there for somewhat incongruous reasons: Ada Mumford had been born in Peckham, lived all her life in London and only had extended family links with Lincolnshire, while Ida Clayton, although local to Kirton, could have been working as a housekeeper for any number of families in the area or simply have chosen not to accompany the Tomlinsons on their trip to the beach that day. It was, in many ways, almost a spider's web of loose connections that came together on one fateful day and took the lives of four young people who were just starting to make their way in the world.

23

'A STRANGER AND A FOREIGNER'

G.F. Watts was undoubtedly a patriotic man and he believed that Great Britain, particularly under the rule and governance of Queen Victoria, most certainly had cause to think of itself as a great and powerful nation; something he intended his monument to reflect. In 1887, when he initially put forward the idea, Watts declared that his memorial would demonstrate 'the character of a nation as a people of great deeds', and he believed that heroic acts undertaken by civilians were the glory of that nation's people, representing 'a grand and honourable feature of the national character'.[432] Watts also considered the prevalence of heroic individuals as an indicator of the condition of the nation as a whole, as he told the *Pall Mall Gazette*: 'The frequency of such noble acts leads me to look hopefully to the future of a nation that can produce such heroes.'[433] The individuals who featured on the Watts Memorial were presented not only as models of exemplary individual character, but also as representatives and examples of a glorious and honourable nation.

Watts was, though, also concerned about the social and moral downturn in Britain's fortunes and its standing in the world. Writing to Lord Wemyss in 1888, the artist expressed a fear that 'every nation stands by with unfriendly feeling ... we are neither loved, which is a pity, nor trusted which is a disgrace, nor feared which is a disaster!'[434] Furthermore, when asked by an interviewer in 1889, whether those who featured on the memorial would be national or international, Watts assertively replied: 'British, decidedly British; they would be the honour of our nation!' In the logic of its creator, the Watts monument would explicitly demonstrate exemplary character and, with its focus on British subjects, implicitly suggest a superior national character which would, in turn, help to bolster and substantiate Britain's position as a social and political world leader.

In Watts' comments there is a sense that he believed heroism to be, more or less, the preserve of the British; or at least he viewed civilian heroism in that way. It was testament to British values and standards that heroism was performed at every level in society, not simply by great military leaders or the nation's armed forces. Consequently, 'exporting' British heroism was part and parcel of stabilising and reinforcing Britain's place in the world and instilling those qualities and virtues in others. Equally, commemorating and publicising cases of British people performing heroic acts in other countries would also bolster pride and patriotism at home and help to remind people of the benevolent side of the British imperial project.

Two of the incidents commemorated on the Watts Memorial really embody this element of Watts' thinking. In both cases, the individuals concerned were born and lived in south-west London, and both were from prosperous and successful families. The incidents occurred outside the UK, one in Belgium and the other in France, but they were prominently reported by British newspapers, which is how Watts came to know of them. In one case, the overseas aspect of the incident is actually proclaimed on the tablet itself, 'drowned near Ostend while saving the life of a stranger and foreigner', and while the statement is not wholly correct, it would surely have left visitors to the memorial in little doubt as to the brave and honourable character of Brits abroad.

It is true to say that 1901 was over 100 years ago and that the *fin de siècle* ideas and attitudes of the first year of a new century were, in many ways, significantly different from those today. Nevertheless, it is easy to imagine that the excitement felt by the four young members of the Cambridge family, as they arrived in Ostend, would not have been dissimilar to that felt by youngsters today when holidaying abroad without their parents. It probably was not their first trip overseas, or their first trip without supervision, but for siblings Frederick, aged 25, John, aged 23, Lucy, aged 22, and Violet, aged 21, the prospect of seven days on the beaches and in the cafés and restaurants of the Belgian town must have been eagerly anticipated.

The four had travelled to Ostend from their home in Croydon, Surrey, where they lived with their parents, Frederick and Lucy Cambridge. Frederick, the son of a Norfolk farmer, was born in South Runcton in 1841. He appears to have received some education in music at the Priory School in Thuxton, and by 1861 he was teaching music at St James' Street Grammar School in King's Lynn. In 1875, Frederick married Lucy Birch, also born in Norfolk, who was the daughter of a brush maker in King's Lynn, and soon after, the couple moved to Croydon where their first child, Frederick Royston, was born on 26 May 1876.

John Cramner Cambridge was their second child, born on 18 August 1877, and then the two girls arrived within the next three years: Lucy Dorothea on 13 January 1879 and Violet Marjorie on 13 May 1880. The family lived for a while at Rydal House on Heathfield Road in Croydon before moving to 1 Upper Coombe Street, where the family would live until at least 1914 and where the vacation party set off from in August 1901. They would probably have got the train to Dover, where they would have boarded a South Eastern Railways paddle steamer to Ostend. They arrived at the Hotel Marion on 7 August and it is possible the trip was partly in celebration of John's forthcoming birthday. Celebration would, however, turn to despair just a day after their arrival.

It was forecast to be warm and sunny on 8 August and the foursome had arrived early on the beach at the West Front to enjoy the fine weather. Suddenly they became aware of distant cries for help and, looking out into the water, they spotted a man and a woman being pulled out to sea on a tidal current.[435] John shouted to his siblings to raise the alarm and bring help, before wading into the surf and swimming out towards the stricken couple. Cambridge managed to reach them and helped to keep them afloat while a lifeboat was launched. When the boat reached the group, the crew were able to rescue the couple, but by that time, John had disappeared beneath the waves and was presumed drowned. This was confirmed later that day when his body was washed up on the eastern beach.

John's death was recorded in the General Record Office's Register of Miscellaneous Foreign Deaths and his funeral was held at the English church in Ostend on 12 August. The church had been consecrated in 1865 and was the responsibility of the Bishop of London, as were all Anglican churches overseas where no other bishop had been appointed. It is not known if John's parents attended the funeral and he was buried in 'non-purchased land', essentially a common grave, with a simple wooden cross marking the spot. Everything happened very quickly and, within the week, the three surviving Cambridge children returned home, leaving the body of their brother to rest in the churchyard. No headstone was ever installed but sometime later a hand-crafted plaster tablet with a wooden border was installed inside the church (see plate 20). It depicts a sunset framed by an arch of palms above an inscription which reads, 'In loving memory of John Cramner Cambridge aged 23 who was drowned at Ostend Aug 8 1901 while rescuing a stranger. Blessed are the pure in heart for they shall see God.'[436] John's aunt was the portrait artist Sarah Birch and it is possible that she may have been responsible for making the tablet.

Despite their loss, life went on for the rest of the family. John's elder brother, Frederick, followed his father and became a professional violinist and teacher of music. In 1912, he married Millicent Dell, the daughter of a corn dealer and the younger sister of John Dell, whom Frederick's sister Violet had married in 1907. The couple do not appear to have had any children. Frederick died on 25 November 1942 and, at the time, was living at 52 Brockswood Lane in Welwyn Garden City, Hertfordshire. He left an estate valued at £5,589 which passed to his widow, Millicent, and John Cambridge Crowley, the eldest son of Frederick's sister, Lucy. Millicent appears to have died in 1969 in Maidstone in Kent.

Lucy Cambridge became a kindergarten teacher and, in 1903, married Walter Noel Crowley, a commercial clerk, in Croydon. They had three children: John Cambridge (b. 1907), Catharine Dorothea (b. 1909) and Christine (b. 1915). Walter Crowley died on 27 September 1949, aged 73, and left £35,117 to his widow and his eldest son.

Lucy died on 15 February 1960 at the Little Hayes Nursing Home in Kenley, Surrey, aged 81. She left an estate valued at £12,401 to her eldest son, John, and her married daughter, Catharine Hodge.

Violet also became a teacher and married John Christopher Dell at St John the Baptist church in Croydon on 6 April 1907. John was the older brother of Millicent Dell, who later married Violet's brother, Frederick. John was a corn dealer, as was his father. The couple had their first child, Elizabeth, in 1908 and then two more, Millicent H. (b. 1912) and Richard Christopher (b. 1914). They lived for some time at 16 Mayfield Road in South Croydon. John died on 8 July 1920 at the Cottage Hospital in Ashford, Kent, and his estate, valued at £4,955, passed to his widow. Violet died on 6 February 1954, aged 73, and, at the time, was living at 12 The Paragon in Bristol. She left an estate valued at £8,588, which passed to her son, Richard Dell, a patent engineer, and Rosamond Sara Green.

John's father, Frederick, died on 17 December 1914, aged 73, and left an estate valued at £520 to his wife and eldest son. John's mother, Lucy, died on 12 July 1932, aged 87, and, at the time, was living at 237 Falloden Way in Finchley. She left £1,520 to her eldest son, Frederick. It must have been satisfying for John and Lucy to see their three children settled and successful, but one can imagine that there was always something of a void in their life and the thought of how different things might have been had their four children not gone away to Ostend that summer.

It was also a series of unfortunate and interlinked circumstances that led to the death of the other individual commemorated on the Watts Memorial who performed his act of heroism overseas. In the last twenty years of the nineteenth century, **Dr Alexander Stewart Brown** became a familiar figure in the Brockley area of south-east London, where he had a medical practice at Holly Lodge on the Brockley Road. He was also a member of the Lewisham vestry and the district board of works as well as a chairman of the works committee, the Lewisham poor law union guardians and the Lewisham parochial guardians.[437] He had stood as a candidate for election to the borough council and was a prominent member of local Conservative clubs and associations. Alexander had been born in Streatham in south London so, geographically, he had not come far, but professionally and personally he had been on quite a journey.

Alexander came from a family with an established medical pedigree; both his father and his grandfather had been general practitioners, so it was logical that he would follow in their footsteps. Alexander's father, also Alexander, married Cecilia Vernon, the daughter of an army clothier, at St Mary's church in Ealing on 3 August 1854, and Alexander Stewart was their first child, baptised at St Leonard's church in Streatham on 17 October 1855. The couple's second child, Mary Ann, was born on 28 November 1857 but died a few days later on 3 December. No further children appear to have followed; at least not by 1861 when the family was living near the White Lion Inn on Streatham High Road. The household had three domestic servants, reflecting the stature of Alexander's profession, but his training and social status did not grant him a long and healthy life and he died on 21 September 1865, aged around 34. Cecilia Brown remarried in Hove, Sussex, on 6 January 1876 to William Moore.

Alexander Stewart Brown underwent his initial medical education at the Royal Medical Benevolent College in Epsom, which had originally been established in 1855 to educate the sons of retired practitioners, but by 1864 it had expanded beyond that remit and was accepting pupils from other backgrounds.[438] In 1871, Alex was a boarder at the school along with 195 other boys between the ages of 10 and 18 as well as around thirty servants, ranging from housemaids to gardeners, eight male masters and a handful of female administrators.

After graduating from Epsom, Alex undertook a number of posts en route to acquiring his various medical qualifications. He was an assistant medical officer at the Female Hospital and Lock Asylum in Harrow Road, which treated venereal diseases, and also an assistant surgeon at the Margate Royal Infirmary. In the period 1874–5 he worked as a prosector for the Royal College of Surgeons, which was a skilled job involving the preparation and exhibition of dissected bodies for use in anatomy demonstrations and teaching.

In 1877 Alex became a registered medical practitioner by qualifying as a Licentiate of the Society of Apothecaries (LSA), the following year he became a Member of the Royal College of Surgeons (MRCS) and by 1881 he was a resident house surgeon at the Warneford Hospital in Oxford. The Warneford had originally been founded as a lunatic asylum by a Northamptonshire vicar named John Vye, but it was renamed in 1843 after Samuel Wilson Warneford, a major benefactor of the institution. Alexander became a Fellow of the Royal College of Surgeons (FRCS) in 1883 and within two years had established his own medical practice at 284 Brockley Road in Lewisham. His life was also growing personally, as well as professionally, and on 6 December 1890, he married Walburga Lever, the daughter of a Sussex gentleman, at All Saints church in Fulham. The couple had one child, Walburga Marian, who was born in June 1891 but died in infancy, and no further children followed.

Over the next ten years, Alex's medical practice grew and became more established, allowing him more time for another of his interests: Freemasonry. The exact origins of the Freemasons are still subject to speculation, but the modern movement can be traced back to 1813 with the formation of the United Grand Lodge of England. Freemasonry is essentially a non-religious, non-political, fraternal and charitable organisation based around a network of lodges and a membership structure consisting of three levels: apprentice, journeyman and master.

Alexander rose to the very highest echelons of Freemasonry and became a high-ranking member of a number of lodges.[439] In 1897, as part of the Masonic honours granted in commemoration of Queen Victoria's Diamond Jubilee, the Prince of Wales conferred upon Alexander the rank of Junior Grand Deacon in the Grand Lodge and Assistant Grand Sojourner in the Grand Chapter, two of the highest offices that a commoner could hold. Alexander was also a generous benefactor, donating large sums of money to numerous charities through Masonic institutions, and he was instrumental in founding the Sancta Maria Lodge that was connected with St Mary's Hospital Medical School in Paddington. Alexander was certainly leading a full and energetic life with many pursuits that kept him well occupied.

On 19 September 1900, Alex was driving his carriage along Ivy Lane in Brockley when his horse suddenly took flight and galloped, out of control, into the Brockley Road, where horse and carriage crashed into a shop window, throwing Alexander head-first onto the ground. He sustained a severe head wound, concussion and some bruising to his neck and spine, which necessitated a period of rest and recovery.[440] On 29 September, apparently as part of the recuperation process, Alex decided to take a short trip to Paris, and he travelled from Brockley to Boulogne with the intention of catching a train from the port to the city.

As Alex was disembarking at Boulogne, one of his fellow passengers leaving the ship fell backwards off the quayside and into the harbour, where he was engulfed in several feet of wet slimy mud, which threatened to suffocate him. Having been warned against jumping from the quay, at the risk of incurring a similar fate, Alex descended some steps and waded out through the shallow water and waist-deep mud until he reached the unconscious man, and dragged him back to the steps. Once there, Alex performed artificial respiration and stayed with the man for several hours until further medical help arrived, during which time Alex had remained in his soaking wet and muddy clothes. It was, apparently, the only suit of clothes he had with him, and so once they had been dried, he decided to abandon his trip to Paris and returned home the same day.

By curious coincidence, it was reported that the man who had fallen into the harbour was a Brockley resident and when he returned home he was treated by Alex at his surgery and made a full recovery. Alex was not, however, so fortunate and it appears that as a result of spending time in the cold water he contracted pneumonia. No doubt he received the best medical treatment that money could buy, but within a week the disease proved fatal and he passed away at Holly Lodge on 17 October 1900. The following Tuesday, 23 October, Alex's funeral took place at Lewisham Cemetery, his body being conveyed there in a Washington car drawn by four horses, followed by his favourite horse and trap in mourning livery.[441] The mourners, 'a large and sympathetic gathering', included representatives from all the various organisations with which Alex was associated, St Mary's Hospital, the London County Council, the Lewisham Guardians and the Brockley Conservative Association, as well as many medical colleagues. The Grand Lodge sent a splendid wreath and, keeping with tradition, the Freemasons present threw sprigs of acacia into the grave at the conclusion of the service. The vicar of All Saints, North Peckham and a Masonic chaplain officiated and the address was fittingly based upon John 15:13: 'Greater love hath no man than this, that a man lay down his life for his friend.'

Following her husband's death, Walburga Brown married George Read, a merchant's clerk, at St Mary's church in Lewisham on 19 March 1907, and by 1911 the couple were living at Holly Bank, 208 Adelaide Road, in Brockley. The couple did not have any children and Walburga died on 6 April 1920 at the London County Mental Hospital in Bexley in Kent. It is not clear if Walburga was an inmate at the hospital or if she was just resident there at the time. Her estate, valued at £2,065, was divided between her husband and James Ernest Lane, a surgeon and acquaintance of Alex's from St Mary's Hospital.

The tablet commemorating John Cambridge is one of the most commented upon by visitors to the memorial and this is because it features the phrase 'drowned near Ostend whilst saving the life of a stranger and a foreigner'. To modern-day viewers, this phrasing might come across as odd or even xenophobic, and it perhaps seems unnecessary or distasteful to stipulate that the person being saved was not British. However, for Watts, this was a key consideration and there is no doubt that the wording of the narrative was purposeful and designed to convey strong and distinct messages about nationalism and patriotism. Cambridge had gone to Ostend with his family, but Watts wanted to make it clear that this was a British man who had lost his life while saving someone from another country, rather than someone he knew. In that way, Watts was able to imply that everyday heroism was a distinctly British trait and that it was something that British people had acquired as a result of their national identity and the ideas and beliefs that were prevalent in the nation. For Watts, Great Britain was, indeed, 'great' and the behaviour of the individuals who featured on his memorial was a sound testament of that.

AFTERWORD

Following the installation of the tablet commemorating Herbert McConaghey in 1931, interest in the Watts Memorial waned once again. In 1939, Britain went to war and the nation's attentions turned to heroism on the battlefield and support on the home front. Undoubtedly, there were thousands of heroic acts undertaken by civilians in London during the war, but, as with Edward Greenoff and Alfred Smith, collective commitment and service to the nation were extolled, rather than individual gallantry, which was, to some extent, downplayed. The monument itself was extremely fortunate to survive the war, and in late 1940 or early 1941 a high-explosive bomb fell very close by in King Edward Street. If it had struck just a few feet to the north-east, the Watts Memorial would have been destroyed and lost for ever.[442]

In 1962, *The Times* published a story lamenting the number of empty spaces on the memorial and it reported that the lack of recent installations was not especially due to funding, but more the fact that suitable candidates were already being honoured through other decorations or memorials. The churchwarden at the time, B. Norman, told the newspaper, 'we had thought about the men concerned with bomb disposal in the area, a lot of whom lost their lives; then the City Corporation thought of a general memorial to Civil Defence Volunteers and while they have done nothing about it yet, this takes it out of our hands'.[443] When G.F. Watts had originally conceived the memorial, civilian heroism was not widely recognised or commemorated (particularly for posthumous cases) and so there was a strong rationale and purpose behind the monument. However, by the 1960s ideas had changed and there were numerous decorations and honours which could be bestowed upon an 'everyday' hero. These had, effectively, assumed the role that the memorial had once fulfilled and there was less foundation or opportunity for that type of commemoration.

Notwithstanding this, in 2009 a new tablet was installed on the Watts Memorial and it was placed on the upper row of the first bay, adjacent to the one commemorating

Alfred Smith. The tablet commemorates **Leigh Pitt**, a 31-year-old print worker, who lost his life in Broadwater Dock near Thamesmead on 7 June 2007. Leigh Pitt lived with his fiancée, Hema Shah, in a flat overlooking the dock and on 7 June 2007, hearing shouts for help, he ran down to the dockside to see what the problem was. When he arrived, he saw a young boy, 9-year-old Harley Bagnall-Taylor, struggling in the water and, without hesitation, plunged into the water and swam to assist him. Meanwhile, other neighbours had found a length of hosepipe and, while Leigh kept Harley's head above the water, the pipe was thrown in and the young boy pulled up and out of the water to safety.

The hosepipe, though, was not strong enough to lift Leigh, who by this time was struggling with exhaustion, and shortly after he disappeared below the surface. At that point, a local police constable, Ken Chow, jumped into the dock and managed to bring Leigh back to the surface. Chow was able to tread water with Leigh for some time, but there was nothing in the dock to hold on to, and before the fire brigade could reach them, Chow had no choice but to release his grip or else he and Leigh would have both drowned. The fire brigade, using ropes and ladders, managed to recover Leigh from the dock, but he died in hospital less than two hours later.

Leigh worked as a subcontractor in the offices of Merrill Lynch, which are in King Edward Street, just across the road from Postman's Park. He and his colleagues were very familiar with the Watts Memorial and following Leigh's death one of his co-workers, Jane Michell, began a campaign to have a new tablet manufactured and installed. The monument is Grade II★ listed, so specific consent from the local authority was required and this was obtained, along with agreement from English Heritage. The new tablet was installed in 2009 and unveiled on 11 June that year, following a memorial service in St Botolph's church. The new tablet has generally been well received and, on first impressions, it appears to fulfil English Heritage's remit that it should be 'in keeping' with the rest of the memorial; the design and colour are a reasonably close match with the Doulton tablets and it has been professionally installed.

However, there are several things which are not quite right with the wording of the text, which reads, 'Leigh Pitt, Reprographic Operator, aged 30. Saved a drowning boy from the canal at Thamesmead but was sadly unable to save himself, June 7 2007.' The narratives on Watts' tablets do sometimes record the occupation of the individual and, of course, they do so using Victorian terminology, examples being lighterman, carman, compositor and fitter's labourer. Most contemporary reports of Leigh's death refer to him as a 'print worker' but it seems that the term 'reprographic operator' has been created instead to try and sound more 'Victorian', and the result is, arguably, somewhat strained and appears cumbersome.

More crucially, though, the phrase 'but was *sadly* unable to save himself' is entirely out of keeping with the rest of the memorial, as no other tablet conveys any sense of sentiment or emotional attachment to the individual. This was because Watts *had no* emotional attachment to the people and the memorial was never intended to serve that purpose; it was not a place for mourning or sentimentality, it was a place for education, inspiration and edification, and for celebrating acts of exemplary behaviour rather than memorialising personal tragedy. There is a distinct sense of detachment in all of the narratives; they are designed to convey information and to stimulate empathy, but they do not instruct the viewer to feel sadness or sorrow.

To a large degree Watts was unconcerned about whether the incident was 'sad' or 'tragic'; the emotions he was trying to evoke were more pride, admiration, humility and a sense of progress and modernity. The artist limited his scope to the reign of Queen Victoria, as he believed that period marked something of a high point in British achievement. He wanted his memorial to be a reflection of that and a rebuttal to doomsayers who dwelt upon the negative aspects of Victorian society. His tablets were not personal tributes to loved ones; they were lessons in 'correct' modes of behaviour and an attempt to show that there was more to the working classes than poverty and deprivation. Watts has been described as 'the last great Victorian' and he created a Victorian memorial based upon very Victorian ideas and attitudes. It is, arguably, no place for twenty-first-century homages underpinned by significantly different motivations.

Leigh Pitt undoubtedly undertook a selfless act and lost his life while attempting to save another, which was tragic and devastating for his friends and family. It is also admirable and understandable that those friends and family wanted to honour his act and his life, and to see that he was remembered for his sacrifice. It is, however, highly questionable that the Watts Memorial was the right location for that tribute. Had wider and more considered consultation been undertaken during the planning process, it is likely that this could have been made clearer and a more appropriate location could have been identified; to the benefit of all parties. What is not often realised is that Watts conceived the memorial to contain 120 tablets, he then meticulously planned a full 120-tablet scheme, and finally, he selected and documented 120 cases with which to complete that scheme; regrettably, he died before he had the chance. The blank spaces on the memorial are not vacant lots waiting for cases to fill them; Watts had already allocated a case to each space. The memorial is not, therefore, half empty, it is simply half finished, and adding additional tablets impedes any possibility of completing it as originally intended.

Following the installation of the tablet commemorating Leigh Pitt, the Corporation of London and the Diocese of London received another application and, realising that insufficient consultation had previously been undertaken, a committee was convened in July 2010 to discuss the implications of authorising a further tablet. This committee contained representatives from all significant interest groups involved with the monument and, after lengthy discussions, it was decided that 'it was no longer appropriate to add further memorials to the wall'. In the policy statement drawn up to explain this decision, the following reasons were given:

(a) The Wall was a personal project by G.F. Watts and his personal influence in the early memorials (and his wife's in the later memorials) is intrinsic to the special interest of The Wall.

(b) The Wall was conceived at a time before the modern honours system had been put in place, which allows for posthumous honours for gallantry.

(c) The language used to describe the acts of heroism commemorated is of its period which, together with the design of the plaques themselves, is what gives the memorial much of its present-day interest. This would inevitably be diluted by the addition of further plaques.

The committee also resolved 'that new memorials attached to the wall would be unlikely to be regarded as acceptable for the reasons set out above'. This is still slightly ambiguous, but it seems highly likely that there will not be any more modern-day cases installed on the memorial.

In 2013, the interest groups who initially met to consider the policy on new installations were reconvened and formalised as a committee for the purposes of protecting, maintaining and promoting the monument. Two prominent bodies on the committee have made ongoing financial commitments to support maintenance and to stage annual events celebrating the park and the memorial. In the long term, it is anticipated that this committee will also undertake fundraising to complete a planned programme of repairs. It would appear that the Watts Memorial to Heroic Self-Sacrifice in Postman's Park is in good hands and, with good luck and good will, it will continue to fascinate and charm visitors for another hundred years and beyond.

List of Tablets and Inscriptions on the Watts Memorial in Postman's Park

The position of the tablet on the memorial wall is indicated at the end of each transcription by the abbreviation 'lwr' (lower row), 'md' (middle row) or 'upr' (upper row), and a number (giving the place in the row from left to right). As an example, the position 'md 3' for the tablet to Mary Rogers is third from the left in the middle row.

First four tablets, unveiled on 30 July 1900

Manufactured by William De Morgan

Thomas Griffin, Fitters Labourer, April 12 1899. In a boiler explosion at a Battersea Sugar Refinery was fatally scalded in returning to search for his mate. [md 1]

Walter Peart, Driver and Harry Dean, Fireman of the Windsor Express on July 18 1898. Whilst being scalded and burnt, sacrificed their lives saving the train. [md 2]

Mary Rogers, Stewardess of the 'Stella', March 30 1899, self sacrificed by giving up her life belt and voluntarily going down in the sinking ship. [md 3]

George, Stephen Funnell, Police Constable, December 22 1899. In a fire at the Elephant and Castle, Wick Road, Hackney Wick. After rescuing two lives went back into the flames, saving a barmaid at the risk of his own life. [md 4]

Nine tablets, in place by 4 May 1902

Manufactured by William De Morgan

Elizabeth Boxall, aged 17 of Bethnal Green, who died of injuries received in trying to save a child from a runaway horse. June 20 1888. [md 5]

Herbert Peter Cazaly, Stationer's Clerk, who was drowned at Kew in endeavouring to save a man from drowning. April 21 1889. [md 6]

Frederick Mills, A. Rutter, Robert Durrant and F. D. Jones, who lost their lives in bravely striving to save a comrade at the sewage pumping works, East Ham, July 1 1895. [Original position md 7, then tablet removed and replacement erected at upr 8 in 1930; see Chapter 2]

Samuel Rabbeth, Medical Officer of the Royal Free Hospital, who tried to save a child suffering from diphtheria at the cost of his own life. October 26 1884. [md 8]

Alice Ayres, daughter of a bricklayer's labourer, who by intrepid conduct saved 3 children from a burning house in Union Street, Borough, at the cost of her own young life. April 24 1885. [md 17]

John Cramner Cambridge, aged 23, a clerk in the London County Council, who was drowned near Ostend while saving the life of a stranger and foreigner. August 8 1901. [md 18]

G. Garnish, a young Clergyman, who lost his life in endeavouring to rescue a stranger from drowning at Putney. January 7 1885. [md 19]

John Clinton, aged 10, who was drowned near London Bridge in trying to save a companion younger than himself. July 16 1894. [md 20]

Joseph William Onslow, Lighterman, who was drowned at Wapping on May 5 1885 in trying to save a boy's life. [md 24]

Eleven tablets, unveiled 13 December 1905

Manufactured by William De Morgan

David Selves, aged 12, off Woolwich supported his drowning playfellow and sank with him clasped in his arms, September 12 1886. [md 9]

William Goodrum, Signalman, aged 60, lost his life at Kingsland Road Bridge in saving workman from death under the approaching train from Kew, February 28 1880. [md 10]

Mrs Yarman, wife of George Yarman, Labourer, at Bermondsey refusing to be deterred from making three attempts to climb a burning staircase to save her aged mother, died of the effects, March 26 1900. [md 11]

Alex Stewart Brown of Brockley, Fellow of the Royal College of Surgeons, though suffering from a severe spinal injury, the result of a recent accident, died from his brave efforts to rescue a drowning man and restore his life, October 9 1900. [md 12]

Richard Farris, Labourer, was drowned in attempting to save a poor girl who had thrown herself into the canal at Globe Bridge, Peckham, May 20 1878. [md 13]

George Lee, Fireman, at a fire in Clerkenwell carried an unconscious girl to the escape, falling six times, and died of his injuries, July 26 1876. [md 14]

William Drake, lost his life in averting a serious accident to a lady in Hyde Park, April 2 1869, whose horses were unmanageable through the breaking of the carriage pole. [md 15]

Ellen Donovan of Lincoln Court, Great Wild Street, rushed into a burning house to save a neighbour's children and perished in the flames, July 28 1873. [md 16]

Sarah Smith, Pantomime artist at Prince's Theatre, died of terrible injuries received when attempting in her inflammable dress to extinguish the flames which had enveloped her companion, January 24 1863. [md 21]

Robert Wright, Police Constable of Croydon, entered a burning house to save a woman knowing that there was petroleum stored in the cellar. An explosion took place and he was killed, April 30 1893. [md 22]

Henry James Bristow, aged eight, at Walthamstow on December 30 1890, saved his little sister's life by tearing off her flaming clothes, but caught fire himself and died of burns and shock. [md 23]

Twenty-four tablets, unveiled 21 August 1908

Manufactured by Doulton of Lambeth

Joseph Andrew Ford, aged 30, Metropolitan Fire Brigade, saved six persons from fire in the Gray's Inn Road, but in his last heroic act he was scorched to death, October 7 1871. [lwr 1]

Amelia Kennedy, aged 19, died in trying to save her sister from their burning house in Edward's Lane, Stoke Newington, October 18 1871. [lwr 2]

Edmund Emery of 272 King's Road, Chelsea, passenger, leapt from a Thames steamboat to rescue a child and was drowned, July 31 1874. [lwr 3]

William Donald of Bayswater, aged 19, Railway Clerk, was drowned in the Lea trying to save a lad from a dangerous entanglement of weed, July 16 1876. [lwr 4]

Frederick Alfred Croft, Inspector, aged 31, saved a lunatic woman from suicide at Woolwich Arsenal Station but was himself run over by the train, January 11 1878. [lwr 5]

Harry Sisley of Kilburn, aged 10, drowned in attempting to save his brother after he himself had just been rescued, May 24th 1878. [lwr 6]

James Hewers, on September 24 1878, was killed by a train at Richmond Station in the endeavour to save another man. [lwr 7]

George Blencowe, aged 16, when a friend bathing in the Lea cried for help, went to his rescue and was drowned, September 6 1880. [lwr 8]

Ernest Benning, Compositor, aged 22, upset from a boat one dark night off Pimlico Pier. Grasped an oar with one hand, supporting a woman with the other but sank as she was rescued, August 25 1883. [lwr 9]

Thomas Simpson died of exhaustion after saving many lives from the breaking ice at Highgate Ponds, January 25 1885. [lwr 10]

William Fisher, aged 9, lost his life on the Rodney Road, Walworth, while trying to save his little brother from being run over, July 12 1886. [lwr 11]

George Simmonds of Islington rushed into a burning house to save an aged widow and died of his injuries, December 1 1886. [lwr 12]

Samuel Lowdell, Bargeman, drowned when rescuing a boy at Blackfriars, February 25 1887. He had saved two other lives. [lwr 13]

William Freer Lucas M. R. C. S., L. L. D., at Middlesex Hospital risked poison for himself rather than lessen any chance of saving a child's life and died, October 8th 1893. [lwr 14]

Edward Blake, drowned while skating at the Welsh Harp Waters, Hendon in an attempt to rescue two unknown girls, February 5 1895. [lwr 15]

Edward Morris, aged 10, bathing in the Grand Junction Canal sacrificed his life to help his sinking companion, August 2 1897. [lwr 16]

Godfrey Maule Nicholson, Manager of a Stratford distillery, George Elliott & Robert Underhill, workmen, successively went down a well to rescue comrades and were poisoned by gas, July 12 1901. [lwr 17]

Solomon Galaman, aged 10, died of injuries, September 6 1901, after saving his little brother from being run over in Commercial Street. 'Mother, I saved him but I could not save myself.' [lwr 18]

James Bannister of Bow, aged 30, rushed over when an opposite shop caught fire and was suffocated in the attempt to save life, October 14 1901. [lwr 19]

Elizabeth Coghlam, aged 26 of Church Path, Stoke Newington, died saving her family and house by carrying blazing paraffin to the yard, January 1 1902. [lwr 20]

Arthur Regelous, Carman ('little Peter'), aged 25, who with Alice Maud Denman, aged 27, died in trying to save her children from a burning house in Bethnal Green, April 20 1902. [lwr 21]

Arthur Strange, Carman of London and Mark Tomlinson, on a desperate adventure to save two girls from a quicksand in Lincolnshire were themselves engulfed, August 25 1902. [lwr 22]

John Slade, Private 4th Battalion Royal Fusiliers, of Stepney. When his house caught fire saved one man and dashing upstairs to rouse other lost his life, December 26 1902. [lwr 23]

Daniel Pemberton, aged 61, Foreman L. S. W. R., surprised by a train when gauging the line hurled his mate out of the track, saving his life at the cost of his own, January 17 1903. [lwr 24]

One single tablet, unveiled 13 June 1919

Manufactured by Doulton of Lambeth

Alfred Smith, Police Constable, who was killed in an air raid while saving the lives of women and girls, June 13 1917. [upr 1]

Three tablets, unveiled 15 October 1930

Manufactured by Doulton of Lambeth

P.C. Harold Frank Ricketts, Metropolitan Police, drowned at Teignmouth whilst trying to rescue a boy bathing and seen to be in difficulty, 11 September 1916. [upr 5]

P.C. Edward, George, Brown Greenoff, Metropolitan Police, many lives were saved by his devotion to duty at the terrible explosion at Silvertown, 19 January 1917. [upr 6]

P.C. Percy, Edwin Cook, Metropolitan Police, voluntarily descended high tension chamber at Kensington to rescue two workmen overcome by poisonous gas, 7 October 1927. [upr 7]

One single tablet, in place by April 1931

Manufactured by Fred Passenger

Herbert Maconoghu, school boy from Wimbledon, aged 13, his parents absent in India, lost his life in vainly trying to rescue two school fellows who were drowned at Glovers Pool, Croyde, North Devon, August 28 1882. [md 7, replacing the original tablet that was moved in 1930; see Chapter 8]

Notes

Introduction

1   Postman's Park is located in the City of London and the nearest postcode is for the church of St Botolph without Aldersgate, EC1A 4EU. The park itself is situated between King Edward Street, EC1 and St Martin's Le-Grand/Aldersgate Street, EC1.

2   The full history and development of the Watts Memorial is documented in detail in John Price, *Postman's Park: G.F. Watts's Memorial to Heroic Self-Sacrifice* (Compton: Watts Gallery, 2008), and all the information about the memorial in this introduction is derived from that volume.

3   For more on the development of the idea of 'everyday' heroism, see John Price, *Everyday Heroism: Victorian Constructions of the Heroic Civilian* (London: Bloomsbury, 2014).

4   For more on G.F. Watts and his works, see Mark Bills and Barbara Bryant, *G.F. Watts: Victorian Visionary* (London: Yale University Press, 2008); Veronica Franklyn-Gould, *G.F. Watts: The Last Great Victorian* (London: Yale University Press, 2004); Colin Trodd and Stephanie Brown, eds, *Representations of G.F. Watts: Art Making in Victorian Culture* (Aldershot: Ashgate, 2004).

5   *The Times*, 5 September 1887.

6   See Price, *Postman's Park* (2008).

Chapter 1

7   Jerry White, *London in the Nineteenth Century* (London: Jonathan Cape, 2007), pp. 172–81.

8   For information on manufacturing in London during the nineteenth century, see Peter G. Hall, *The Industries of London since 1861* (London: Routledge, 2005); L.D. Schwarz, *London in the Age of Industrialisation: Entrepreneurs, Labour Force, and Living Conditions, 1700–1850* (Cambridge: Cambridge University Press, 2003).

9   See Fiona Wood, 'Garton, Sir Richard Charles (1857–1934)', *Oxford Dictionary of National Biography* (Oxford: Oxford University Press, 2004) and Bryan Mawer, *Sugarbakers: From Sweat to Sweetness* (London: Anglo-German Family History Society, 2011).

10 The inquest was reported in the following publications and the details from these have been used to construct the account given in this chapter: *Daily News*, 18 April 1899; *Lloyd's Weekly*, 23 April 1899; *London Evening Standard*, 18 April 1899; *The Morning Post*, 18 April 1899. Watts derived his information about the incident from *The Times*, 18 April 1899.

11 *London Evening Standard*, 18 April 1899.

12 *Lloyd's Weekly*, 23 April 1899.

13 Margaret and William's seven children were: Mary Elspeth (b. 1911), Horace W. (b. 1912), Arthur F. (b. 1916), Frances M. (b. 1919), Edna B. (b. 1922), Sheila G. (b. 1926) and Joyce K. (b. 1927). Sarah and Charles' two children were Frances Mary (b. 1909) and Charles Leonard (b. 1911). Hannah and John do not appear to have had any children.

14 *London Evening Standard*, 18 April 1899.

15 Brian Strong, ed., *Remembering Three Mills* (London: River Lee Tidal Mill Trust Ltd, 2008); Martin Watts, *The House Mill, Bromley by Bow, London* (London: River Lee Tidal Mill Trust Ltd, 1998).

16 Olivia Williams, *Gin Glorious Gin: How Mother's Ruin Became the Spirit of London* (London: Headline, 2014).

17 W.R. Powell, ed., 'West Ham: ancient mills', in *A History of the County of Essex*, Vol. 6 (Oxford: Oxford University Press, 1973), pp. 89–93.

18 Geraldine Coates, *Beefeater London: The Story of London's Gin* (Edinburgh: Contagious Publishing, 2007).

19 Derek Birley, *A Social History of English Cricket* (London: Aurum, 1999).

20 The couple's other children were: Ellen Isabel (b. 8 Oct. 1859), Edith Mary (b. 8 Feb. 1861), William Graham (b. 11 Mar. 1862), John Sanctuary (b. 19 May 1863), Arthur Carleton (b. 2 Jul. 1864), Richard Francis (b. 7 Oct. 1865), Hugh Blomfield (b. 13 Nov. 1866), Reginald (b. 26 Nov. 1867), Isabel Winifred Maud (b. 8 Dec. 1868), Mary Stephanie (b. 26 Dec. 1869), Gertrude Ann (b. 1 Apr. 1871), Marion Theodora (b. 22 Jul. 1873) and Clement Octavius Edward (b. 7 Aug. 1874).

21 The incident in which the men died was extensively reported in *The Times* and the details from the editions of 13, 15 and 16 July 1901 have been used to construct the account given in this chapter.

22 The coroner's inquest was reported in *The Times*, 15 July 1901, and the quotes that follow are all taken from that edition.

23 Obituary in *The Times*, 26 July 1909.

24 Bradford had married Godfrey's elder sister, Edith Mary, in 1898.

25 The monument also carries a panel commemorating other accidents at the distillery, the text of which reads: 'Remember also these others who were accidentally killed in the course of their duties. Alfred Green, Stillman, James Ede, Officer H. M. Excise, 29 June 1908. William Hayzer, Labourer, 6 Oct 1916. John Henry Sodo, Labourer, 17 Nov 1947. The cross of Christ placed upon this spot bears daily witness to the solemn hour in which God called them home. Greater love hath no man than that a man lay down his life for his friends.'

Chapter 2

26 Excellent studies of London's Victorian sewers include: Paul Dobraszczyk, *Into the Belly of the Beast: Exploring London's Victorian Sewers* (Reading: Spire, 2009) and

Stephen Halliday, *The Great Stink of London: Sir Joseph Bazalgette and the Cleansing of the Victorian Metropolis* (Stroud: Sutton, 1999).

27 Halliday, *The Great Stink of London*, pp. 78–107.

28 The incident in which the men died was reported in the following publications and the details from these have been used to construct the account given in this chapter: *The Bristol Mercury and Daily Post*, 2 July 1895; *East Ham Echo*, 12 July 1895; *Lloyd's Weekly*, 7 July 1895; *Manchester Times*, 5 July 1895. Watts derived his information about the incident from *The Times*, 1, 3 and 19 July 1895.

29 Ellen lived at 95 Queens Road, Bury St Edmunds, and then 75 Mill Road.

30 By coincidence, the house in which Alice Ayres perished in 1885 was at the junction of Union Street and Gravel Lane in Southwark (see Chapter 12).

31 The inquest was reported in the following publications and the details from these have been used to construct the account given in this chapter: *East Ham Echo*, 12 July 1895; *Lloyd's Weekly*, 7 July 1895; *Reynolds's News*, 7 July 1895.

32 The conclusion of the inquest into the deaths of Digby, Durrant, Mills and Rutter was reported in *The Morning Post*, 19 July 1895, and all quotes from the inquest that follow are taken from that edition.

33 The conclusion of the inquest into the death of Jones was reported in the *East Ham Echo*, 9 August 1895, and all quotes from the inquest that follow are taken from that edition.

34 *East Ham Echo*, 12 July 1895.

35 *Daily News*, 4 July 1895; *Pall Mall Gazette*, 4 July 1895.

36 *East Ham Echo*, 2 August 1895.

37 *East Ham Echo*, 9 August 1895.

38 *East Ham Echo*, 22 September 1895.

39 Robert Durrant junior's regimental number was 194639.

40 The couple's first child, Robert Arthur, was born in Suffolk in 1898 and the three children born in Alberta in Canada were: Bessie (b. 1907), Freeman (b. 1909) and Bertil (b. 1913).

41 Maud and William's four children were: Charles Henry (b. 1899), Ellen Miriam (b. 1901), Violet Mabel (b. 1902) and William (b. 1904).

42 Maud and John's six children were: John William junior (b. 1908), Elizabeth (b. 1915), William A. (b. 1920), Henry A. (b. 1921), Thomas G. (b. 1923) and Violet J. (b. 1925).

43 The couple's surviving child was Wilfred George (b. 1901).

44 *Lloyd's Weekly*, 21 July 1895.

45 The details of this are discussed in full in John Price, *Postman's Park: G.F. Watts's Memorial to Heroic Self-Sacrifice* (Compton: Watts Gallery, 2008).

Chapter 3

46 Norman McCord, *British History 1815–1906* (Oxford: Oxford University Press, 1991), pp. 228–30.

47 Watts derived his information about the Lucas incident from *The Times*, 16 October 1893, and it was also reported in the *Birmingham Daily Post*, 17 October 1893, the *Daily Telegraph*, 16 October 1893, and *Lloyd's Weekly*, 22 October 1893.

48 Watts derived his information about the Rabbeth incident from *Lloyd's Weekly*, 26 October 1884, and it was also reported in the *British Medical Journal*, 25 October 1884, the *Glasgow Herald*, 21 October 1884, and the *Pall Mall Gazette*, 21 October 1884.

49 *British Medical Journal*, 28 October 1893.

50 *British Medical Journal*, 28 October 1893.

51 *The Spectator*, 1 November 1884.

52 *Illustrated Police News*, 28 October 1893; *British Medical Journal*, 28 October 1893.

53 *British Medical Journal*, 25 October 1884.

54 *Hampshire Advertiser*, 18 October 1893.

55 *British Medical Journal*, 8 November 1884.

56 W.I. McDonald, 'Jenner, Sir William, first baronet (1815–1898)', *Oxford Dictionary of National Biography* (Oxford: Oxford University Press, 2004); D.A. Power, 'Bowman, Sir William, first baronet (1816–1892)', rev. Emilie Savage-Smith, *Oxford Dictionary of National Biography* (Oxford: Oxford University Press, 2004); Nick Hervey, 'Gull, Sir William Withey, first baronet (1816–1890)', *Oxford Dictionary of National Biography* (Oxford: Oxford University Press, 2004).

57 *British Medical Journal*, 18 and 25 April 1885.

58 *The Times*, 23 October 1893.

59 *The Times*, 23 October 1893.

60 *The Times*, 27 October 1884.

61 *The Times*, 29 October 1884.

62 *The Times*, 30 October 1884.

63 *The Times*, 4 November 1884.

64 *The Times*, 29 and 30 October 1884.

65 *The Times*, 17 October 1893.

66 *The Times*, 4 November 1884.

Chapter 4

67 Peter Ackroyd, *Thames: The Biography* (London: Random House, 2009), pp. 9–11.

68 Ackroyd, *Thames*, pp. 123–7.

69 Dick Fagan and Eric Burgess, *Men of the Tideway* (London: Hale, 1996); Jack Gaster, *Time and Tide: The Life of a Thames Waterman* (London: Amberley, 2010); James Legon, *My Ancestors were Watermen: A Guide to Tracing Your Watermen and Lightermen Ancestors* (London: Society of Genealogists, 2014).

70 Henry Humpherus, *History of the Origin and Progress of the Company of Watermen and Lightermen of the River Thames* (London: Prentice, 3 vols, 1874–6).

71 Watts derived his information about the incident from *Lloyd's Weekly*, 10 May 1885, and the details from that report, along with reports of the inquest, have been used to construct the account given in this chapter.

72 The inquest was reported in *Lloyd's Weekly*, 10 May 1885, and *Reynolds's News*, 10 May 1885.

73 Beatrice and George's nine children were: Lillian Beatrice (b. 1906), George John (b. 1908), Rose L. (b. 1911), Ivy A. (b. 1913), Charles L. (b. 1915), Albert E. (b. 1917), Doris M. (b. 1919), Minnie C. (b. 1921) and Leonard S. (b. 1926).

74 Henry Mayhew, 'London watermen, lightermen and steamboat-men', in *London Labour and the London Poor*, vol. 3 (London: Griffin, Bohn and Co., 1861).

75 Watts derived his information about the incident from *The Times*, 24 April 1887, and the details from that report, along with reports and records of the inquest, have been used to construct the account given in this chapter. For the original inquest records, see London Metropolitan Archives, CLA/042, 'Records of the Southwark Coroner's Court' (1837–1932).

76 *The Times*, 24 April 1887.

77 *Aberdeen Weekly Journal*, 30 April 1887.

78 Mary Jane and Arthur's seven children were: Emma Jane (b. 1896), Nellie (b. 1900), George (b. 1903), Daisy (b. 1905), Ernest (b. 1909), Arthur J. (b. 1912) and Richard C. (b. 1914).

79 Mayhew, 'London watermen, lightermen and steamboat-men'.

Chapter 5

80 Peter Ackroyd, *Thames: The Biography* (London: Random House, 2009), pp. 252–61.

81 Jerome K. Jerome, *Three Men in a Boat: To Say Nothing of the Dog* (Bristol: J.W. Arrowsmith, 1889).

82 Edward Mogg, *Mogg's New Picture of London and Visitor's Guide to its Sights* (London: E. Mogg, 1844).

83 Watts derived his information about the incident from *The Times*, 8 September 1883, and the details from that report, along with reports of the inquest, have been used to construct the account given in this chapter.

84 Jerry White, *London in the Nineteenth Century* (London: Jonathan Cape, 2007), p. 253.

85 The inquest was reported in *The Times*, 6 April 1889 and the *Richmond and Twickenham Times*, 27 April 1889 and the quotes that follow are all taken from those editions.

86 Watts derived his information about the Cazaly incident from *The Times*, 6 April 1889, and the details from that report, along with reports of the inquest, have been used to construct the account given in this chapter.

87 The inquest was reported in *The Times*, 6 April 1889 and the *Richmond and Twickenham Times*, 27 April 1889, and the quotes that follow are all taken from those editions.

88 Watts derived his information about the incident from *Lloyd's Weekly*, 11 January 1885.

89 *Putney and Wandsworth Borough News*, 10 January 1885; *Reynolds's News*, 11 January 1885; *Leeds Mercury*, 10 January 1885; *Aberdeen Weekly Journal*, 10 January 1885.

90 *Mid-Surrey Gazette*, 10 January 1885.

91 *Crockford's Clerical Directory* (London: Church House Publishing, 1882–5).

Chapter 6

92 James Ewing Ritchie, *The Night Side of London* (London, 1858).

93 Craig Barclay, 'Heroes of peace: the Royal Humane Society and the award of medals in Britain 1774–1914', unpublished Ph.D. thesis (York: University of York, 2009).

94 Royal Humane Society, *Annual Report* (London, 1837–1910).

95 Gavin Weightman and Steve Humphries, *The Making of Modern London* (London: Ebury, 2007), pp. 55–6.

96 Peter Ackroyd, *Thames: The Biography* (London: Random House, 2009), pp. 203–4.

97   Henry Mayhew, 'London watermen, lightermen and steamboat-men', in *London Labour and the London Poor*, vol. 3 (London: Griffin, Bohn and Co., 1861).

98   Watts derived his information about the incident from *The Times*, 4 August 1874, and *Lloyd's Weekly*, 2 August 1874, and the details from those reports, along with reports of the inquest, have been used to construct the account given in this chapter.

99   The inquest was reported in the *Pall Mall Gazette*, 4 August 1874, *Reynolds's News*, 9 August 1874, and *The Times*, 4 August 1874; the quotes that follow are all taken from those editions.

100 *Illustrated London News*, 15 August 1874.

101 Ackroyd, *Thames*, pp. 43–51.

102 Margaret Ashby, *The Book of the River Lea* (Buckingham: Barracuda, 1991); J.G.L. Burnby and M. Parker, *The Navigation of the River Lee, 1190–1790* (Enfield: Edmonton Hundred Historical Society, 1978); Jim Clifford, 'The River Lea in West Ham: a river's role in shaping industrialization on the eastern edge of nineteenth-century London', in Stéphane Castonguay and Matthew Evenden, eds, *Urban Rivers: Remaking Rivers, Cities, and Space in Europe and North America* (Pittsburgh, PA: University of Pittsburgh Press, 2012), pp. 34–56.

103 Peter Ackroyd, *London: The Biography* (London: Chatto and Windus, 2000), p. 677.

104 Watts derived his information about the incident from *The Times*, 20 July 1876, and *Lloyd's Weekly*, *23 July 1876*, and the details from those reports, along with reports of the inquest, have been used to construct the account given in this chapter.

105 The inquest was reported in the *Daily News*, 19 July 1876, and *The Times*, 20 July 1876.

106 Ian A. Burney, 'Making room at the public bar: coroners' inquests, medical knowledge and the politics of the constitution in early-nineteenth-century England', in James Vernon, ed., *Re-reading the Constitution: New Narratives in the Political History of England's Long Nineteenth Century* (Cambridge: Cambridge University Press, 1996), pp. 123–53.

107 William and Mary's eight children were: Helen (b. 1868), Mary junior (b. 1871), Edith (b. 1872), Charles (b. 1874), Clara (b. 1876), Annie (b. 1878), Ella (b. 1880) and Marjorie Amy (b. 1883).

108 Watts derived his information about the incident from *Lloyd's Weekly*, 12 September 1880, and the details from that report, along with a report from the *London Evening Standard*, 8 September 1880, and reports of the inquest, have been used to construct the account given in this chapter.

109 It is not entirely clear when the Webb family moved from one address to the other, but both were very close to the home of Walter Sale.

110 The five children were: Ada (b. 1868), Ellen Beatrice (b. 1870), Alice (b. 1872), Albert William (b. 1874) and Margaret (b. 1878).

111 The inquest was reported in the *London Evening Standard*, 9 September 1880, and the quotes that follow are taken from that edition.

112 In addition to Charles Henry (b. 1890), Louisa and Charles' children were: George Albert (b. 1893), Richard William (b. 1895), Queenie (b. 1899) and Phillip Sidney (b. 1903).

113 Derek Pratt, *Discovering London's Canals* (Aylesbury: Shire, 2nd edn, 1981).

114 Watts derived his information about the incident from *Lloyd's Weekly*, 26 March 1878, and the details from that report, along with reports from the *Illustrated Police News*, 25 May 1878, and *The Times*, 18 May 1878, as well as reports of the inquest, have been used to construct the account given in this chapter.

115 Henry and Elizabeth's three children were: Mary (b. 1842), Harriet (b. 1843) and George (b. 1850).

116 *The Times*, 18 May 1878.

117 The inquest was reported in *Lloyd's Weekly*, 26 March 1878, the *Illustrated Police News*, 25 May 1878 and *The Times*, 18 May 1878, and the quotes from the inquest that follow are taken from those editions.

Chapter 7

118 James Walvin, *A Child's World: A Social History of English Childhood 1800–1914* (Harmondsworth: Penguin, 1982), p. 12.

119 Thomas Hughes, *Tom Brown's School Days* (Cambridge: Macmillan and Co., 1857); Charles Dickens, *Oliver Twist; or the Parish Boy's Progress* (London: Richard Bentley, 1838).

120 Walvin, *A Child's World*, p. 13.

121 Walvin quoted national death-rate figures of 153 per 1,000 for babies under 1 in 1839–40, and in York in the period 1839–43, 42 per cent of all deaths were children under the age of 5. He also highlighted that, in Bath in the same period, one child in two from working-class homes died before the age of 5, whereas the figure for middle-class homes was one in eleven.

122 Henry Mayhew, 'Of the children street-sellers of London', in *London Labour and the London Poor*, vol. 1 (London: Griffin, Bohn and Co., 1861).

123 Watts derived his information about the incident from *The Times*, 10 January 1891, and the details from that report, along with reports of the inquest, have been used to construct the account given in this chapter.

124 The inquest was reported in *The Times*, 10 January 1891, and *Aberdeen Weekly Journal*, 13 January 1891; the quotes in this paragraph are taken from those editions.

125 Gustave Doré, *Ludgate Hill, a Block in the Street* (1872).

126 See Henry Mayhew, 'London omnibus drivers and conductors', 'London cab drivers' and 'London carmen and porters', in *London Labour and the London Poor*, vol. 3 (London, 1861).

127 See Chapter 20.

128 Charles Maurice Davies, *Mystic London* (London: Tinsley Bros., 1875), p. 86.

129 Watts derived his information about the incident from *The Times*, 17 July 1886, and *Lloyd's Weekly*, 18 July 1886, and the details from those reports, along with reports of the inquest, have been used to construct the account given in this chapter.

130 The inquest was reported in *The Times*, 17 July 1886, and *Lloyd's Weekly*, 18 July 1886.

131 For attitudes towards the death of children, see Walvin, *A Child's World*, ch. 2.

132 Eliza and George's six children were: Clara Florence (b. 1892), George Edward (b. 1894), Annie Edith (b. 1899), William Joseph (b. 1901), Edward Albert (b. 1904) and Florence Marian (b. 1907).

133 *East London Advertiser*, 14 September 1901. Watts derived his information about the incident from the *Daily Mail*, 9 September 1901, and the details from that report, as well as the one from the *East London Advertiser*, have been used to construct the account given in this chapter.

134 For a concise discussion of Jewish immigration into east London, see Jerry White, *London in the Nineteenth Century* (London: Jonathan Cape, 2007), pp. 152–9.

135 Jerry White, *London in the Nineteenth Century* (London: Jonathan Cape, 2007), p. 154.

136   Henry Walker, *Sketches of Christian Work and Workers* (London: Religious Tract Society, 1896).

137   *East London Advertiser*, 14 September 1901.

138   Watts derived his information about the incident from *Lloyd's Weekly*, 2 June 1878, and *The Times*, 29 May 1878, and the details from those reports, as well as reports from the inquest, have been used to construct the account given in this chapter.

139   The inquest was reported in the *Illustrated Police News*, 8 June 1878, *Jackson's Oxford Journal*, 1 June 1878, and *The Times*, 29 May 1878.

140   Edwin and Charlotte's five children were: George Richard (b. 1885), Ethel Rose (b. 1886), Henry Sidney (b. 1892), Elsie Ellen Frances (b. 1899) and Albert Edward (b. 1902).

Chapter 8

141   The growth of the idea of 'everyday' heroism is explored in John Price, *Everyday Heroism: Victorian Constructions of the Heroic Civilian* (London: Bloomsbury, 2014).

142   Craig Barclay, 'Heroes of peace: the Royal Humane Society and the award of medals in Britain 1774–1914', unpublished Ph.D. thesis (York: University of York, 2009); see also Price, *Everyday Heroism*.

143   The medal was awarded to 10-year-old Jack Hewitt, who jumped into the River Ouse from a landing stage in Goole in Yorkshire to save his 9-year-old friend who could not swim.

144   William Martin, *Heroism of Boyhood* (London: Darton and Hodge, 1865); Alfred H. Miles, *Fifty-Two Stories of Heroism in Life and Action for Boys* (London: Hutchinson and Co., 1899); Charles D. Michael, *Deeds of Daring: Stories of Heroism in Every Day Life* (London: S. W. Partridge and Co., 1900).

145   Charles D. Michael, *Heroines: True Tales of Brave Women – a Book for British Girls* (London: S.W. Partridge and Co., 1904); Alfred. H. Miles, *A Book of Brave Girls at Home and Abroad: True Stories of Courage and Heroism* (London: Hutchinson and Co., 1909).

146   *Jackson's Oxford Journal*, 28 July 1894.

147   The incident was reported in *Jackson's Oxford Journal*, 28 July 1894, and the details from that report, as well as reports of the inquest, have been used to construct the account given in this chapter.

148   *Jackson's Oxford Journal*, 28 July 1894.

149   *Illustrated Police News*, 28 July and 4 August 1894.

150   *Illustrated Police News*, 4 August 1894.

151   *Illustrated Police News*, 11 August 1894.

152   A concise account of the sinking of the *Princess Alice* is given in Jonathan Schneer, *The Thames: England's River* (London: Little, Brown, 2005), pp. 149–59. More in-depth coverage can be found in Joan Lock, *The Princess Alice Disaster* (London: Robert Hale, 2013).

153   Daniel's other siblings were George junior (b. 1848), Emma junior (b. 1849), Richard (b. 1851), Caroline (b. 1853), Frances (b. 1856), Eliza (b. 1858), Charles Alfred (b. 1859), Samuel (b. 1862), Arthur (b. 1864), Selina (b. 1865, d. 1867), Melville (b. 1867), Albert Edward (b. 1870) and William James (b. 1875). The family also lived at 18 Parson's Hill in Woolwich (1847) and 4 Upper Ann Street in Plumstead (1861) and occupied 160 Ann Street until 1907.

154   Watts derived his information about the incident from *Lloyd's Weekly*,

12 September 1886, and the details from those reports, along with the report from the *Daily News*, 6 September 1886, as well as reports of the inquest, have been used to construct the account given in this chapter.

155 The inquest was reported in *Lloyd's Weekly*, 12 September 1886.

156 The couple's nine children were: Mary Ann junior (b. 1870), George junior (b. 1872), Emma (b. 1874), Harriett League (b. 1877), Arthur (b. 1879), Herbert (b. 1882), Phoebe (b. 1885), William (b. 1890) and Frances (b. 1892).

157 Alan H. Faulkner, *The Grand Junction Canal* (Newton Abbot: David and Charles, 1973); Derek Pratt, *Discovering London's Canals* (Aylesbury: Shire, 2nd edn, 1981).

158 Watts derived his information about the incident from *Lloyd's Weekly*, 8 August 1897, and the details from that report, along with reports of the inquest, have been used to construct the account given in this chapter.

159 The inquest was reported in the *Illustrated Police News*, 21 August 1897, and the quotes that follow are taken from that edition.

160 John Price, *Postman's Park: G. F. Watts's Memorial to Heroic Self-Sacrifice* (Compton: Watts Gallery, 2008), p. 34.

161 For a broad history of the Imperial Civil Service, see Lewis O'Malley, *The Indian Civil Service, 1601–1930* (London: Frank Cass and Co., 2nd edn, 1965).

162 The incident was reported in the *Devon Evening Express*, 29 August 1882, *Ilfracombe Chronicle*, 2 September 1882, *Reynolds's News*, 10 September 1882, and *The Times*, 7 September 1882, and the details from those reports, as well as reports of the inquest, have been used to construct the account given in this chapter.

163 *Lloyd's Weekly*, 10 September 1882.

164 The inquest was reported in *Berrow's Worcester Journal*, 9 September 1882, the *Daily News*, 7 September 1882, the *Devon Evening News*, 6 September 1882 and *Lloyd's Weekly*, 10 September 1882, and the quotes that follow are taken from those editions.

Chapter 9

165 There are numerous excellent histories of the Metropolitan Police, including David Ascoli, *The Queen's Peace: The Origins and Development of the Metropolitan Police, 1829–1979* (London: Hamish Hamilton, 1979); Clive Emsley, *The Great British Bobby: A History of British Policing from the 18th Century to the Present* (London: Quercus, 2009); Gary Mason, *The Official History of the Metropolitan Police: 175 Years of Policing London* (London: Carlton, 2004); Phillip T. Smith, *Policing Victorian London: Political Policing, Public Order and the London Metropolitan Police* (Westport, CT: Greenwood Press, 1985).

166 Emsley, *The Great British Bobby*, p. 119.

167 Robert Wright's divisional number was 538 and his warrant number 75107.

168 For descriptions of barrack life, see Emsley, *The Great British Bobby*, pp. 121–3.

169 Watts derived his information about the incident from *The Times*, 1 and 4 May 1893, and the details from those reports, along with the reports from *Lloyd's Weekly*, 7 May 1893, *Reynolds's News*, 7 May 1893 and *London Evening Standard*, 1 May 1893, as well as reports of the inquest, have been used to construct the account given in this chapter.

170 The inquest was reported in *Lloyd's Weekly*, 7 May 1893, *London Evening Standard*, 4 May 1893, and *The Times*, 4 May 1893, and the quotes that follow are taken from those editions.

171 *Lloyd's Weekly*, 7 May 1893.

172 Robert and Mary's eight children were: Isabella (b. 1889), Storey (b. 1890, d. 1894), John Storey (b. 1897), Albert Edward (b. 1898), James Robert (b. 1900, d. 1908), William Storey (b. 1902), Annie (b. 1904) and Mary Ellen (b. 1910).

173 John and Matilda's nine children were: Ada Mary (b. 1893), Daisy (b. 1895), Ida Elizabeth (b. 1897), John Robert (b. 1899), twins Albert Edward and James Henry (b. 1902), Thomas William (b. 1905), Bertie (b. 1908) and Stanley (b. 1911).

174 *The Times*, 5 January 1900.

175 George Funnell's regimental number was OX2128.

176 George Funnell's divisional number was 261 and his warrant number 79122.

177 Watts derived his information about the incident from *The Times*, 5 January 1900, and the details from that report, along with a report from the *Pall Mall Gazette*, 29 January 1900, and reports of the inquest, have been used to construct the account given in this chapter.

178 The inquest was reported in *Lloyd's Weekly*, 7 January 1900, the *News of the World*, 14 January 1900, *The Times*, 5 January 1900 and the *Weekly Despatch*, 7 January 1900; the quotes that follow are taken from those editions.

179 *News of the World*, 25 March 1900; *The Times*, 23 March 1900. For information on the Society for the Protection of Life from Fire, see Chapter 16.

180 *The Times*, 29 January 1900.

181 Leonard Funnell's regimental number was 189331.

182 For more on this subject, see Nicolette Gullace, 'White feathers and wounded men: female patriotism and memory of the Great War', *Journal of British Studies*, vol. 36 (April 1997).

183 Jerry White's book, *Zeppelin Nights: London in the First World War* (London: Bodley Head, 2014) is a rich resource on the experiences of Londoners, including air raids, during the Great War.

184 For specific information on air raids in the First World War, see Thomas Fegan, *The 'Baby Killers': German Air Raids on Britain in the First World War* (Barnsley: Leo Cooper, 2002).

185 Accounts of the bombing raid on London appeared in *The Times*, 14 and 15 June 1917. The incident involving PC Smith was documented in the *Police Review and Parade Gossip*, 22 June 1917 and *On and Off Duty*, 2 July 1917, and the details from those reports have been used to construct the account given in this chapter.

186 Alfred Smith's divisional number was 59 and his warrant number 89106.

187 *Police Review and Parade Gossip*, 22 June 1917.

188 House of Commons debate, 28 June 1917, published in *Hansard*, vol. 95, cc. 513–14.

189 I am indebted to Rob Jeffries for documents, images and personal information relating to PC Alfred Smith.

190 For more on the Carnegie Hero Fund Trust, see John Price, *Everyday Heroism: Victorian Constructions of the Heroic Civilian* (London: Bloomsbury, 2014).

Chapter 10

191 Letter from T.H. Ellis to Mary Watts, dated 1 October 1927, in Heroic Self-Sacrifice Memorial Committee (HSSMC) *Minutes Book*, London Metropolitan Archives, P69/BOT1/B/036/MS18628 (1904).

192 Meeting of May 1929, appeal dated 14 May 1929, HSSMC, *Minutes Book*.

193 Meeting of 26 May 1930, HSSMC, *Minutes Book*.

194 Jay Winter's book, *Sites of Memory, Sites of Mourning: The Great War in European Cultural History* (Cambridge: Cambridge University Press, 1995) remains one of the best explorations of memory and remembrance of the First World War.

195 For correspondence relating to the three tablets erected to Metropolitan Police officers, see *Metropolitan Police Commendations, Awards and Testimonials*, The National Archives (TNA): Public Record Office (PRO) MEPO 2/1925.

196 Letter from B.A.G. Norman to Mary Watts, dated 30 October 1929, HSSMC, *Minutes Book*.

197 *The Times*, 16 October 1930; *City Press*, 17 October 1930.

198 Harold's divisional number was 174 and his warrant number 102307.

199 The incident was reported in the *Teignmouth Post*, 13 September 1916, the *Teignmouth Gazette*, 13 September 1916, and *The Times*, 12 September 1916, and the details from those reports, as well as reports of the inquest, have been used to construct the account given in this chapter.

200 The inquest was reported in the *Teignmouth Post*, 13 September 1916, and the *Teignmouth Gazette*, 13 September 1916; the quotes that follow are taken from those editions.

201 Reported in the *Teignmouth Gazette*, 13 September 1916.

202 For information on the King's Police Medal and other decorations, see J.H.F. Kemp, *The Metropolitan Police: The Men and their Medals* (London: Ethandune Medal Publications, 2009). See also Dick Kirby, *The Brave Blue Line: 100 Years of Metropolitan Police Gallantry* (Barnsley: Wharncliffe True Crime, 2011); Jean Sweetser and Colin Gillespie, *The Tottenham Outrage* (London: Page Green Centre, 1983).

203 The two key studies of the Silvertown explosion are Howard Bloch and Graham Hill, eds, *The Silvertown Explosion, 1917* (London: All Points East, 1997) and Gerard Melia, *The Silvertown Disaster*, ed. J. Levine (London: Longman, 1984).

204 Greenoff's divisional number was 389 and his warrant number 96389.

205 Despite being subject to wartime censorship, accounts of the Silvertown explosion appeared in *The Times*, 22 and 23 January 1917, and it was extensively covered by the *Stratford Express* on 27 January 1917 and 3 and 10 February 1917. The incident involving PC Greenoff was documented in the *Police Review and Parade Gossip*, 9 February 1917, and the *Stratford Express*, 3 February 1917, and the details from those reports, along with the narrative in Miles Henslow's book (see n. 16), have been used to construct the account given in this chapter.

206 Miles Henslow, *Fifty Great Disasters and Tragedies that Shocked the World* (London: Odhams, 1937), ch. 31.

207 The funeral was reported in the *Stratford Express* on 10 February 1917.

208 Rob Cochrane, *Pioneers of Power: The Story of the London Electricity Supply Corporation, 1887–1948* (London: London Electricity Board, 1987).

209 The incident was reported in *The Times*, 8 October 1927, and the details from that report, as well as reports of the inquest, have been used to construct the account given in this chapter.

210 Cook's divisional number was 474 and his warrant number 108962.

211 These three children were Sidney Isaac (b. 1895), Leslie Gordon (b. 1897) and Cecil Ernest (b. 1899, d. 1901).

212 Cook's regimental number was 14927.

213 *The Times*, 8 October 1927.

214 The inquest was reported in *The Times*, 12 October 1927, and the quotes that follow are taken from that report.

215 *The Times*, 8 and 12 October 1927.

Chapter 11

216 The best secondary text on the sinking of the *Stella* is John Ovenden and David Shayer, *The Wreck of the Stella: Titanic of the Channel Islands* (St Peter Port: Guernsey Museums and Galleries, 1999). Contemporary accounts from survivors appear in: Marie H. Bailey, *A Terrible Experience: The Wreck of the Stella, by a Survivor* (London: M. Bailey, *c.*1900); Alfred H. Miles, *The Bravest Deed I Ever Saw* (London: Hutchinson and Co., 1905); Edward R. Snow, *Women of the Sea* (London: Alvin Redman, 1963).

217 'Employments for women', *Myra's Journal*, 1 October 1889, p. 528.

218 I am indebted to Elizabeth Peacey for documents and personal information relating to Mary Rogers.

219 *Marine Register of Deaths*, January 1881, official number 68827.

220 *Western Mail*, 3 April, 1899; *The Times*, 14 April 1899.

221 *Northern Echo*, 5 April 1899; *Jersey Weekly Press and Independent*, 8 April 1899.

222 Quotes taken from reports in the *Daily News*, 1 April 1899, the *Glasgow Herald*, 1 April 1899, and *The Times*, 4 and 5 April 1889.

223 Watts derived his information about Mary Rogers from *The Times*, 10 April 1899.

224 Parton's account appears in Miles, *The Bravest Deed I Ever Saw* and Williams' in Snow, *Women of the Sea*.

225 *The Times*, 13 April 1899.

226 For biographies and discussions of Cobbe, see Barbara Caine, *Victorian Feminists* (Oxford: Oxford University Press, 1992); Susan Hamilton, *Frances Power Cobbe and Victorian Feminism* (Basingstoke: Palgrave Macmillan, 2006); Lori Williamson, *Power and Protest: Frances Power Cobbe and Victorian Society* (London: Rivers Oram, 2005).

227 *The Times*, 17 April 1899.

228 Annie Bryans, *A Souvenir of the Unveiling of the Memorial Fountain in Southampton* (Southampton, 1901).

229 Peter Kennerley, *The Building of Liverpool Cathedral* (Lancaster: Carnegie, 2004); John Thomas, 'The "beginnings of a noble pile": Liverpool Cathedral's Lady Chapel, 1904–10', *Architectural History*, vol. 48 (2005), pp. 257–90.

230 For details, see Liverpool Anglican Cathedral, *Noble Women Windows in the Lady Chapel, Liverpool Cathedral* (Liverpool: Liverpool Anglican Cathedral, 1951).

231 William McNeill, *The Noble Women of the Staircase and Atrium Windows in the Lady Chapel of the Liverpool Cathedral* (Liverpool: Daily Post Printers, 1915).

232 Published in Bryans, *A Souvenir* (1901).

233 Joseph Gwyer, *The Disaster to the Stella in the Channel* (Penge: T.H. Bentley and Co., 1899).

234 William McGonagall, *More Poetic Gems* (Dundee: David Winter and Son, 1962).

235 The published 'Board of Trade inquiry into loss of SS "Stella" on the Casquets' is available from The National Archives (TNA), Public Record Office (PRO), ref. RAIL 411/411 (1899). All the details which follow are taken from the published report.

236 See Hugh Cunningham, *Grace Darling: Victorian Heroine* (London: Continuum, 2007).

237 See John Price, *Everyday Heroism: Victorian Constructions of the Heroic Civilian* (London: Bloomsbury, 2014).

238 Lucy Delap, '"Thus does man prove to be the master of things": shipwrecks, chivalry and masculinities in nineteenth- and twentieth-century Britain', *Cultural and Social History*, vol. 3 (2006), pp. 45–77.

239 *Derby Mercury*, 19 April 1899.

240 *Jersey Times*, 8 April 1899.

Chapter 12

241 Laura M. Lane, *Heroes of Everyday Life* (London: Cassell and Co., 1888). Lane mistakenly cited the date of the fire as 26 April 1886, so the correct date, the night of 23 April/ early hours of 24 April 1885, has been inserted to amend this error.

242 For detailed accounts of the incident, see *Southwark Recorder and Bermondsey and Rotherhithe Advertiser*, 2 May 1885; *South London Press*, 2 May 1885; *South London Observer*, 29 April 1885.

243 The tablet commemorating Alice Ayres was also one of the first thirteen that Watts had erected on the memorial.

244 Patrick Marber, *Closer* (London: Methuen, 1997). The play premiered at the Cottesloe, National Theatre, in May. The motion picture, directed by Mike Nichols, had its worldwide release in December 2004 (UK, January 2005) and starred Jude Law, Clive Owen, Natalie Portman and Julia Roberts. The monument itself features in several scenes towards the beginning and end of the film.

245 John and Mary Ann's six children were: Frederick (b. 1851), Emily (b. 1853), John (b. 1854), Lydia (b. 1857), Alice (b. 1859) and Ada (b. 1861).

246 Between 1861 and 1871, John and Mary had two more children: David (b. 1863) and Alfred (b. 1864). Sometime between 1871 and 1881, the cottage the family was living in became number 33 Magdala Road.

247 Invalid Asylum for Respectable Females, *Fifth Report for 1831 of the Invalid Asylum for Respectable Females in London and its Vicinity* (London, 1832).

248 The inquests were reported in *The Times*, 30 April 1885 and 3 May 1885.

249 *The Times*, 30 April 1885.

250 *The Times*, 30 April 1885.

251 *Southwark Standard and South London News*, 2 May 1885.

252 The funeral was extensively reported, including in *The Times*, 5 May 1885.

253 *South London Chronicle and Southwark and Lambeth Ensign*, 16 May 1885.

254 The Red Cross Hall and the mural project are examined in detail in John Price, 'Octavia Hill's Red Cross Hall and its murals to heroic self-sacrifice', in Elizabeth Baigent and Ben Cowell, eds, *'Nobler Imaginings and Mightier Struggles': Octavia Hill and the Remaking of British Society* (London: Institute of Historical Research, 2015).

255 Octavia Hill, *Letter to My Fellow Workers* (London: James Martin, 1893). Also available in Robert Whelan, ed., *Letters to My Fellow Workers* (London: Kyrle Books, 2005), pp. 333–49.

256 Emilie Barrington, 'The Red Cross Hall', *English Illustrated Magazine*, vol. x (June 1893), 610–8.

257 M. Bettison, 'Luffman, Lauretta Caroline Maria (1846–1929)', *Australian Dictionary of Biography*, vol. 10 (1986), p. 167.

258 Peter J. Keating, *The Working Classes in Victorian Fiction* (London: Routledge and Kegan Paul, 1971).

259 Sir Francis Doyle, 'The story of a modern heroine', *Pall Mall Gazette*, 31 October 1887.

260 Luara Ormiston Chant, 'In memory of Alice Ayres', *The Englishwoman's Review*, 15 June 1885.

261 H.D. Rawnsley, *Ballads of Brave Deeds* (London: J. M. Dent and Co., 1896), pp. 10–12.

262 *The Times*, 5 May and 30 April 1885.

263 See John Price, *Everyday Heroism: Victorian Constructions of the Heroic Civilian* (London: Bloomsbury, 2014).

264 *Illustrated Police News*, 2 February 1889.

265 *Southwark Recorder and Bermondsey and Rotherhithe Advertiser*, 2 May 1885; *South London Press*, 2 May 1885; *South London Observer*, 29 April 1885.

266 *The Times*, 3 June 1885.

267 Edward Walford, *Old and New London*, vol. 5 (London: Cassell and Co., 1878), pp. 309–24.

268 *The Times*, 27 March 1886.

269 Borough of Southwark Council, *Minutes*, vol. 36 (1936), Southwark Local Studies Library.

Chapter 13

270 Frederick S. Williams, *Our Iron Roads: Their History, Construction and Social Influences* (London: Bemrose and Sons, 1883), p. 285.

271 Christian Wolmar, *Fire and Steam: A New History of the Railways in Britain* (London: Atlantic, 2007), p. xi.

272 Henry Mayhew, 'On the transit of Great Britain and the metropolis', in *London Labour and the London Poor* (London: Griffin, Bohn and Co., 4 vols, 1861).

273 This was based on a rather conservative estimate that each worker supported a family of three.

274 Wolmar, *Fire and Steam*, p. 152.

275 James Stevens Curl, ed., *Kensal Green Cemetery: The Origins and Development of the General Cemetery of All Souls, Kensal Green, London, 1824–2001* (Chichester: Phillimore and Co., 2001); Henry Vivian-Neal, *A Railway Pantheon* (London: Friends of Kensal Green Cemetery, 2005).

276 There is also evidence to suggest that Walter had already married a Sarah Ann Jermy in 1847 and that the couple had a son, James Henry William (b. 1847). In 1857, Sarah Ann Peart, as she was, married Robert Crow, declaring that she was a widow when James was still very much alive and living in Islington with Mary Norman.

277 Information derived from The National Archives (TNA), Public Record Office (PRO), RAIL 264/24, nos. 1501–1750, 'Registers of drivers and firemen, showing date of entering service, promotions, type of work, fines etc.'

278 Information derived from The National Archives (TNA), Public Record Office (PRO), RAIL 264/33, nos. 3751–4000, 'Registers of drivers and firemen, showing date of entering service, promotions, type of work, fines etc.'

279 Watts derived his information about the incident from *Lloyd's Weekly*, 24 July 1898, and *The Times*, 30 July 1898, and details from those reports, along with the reports from

the *Illustrated London News*, 30 July 1898, *Reynolds's News*, 24 July 1898, the *Illustrated Police News*, 30 July 1898 and the *Pall Mall Gazette*, 19 and 20 July 1898, as well as reports of the inquest, have been used to construct the account given in this chapter.

280 The inquest was reported in the *London Evening Standard*, 23 July 1898, *Lloyd's Weekly*, 24 July 1898, the *Morning Post*, 23 July 1898, and *Reynolds's News*, 24 July 1898; the quotes from the inquest that follow are taken from those editions.

281 The full report is available at The National Archives (TNA), Public Record Office (PRO), RAIL 1053/87/37, 'Great Western Railway: report on the accident that occurred on 18 July 1898 to a passenger train near Acton'. A summary of the findings was published in several newspapers including the *Pall Mall Gazette*, 27 August 1898.

282 *Pall Mall Gazette*, 20 July 1898; *Illustrated Police News*, 30 July 1898.

283 *Penny Illustrated Paper*, 30 July 1898.

284 Reported in the *Penny Illustrated Paper*, 30 July 1898.

285 Phillip Carter, 'Axon, John (1900–1957), railwayman', *Oxford Dictionary of National Biography* (Oxford: Oxford University Press, 2010).

286 Ewan MacColl et al., *The Ballad of John Axon*, first broadcast on the BBC Home Service, July 2, 1958, released by Argo Records in 1965.

Chapter 14

287 The couple's other seven children were: Mary (b. 1823), John (b. 1825), Emily (b. 1828), Robert (b. 1894), Jehosaphar (b. 1832), Harriet (b. 1835) and James (b. 1838).

288 In addition to Elijah and Deborah, William and Caroline's four children were: Caroline junior (b. 1855), Charlotte (b. 25 Mar. 1859), William Edward (b. 1 Jan. 1860) and Charles (b. 15 Apr. 1866).

289 Watts derived his information about the incident from *Lloyd's Weekly*, 7 March 1880, and the details from that report, along with reports of the inquest, have been used to construct the account given in this chapter.

290 The inquest was reported in *The Times*, 3 March 1880.

291 In addition to Jane junior, the couple's five children were: Emma (b. 1870), Alice (b. 1871), Harriet (b. 1876), William Thomas (b. 1879) and Ellen Annie (b. 1882). They lived at 12 Mason Street and 86 Cornwall Road in Lambeth.

292 William and Emmeline's seven children were: William Edward (b. 1885), Charles (b. 1886), Alice (b. 1891), George (b. 1892), Edward (b. 1894), Joseph (b. 1896) and Esther (b. 1899), and they lived at 16 Jane Street in Southwark. William and Alice's three children were Elijah Alfred (b. 1905), Alfred (b. 1906) and Olive Miriam (b. 1908), and they lived at 125 Broadwall in Southwark.

293 Caroline and James' six children were: Florence Jane (b. 1877), James William (b. 1878), Charles (b. 1881), Albert (b. 1883), Alfred (b. 1885) and George Thomas (b. 1888). They lived at Stones Buildings near Regent Street in Lambeth, 1 Wilson Street in Bromley and 35 Cobden Street, also in Bromley.

294 Jane's other three children were: Charles, aged 20, Henry, aged 14 and 13-year-old Thomas.

295 Watts derived his information about the incident from the *Morning Post*, 21 January 1903, and the details from that report, along with reports of the inquest, have been used to construct the account given in this chapter.

296 The inquest was reported in the *Morning Post*, 21 January 1903, the *Richmond Herald*, 24 January 1903, and *The Times*, 21 January 1903; the quotes that follow are taken from that edition.

Chapter 15

297 Christian Wolmar, *Fire and Steam: A New History of the Railways in Britain* (London: Atlantic, 2007), p. 50.

298 Home Office case notes file, 'ALBERT MEDAL: Guard Sullivan – refused' (1908), The National Archives (TNA): Public Record Office (PRO): HO45/10382/167940.

299 Watts derived his information about the incident from *Lloyd's Weekly*, 13 January 1878, and *The Times*, 14 and 16 January 1878, and the details from those reports, along with reports from the *London Evening Standard*, 14 January 1878, the *Morning Post*, 14 January 1878, and the *Woolwich Gazette*, 19 January 1878, as well as reports of the inquest, have been used to construct the account given in this chapter.

300 The inquest was reported in *The Times*, 16 January 1878, the *Morning Post*, 16 January 1878, and the *Pall Mall Gazette*, 16 January 1878; the quotes that follow are taken from those editions.

301 *Penny Illustrated Newspaper*, 26 January 1878.

302 The additional three children were: George Howarth C. (b. 1912), Charles H. (b. 1915) and Donald L. (b. 1921).

303 Wolmar, *Fire and Steam*, pp. 38–42.

304 Watts derived his information about the incident from *Lloyd's Weekly*, 29 September 1878, and the details from that report, along with reports from the *Bristol Mercury and Daily Post*, 28 September 1878, and the *York Herald*, 25 September 1878, and reports of the inquest, have been used to construct the account given in this chapter.

305 The inquest was reported in *Lloyd's Weekly*, 29 September 1878, and the *Richmond and Twickenham Times*, 28 September 1878; the quotes that follow are taken from those editions.

Chapter 16

306 For a broad overview of the impact of fire upon the history of London, see Anna Milford, *London in Flames: The Capital's History through its Fires* (West Wickham: Comerford and Miller, 1998).

307 For the history of insurance company fire brigades, see Brian Wright, *Insurance Fire Brigades 1680–1929: The Birth of the British Fire Service* (Stroud: Tempus, 2008).

308 Brian Henman, *True Hero: The Life and Times of James Braidwood, Father of the British Fire Service* (Romford: Braidwood, 2000).

309 There are several excellent histories of the Metropolitan/London Fire Brigade, including the following which have been employed in researching this chapter and from which all statistics are derived: Shane Ewan, *Fighting Fires: Creating the British Fire Service 1800–1978* (London: Palgrave Macmillan, 2010); W.F. Hickin, *Organised Against Fire: A Short Organisational History of the London Fire Brigade and its Predecessors from 1833 to 1996* (London: W.F. Hickin, 1996); Sally Holloway, *Courage High: A History of Firefighting in London* (London: HMSO, 1992); William E. Jackson, London's Fire

Brigades (London: Longmans, 1966); John B. Nadal, *London's Fire Stations* (Huddersfield: Jeremy Mills, 2006).

310 Ewan, *Fighting Fires*, p. 74.

311 The funeral was reported in the *Illustrated London News*, 21 October 1871, the *Illustrated Police News*, 21 October 1871, and *Reynolds's News*, 22 October 1871.

312 Watts derived his information about the incident from *The Times*, 9 October 1871, and the details from that report, along with a report in the *Illustrated London News*, 14 October 1871, and reports of the inquest, have been used to construct the account given in this chapter.

313 The two sittings of the inquest were reported in the *Daily News*, 19 October 1871, *Lloyd's Weekly*, 15 October 1871, the *Pall Mall Gazette*, 12 October 1871, *Reynolds's News*, 22 October 1871, and *The Times*, 12 October 1871; the quotes that follow are taken from those editions.

314 *The Era*, 15 October 1871.

315 *The Times*, 18 October 1871.

316 *Reynolds's News*, 22 October 1871.

317 Cited in Holloway, *Courage High*, pp. 33–4.

318 Ewan, *Fighting Fires*, pp. 86–7.

319 *The Graphic*, 28 October 1871.

320 *Lloyd's Weekly*, 13 August 1876; *The Times*, 10 August 1876.

321 Watts derived his information about the incident from *The Times*, 25 July 1876 and 10 August 1876, and the details from those reports, along with reports from the *Daily News*, 27 July 1876, *Lloyd's Weekly*, 30 July 1876, and *Reynolds's News*, 30 July 1876, and reports of the inquest, have been used to construct the account given in this chapter.

322 *Lloyd's Weekly*, 13 August 1876.

323 The inquest was reported in *Lloyd's Weekly*, 13 August 1876, *Reynolds's News*, 30 July 1876, and *The Times*, 10 August 1876; the quotes that follow are taken from those editions.

324 For further reading on this concept, see James S. Curl, *The Victorian Celebration of Death* (Newton Abbot: David and Charles, 1972).

325 The funeral was reported in *Freeman's Journal and Daily Commercial Advertiser*, 14 August 1876, *Lloyd's Weekly*, 13 August 1876, the *Pall Mall Gazette*, 11 August 1876, and the *Daily News*, 11 August 1876.

326 *Daily News*, 11 August 1876.

Chapter 17

327 'Of the fires of London', in Henry Mayhew, *London Labour and the London Poor*, vol. 2 (London: Griffin, Bohn and Co., 4 vols, 1861).

328 Watts derived his information about the incident from *The Times*, 6 December 1886, and the details from that report, along with reports in the *Daily News*, 2 December 1886, and the *London Evening Standard*, 2 December 1886, and reports of the inquest, have been used to construct the account given in this chapter.

329 *London Evening Standard*, 3 December 1886.

330 The inquest was reported in *The Times*, 6 December 1886.

331 Watts derived his information about the incident from the *Daily Mail*, 16 October 1901,

and the details from that report, along with a report from the *East London Observer*, 19 October 1901, as well as reports of the inquest, have been used to construct the account given in this chapter. The tablet on the Watts Memorial incorrectly records the date of the fire as 4 October.

332 The inquest was reported in the *East London Observer*, 26 October 1901, and *The Times*, 23 October 1901; all the quotes that follow are taken from those editions.

333 Letter published in the *East London Observer*, 19 October 1901 and 26 October 1901.

334 Letter published in the *East London Observer*, 26 October 1901.

335 John Slade's regimental number was 7308 for the 2nd Battalion and 7305 for the 4th.

336 Watts derived his information about the incident from the *Daily Mail*, 2 January 1903, and the details from that report, along with reports from the *East London Observer*, 27 December 1902, and *The Times*, 27 December 1902, as well as reports of the inquest, have been used to construct the account given in this chapter.

337 The inquest was reported in the *Daily Mail*, 2 January 1903, the *East London Observer*, 3 January 1903, and the *East End News and Chronicle*, 6 January 1903; the quotes that follow are taken from those editions.

Chapter 18

338 See, for example, Catherine Hall, 'The early formation of Victorian domestic ideology', in Sandra Burman, ed., *Fit Work for Women* (London: Croom Helm for Oxford University Women's Studies Committee, 1979), pp. 15–32; Leonore Davidoff and Catherine Hall, eds, *Family Fortunes: Men and Women of the English Middle Class, 1780–1850* (London: Routledge, 2002); Martha Vicinus, ed., *Suffer and Be Still: Women in the Victorian Age* (Bloomington: Indiana University Press, 1972); Catherine Hall, ed., *White, Male and Middle Class: Explorations in Feminism and History* (Cambridge: Polity, 1992).

339 For example, Francis B. Smith, 'Sexuality in Britain, 1800–1900: some suggested revisions', in Martha Vicinus, ed., *A Widening Sphere: Changing Roles of Victorian Women* (Bloomington: Indiana University Press, 1977), pp. 188–93; M. Jeanne Peterson, 'No angels in the house: the Victorian myth and the Paget women', *American History Review* (1984), p. 693.

340 M. Vicinus, 'What makes a heroine? Girls' biographies of Florence Nightingale', in Vern L. Bullough, Bonnie Bullough and Marietta P. Stanton, eds, *Florence Nightingale and Her Era: A Collection of New Scholarship* (New York: Garland 1980), pp. 96–107; Mark Bostridge, *Florence Nightingale: The Woman and Her Legend* (London: Penguin, 2009); Katie Pickles, *Transnational Outrage: The Death and Commemoration of Edith Cavell* (Basingstoke: Palgrave Macmillan, 2007); Shane M. Barney, 'The mythic matters of Edith Cavell: propaganda, legend, myth and memory', *Historical Reflections*, vol. 31, no. 2 (2005), pp. 217–33; Anne Summers, *Female Lives, Moral States: Women, Religion and Public Life in Britain, 1800–1930* (Newbury: Threshold, 2000); Jane Jordan, *Josephine Butler* (London: John Murray, 2001); Hugh Cunningham, *Grace Darling: Victorian Heroine* (London: Hambledon Continuum, 2007).

341 J. Price, *Everyday Heroism: Victorian Constructions of the Heroic Civilian* (London: Bloomsbury, 2014), pp. 64–5.

342 See Price, *Everyday Heroism*, ch. 1.

343 For a more detailed discussion of this topic, see John Price, 'Octavia Hill's Red Cross Hall and its murals to heroic self-sacrifice', in Elizabeth Baigent and Ben Cowell, *'Nobler Imaginings and Mightier Struggles': Octavia Hill and the Remaking of British Society* (London: Institute of Historical Research, 2015).

344 Edward Mogg, *Mogg's New Picture of London and Visitor's Guide to its Sights* (London: E. Mogg, 1844).

345 Watts derived his information about the incident from consecutive editions of *The Times* between 26 and 30 January 1663 and the details from those reports, along with reports from *Lloyd's Weekly*, 1 February 1863, and *Reynolds's News*, 25 January 1863, and reports of the inquest, have been used to construct the account given in this chapter.

346 The inquest was reported in the *Daily News*, 2 February 1863, and *The Times*, 2 February 1863; all the quotes from the inquest that follow are taken from those editions.

347 Reports of the funeral appeared in the *Daily News*, 6 February 1863, and *Lloyd's Weekly*, 8 February 1863.

348 For more on 'sweated' labour, see Duncan Bythell, *The Sweated Trades: Outwork in Nineteenth-Century Britain* (London: Batsford, 1978); James. A. Schmiechen, *Sweated Industries and Sweated Labour: The London Clothing Trades, 1860–1914* (London: Croom Helm, 1984).

349 *Census of England and Wales* (1881), vol. IV, *General Report*, British Parliamentary Paper, 1883 lxxx (C.3797) 583.

350 Watts derived his information about the incident from *Lloyd's Weekly*, 29 October 1871, and the details from that report, along with reports from the *Birmingham Daily Post*, 19 October 1871, and *Jackson's Oxford Journal*, 21 October 1871, and reports of the inquest, have been used to construct the account given in this chapter.

351 The inquest was reported in the *Lloyd's Weekly*, 29 October 1871, and *The Times*, 21 October 1871; all of the quotes from the inquest that follow are taken from those editions.

352 George and Elizabeth had a total of eight children: Amelia Agnes (b. 1872), Alice Maud (b. 1876), George Edward (b. 1878), Ralph (b. 1880), Frederick John (b. 1882), Harry James (b. 1884), William (b. 1886) and Ellen Elizabeth (b. 1887).

353 Figure derived from Brian R. Mitchell and Phyllis Deane, *Abstract of British Historical Statistics* (Cambridge: Cambridge University Press, 1976).

354 Kathryn Gleadle, *British Women in the Nineteenth Century* (Basingstoke: Palgrave, 2001), pp. 104–6.

355 Watts derived his information about the incident from the *London Evening Standard*, 2 January 1902, and the *Daily Telegraph*, 2 January 1902, and the details from those reports, along with reports in the *Hackney and Kingsland Gazette*, 3 January 1902, the *Nottingham Evening Post*, 2 January 1902, the *Sheffield Evening Telegraph*, 2 January 1902, and reports of the inquest, have been used to construct the account given in this chapter.

356 The inquest was reported in the *Hackney and Kingsland Gazette*, 3 January 1902, and the quotes that follow are taken from that edition.

357 *Exeter and Plymouth Gazette*, 2 January 1902.

358 These included the *Nottingham Evening Post*, 2 January 1902, and the *Sheffield Evening Telegraph*, 2 January 1902.

Chapter 19

359 Frank Mundell, *Heroines of Daily Life* (London: Sunday School Union, 1896), p. 46.

360 'Female heroism, exemplified by anecdotes', *The Englishwoman's Domestic Magazine* (London, date unknown), p. 11.

361 Mundell, *Heroines of Daily Life*, p. 30.

362 Watts derived his information about the incident from the *Daily Mail*, 21 April 1902, the *Pall Mall Gazette*, 21 April 1902, and *The Sun*, 22 April 1902, and the details from those reports, along with reports from the *East London Observer*, 26 April 1902, and *The Times*, 21 April 1902, and reports of the inquest, have been used to construct the account given in this chapter.

363 Charles and Elizabeth's eleven children were: William John (b. 8 Mar. 1859), Elizabeth (b. 1859), John (b. 29 Mar. 1861), Henry (b. 28 Jan. 1863), Samuel (b. 12 Jan. 1865), Charles (b. 23 Feb. 1867), Mary Ann (b. 1869), Frederick William (b. 16 Jan. 1871), Reuben (b. 2 Jul. 1873), Alfred (b. 1875) and Ann (b. 4 Oct. 1876). They lived at several addresses in Hackney and Shoreditch during that time, including 1 Georges Place, 12 Collingwood Street and 8 Georges Place.

364 Rose Regelous had married Samuel James Reynold, a carman, on 6 August 1893.

365 The inquest was reported in the *East London Observer*, 26 April 1902, and *The Times*, 23 April 1902; all the quotes from the inquest that follow are taken from those editions.

366 The funeral of Alice Denman and her children was reported in *The Times*, 29 April 1902, and the local press.

367 The funeral of Arthur Regelous was reported in *Lloyd's Weekly*, 27 April 1902, and the local press.

368 Letter published in the *East London Observer*, 3 May 1902; donation lists were published in the *East London Observer* every week until the fund closed in June 1902.

369 The fountain is still extant in Museum Gardens next door to the Museum of Childhood on Cambridge Heath Road in Bethnal Green.

370 Borough of Bethnal Green Council, 'Proceedings: 9 November 1901 to 10 November 1902', vol. 2.

371 Watts derived his information about the incident from the *Daily Mail*, 31 March 1900, and the details from that report, along with reports from *Lloyd's Weekly*, 25 March 1900, and the *Pall Mall Gazette*, 26 March 1900, and the inquest report, have been used to construct the account given in this chapter.

372 The inquest was reported in the *Daily Mail*, 31 March 1900. The original inquest documentation and depositions were also consulted at the London Metropolitan Archives (ref. CLA/042).

373 Information derived from the original inquest documentation and depositions, consulted at the London Metropolitan Archives (ref. CLA/042).

374 James E. Ritchie, 'The low lodging house', in *Days and Nights in London* (London, 1880).

375 Ritchie, 'The low lodging house'.

376 Figures taken from the inquest report published in *The Times*, 1 August 1873.

377 Arthur Morrison, *A Child of the Jago* (London: Methuen and Co., 1896).

378 Watts derived his information about the incident from *The Times*, 1 August 1873, and the details from that report, along with reports from the *Bradford Observer*, 30 July 1873, the *Daily News*, 29 July 1873, *Reynolds's News*, 3 August 1873, and the *York Herald*, 2 August 1873, and reports of the inquest, have been used to construct the account given in this chapter.

379 Examples of this include the *Bradford Observer*, 30 July 1873, the *Daily News*, 29 July 1873, *Reynolds's News*, 3 August 1873, and the *Yorkshire Post*, 30 July 1873.

380 Information derived from the original inquest depositions, consulted at the London Metropolitan Archives (ref. COR/B/084).

381 *Reynolds's News*, 3 August 1873.

382 *The Times*, 30 July 1873.

383 Metropolitan Board of Works, 'Annual report of the St. Giles district' (1873).

Chapter 20

384 Henry Mayhew, 'Of the horse dung of the streets of London', in *London Labour and the London Poor*, vol. 2 (London: Griffin, Bohn and Co., 4 vols, 1861).

385 There do not appear to be any press reports of the initial accident, only later reports after Elizabeth's death.

386 In addition to Elizabeth, Joseph and Jane's other nine children were: Charles Henry Joseph (b. 1856), Joseph James (b. 1857), Louisa (b. 3 Jan. 1862, d. Oct.–Dec. 1871), Amelia (b. 2 Jan. 1864, d. Oct.–Dec. 1871), Sarah Anne (b. 31 Dec. 1865), Edward Henry (b. 1868), Elizabeth Mary (b. 1871), James (b. 1873) and John Frederick (b. 1875).

387 Watts derived his information about the incident from the report of the inquest in *Lloyd's Weekly*, 24 June 1888, and the details from that report, along with other reports on the inquest including the *Eastern Argus and Borough of Hackney Times*, 30 June 1888, have been used to construct the account given in this chapter.

388 Five months later, Ross would preside over the inquest on Mary Jane Kelly, the fifth and final victim of the Whitechapel murderer.

389 *Lloyd's Weekly*, 1 July 1888.

390 Joseph and Eliza had at least four children: Joseph junior (b. 1884), Sarah (b. 1888), William (b. 1892) and Mary Ann (b. 1894).

391 *Lloyd's Weekly*, 10 June 1888.

392 Edward and Elizabeth's three children were: Lilian (b. 1897), Eliza (b. 1900) and Violet (b. 1914).

393 James and Eliza's five children were: James junior (b. 1912), John (b. 1914), Doris (b. 1917), George (b. 1920) and Jessie (b. 1922).

394 John and Eliza's four children were: Eliza Jane (b. 1899), Elizabeth Annie (b. 1900), Beatrice Maria (b. 1904) and John Henry (b. 1910).

395 Sarah and William's additional four children were: Clara Jane (b. 1897), Elizabeth Emily (b. 1898), Mary Ann (b. 1900) and James (b. 1905).

396 Susie Timms, *Titiens: Her Majesty's Prima Donna* (London: Bezazzy, 2005).

397 Watts derived his information about the incident from *The Times*, 12 April 1869, and the details from that report, along with reports in *Lloyd's Weekly*, 4 April 1869, and the *Pall Mall Gazette*, 12 April 1869, have been used to construct the account given in this chapter.

398 Edward and Sarah's other seven children were: Elizabeth (b. 1809), Thomas (b. 1814), James (b. 1818), Francis (b. 1819), Sarah (b. 1821), Edward (b. 1823) and John (b. 1825).

399 The inquest was reported in *The Times*, 12 April 1869, and the *Pall Mall Gazette*, 12 April 1869; the quotes from the inquest that follow are taken from that edition.

Chapter 21

400 Charles Manby Smith, *Curiosities of London Life* (London, 1853).

401 Austin Dobson and John Evelyn, *The Diary of John Evelyn*, vol. 2: Primary Source edn (London: Nabu, 2014).

402 Joanne Hawley, 'The development of indoor ice skating rinks in London before World War II', unpublished MA thesis (London: City University, 1984).

403 *Penny Illustrated Paper*, 22 January 1876.

404 Diana Coke, *Saved from a Watery Grave* (London: Royal Humane Society, 2000).

405 In addition to Thomas junior, Thomas senior and Maria Simpson had six children: Eliza (b. 1842), Maria junior (b. 1844), Martha (b. 1846), William (b. 1849), Sarah (b. 1857) and Alice (b. 1860).

406 *Daily News*, 26 January 1885.

407 Watts derived his information about the incident from *Lloyd's Weekly*, 1 February 1885, and *The Times*, 26 January 1885, and the details from that report, along with a report from the *Daily News*, 26 January 1885, and reports of the inquest, have been used to construct the account given in this chapter.

408 Burke was reported to be living at 18 Anatola Road, Dartmouth Park Hill.

409 Francis Annett was reported to be living at 4 Ashbrook Road, Holloway.

410 Pepper was reported to be living at 38 Mansfield Road.

411 The inquest was reported in *The Times*, 29 January 1885, and the *Pall Mall Gazette*, 29 January 1885; all the quotes from the inquest that follow are taken from those editions.

412 *Lloyd's Weekly*, 10 February 1895.

413 *The Observer*, 10 February 1895.

414 *Daily News*, 11 February 1895.

415 Alan Faulkner, *The Regent's Canal: London's Hidden Waterway* (Burton-on-Trent: Waterways World, 2005); Herbert Spencer, *London's Canal: The History of Regent's Canal* (London: Lund Humphries, 2nd edn, 1976).

416 *Lloyd's Weekly*, 10 February 1895.

417 *Lloyd's Weekly*, 10 February 1895.

418 The account given in this chapter is derived from the *Daily News*, 11 February 1895, *Lloyd's Weekly*, 10 February 1895, and *The Observer*, 10 February 1895.

419 The site is now known as Willesden Old Burial Ground and is located on Neasden Lane, NW10.

Chapter 22

420 The development of the Watts Memorial in Postman's Park is fully explored in John Price, *Postman's Park: G.F. Watts's Memorial to Heroic Self-Sacrifice* (Compton: Watts Gallery, 2008).

421 G.F. Watts, 'Letter to James Smith, 1 December 1893', National Portrait Gallery, Heinz Archive, *G.F. Watts Correspondence*, vol. 14, f. 27.

422 Mary Seton Watts, 'Diary entries for 2 and 8 February 1891; 23 May 1891', Watts Gallery Archive, *Mary Seton Watts Diaries*.

423 Jennifer S. Alexander, 'Mapperley Hospital and George Thomas Hine (1841–1916), Consulting Architect to the Commissioners in Lunacy', *Transactions of the Thoroton Society of Nottinghamshire*, vol. 112 (2008), pp. 199–219.

424 Richard S. Lambert, *The Universal Provider: A Study of William Whiteley and the Rise of the London Department Store* (London: George G. Harrap and Co. Ltd, 1958); Linda Stratmann, *Whiteley's Folly: The Life and the Death of a Salesman* (Stroud: Sutton, 2004).

425 Watts derived his information about the incident from the *Boston Post*, 30 August 1902,

and the *Yorkshire Post*, 28 August 1902, and the details from those reports, along with a report which appeared in *The Times*, 27 August 1902, and reports of the inquest, have been used to construct the account given in this chapter.

426 The inquests were reported in the *Boston Post*, 30 August 1902, *The Times*, 28 and 29 August 1902, and the *Yorkshire Post*, 28 August 1902; the quotes from the inquest that follow are taken from those editions.

427 Elizabeth and John's eight children were: Henry (b. 1890), Frank (b. 1893), Alice (b. 1895), Lizzie Ellen (b. 1896), Lucy May (b. 1899), George Wilfred (b. 1900), Edith Lottie (b. 1902) and Albert Bradley (b. 1907).

428 Alfred and Miriam's thirteen children were: Roy (b. 1907), Cecil (b. 1908), Allen (b. 1912), John (b. 1914), Ethel (b. 1915), Frank (b. 1916), James (b. 1918), Hilda (b. 1919), Edgar (b. 1920), Violet (b. 1923), Dorothy (b. 1925) and twins Bessie and Bryan (b. 1926).

429 George and Ada's six children were: Gladys May (b. 1908), Evelyn (b. 1911), twins George F. and George W. (b. 1913), Mark (b. 1917) and Phyllis (b. 1919).

430 Information derived from The National Archives (TNA), Public Record Office (PRO), RAIL 264/55, nos. 9251–500, 'Registers of drivers and firemen, showing date of entering service, promotions, type of work, fines etc.'.

431 Thomas T. Carter, *The First Ten Years of the House of Mercy, Clewer* (London: Joseph Masters, 1861).

Chapter 23

432 *Christian World*, 22 December 1898; *Daily Mail*, 7 July 1898; *The Times*, 5 September 1887.

433 *Pall Mall Gazette*, 1 November 1887.

434 Letter to the Earl of Wemyss, 8 May 1888, quoted in Veronica Franklin-Gould, *G.F. Watts: The Last Great Victorian* (London: Yale University Press, 2004), p. 226.

435 The account of the incident provided in this chapter is derived from reports in *The Times*, 9 and 10 August 1901; it is not clear where Watts obtained his information about the incident.

436 I am indebted to Helen Simpson for information and images relating to John Cambridge and the plaque in the English church.

437 An obituary for Alexander Brown was published in the *Lewisham Gazette*, 19 October 1900.

438 William Freer Lucas also attended the Royal Medical College in Epsom; see Chapter 3.

439 Obituaries in the *Lewisham Gazette*, 19 October 1900, and the *Freemason's Chronicle*, 10 November 1900.

440 Watts derived his information about the incident from *Lloyd's Weekly*, 21 October 1900, and the details from that report, along with reports in the *Brockley News*, 19 October 1900, and the *Lewisham Gazette*, 19 October 1900, have been used to construct the account given in this chapter.

441 *Lewisham Gazette*, 26 October 1900.

Afterword

442 'Aggregate Night Time Bomb Census, 7th October 1940 to 6 June 1941', The National Archives (TNA), Public Record Office (PRO), H0193/13.

443 *The Times*, 5 December 1962.

BIBLIOGRAPHY

Manuscripts, newspapers and periodicals

London Metropolitan Archives, CLA/042, 'Records of the Southwark Coroner's Court' (1837–1932)

London Metropolitan Archives, COR/B/084, 'Middlesex Central Coroners District, Depositions' (1873)

London Metropolitan Archives, P69/BOT1/B/036/MS18628 'Heroic Self-Sacrifice Memorial Committee minute book' (1904)

The National Archives (TNA), Ho 45/10382/167940, 'ALBERT MEDAL: Guard Sullivan – refused' (1908)

The National Archives (TNA), Ho 193/13, 'Aggregate Night Time Bomb Census, 7th October 1940 to 6 June 1941' (1940–1)

The National Archives (TNA), MEPO 2/1925, 'Metropolitan Police commendations, awards and testimonials' (1930)

The National Archives (TNA), RAIL 264/24, nos. 1501–750, 'Registers of drivers and firemen, showing date of entering service, promotions, type of work, fines etc.' (1875–7)

The National Archives (TNA), RAIL 264/33, nos. 3751–4000, 'Registers of drivers and firemen, showing date of entering service, promotions, type of work, fines etc.' (1886–8)

The National Archives (TNA), RAIL 264/55, nos. 9251–500, 'Registers of drivers and firemen, showing date of entering service, promotions, type of work, fines etc.' (1902)

The National Archives (TNA), RAIL 411/411, 'Board of Trade inquiry into loss of SS "Stella" on the Casquets' (1899)

The National Archives (TNA), RAIL 1053/87/37, 'Great Western Railway: report on the accident that occurred on 18 July 1898 to a passenger train near Acton' (1898)

National Portrait Gallery, Heinz Archive, 'G.F. Watts correspondence' (1893)

Southwark Local History Library and Archive, 'Borough of Southwark Council minute book', vol. 36 (1936)

Watts Gallery Archive, 'Mary Seton Watts, diaries' (1891)

Aberdeen Weekly Journal
Berrow's Worcester Journal
Birmingham Daily Post
Boston Post
Bradford Observer
Bristol Mercury and Daily Post
British Medical Journal
Brockley News
Christian World
Daily Mail
Daily News
Daily Telegraph
Derby Mercury
Devon Evening Express
Devon Evening News
*Eastern Argus and Borough of Hackney
    Times*
East End News and Chronicle
East Ham Echo
East London Advertiser
East London Observer
English Illustrated Magazine
The Englishwoman's Domestic Magazine
The Englishwoman's Review
The Era
Exeter and Plymouth Gazette
*Freeman's Journal and Daily
    Commercial Advertiser*
Freemason's Chronicle
Glasgow Herald
The Graphic
Hackney and Kingsland Gazette
Hampshire Advertiser
Ilfracombe Chronicle
Illustrated London News
Illustrated Police News
Jackson's Oxford Journal
Jersey Times
Jersey Weekly Press and Independent

Lewisham Gazette
Lloyd's Weekly
London Evening Standard
Manchester Times
Mid-Surrey Gazette
Morning Post
Myra's Journal
News of the World
Northern Echo
Nottingham Evening Post
The Observer
On and Off Duty
Pall Mall Gazette
Penny Illustrated Paper
Police Review and Parade Gossip
Putney and Wandsworth Borough News
Reynolds's News
Richmond and Twickenham Times
Richmond Herald
Sheffield Evening Telegraph
*South London Chronicle and Southwark and
    Lambeth Ensign*
South London Observer
South London Press
*Southwark Recorder and Bermondsey and
    Rotherhithe Advertiser*
*Southwark Standard and South London
    News*
The Spectator
Stratford Express
The Sun
Teignmouth Gazette
Teignmouth Post
The Times
Weekly Despatch
Western Mail
Woolwich Gazette
York Herald
Yorkshire Post

Books and articles

Peter Ackroyd, *London: The Biography* (London: Chatto and Windus, 2000)

Peter Ackroyd, *Thames: The Biography* (London: Random House, 2009)

Peter Ackroyd, *London Under* (Oxford: ISIS, 2011)

Jennifer S. Alexander, 'Mapperley Hospital and George Thomas Hine (1841–1916), Consulting Architect to the Commissioners in Lunacy', *Transactions of the Thoroton Society of Nottinghamshire*, vol. 112 (2008), pp. 199–219

David Ascoli, *The Queen's Peace: The Origins and Development of the Metropolitan Police, 1829–1979* (London: Hamish Hamilton, 1979)

Margaret Ashby, *The Book of the River Lea* (Buckingham: Barracuda, 1991)

Marie H. Bailey, *A Terrible Experience: The Wreck of the Stella, by a Survivor* (London: M. Bailey, *c*.1900)

Craig Barclay, 'Heroes of peace: the Royal Humane Society and the award of medals in Britain 1774–1914', unpublished Ph.D. thesis (York: University of York, 2009)

Shane M. Barney, 'The mythic matters of Edith Cavell: propaganda, legend, myth and memory', *Historical Reflections*, vol. 31, no. 2 (2005), pp. 217–33

Emilie Barrington, 'The Red Cross Hall', *English Illustrated Magazine*, vol. x (June 1893)

Chaim I. Bermant, *Point of Arrival: A Study of London's East End* (London: Eyre Methuen, 1975)

M. Bettison, 'Luffman, Lauretta Caroline Maria (1846–1929)', *Australian Dictionary of Biography*, vol. 10 (1986)

Mark Bills and Barbara Bryant, *G.F. Watts: Victorian Visionary* (London: Yale University Press, 2008)

Derek Birley, *A Social History of English Cricket* (London: Aurum, 1999)

Howard Bloch and Graham Hill, eds, *The Silvertown Explosion, 1917* (London: All Points East, 1997)

Charles Booth, *London Life and Labour* (London: Macmillan, 1892)

Mark Bostridge, *Florence Nightingale: The Woman and Her Legend* (London: Penguin, 2009)

Marc Brodie, *The Politics of the Poor: The East End of London, 1885–1914* (Oxford: Clarendon Press, 2004)

Annie Bryans, *A Souvenir of the Unveiling of the Memorial Fountain in Southampton* (Southampton, 1901)

Robert Bucholz and Joseph Ward, *London: A Social and Cultural History, 1550–1750* (Cambridge: Cambridge University Press, 2012)

J.G.L. Burnby and M. Parker, *The Navigation of the River Lee, 1190–1790* (Enfield: Edmonton Hundred Historical Society, 1978)

Ian A. Burney, 'Making room at the public bar: coroners' inquests, medical knowledge and the politics of the constitution in early-nineteenth-century England', in James Vernon, ed., *Re-reading the Constitution: New Narratives in the Political History of England's Long Nineteenth Century* (Cambridge: Cambridge University Press, 1996)

Duncan Bythell, *The Sweated Trades: Outwork in Nineteenth-Century Britain* (London: Batsford, 1978)

Barbara Caine, *Victorian Feminists* (Oxford: Oxford University Press, 1992)

Phillip Carter, 'Axon, John (1900–1957), railwayman', *Oxford Dictionary of National Biography* (Oxford: Oxford University Press, 2010)

Thomas T. Carter, *The First Ten Years of the House of Mercy, Clewer* (London: Joseph Masters, 1861)

Jim Clifford, 'The River Lea in West Ham: a river's role in shaping industrialization on the eastern edge of nineteenth-century London', in Stephane Castonguay and Matthew Evenden, eds, *Urban Rivers: Remaking Rivers, Cities, and Space in Europe and North America* (Pittsburgh, PA: University of Pittsburgh Press, 2012)

Geraldine Coates, *Beefeater London: The Story of London's Gin* (Edinburgh: Contagious Publishing, 2007)

Rob Cochrane, *Pioneers of Power: The Story of the London Electricity Supply Corporation, 1887–1948* (London: London Electricity Board, 1987)

Diana Coke, *Saved from a Watery Grave* (London: Royal Humane Society, 2000)

Crockford's Clerical Directory (London: Church House Publishing, 1882–5)

Hugh Cunningham, *Grace Darling: Victorian Heroine* (London: Continuum, 2007)

James S. Curl, *The Victorian Celebration of Death* (Newton Abbot: David and Charles, 1972)

James S. Curl, ed., *Kensal Green Cemetery: The Origins and Development of the General Cemetery of All Souls, Kensal Green, London, 1824–2001* (Chichester: Phillimore and Co., 2001)

Joseph Cwyer, *The Disaster to the Stella in the Channel* (Penge: T.H. Bentley and Co., 1899)

Leonore Davidoff and Catherine Hall, eds, *Family Fortunes: Men and Women of the English Middle Class, 1780–1850* (London: Routledge, 2002)

Charles Maurice Davies, *Mystic London* (London: Tinsley Bros, 1875)

Anna Davin, *Growing Up Poor: Home, School and Street 1870–1914* (London: Rivers Oram, 1996)

Lucy Delap, '"Thus does man prove to be the master of things": shipwrecks, chivalry and masculinities in nineteenth- and twentieth-century Britain', *Cultural and Social History*, vol. 3 (2006), pp. 45–77.

Charles Dickens, *Oliver Twist; or the Parish Boy's Progress* (London: Richard Bentley, 1838)

Austin Dobson and John Evelyn, *The Diary of John Evelyn*, vol. 2: Primary Source edn (London: Nabu, 2014)

Gustave Doré and Blanchard Jerrold, *London: A Pilgrimage* (1870) (London: Anthem, 2006)

Harold J. Dyos and Michael Wolff, eds, *The Victorian City*, vol. 1 (London: Routledge, 1973)

Clive Emsley, *The Great British Bobby: A History of British Policing from the 18th Century to the Present* (London: Quercus, 2009)

Shane Ewan, *Fighting Fires: Creating the British Fire Service 1800–1978* (London: Palgrave Macmillan, 2010)

Dick Fagan and Eric Burgess, *Men of the Tideway* (London: Hale, 1996)

Alan H. Faulkner, *The Grand Junction Canal* (Newton Abbot: David and Charles, 1973)

Alan Faulkner, *The Regent's Canal: London's Hidden Waterway* (Burton-on-Trent: Waterways World, 2005)

William Fishman, *East End 1888* (Nottingham: Five Leaves, 2005)

Veronica Franklyn-Gould, *G. F. Watts: The Last Great Victorian* (London: Yale University Press, 2004)

Jack Gaster, *Time and Tide: The Life of a Thames Waterman* (London: Amberley, 2010)

Kathryn Gleadle, *British Women in the Nineteenth Century* (Basingstoke: Palgrave, 2001)

Nicolette Gullace, 'White feathers and wounded men: female patriotism and memory of the Great War', *Journal of British Studies*, vol. 36 (April 1997)

Catherine Hall, 'The early formation of Victorian domestic ideology', in Sandra Burman, ed., *Fit Work for Women* (London: Croom Helm for Oxford University Women's Studies Committee, 1979), pp. 15–32

Catherine Hall, ed., *White, Male and Middle Class: Explorations in Feminism and History* (Cambridge: Polity, 1992)

Peter G. Hall, *The Industries of London since 1861* (London: Routledge, 2005)

Susan Hamilton, *Frances Power Cobbe and Victorian Feminism* (Basingstoke: Palgrave Macmillan, 2006)

Joanne Hawley, 'The development of indoor ice skating rinks in London before World War II', unpublished MA thesis (London: City University, 1984)

Brian Henman, *True Hero: The Life and Times of James Braidwood, Father of the British Fire Service* (Romford: Braidwood, 2000)

Miles Henslow, *Fifty Great Disasters and Tragedies that Shocked the World* (London: Odhams, 1937)

Nick Hervey, 'Gull, Sir William Withey, first baronet (1816–1890)', *Oxford Dictionary of National Biography* (Oxford: Oxford University Press, 2004)

W. F. Hickin, *Organised Against Fire: A Short Organisational History of the London Fire Brigade and its Predecessors from 1833 to 1996* (London: W. F. Hickin, 1996)

Octavia Hill, *Letter to My Fellow Workers* (London: James Martin, 1893)

Sally Holloway, *Courage High: A History of Firefighting in London* (London: HMSO, 1992)

Philip Howard, *London's River* (London: Hamilton, 1975)

Thomas Hughes, *Tom Brown's School Days* (Cambridge: Macmillan and Co., 1857)

Henry Humpherus, *History of the Origin and Progress of the Company of Watermen and Lightermen of the River Thames* (London: Prentice, 3 vols, 1874–6)

Invalid Asylum for Respectable Females, *Fifth Report for 1831 of the Invalid Asylum for Respectable Females in London and its Vicinity* (London, 1832)

Stephen Inwood, *A History of London* (London: Macmillan, 1998)

Stephen Inwood, *City of Cities* (London: Macmillan, 2005)

William E. Jackson, *London's Fire Brigades* (London: Longmans, 1966)

Jerome K. Jerome, *Three Men in a Boat: To Say Nothing of the Dog* (Bristol: J. W. Arrowsmith, 1889)

Jane Jordan, *Josephine Butler* (London: John Murray, 2001)

Peter J. Keating, *The Working Classes in Victorian Fiction* (London: Routledge and Kegan Paul, 1971)

J. H. F. Kemp, *The Metropolitan Police: The Men and their Medals* (London: Ethandune Medal Publications, 2009)

Peter Kennerley, *The Building of Liverpool Cathedral* (Lancaster: Carnegie, 2004)

Dick Kirby, *The Brave Blue Line: 100 Years of Metropolitan Police Gallantry* (Barnsley: Wharncliffe True Crime, 2011)

Richard S. Lambert, *The Universal Provider: A Study of William Whiteley and the Rise of the London Department Store* (London: George G. Harrap and Co. Ltd, 1958)

Laura M. Lane, *Heroes of Everyday Life* (London: Cassell and Co., 1888)

James Legon, *My Ancestors were Watermen: A Guide to Tracing Your Watermen and Lightermen Ancestors* (London: Society of Genealogists, 2014)

Liverpool Anglican Cathedral, *Noble Women Windows in the Lady Chapel, Liverpool Cathedral* (Liverpool: Liverpool Anglican Cathedral, 1951)

Joan Lock, *The Princess Alice Disaster* (London: Robert Hale, 2013)

Ewan MacColl et al., *The Ballad of John Axon* (Argo Records, 1965)

William McNeill, *The Noble Women of the Staircase and Atrium Windows in the Lady Chapel of the Liverpool Cathedral* (Liverpool: Daily Post Printers, 1915)

Patrick Marber, *Closer* (London: Methuen, 1997)

John Marriott, *The Metropolitan Poor: Semi-factual Accounts, 1795–1910* (London: Pickering and Chatto, 1999)

William Martin, *Heroism of Boyhood* (London: Darton and Hodge, 1865)

Gary Mason, *The Official History of the Metropolitan Police: 175 years of Policing London* (London: Carlton, 2004)

Bryan Mawer, *Sugarbakers: From Sweat to Sweetness* (London: Anglo-German Family History Society, 2011)

Henry Mayhew, *London Labour and the London Poor* (London: Griffin, Bohn and Co., 4 vols, 1861)

W.I. McDonald, 'Jenner, Sir William, first baronet (1815–1898)', *Oxford Dictionary of National Biography* (Oxford: Oxford University Press, 2004)

William McGonagall, *More Poetic Gems* (Dundee: David Winter and Son, 1962)

Gerard Melia, *The Silvertown Disaster*, ed. J. Levine (London: Longman, 1984).

Charles D. Michael, *Deeds of Daring: Stories of Heroism in Every Day Life* (London: S.W. Partridge and Co., 1900)

Charles D. Michael, *Heroines: True Tales of Brave Women – A Book for British Girls* (London: S.W. Partridge and Co., 1904)

Alfred H. Miles, *Fifty-Two Stories of Heroism in Life and Action for Boys* (London: Hutchinson and Co., 1899)

Alfred H. Miles, *The Bravest Deed I Ever Saw* (London: Hutchinson and Co., 1905)

Alfred H. Miles, *A Book of Brave Girls at Home and Abroad: True Stories of Courage and Heroism* (London: Hutchinson and Co., 1909)

Anna Milford, *London in Flames: The Capital's History through its Fires* (West Wickham: Comerford and Miller, 1998)

Brian R. Mitchell and Phyllis Deane, *Abstract of British Historical Statistics* (Cambridge: Cambridge University Press, 1976)

Edward Mogg, *Mogg's New Picture of London and Visitor's Guide to its Sights* (London: E. Mogg, 1844)

Arthur Morrison, *A Child of the Jago* (London: Methuen and Co., 1896)

Frank Mundell, *Heroines of Daily Life* (London: Sunday School Union, 1896)

John B. Nadal, *London's Fire Stations* (Huddersfield: Jeremy Mills, 2006)

Lynda Nead, *Victorian Babylon: People, Streets and Images in Nineteenth Century London* (New Haven: Yale University Press, 2000)

Lewis O'Malley, *The Indian Civil Service, 1601–1930* (London: Frank Cass and Co., 2nd edn, 1965)

John Ovenden and David Shayer, *The Wreck of the Stella: Titanic of the Channel Islands* (St Peter Port: Guernsey Museums and Galleries, 1999)

M. Jeanne Peterson, 'No angels in the house: the Victorian myth and the Paget women', *American History Review* (1984)

Katie Pickles, *Transnational Outrage: The Death and Commemoration of Edith Cavell* (Basingstoke: Palgrave Macmillan, 2007)

Dale Porter, *The Thames Embankment: Environment, Technology, and Society in Victorian London* (Akron: University of Akron Press, 1998)

Roy Porter, *London: A Social History* (London: Penguin, 2000)

Alex Potts, 'Picturing the modern metropolis: images of London in the nineteenth century', *History Workshop Journal*, vol. 26 (1988), pp. 28–56

W.R. Powell, ed., *A History of the County of Essex*, vol. 6 (Oxford: Oxford University Press, 1973)

D.A. Power, 'Bowman, Sir William, first baronet (1816–1892)', rev. Emilie Savage-Smith, *Oxford Dictionary of National Biography* (Oxford: Oxford University Press, 2004)

Derek Pratt, *Discovering London's Canals* (Aylesbury: Shire, 2nd edn, 1981)

John Price, *Postman's Park: G.F. Watts's Memorial to Heroic Self-Sacrifice* (Compton: Watts Gallery, 2008)

John Price, *Everyday Heroism: Victorian Constructions of the Heroic Civilian* (London: Bloomsbury, 2014)

John Price, 'Octavia Hill's Red Cross Hall and its murals to heroic self-sacrifice', in Elizabeth Baigent and Ben Cowell, *'Nobler Imaginings and Mightier Struggles': Octavia Hill and the Remaking of British Society* (London: Institute of Historical Research, 2015)

Hardwicke D. Rawnsley, *Ballads of Brave Deeds* (London: J.M. Dent and Co., 1896)

Peter Reese, *Target London: Bombing the Capital, 1915–2005* (Barnsley: Pen and Sword Military, 2011)

James E. Ritchie, *The Night Side of London* (London, 1858)

James E. Ritchie, *Days and Nights in London* (London, 1880)

Ellen Ross, *Slum Travellers: Ladies and London Poverty, 1860–1920* (Berkeley: University of California Press, 2007)

Royal Humane Society, *Annual Report* (London, 1837–1910)

James A. Schmiechen, *Sweated Industries and Sweated Labour: The London Clothing Trades, 1860–1914* (London: Croom Helm, 1984)

Jonathan Schneer, *London 1900: The Imperial Metropolis* (New Haven: Yale University Press, 1999)

Jonathan Schneer, *The Thames: England's River* (London: Little, Brown, 2005)

L.D. Schwarz, *London in the Age of Industrialisation: Entrepreneurs, Labour Force, and Living Conditions, 1700–1850* (Cambridge: Cambridge University Press, 2003)

Francis Sheppard, *London: A History* (Oxford: Oxford University Press, 1998)

Charles Manby Smith, *Curiosities of London Life* (London, 1853)

Francis B. Smith, 'Sexuality in Britain, 1800–1900: some suggested revisions', in Martha Vicinus, ed., *A Widening Sphere: Changing Roles of Victorian Women* (Bloomington: Indiana University Press, 1977), pp. 188–93

Phillip T. Smith, *Policing Victorian London: Political Policing, Public Order and the London Metropolitan Police* (Westport, CT: Greenwood Press, 1985)

Edward R. Snow, *Women of the Sea* (London: Alvin Redman, 1963)

Herbert Spencer, *London's Canal: The History of Regent's Canal* (London: Lund Humphries, 2nd edn, 1976)

Gareth Steadman Jones, *Outcast London: A Study in the Relationship between Classes in Victorian Society* (Oxford: Clarendon Press, 1971)

Linda Stratmann, *Whiteley's Folly: The Life and the Death of a Salesman* (Stroud: Sutton, 2004)

Brian Strong, ed., *Remembering Three Mills* (London: River Lee Tidal Mill Trust Ltd, 2008)

Anne Summers, *Female Lives, Moral States: Women, Religion and Public Life in Britain, 1800–1930* (Newbury: Threshold, 2000)

Jean Sweetser and Colin Gillespie, *The Tottenham Outrage* (London: Page Green Centre, 1983)

Richard Tames, *London, a Cultural History* (Oxford: Signal, 2006)

John Thomas, 'The "beginnings of a noble pile": Liverpool Cathedral's Lady Chapel, 1904–10', *Architectural History*, vol. 48 (2005), pp. 257–90

Susie Timms, *Titiens: Her Majesty's Prima Donna* (London: Bezazzy, 2005)

Colin Trodd and Stephanie Brown, eds, *Representations of G. F. Watts: Art Making in Victorian Culture* (Aldershot: Ashgate, 2004)

Martha Vicinus, ed., *Suffer and Be Still: Women in the Victorian Age* (Bloomington: Indiana University Press, 1972)

Martha Vicinus, 'What makes a heroine? Girls' biographies of Florence Nightingale', in Vern L. Bullough, Bonnie Bullough and Marietta P. Stanton, eds, *Florence Nightingale and her Era: A Collection of New Scholarship* (New York: Garland, 1980), pp. 96–107

Henry Vivian-Neal, *A Railway Pantheon* (London: Friends of Kensal Green Cemetery, 2005)

Edward Walford, *Old and New London*, vol. 5 (London: Cassell and Co., 1878)

Henry Walker, *Sketches of Christian Work and Workers* (London: Religious Tract Society, 1896)

James Walvin, *A Child's World: A Social History of English Childhood 1800–1914* (Harmondsworth: Penguin, 1982)

Philip Ward-Jackson, *Public Sculpture of Historic Westminster* (Liverpool: Liverpool University Press, 2011)

Philip Ward-Jackson, *Public Sculpture of the City of London* (Liverpool: Liverpool University Press, 2003)

Martin Watts, *The House Mill, Bromley by Bow, London* (London: River Lee Tidal Mill Trust Ltd, 1998)

Gavin Weightman and Steve Humphries, *The Making of Modern London* (London: Ebury, 2007)

Robert Whelan, ed., *Letters to My Fellow Workers* (London: Kyrle Books, 2005)

Jerry White, *London in the Nineteenth Century* (London: Jonathan Cape, 2007)

Jerry White, *Zeppelin Nights: London in the First World War* (London: Bodley Head, 2014)

Frederick S. Williams, *Our Iron Roads: Their History, Construction and Social Influences* (London: Bemrose and Sons, 1883)

Olivia Williams, *Gin Glorious Gin: How Mother's Ruin Became the Spirit of London* (London: Headline, 2014)

Lori Williamson, *Power and Protest: Frances Power Cobbe and Victorian Society* (London: Rivers Oram, 2005)

Jay Winter, *The Great War and the British People* (London: Macmillan, 1985)

Jay Winter, *Sites of Memory, Sites of Mourning: The Great War in European Cultural History* (Cambridge: Cambridge University Press, 1995)

Christian Wolmar, *Fire and Steam: A New History of the Railways in Britain* (London: Atlantic, 2007)

Fiona Wood, 'Garton, Sir Richard Charles (1857–1934)', *Oxford Dictionary of National Biography* (Oxford: Oxford University Press, 2004)

Brian Wright, *Insurance Fire Brigades 1680–1929: The Birth of the British Fire Service* (Stroud: Tempus, 2008)

INDEX

Abbott, Harriett, 56
Ackroyd, Peter, 48, 55
Acton, 158-59
Adams, William James, 37
Aitken, William, 219
Alge, Elizabeth, 73
Allen, Matthew, 102
Alsop, Maria, 264
Anderson, Martha, 100
Angel, Dr Andrea, 125, 127
Annett, Francis, 256-57
Anthony: John Henry Davey, 187;
    Sarah, 187
Arbuckle, Mr, 20
Archdeacon: Montague Aloysius, 62;
    Rosalie Louisa Henrietta, 62
Arlott: Eliza, 77-79; Eliza Sarah,
    77-78; Sarah, 78
Armstrong, John, 160-61
Arnold: Emily, 82; James, 82; Mr, 231
Attwater, Walter, 25
Attwood, Alfred, 160
Australia, 103
Austria, 86
Axon, John, 164
Ayres: Ada, 152; Alfred, 152; Alice,
    141, 143-53, 170; Charles
    Frederick, 152; David, 144, 153;
    Eliza Marian, 84; Emily, 144, 152;
    Hugh Stanley, 152; John, 144;
    John jnr., 144; Lydia, 152; Mary
    Ann, 152; Mary Ann jnr., 144
Backhurst, Bessie, 106
Baddeley, W., 202
Baden-Powell: Robert, 26, 139;
    Warington, 139
Badger, Jane Elizabeth, 68
Badkin: Alleyne Shafto, 59; Walter, 59
Bagnall-Taylor, Harley, 276
Bailey: Alice, 26; Arthur, 26; George,

224; John William, 37; Richard, 26
Baker: Allen, 115-16; Daniel, 96; Dr
    Thomas, 180-81; Edward, 159;
    Elizabeth, 77; P.C. Thomas, 110;
    Thomas, 182
Baldwin, Mary Ann, 97
Ball, Richard George, 128-31
Banham, James, 85
Banks, Edward James, 256-57
Bannister: Charles Akhurst, 207;
    Charlotte Ann, 207; Emma, 207;
    Ernest Albert, 207, 210; James
    Charles Akhurst, 207-10; James
    Richard, 207, 210; Mary Ann, 210;
    Mary Ann Elizabeth, 210; Mary
    Ann Emily, 207; May Eleanor,
    207; Susannah Elizabeth, 207
Barber, Joseph, 23
Barfield, James, 160
Barnes, 43
Barnes: James, 227; Mary Ann, 30
Barnet, 73, 126
Barnett: Caroline, 175; Edward, 107;
    James, 175
Barrington, Mrs Emilie, 147-48
Bartholomew, Mr, 183
Bass, Hannah, 23
Batholomew, Charles, 182
Batten, Inspector, 177
Battersea, 18-19, 64, 110
Baxter: Herbert, 212-13; Wynne,
    208, 213
Bayliss, P.C., 108
Bayne: Ada, 95; Ann, 95; Emily, 95;
    James, 95-96; Julia, 95; Lily, 95;
    Peter, 95; Rose, 95
Bayswater, 264
Bazalgette, Joseph, 28-29
Bedford, John St Clare, 69, 251
Bedfordshire, 70, 97, 129, 225

Bee, Kay, 162
Belfast, 190
Belgium, 171, 269-71, 274
Belgravia, 251
Bellini, Vincenzo, 250
Bengal, 100
Bennett: Henry, 106; Mr, 108
Benning: Ada, 58; Albert, 57-58;
    Alice, 57-58; Charles, 56, 58;
    Charles Barlas, 56-58; Charlie,
    58; Edith, 59; Edith Frances Jane,
    56; Emily, 58; Ernest, 59; Ernest
    Bradley, 56-57; Frederick, 56-58;
    Granger William, 59; Harriett,
    58; John, 58; Margaret, 57, 59;
    Margaret Ethel, 56
Berdoe, Dr Edward, 248
Berkshire, 114, 152, 157-58, 160,
    176, 267
Bermondsey, 17, 29, 31, 33, 49, 76,
    85, 116, 238-40, 244
Bethnal Green, 51-52, 86-88, 110,
    171, 174, 198, 204, 206, 211-12,
    230, 233, 235, 237, 236, 247-50
Betten, Mr & Mrs, 180
Bhownagree, Mancherjee, 236
Biggs: Alice Isabella, 234; Alice
    Rebecca, 235; Frederick, 19, 235;
    Frederick John, 234; Frederick
    William, 234; George, 235;
    George Frederick, 234
Bilton, Sergeant, 122
Binney, Charles, 101-2, 169
Birch, Lucy, 269; Sarah, 270
Birmingham, 34, 68, 70
Bishop, Kate, 162
Bishopp, Dr George, 251
Bishopsgate, 77
Bisson, Daniel, 21
Blackfriars, 29

Blackmore, Elizabeth, 158

Blake: Edward, 258-59, 261; Stewart, 35

Blann: Arthur Henry, 112; Henry Arthur, 112; Jane, 112; Reginald Eric, 112

Blencowe: Albert William, 75; Alice, 75; Elizabeth Charlotte Ann, 73; Ellen, 75; Ethel May, 75; George, 73-75; George jnr., 73; George Henry Albert, 75; George snr., 73; Ivy Ada Bathsheba, 75; Louisa, 75; Louisa Edith, 73; Margaret, 75

Bloomfield: Margaret, 238; Mary, 238; Thomas, 238

Bloomsbury, 243

Bolding, Irene May, 126

Bond, P.C., 107-8

Booth, Charles, 80

Borough, 143, 147

Boss, Philip, 225

Bouillancy, P.C., 212-13

Boulton, Jane Lilian, 110

Bow, 21, 70, 73, 207-9

Bowden, Eliza, 156

Bowman: John, 21; Sir William, 44

Boxall: Amelia, 247; Charles, 249; Edward, 249; Elizabeth, 247-48, 250; James, 249; Jane, 247, 249; John, 250; Joseph, 247-49; Joseph James, 249; Louisa, 247; Sarah Ann, 250

Bradford: Eliza, 249; Sir Edward, 25-26

Bradley, John, 266

Braidwood, James, 189, 191, 200

Braxton-Hicks: Athelstan, 62; John, 62

Breitman, Lazarus, 86

Brewer, Frederick, 22

Bridgeman, Sydney, 61-62

Brien: Amy, 226; Robert, 226; Stanley, 226-27; William, 226-27

Bristow: Beatrice, 82-83; Edward James, 83; Elizabeth Winifred, 83; Elsie, 83; Emily, 83; Emily Sophia, 82; Henry, 14, 81, 83, 91, 94; Henry James, 82; Jessie, 83; 91; Jessie Eliza, 82; Jessie Louisa, 82; Rose Olive, 83; Sophia, 83; Sydney, 83; Sydney Albert, 82; William, 83

Brixton, 77

Broad: Harry, 255; Thomas, 255; Wilfred, 255

Broan, Alice Jane, 174

Bromley, 23, 97, 152, 174-75, 184, 207

Brook: Louisa, 102; Margaret, 100

Brooks: Henry, 58; Herbert, 56-57;

John, 35

Broughton, Dr, 131

Brown: Cecilia, 272; Dr Alexander Stewart, 247, 263, 271-73; Emily Sarah, 125; James, 98-99, 155, 210; John Samuel, 128; Mary Ann, 271; P.C., 177; Sarah, 49; Tom, 80; Walburga, 274; Walburga Marian, 272; William, 192

Brunel, Isambard Kingdom, 155

Bryans: Annie, 137; Herbert, 137

Buck, Master, 52

Buckinghamshire, 129, 157

Burke, Thomas, 256

Burma, 110

Burt, Ruth, 120

Butler: Alfred, 227; Harriett, 98; Josephine, 216

Bywaters, Mary Ann, 110

Caborne, W.F., 139

Camberwell, 76, 78, 85, 187, 217

Cambridge: Frederick Royston, 269-71; John Cramner, 155, 171, 263, 269-70, 274; Lucy Dorothea, 269-71; Millicent, 270; Violet Marjorie, 269-70

Cambridgeshire, 152

Camden, 23, 96

Canada, 37, 77, 184, 287

Canning Town, 175

Cardiff, 164

Carnegie, Andrew, 92, 116

Carter: George, 194; William, 78

Carttar, Charles, 182

Cartwright: Miriam, 40; Richard, 40

Carver, William, 30

Catlin, Lucy, 77

Cave, Sir George, 115-16

Cazaly: Bessie Marian, 62; Charlotte, 60, 62; Edward John, 62; Henrietta Charlotte Elizabeth, 60; Herbert Peter, 59-60, 62; Herbert Peter Adolphus, 62; James, 62; James Adolphus, 60; Marianne, 62; Marianne Jane, 60, 62; Peter, 60, 62

Cemeteries: Abney Park, 62, 115, 191, 200, 224, 236; Barnes, 43; Brompton, 251; Chingford, 236; Cité Bonjean, Armentières, 130; Dawlish, 170; Greenwich, 213; Hampstead, 90; Isleworth, 146; Kensal Green, 155-56, 170, 251; Lambeth, 152; Lewisham, 273; Manor Park, 53, 75, 85, 95, 168; Mortlake, 186; Nunhead, 221; Old Barnes, 167; Southampton Old, 142; St Marylebone, 126; St Pancras, 257; Teignmouth, 123; Twickenham, 177; West Ham, 75;

Woodgrange Park, 25-26; Wood Green, 62

Chaloner: Eliza, 206; Ernest Albert, 205; Grace, 205; Lucy Constance, 206; Richard Henry, 205-6; Rose, 206

Chambers, Mary, 105

Chance, George, 152

Chandler: Annie, 126; Charlotte May Ada, 90; Edith, 144, 151-52; Elizabeth, 145-46; Ellen, 144, 151-52; Frederick, 106, 152; Henry, 144-46, 151; Mary Ann, 146

Channel Islands, 133, 135, 139-42

Chant, Laura Ormiston, 149

Charing Cross, 17, 144

Charlton, 183

Chelsea, 32, 68-69, 77, 157

Cheshire, 124

China, 240

Chiswick, 153

Chow, P.C. Ken, 276

Churcher, Richard, 40

Clack: Arthur, 259; Charles Edward, 259; Edwin, 241, 259-60; Edwin Charles, 259, 261; Edwin Charles jnr., 259; Edwin jnr., 260; Ernest, 259; Ivy, 261; Ivy Florence, 260; Nathaniel, 259; Walter, 259; William Henry, 259; William Henry jnr., 259

Clapham, 19, 29, 77, 106

Clapton, 57

Clark, Edward Charles, 258-59

Clarke, George, 194

Clay: Mary, 71; Samuel, 71-72

Clayton, Ida, 265-67

Clements, Alice Mary, 70

Clerkenwell, 21, 86-87, 110, 144, 197-98, 206

Clinton: Arthur, 93-94; Frederick Fry Joseph, 93; John, 93-95, 98, 168; May Florence, 94; Theresa, 93-94; Thomas, 93-94

Cobbe, Francis Power, 137

Coe, Elizabeth, 91

Coghlan: Ann, 228; Annie, 226-27; Dennis, 226; Elizabeth, 225-27; Emily Amelia, 226

Cohen, Abraham, 88

Coke, Sidney, 260

Colindale, 11

Collier: Dorothy Maud, 25; George, 74

Collins, Wilkie, 155

Colwell: Ada, 126; Beryl M., 126; Betty Mina, 126; Clara Eileen, 126; Herbert, 126

Connely: Alice Mary, 97; Phyllis, 97

Cook: Ada, 129; Alice Annie, 129; Ambrose, 129; Arthur Harry, 129-30; Edith, 131; Florence Ada, 129; Frederick, 129; Harry, 129; Helena Thorpe, 129; Isaac, 129; Jessie, 91; Leonard, 129

Cooke, G.W., 193

Cooper: Fanny, 175; Herbert John, 152; James, 152; William, 60

Cope, Maria, 255

Corby, Emma Clayden, 32

Corking, John, 57-58

Cornford, Edward, 101

Cornwall, 163

Corston: Ann, 173; Caroline, 173; Charles, 173

County Durham, 53, 57

County Tyrone, 100

Court, Hannah, 41

Covent Garden, 120, 129

Cowan, Mrs, 242

Craft: Daniel Newman, 180; Dorothy Mary, 184; Elizabeth, 183; Frederick, 14, 180, 182-83, 187, 241, 261; Frederick Alfred, 180; Frederick jnr., 183; Frederick Thomas, 180; Henry Jennings, 180; Mabel, 184; Thomas George, 180; William, 183; William Harry, 180

Crane, Walter, 147

Cricklewood, 91

Cronin, John, 50

Cross, Deborah, 31

Crossness, 95

Crowley: Catharine Dorothea, 270; Christine, 270; John, 271; John Cambridge, 270; Lucy, 271; Walter, 270; Walter Noel, 270

Crutcher, Catherine Hayward, 33

Cubitt, William, 209

Cumbria, 164, 184

Curtis, Sarah Ann, 53

Cuss, Eliza, 250

Dafforne, Charles Frederick, 44

Dagnall, Harry, 7

Dane, Septimus, 208-9

Danford-Thomas, George, 160, 257-58, 260

Danzey, P.S. John, 110-11

Dare, William, 50

Darling, Grace, 138-39, 141, 143, 216

Darnill, Thomas, 185-86

Daven: Jane, 174; Jane jnr., 174

Davies: Charles Maurice, 84; Walter Cromwell, 75

Davis, Sarah, 251

Dawkins, Albert, 23-24

Day: Arthur, 227; Dennis jnr., 227; Edward Charles, 227; Elsie,

227; Florence, 227; Henry, 227; Leonard, 227; Violet, 227; William Henry, 227

Dean: Alice Rebecca, 234-35; Elizabeth, 162-63; Elsie, 158, 164; Gertrude, 158, 164; Henrietta Ann, 235; Henry John Lancey, 156-59, 161-62, 166, 170; James, 157; Lancey, 163-64; Mary Ann, 157-58; Richard, 157-58

Deboeck: George Thomas, 211; Mary Elizabeth, 211

Deighton, W. G., 42

Dell: Elizabeth, 271; John, 270; John Christopher, 271; Millicent, 270-71; Millicent H., 271; Richard, 271; Richard Christopher, 271

De Morgan, William, 15, 63, 99-100, 119, 142, 241

Denman: Alice Maud, 13, 171, 231-32, 234, 236-37; Charles, 230-31; Charles George, 231, 234; Daisy Alice, 238; Elizabeth, 237; Ethel, 234; Ethel Mary, 231; Leslie H, 238; Lillian May, 231, 236-37; Percival, 231, 236; Percival Owen, 231, 236-37; William, 230

Deptford, 29, 53, 76, 89

Derbyshire, 91, 164, 229

Devon, 93, 101-2, 120-3, 156-58, 164, 169

Digby, Walter, 29-31, 34, 38

Dobell, Horace, 45

Donald: Amy, 71, 73; Helen, 71; John, 71; Marian, 73; Marian jnr., 71; Mary, 72-73; William, 71-72; William Percy, 71-73

Donaldson, Mr, 72

Donnell, Martha, 100

Donovan: Ann, 244; Ann Ellen, 243; Daniel, 244; Ellen, 243-44; James, 243; Johanna, 243; John, 161, 243-44; Mary Ann, 243

Doré, Gustave, 83

Dorset, 120, 123-24, 267

Douglas, Henry, 194

Dowling, John, 30

Doyle, Sir Francis, 148

Drake: Charles, 25; Edward, 251; Mary, 250-51; Miss, 135; William, 250-51

Draper, Emma, 153

Drayne: Cynthia, 261; Enoch, 261

Dredge, Sophia, 134

Drew: Charles Luxmoore, 98; Stanley, 121-22

Driscoll, Mary Ann, 207

Dukes, Dr, 108

Dunfermline, 116

Dunn: Ellen, 19; John, 19

Durrant: Augustin, 31; Ellen Elizabeth, 37; Joan, 37; Laura, 37; Mary Ellen, 37; Maud, 37; Robert, 31-32, 34, 38; Robert George, 37; Robert George Edward, 32

Ealing, 58, 176

Eames, Ada Lily, 73

East Africa, 130

East Ham, 29-38, 119, 127, 167, 175, 196

East Indies, 105, 110

East Sheen, 185-86

Ebbage: Barbara A, 126; Barbara A., 126; Edward J., 126; Lynda, 126

Eddison, Ada, 217

Edmonton, 51, 75, 82-83, 180, 225, 228

Edwards, P.C., 212-13

Elborough, Mr, 109

Elephant & Castle, 84, 111

Ellard: Albert, 97; Daisy, 97; Ernest, 97; Sydney, 97; Thomas, 97

Elliott: Dorothy, 23, 25; Ellen, 25; Ellen Elizabeth, 23; Esther Emma, 23; Flora Ida Emma, 23; Frederick, 26; Frederick George, 23, 25; George Frederick, 23; George Frederick snr., 23; James Alfred, 23; Rachel Mary, 23; Walter, 23

Ellis: family, 251; T.H., 118

Ellison, Ada, 219

Elms, P.C. Morris, 192

Elrick, James, 111

Emery: Alice May, 70; Charles, 68-70; Charles Edward, 68, 70; Edmund, 68; Edward, 68, 70; Frank, 68, 70; Frank jnr., 70; Frank Frewin, 68; George, 208-9; Jane, 68; Joseph Rudolph, 68; Lionel Frederick, 68; Octavius William, 68

Emsley, Clive, 105

Essex, 25, 30, 32, 37, 51, 76, 95, 113, 187, 191, 196, 211, 232-33

Evelyn, John, 253

Eves, Alfred, 151

Exeter, 85, 158

Eyre: Elizabeth, 239-41; George James, 239

Fardon, Edward, 42

Farne Islands, 138

Farris: Catherine, 77; Charlotte, 77; Eliza, 77; Henry, 77; Henry jnr., 77; James, 77; Richard, 77-79; Sarah, 77; Walter, 77

Faulkner, Miriam Wade, 266

Finchley, 125-26, 271

Finsbury, 75, 114

First World War, 15, 83, 113, 118, 124, 126

Fisher: Alice Olivia, 89; Annie

Caroline, 84–85, 114; Arthur Sidney, 89; Doris Beatrice, 85; Edwin Charles, 89; Eliza, 85; Eliza Ann, 84–85; Eliza Clara, 85; Florence Alice, 85; Florence Maud, 84; George William, 89; Henry, 85; Henry George, 84–85; James, 85–86, 91; James Charles, 84; Jane Elizabeth, 84; Matilda Amelia, 89; William, 84–86, 91, 247; William Joseph, 84

Fitzrayne, Dr, 53

Flynn, William, 213

Ford: Alfred, 191; Arthur P.R., 196; Caroline, 191; Emmeline, 195–96; Emmeline jnr., 195; Emmeline Louisa, 191, 196; Frederick, 195–96; Frederick George, 191; George Albert, 191; Henry, 191; Jane, 196; Jane jnr., 191; Joseph, 191, 196; Joseph Andrew, 171, 191–92, 196, 200–201, 203; Louisa, 191; William John, 191

Forest Gate, 53, 95

Forward, Dorothy, 124

Fowler, Mr & Mrs, 110–11

Fox, C.E., 237

Foxwell: Caroline, 134; Charles, 134; Elizabeth, 134; Emily, 134; James, 134–35; Mary Ann, 134; Samuel, 134; Sophia, 135; Sophia jnr., 134; William, 134

France, 273

Francombe: Elizabeth Mary, 198–99; Mary Anne, 198–99; Walter, 198–99

Franklin, Dr, 199

Fraser, James, 121

Freegard, Alice, 57

French, William, 58

Frost: Alice, 91; Hilda, 91; William, 91

Fry: Elizabeth, 216; Harriett, 93

Funnell: Emily, 110; George John, 110; George Stephen, 110–13; George Stephen jnr., 110, 112–13; Jane, 112–13; Leonard Albert, 110, 112–13

Fursdon, Private, 122

Galaman: Becky, 86; Solomon, 86

Galman: Becky, 86; Sarah, 86

Gamble, Henry, 15

Gamgee, Professor John, 253

Gant, Frederick, 45–46

Gardner, Dr, 61

Garner, Mr, 130

Garnish: Golding Albert, 64; Rev. G., 63, 65

Garrard, Mary Ellen, 32

Garrett, Frederick Thomas, 37

Garton, William, 18

Gash, Charlotte, 263

Gaze, Alice Susan, 174

Gellman: Alexander, 88; Annie, 87–88; Benjamin, 87–88; Charles, 87; David, 87; Elizabeth, 86, 88; Ethel, 88; Israel, 86–88; Nathan, 86–88; Samuel, 87–88, 91; Sarah, 87–88; Solomon, 86–88, 91, 247; Tilly, 88

Gerety, Joseph, 59

German, Edith, 131

Gerton, Charles, 235

Gibson: Andrew, 217; Sarah, 216–18, 221, 228; Sarah snr., 217

Gillemand, Mr, 108

Gilpin: Elizabeth, 120–22; Kate Ellen, 120; William, 120–21

Gloucestershire, 48, 68, 186

Godfry, Ernest, 191

Goodchild, P.C., 208, 210

Goodman, Edith, 265

Goodridge, William, 110

Goodrum: Caroline, 174–75; Charles, 174–75; Charlotte, 175; Deborah, 173; Elijah, 173–74; Florence, 175; Frances, 172; George, 174; James, 172–73; William, 172–74, 178; William Edward, 174

Goodwin, Inspector, 257

Goschen, George, 160, 162

Grant: Edgar J, 164; Tom W.E., 164; Vera, 164

Grass, John, 173

Gray, Alice, 163

Green: Alice, 176; George, 176; Jane, 176

Greenoff: Ada, 125–26; Doris Amelia, 125; Edward Arthur Cecil, 125–26; Edward G, 126; Elsie Irene, 126; Emily Alethea, 125; Ernest Charles, 125; John, 126; Lilian Elsie, 125; P.C. Edward George Brown, 115, 125–27, 169, 275; Samuel Albert, 125; Samuel Edward, 125; Stanley William, 125; Sydney Albert, 125

Greenwich, 67, 96, 217

Griffin: Fred, 18; Hannah, 20; Isaac, 18; Jane, Sarah, 18; Mary Jane, 18; Thomas, 18–21, 166; Walter, 18, 20; William Irson, 18, 20

Grimes, Maria Marian, 71

Grimsley, family, 70

Gull, Sir William, 44

Gwyer, Joseph, 138

Hacker, Sidney, 122

Hackney: 13, 57–58, 73–74, 77, 82–83, 110–11 173–75, 206, 224–26, 232–34, 236–38, 247–48, 250

Haggerston, 205

Hall: Dr, 111; P.C. William, 96

Hammersmith, 71, 131

Hampshire, 22, 25, 59

Hampstead, 91, 255–56

Hansell, Peter, 45

Hardie, Mary Ellen, 101

Harfield: Frank, 152; Frederick, 152; Harry, 152; Harry David, 152; John, 152; Victor, 152

Haringey, 25

Harker, Leonard Christopher, 210

Harland: Anne, 191; Emmeline Eliza, 191; Ernest, 196

Harle, Dr, 205

Harlesden, 90

Harper, Mr, 20

Harris: Mary-Ann, 144; William, 219

Harrison, Mahala, 152

Harvey: Ann, 187; Charles, 187

Harwicke, Dr William, 243

Harwood, Thomas, 176

Hatfull, Henry, 207

Hathorn, Amelia Emma, 198

Hatton Garden, 60

Hawkes: Derek, 25; John W jnr., 25; Norman, 25

Haworth, Mary Ann Matilda, 184

Hay, Lennox Theobald, 102

Healy, William, 181–82

Heddon, Thomas, 101

Hedges, Calvin Lawrence, 50

Hendon, 88, 116, 123, 131, 249, 258–60

Hensey, Ellen Esther, 224

Henslow, Miles, 126

Hertfordshire, 25, 70, 270

Hewers, James, 185

Hewett, Ann, 264

Hewins: Ann, 186; Charles, 186; Emma, 185, 187; James, 14, 185–87; John, 186; Susan, 187

Highgate, 254–57

Hill, Octavia, 147, 153

Hilliard, George, 24

Hills, Dr, 90

Hitchcock: Tom, 122; William, 122

Hocking, Gertrude, 163

Hockley, Daisy, 237

Hodge, Catharine, 271

Hodges, John, 159

Holborn, 41, 144, 191–92, 244

Hollington, Mr, 33

Holmes, Mary, 105

Homerton, 110

Hooper, Alice, 121–22

Hornsey, 75

Hounslow, 176, 178

Howe, Mrs, 85

Howlett, Edith, 261

Hoxton, 82, 114, 198

Hudson, Thomas, 76, 78-79, 177
Hume, Sarah, 77
Hunt: Fanny, 264; Mary Ann, 230
Huntingdonshire, 23
Huskisson, William, 185
Hussey: David, 242; Mary, 242, 244
Hyne: Alice, 235; Thomas Collings, 235
Ilford, 76, 196
Illingworth, Dr, 131
India, 26, 100, 102-3, 110
Inglis, Mr, 150
Ireland, 93, 100, 110, 184, 226, 238, 243
Isle of Dogs, 49
Isleworth, 144
Islington, 56, 58, 75, 88, 115, 152, 156, 204, 205 226, 237, 255
Jackson, Dr, 109
Jarlett, George, 85
Jarman: Elizabeth, 239; Ellen, 238; George Thomas, 238-40; John, 238; Mary, 238-41, 261; Matilda, 238
Jarrett, William, 158-60
Jarvis: Cecil Jackman, 164; Evelyn Gertrude, 164; Gertrude, 164; Thomas, 164; Thomas Frederick Lancey, 164; Thomas Huxham, 164
Jeffries: Henry, 59-62; Rob, 11, 169
Jenner, Sir William, 44
Jennings: Elizabeth, 42; Fredericka, 42; Henry, 42, 180; Jessie, 42; Leon Rex, 42; Walter, 42
Jepson, John Charles, 185-87
Jiggins: Alfred Thomas, 83; Beatrice, 83; Florence, 83; Marie, 83; Walter John, 83; Winifred, 83
Johnson: Dr, 122; Margaret, 164; Mary Tyles, 164
Jones: Alfred William, 32; Catherine, 37; David, 204; Emma Maria, 32; Ernest, 32; Frederick David, 32-33, 35, 37-38; George Frederick, 32, 37; George William, 33; Lizzie, 259-60; Stephen, 74; Winifred Elsie, 33; Winifred Margaret, 33
Joyner, P.S., 129-30
Keeling: Edward, 228; Frederick William, 228; Frederick William jnr., 228; George, 228; George Frederick, 228; Leonard, 228
Kemp: Elizabeth, 249; Reginald, 177
Kennedy: Alice Margaret, 225; Amelia, 222-24; Annie, 225; Elizabeth, 222, 224; Elizabeth Frances, 222-23; Emily, 228; Florence Mary, 225; Frank Harry,

225; Frederick George, 222; George Edward, 222, 224; George Edward jnr., 222-25; John Wiston, 222-24; Kate Thompson, 225
Kensal Green, 29, 98, 156-57, 259
Kensington, 22, 70, 93, 106, 120, 127-28, 185-86
Kent, 24, 67, 71, 85, 95, 106, 110, 113, 180, 183-84, 248, 269, 270-1
Kent, Elizabeth, 180
Kentish Town, 56, 125, 151, 226, 255
Kerrison: Jane, 31; William, 31
Kew, 55-56, 58-62, 153
Keys, Councillor, 35
Kidd, Eliza, 26
Kilburn, 89, 152, 259-61
Kimmis: Elizabeth Christina, 97
King, Charles, 30, 34, 41
Kirchoffer, Samuel, 22
Knappett, Eliza, 26
Knight: Lilian Ethel, 123; Maud, 123
Knox, Henry, 139
Lacher, Dr, 82
Lambeth, 60, 68, 84, 93-94, 99, 119, 152, 164, 174-75, 211, 217
Lancashire, 112
Lancey, Mary, 157
Land, George, 51
Lane: James Ernest, 274; Laura, 148
Langham, Samuel Frederick, 58, 94, 240
Lankester, Dr Edwin, 192, 218-21
Large, William, 57-58
Law, James, 53
Leak, John, 105
Lee: Caroline Ann, 197; Edward, 197; Emily, 197, 200; Emma, 197-98; George, 197-201, 203; John, 197; Joseph, 197; Louisa, 198; Maria, 197; Martha, 198; Sarah, 197, 200; Thomas, 197-98
Lees-Smith, Hastings, 119
Lefevre, Peter, 21
Leggett, Arthur, 37
Leicestershire, 20
Lemmey, Inspector, 107-8
Lester, Emily, 206
Lever, Walburga, 272
Levett, James, 69
Lewis: Captain, 140; Charles, 34; George, 89; Harry, 233-34; Matilda, 89; Minnie, 111; Sophia, 89
Lewisham, 180, 227, 271, 274
Limehouse, 30, 97, 191
Lincolnshire, 38, 105, 109, 186, 263-64, 265-67
Lindus, Henry William, 220-21
Lister: Cecil, 20; Mary, 144; Sir Joseph, 44

Liverpool, 40
Locker, Arthur, 196
Long, Councillor, 35
Loosemore, Frank, 121-22
Lowdell: Alice Matilda, 53; Annie, 53; Charles Clemens, 52; Ellen, 51, 53; Emma, 52-53; Emma Jane, 53; Ethel Maud, 53; George, 52; John, 52-53; John Champion, 51; John William, 51; Joseph, 52-53; Mary Ann, 52; Mary Jane, 53; Samuel Champion, 51-53; Sarah, 53; Thomas Joseph, 51
Lucas: Alice Gertrude, 40; Catherine Mary, 40; Charles Frederick, 40; Charlotte Elizabeth, 40; Dorothy Joan, 40; Ella Cartwright, 40; Frances Miriam, 40; James Hubert, 40; Miriam, 40; Richard Clement, 40; Thomas Riley, 40; Walter Sheward, 40; William, 40, 42, 44; William Freer, 40, 43, 168, 283
Ludlow, Henry Newman, 207-10
MacColl, Ewan, 164
MacDonald, Dr Roderick, 248
Macfarlane, Janet Marion, 184
Maconoghu, Herbert, 284
Mahoney, James, 238
Maida Vale, 98, 156
Maidment, William, 194
Mallam, Dr, 74
Mandarin, Col. Francis Arthur, 160-61
Manduit, Evelyn Dorothy, 103
Marber, Patrick, 144
Marsham, Robert Henry, 139
Martin, William, 92
Marval, Alice, 138
Marylebone, 68, 70, 160
Maryon, Alice, 110-11
Mayfair, 22, 251
Mayhew, Henry, 52, 54, 67, 80-81, 84, 155, 202, 211, 246
Mays, Edith Mary, 97
McConaghey: Edith, 100, 102; Ethel Mary, 100, 102; Evelyn Delphine, 103; Evelyn Dorothy Newburgh, 102; Francis, 100, 102-3; Herbert Moore, 81, 100-102, 169, 261, 263, 275, 284; Martha, 102; Matthew Allen, 100, 102
McGeorge, George , 101-2, 169
McGonagall, William, 139, 149
McNeill, William, 138
Mears, Edward, 159-60
Meek, Isabella Sarah, 22
Melhado, Clare, 42
Mellership, Mary Ann, 96
Meredith, Frederick, 162

Merrett, Mr, 236
Merrick, Eliza Jane, 249
Merritt, Eliza Mary, 24
Metropolitan Fire Brigade, 14, 24, 92, 107, 127, 129, 130, 188-91, 193-95, 197-98, 200, 203, 209, 213, 223, 235, 276
Metropolitan Police, 58, 60, 69, 93, 96, 116, 126
Meyrick: Emily, 125; George, 125
Michael, Charles D., 92, 93
Michell, Jane, 276
Middlesex, 59, 61, 65, 144, 163, 176, 180, 162, 267
Midlothian, 184
Mile End, 51, 71, 73, 206, 201, 233
Miles, A. H., 92, 93
Milliner, Sarah, 224
Mills: Betsy, 30, 38; Charles, 38; Charles Henry, 30; Frederick, 30, 38; Mary Ann, 38; Mary E, 30
Mingaye, Charles, 144
Minnett, P.C., 60-62
Mitchell, Robert Samuel Elliott, 123
Moody: Ellen, 98; Mabel, 98; Richard, 98; Sidney, 98
Moore: Charles Frank, 75; Elizabeth, 60; Ellen, 52; Francis, 59; Joseph, 180-82, 187; Vera Beatrice, 75; William, 272
More, Sydney, 131
Morgan, Edward, 218-19
Morgenstein: Hannah, 88; Isaac, 88
Morris: Catherine, 99; Edward, 98-99; Harriett, 99; Rev. A., 183
Morrison, Arthur, 242
Morrow, Ellen, 97
Mortimer: Campbell, 93-94, 98; Daisy, 94; Margaret, 94; Margaret jnr., 94; Willie, 94
Mortlake, 55, 186
Morton: Alexander George, 237; Ethel, 237; Lillian R., 237
Mothersole: Ellen, 32; Ellen Elizabeth, 32; Flora, 32; Harry, 32; Laura, 32; Maude, 32; Robert George, 31-32
Mumford: Ada, 264-67; John, 264
Mundell, Frank, 229
Murrell: Alfred, 230; Alice Maud, 230-31; Frank Charles, 230; George, 230; Henry Charles, 230; Louisa, 230; Marie Jane, 230; Mary Ann, 230; Minnie, 150; Owen, 230; Samuel, 230; William, 230
Myers, Walter, 50
Nash, Ellen, 211
Naughton, Tina, 11
Neal: Ada, 58; Annie, 129

Neale, Emma, 23
Newbury, Sidney Thomas, 127
Newham, 38, 167, 169
Newington, 84-86
Newman, Eliza, 180-83, 187
Nicholson: Edith Mary, 26; Godfrey Maule, 22, 25-26, 283; Isabella, 26; John, 21-22; William, 21-22, 26; William Graham, 26
Nightingale, Florence, 137, 216
Nixon, William J., 249
Norfolk, 31, 37, 110, 124, 129, 152, 156, 172-73, 269
Norman: Benjamin, 99-100, 275; Mary, 156
Northamptonshire, 18, 20, 23, 68, 97
Notman: Emily, 213; George Edward, 213; George jnr., 213; Henry George, 214; James, 214; Sarah Ann jnr., 213
Nottinghamshire, 238, 266
Notting Hill, 98-99, 128-29, 131
Nunan, Thomas, 235
Oakley, Eliza, 203
Oierke, Gustavas, 22
Old Ford, 29, 70-71
Oliver: Arthur, 53; Ellen, 53; Emma, 53; Jane, 53; Rose, 53; William, 53; William jnr., 53
Olivia, Alice, 89-90
Onslow: Beatrice Louisa, 50-51; Elizabeth Ann, 50; Jane Louisa, 49; John Bowen, 50; John Goodacre, 49; Joseph William, 49-51, 53; Mary Ann, 51, 53; Sarah Ann, 49
Oram, Matilda, 109
Overton, Edward, 130
Oxfordshire, 157, 175, 272
Paddington, 156-59, 257, 259, 264, 266, 273;
Palmer: Elizabeth, 100; Francis, 56-58; James, 94
Pancras, 131
Paravicini, Dr, 226
Parsons: Arthur, 265; William, 265
Parson's Green, 131
Parton, James, 136
Passenger: Charles, 100; Fred, 100
Paterson, Ruth E., 37
Paul, William Lee, 37
Payne, Mr, 199
Peacey, Elizabeth, 11
Pead: George Durdant, 175; George William, 175; Robert Edward, 175
Peale, Stephen, 58
Peaper: Agnes Lucy, 51; Ernest Nelson, 51; Frederick George, 51; Henry Charles Frederick, 51; John Montague, 51; John William,

51; Montague Byatt, 51
Pearce, Dr, 94
Pearcy: Mary, 37; William, 37
Pearmain, Rose, 233
Peart: Ada, 162; Daisy Alice Ada, 157, 163; Emily Lydia, 157, 163; Gerald, 163; Gertrude, 163; James, 156, 163; James Ernest, 157; Marjorie, 163; Mary, 156; Robert, 156, 163; Sidney M., 163; Sidney Robert, 157, 162-63; Walter, 156, 158, 160-62, 166, 170, 178; Walter jnr., 163; Walter Norman, 157
Peckham, 76-77, 187, 264, 267
Peel, Sir Robert, 104-5
Peever, Alec, 26
Pelley, James William, 198-99
Pemberton: Ada, 176, 178; Alfred, 175; Alice, 177-78; Alice jnr., 176; Daniel, 14, 175-77; Daniel jnr., 176, 178; Fanny, 175; George, 175, 178; James, 175; Jane, 178; Samuel, 175; Stephen, 175; Vincent, 175
Pembrokeshire, 53
Pendrill, Alfred, 58
Pepper, Dr, 256
Percy, William, 71
Perkins, Anne, 217-19
Perrault, Charles, 217
Perrin, Ida, 100
Perry: John, 197; Sarah, 197
Phillips, Elizabeth Jarret, 180
Philpin, John, 161
Piccadilly, 29
Pickett: John, 26; Thomas, 23, 25-26
Pierce, Mr, 59
Pimlico, 69-70
Pinckney: Eliza, 204; Joseph, 204
Pitt, Leigh, 276-77
Plant, Mary Ann, 50
Plumstead, 95-97, 181-82
Ponders End, 180
Poplar, 26, 33, 52-53, 73, 173-75, 207, 210, 249
Portman, Natalie, 144
Postman's Park, 7, 14-15, 21, 38, 65, 109, 118, 136, 142, 147, 165, 215, 254, 258, 263, 276, 278
Potter, Mr, 101
Powell: Cicely, 267; William, 267
Pressman: Arthur P.R. Ford, 196; Elizabeth, 196; Irene Elizabeth, 196; Reuben William, 196; Winifred Emmeline, 196
Preston, Ida, 134-35
Price: Carol, 11; Florence Gertrude, 174
Pritchard, Inspector, 93-94
Pullen, Frank, 256
Purkiss, Anne, 165

Pursey: Hannah, 114; Thomas, 114;
  William, 114
Purt, P.C. Simeon, 107
Putney, 29, 41, 43, 55, 59-60, 63-64
Pye, Master, 89-90
Queen Victoria, 118, 268, 272, 277
Quest: Amy Florence, 259; George,
  259, 261
Rabbeth: Annie, 41, 43-44; George
  Michael, 44; Hannah, 41; John
  Edward, 41, 43-44; Samuel, 41-47,
  87, 167
Randle, William, 219
Rastin: Charles, 183-84; Charles snr.,
  184; Elizabeth, 183; Mary, 183;
  Mary Elizabeth, 184; Robert, 183
Ravensbourne River, 70
Rawnsley, Hardwicke, 149
Read: George, 274; P.C. Arthur,
  110-11
Redding: Amy, 97; Maud, 97; Percy,
  97; Thomas, 97; Thomas jnr., 97;
  Willie, 97
Redshaw, James, 109
Redwood, Mr, 90
Reeks, Captain William, 133, 135,
  139-41
Regelous: Arthur William, 171, 232-
  37; Edith, 233; Ernest Alfred, 233;
  Florence Mary, 233; Frederick,
  233; George, 232-33; George
  Robert, 233; Henry Charles, 233;
  John, 236; Peter, 237; Rose, 233;
  Rose Emma, 233; William, 232
Rensbery, Mr, 108
Reynolds: Doris Marian Annie, 86;
  Florence Adelaide, 86; Henry,
  86; Henry Frederick Fisher, 86;
  Henry William, 86; Mr, 135
Rhondda Fawr Valley, 131
Rickards, Charles, 262
Ricketts: Albert, 120, 124; Ambrose,
  120, 123; Ambrose Henry, 120;
  Arthur, 124; Arthur George, 120;
  Charlotte, 120, 123; Ethel May,
  120; Kate, 120-21, 123; Mabel,
  120, 123; P.C. Harold Frank, 120-
  23, 132, 155; Ruth, 120
Riggs: Ernest J., 123; Vera, 123
Riley, Lily, 232, 234
Ritchie, James Ewing, 66, 241-42
River: Brent, 259; Crane, 144; Fleet,
  70; Lea, 67, 70-74; Lodden, 70;
  Thames, 17, 28-29, 48, 50, 54-55,
  63, 65-67, 70, 93, 95-97, 144, 146,
  153, 253, 259, 282, 288, 312, 314;
  Wandle, 70; Welland, 265
Rogers: Alfred, 160; Ernest, 230-33,
  235-37; Frederick, 134, 137;
  Mary Ann, 134-35, 138, 141-42,

150, 155; Mary Ellen, 134, 137;
  Richard, 134; William, 20
Rolls: Beatrice, 82; Henry, 82; Jessie,
  82; Jessie Louisa, 82; Thomas
  Sanders, 82; William, 82
Ronaldson, A., 139
Roper, Jane, 247
Rosenthal family, 86
Ross & Cromarty, 248
Ross: Dr George, 245; Sir John, 155
Rothen, Frederick Henry, 109
Rotherhithe, 76
Rothery, Eliza, 32
Rouse: Eric Ernest, 163; Lillian
  Alice, 163
Rout, Henry, 222
Rowell, Thomas, 181
Rowley, Inspector, 62
Roxby, Robert, 219
Runnalls, Charles Henry, 75
Russia, 86
Rutter: Arthur, 31, 34-35, 38; Ellen,
  38; George, 31, 38; George
  William, 31, 38; Mary, 31, 38
Sale: Thomas, 73; Walter, 73-74
Salisbury, Emmeline, 174
Savage, Mr, 34
Scadding: Ada Jane, 157; James, 157,
  162; Mary, 162
Schroeder, Walter, 19
Scotland, 116, 184
Scott, John James, 162
Scott-Battams, Dr, 46
Seeger, Peggy, 164
Sellwood, Susannah, 68
Selves: Albert, 96-97; Arthur, 96;
  Caroline, 97; Daniel Thomas,
  95-96, 176; Emma, 96-97;
  Frances, 97; George, 95-96;
  George jnr., 96; Melville, 97;
  Richard, 97; Samuel, 97; Thomas,
  96; William, 96-97
Shadwell, 46, 51
Shah, Hema, 276
Sharp: Doris Catherine, 53; Dr, 181;
  Elizabeth, 53; Joseph, 53; Richard
  Joseph, 53
Sharpe, Caroline, 41
Shaw: Captain Eyre Massey, 190,
  193-95, 197, 199; Mary, 41
Shelvey: Henry Arthur John, 266;
  Henry John, 266
Shepherd's Bush, 120, 129
Sheppard, Harry, 30
Shoreditch, 60, 82-83, 230
Shoreham, 129
Silvertown, 70, 124-126, 132
Simmonds: Charles, 98; James, 30;
  Jeanette, 56-58, 99
Simons: Edith Emily, 206; Eliza,

203-5; Eliza jnr., 204-5; Emily,
  204; Frederick George, 203-6;
  Frederick George jnr., 204-5;
  James, 204-6; James Victor, 206;
  Richard Henry, 203-4; Sarah
  Maria, 204; William Richard, 203
Simpson: Helen, 11, 171; Maria, 255;
  Thomas, 254-58
Sisley: Alice, 90-91; Amy, 97; Arthur,
  91; Charlotte, 90; Edith, 97;
  Edwin, 90; Elsie Ellen, 90; Frank
  Herbert, 89-91; George, 89-91;
  Harry, 89-91; Kathleen Irene,
  91; Leslie, 91; Marjorie Jessie, 91;
  Matilda, 90-91; Maud Sophia,
  89-91; Phyllis, 97; Sophia, 89-90;
  Thomas Henry, 90; William,
  89, 97
Skelton: Eliza, 222; Elizabeth, 224;
  Harriet, 222; Ralph, 224
Slade: Jemima, 211, 214; John, 211-
  12; Mary, 212-13; Rose, 211-12;
  Sarah Ann, 212-13; Thomas, 211,
  213; Thomas John, 211; Walter,
  212
Smale, Mr, 24
Small, Dr, 181-82
Smith: Dr, 34; Fanny, 91; George,
  115-16; Mary Ann, 114; May
  Emma Amelia, 115-16; P.C.
  Alfred, 114-15, 117, 169, 275-76;
  Roy, 116; Susan, 185
Smithfield, 115, 200
Soames, Mr, 25
Society for the Protection of Life
  from Fire, 92, 112, 189, 193-94,
  203
Somerset, 134
Somerstown, 89
Sorrell: Frank Herbert, 163; Keith
  Hydra, 163; Mary, 186; Maureen,
  163
South: Sarah, 250; William, 250
South Africa, 109, 211-12
Southall, 163
South America: 28; Argentina, 88
Southampton, 18, 133-35, 137, 140,
  142, 229
South Croydon, 271
Southwark, 31-33, 85, 93, 109, 145-
  48, 152-53, 174, 180, 187, 211-12,
  238-39
Spain: Bay of Cádiz., 51
Spencer, Joseph, 106
Spittles, Charles, 62
Squire, Susan, 207
SS *Stella*, 133-36, 138-40, 142, 170
Staddon, Thomas, 101
Stamford Hill, 236
Stansfield, George, 90

Stanton, George, 244-45
Stapleton, Joseph, 26
Starling, Thomas, 226
Stephenson, George, 185
Stepney, 50-51, 71, 73, 174, 194, 196, 211-12, 249
Stevens, Mr, 232-33
Stewart, Louisa, 138
St Giles, 191, 243-45
St John's Wood, 98
St Mary-at-Hill, 49
Stockman, Maria Emily, 259
Stockport, 164
Stoke Newington, 56, 77, 115, 222, 225-26, 236
Stone: Mr, 177; William, 46; William Robert, 261
St Pancras, 23, 41, 56, 96, 125, 210, 255, 256-257
Strange: Arthur David, 155, 264-67; Cecily, 267; Ellen, 267; Fanny, 266; Fanny jnr., 264; Gertrude Mary, 264, 266; John, 264, 266; Maria, 267; Olive, 267; William, 267
Stratford, 21, 24, 70, 73-74, 213
Streatham, 174, 271
Suffolk, 31-32, 37-38, 82, 124, 156, 191, 238
Surrey, 19, 40, 42, 55, 59, 63, 65, 75-76, 100, 102, 106, 112, 114, 120, 126, 150, 152, 168 185-86, 210, 222, 226, 238, 269-71
Sussex, 40, 73, 75, 102, 191, 272
Sweeper, John, 97
Tagart, Francis, 251
Taylor: Ann, 226; Eliza, 227; Frederick, 208, 210
Thackway, Frederick Henry, 237
Thamesmead, 276
Thomas, Andrew, 192
Thompson: Ann, 77; Jane, 225
Thornton, Elizabeth, 230
Thorold, Miss, 42
Thorpe, Ada Mina, 125
Tilbury, 103
Tippler, Samuel, 19
Tite, Henry Edward, 123
Titiens, Therese, 250-52
Titlow, May Emma Amelia, 115
Tollett, Bathsheba Mary, 75-76
Tomlinson: Alfred, 264, 266; Cecily Mary Janet, 264; Charlotte, 265-66; Charlotte jnr., 264; Clara, 264; Dorothy Charity, 264; Elizabeth, 264, 266; Ellen Mabel, 264; Fred, 264; George, 264, 266; Hannah, 264; Jabez, 263-66; James, 264, 266; Mark, 155, 263-67; Mary, 264; May Faith, 264; Olive Hope, 264; Samuel, 264; William John,

264
Tooting, 85
Tottenham, 32, 75, 124
Tower Hamlets, 207
Townsend, Mary Elizabeth, 137
Trimming, Alfred, 194
Trower, Henry Seymour, 112
Trubbett, Charles, 134
Turner, Percival, 123
Turnham Green, 153
Tuxford, Dr Arthur, 266
Underhill: Alice, 24; Eliza, 26; Richard William, 24; Robert snr., 24, 26; Robert Arthur, 24, 26; William Graham, 25
USA: 91; New Jersey, 164; New York, 88, 184
Vanning, Job, 24
Vauxhall, 29
Veares: Henry, 210; Henry jnr., 210; Iris M., 210
Vernon, Cecilia, 271
Veysey, J., 123
Viant, Samuel, 119
Vickery: Elizabeth, 164; John, 163-64
Vine family, 31
Voss, R., 237
Vye, John, 272
Wabe: Alfred John, 71; Aylmer jnr., 71; Aylmer Horatio, 71; Maria, 71
Walker, Mrs, 229
Walker, Henry, 87
Walsh, Annie Emma, 85
Walthamstow, 82
Walvin, James, 80
Walworth, 84-86, 93, 95
Wandsworth, 19, 63, 85
Wapping, 49-50
Ward: Dr, 186; Elizabeth, 238; Mr, 255
Warman, P.C. William, 61
Warneford, Samuel Wilson, 272
Waterloo, 55-6, 58, 141, 177
Watts: Albert Ernest E., 75; Edward G., 75; Elizabeth, 75; George Frederic, 7, 14-16, 21, 38-39, 58, 63-64, 92, 100, 113, 117-18, 131-32, 134, 136-37, 144, 147, 154, 175, 178, 197, 200-201, 214, 216, 228, 241, 250, 252, 254, 258, 261-63, 268-69, 274-78; Mary, 15, 118-19, 262
Watts Memorial, 7-8, 13-16, 26, 39-41, 48-49, 51, 63-64, 68, 73, 79, 81, 84, 86, 89, 91-93, 95-96, 99-100, 113, 116, 118, 123-24, 127, 141-44, 154, 156, 165, 172, 174-75, 178, 180, 185, 189, 197, 200, 203, 206, 214-16, 228, 238, 243, 247, 250, 254, 258, 261, 263,

268-69, 271, 275, 277-78
Weavers, John, 111
Webb: Dr, 131; John, 160; Master, 89; P.C., 256; Richard, 73; Stephen, 73-74
Webster, Fred, 159-60
Wells, William, 207
Wemyss, Lord, 268
Wenborne, George, 125, 127
Westcott, Dr William Wynn, 111, 235
West Ealing, 163
West Ham, 17, 26, 31, 38, 59, 175, 196, 207
West Indies, 184
Westlake: Ethel, 121; Florence, 121-22
Westminster, 28, 41, 55, 59, 67, 84, 104-6, 139, 144, 222, 264
Weston, Mary, 251
Whaley, Charlotte, 60
Wheal, Robert, 33, 38
Wheeler: Ellen, 32; Frederick, 32
Whitechapel, 87-88, 125, 238, 247
White: Elsie Honor, 124; Eric, 124; Jerry, 17, 57; Joan, 124; Kitty, 124
Whitefriars, 60
Whiteley, William, 264-677
White, Professor, 256-57
Whiterod, Ellen, 31
Whur, Robert, 264
Wilkinson: Kitty, 138; Sarah, 181-82
Willesden, 37, 75, 89, 91, 119, 152, 260-61
Williams: David Richard, 128, 130-31; Greta, 136
Willis, Charles, 175
Wilson, Hannah, 18
Wiltshire, 161
Wimbledon, 100
Winkworth, Jonathan, 30
Winter, Jane, 191
Woakes, Dr Edward, 145
Wolmar, Christian, 154
Wolverhampton, 157
Wood, Emma, 51
Wood Green, 17
Woodman, William, 19
Woolwich, 95-97, 125, 132, 180-84, 212-13
Worcestershire, 250
Worman, Herbert, 33, 38
Wright: Ada Ellen, 106, 109; Bessie, 109; Ellen, 105; John, 105; John Thomas, 105; Maria Elizabeth, 105; Mary, 109; Mary Ann, 105; P.C. Robert, 105-9, 113, 166, 250-51; Robert snr, 105, 109
Yarman, See Jarman
Yorkshire, 32
Yull, Thomas Percival, 71-72

9 780750 956437

Lightning Source UK Ltd.
Milton Keynes UK
UKOW06f1338010515

250739UK00001B/1/P

9 780750 956437